LINCOLN
and
GRANT

Expand your library with other titles from
Regnery History's featured collections

CIVIL WAR

Backstage at the Lincoln Assassination:
The Untold Story of the Actors and
Stagehands at Ford's Theatre
by Thomas A. Bogar

Lee vs. McClellan:
The First Campaign
by Clayton R. Newell

Lincoln and Grant:
The Westerners Who Won the Civil War
by Edward H. Bonekemper III

The Real Custer:
From Boy General to Tragic Hero
By James S. Robbins

COLD WAR CLASSICS

Operation Solo:
The FBI's Man in the Kremlin
by John Barron

The Venona Secrets:
Exposing Soviet Espionage and
America's Traitors
by Herbert Romerstein and Eric Breindel

Witness
by Whittaker Chambers

EARLY AMERICA

Founding Rivals:
Madison vs. Monroe, the Bill of Rights,
and the Election That Saved a Nation
by Chris DeRose

George Washington
and Benedict Arnold:
A Tale of Two Patriots
by Dave R. Palmer

Ships of Oak, Guns of Iron:
The War of 1812 and the Forging
of the American Navy
by Ronald D. Utt

THE GENERALS

Curtis LeMay:
Strategist and Tactician
by Warren Kozak

George S. Patton:
Blood, Guts, and Prayer
by Michael Keane

Hap Arnold:
Inventing the Air Force
by Bill Yenne

Omar Bradley:
General at War
by Jim DeFelice

Look for these other collections by Regnery History

WORLD WAR II & THE PRESIDENTS

www.RegneryHistory.com

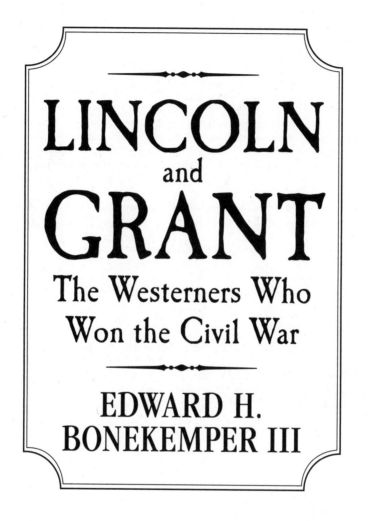

LINCOLN
and
GRANT

The Westerners Who
Won the Civil War

EDWARD H.
BONEKEMPER III

REGNERY
HISTORY

Regnery History™ is a trademark of Salem Communications Holding Corporation; Regnery® is a registered trademark of Salem Communications Holding Corporation.

Library of Congress Cataloging-in-Publication Data

Bonekemper, Edward H.
  Lincoln and Grant : the westerners who won the Civil War / Edward H. Bonekemper, III.
    pages cm
  ISBN 978-1-62157-285-5
  1. Lincoln, Abraham, 1809-1865--Military leadership. 2. Grant, Ulysses S. (Ulysses Simpson), 1822-1885--Military leadership. 3. United States--History--Civil War, 1861-1865--Campaigns. 4. Civil-military relations--United States--History--19th century. 5. Command of troops--History--19th century. I. Title.
  E457.2.B674 2014
  973.7092'2--dc23
                                            2014036079

Published in the United States by
Regnery History
An imprint of Regnery Publishing
A Division of Salem Media Group
300 New Jersey Ave NW
Washington, DC 20001
www.Regnery.com

Manufactured in the United States of America

10 9 8 7 6 5 4 3 2

Books are available in quantity for promotional or premium use. For information on discounts and terms, please visit our website: www.Regnery.com.

DEDICATION

---◆---

This book is dedicated to President Abraham Lincoln and Lieutenant General Ulysses S. Grant, who played major roles in shaping a unified and freedom-loving nation.

> It is not the least of "the crowning mercies" of these days that our political and military chiefs are men upon whose simple, earnest, unselfish devotion to their country no taint of suspicion was ever breathed; and our children will be forever grateful that our national salvation was achieved by the people under two such leaders as ABRAHAM LINCOLN and ULYSSES S. GRANT.
>
> *Harpers Weekly*, April 22, 1865

CONTENTS

LIST OF MAPS

INTRODUCTION

———◆———

I n the course of writing two earlier books, *A Victor, Not a Butcher: The Overlooked Military Genius of Ulysses S. Grant* and *Grant and Lee: Victorious American and Vanquished Virginian*, I discovered the increasingly close working relationship between President Abraham Lincoln and General Ulysses S. Grant as the Union moved toward victory in the Civil War. Astounded to discover that there has been no book-length treatment exclusively about their significant relationship, I decided to examine their backgrounds, experiences, and wartime interactions in order to demonstrate how these two men, working together, won the Civil War.

This book is the result. It is not intended to be a thorough biography of either man but rather a sufficient study of their lives and Civil War activities to understand and appreciate their extraordinary individual and collaborative achievements. It examines Lincoln and Grant's similarities and differences, and describes how their relationship grew into one of the most significant in American history. It terminates with Lincoln's death on April 15, 1865.[1]

The relationship of the president as commander-in-chief with his generals in uniform had been and remains a critical issue in American government. In doing little more than designating the president as commander-in-chief and giving Congress the power to declare war, the U.S. Constitution does not provide any real guidance on the issue of waging war. The War of 1812 lacked national military organization or coordination on the part of the United States. The Mexican-American War saw President James K. Polk first appoint Zachary Taylor as his leading general to keep Winfield Scott out of the limelight and then replace Taylor with Scott after Taylor's military successes—all primarily for political reasons.

Therefore, Lincoln was treading in essentially uncharted territory as he undertook a gigantic war and experimented with civilian-military relations. As will be seen, Lincoln's relationship with generals-in-chief Winfield Scott, George B. McClellan and Henry Halleck were less than satisfactory. Between the terms of the latter two, Lincoln and Secretary of War Edwin Stanton even tried running the war without a designated general-in-chief. It was only with the elevation of Grant to that position in March 1864 and with the quickly developing cooperation between Lincoln and Grant that an effective civilian-military relationship became a reality. Their development of a civilian-controlled, militarily effective relationship, with virtually no precedent upon which to build, was astounding and provided a model for future American wars.[2]

Lincoln and Grant's positive relationship was enhanced by many similarities in their personalities and life experiences. Both were born in modest circumstances west of the Appalachian Mountains in what was regarded in the early nineteenth century as the American frontier. They were men of the river—born near the Ohio River, they understood the uses and value of the nation's inland river systems. They were humble, self-effacing individuals who worked their ways from the bottom to the top of American society. Both battled internal demons but stubbornly pursued the critical goals of their lives. They overcame numerous obstacles and eventually prevailed as two of America's greatest leaders at a time when the nation needed them most.

Parallel experiences in their personal lives included: marriages into slave-owning families, distracting interferences in their lives from other relatives (Lincoln's wife and Grant's father and father-in-law), their self-taught mastery of the English language, and their different but effective interpersonal skills.

They also shared some personality traits. James M. McPherson described Grant: "shy with strangers, uncomfortable in the limelight, notoriously taciturn, Grant earned a reputation as 'the American Sphinx.' Yet wherever he went, things got done—quietly, efficiently, quickly, with no wasted motion. In crisis situations during combat, Grant remained calm. He did not panic. He persevered and never accepted defeat even when he appeared to be beaten."[3] Although Lincoln was more introspective than shy, much of this description could be applied to him as well; he faced his own forms of combat.

Significantly, some of Lincoln's positive attributes contrasted with, and complemented, those of Grant. For example, Lincoln was a political genius[4] while Grant had military acumen.[5] Unlike the Confederacy's President Jefferson Davis, Lincoln did not insist on micromanaging the war. In fact, Lincoln delegated more and more military authority to Grant as the general earned the president's confidence. For his part, Grant yielded to Lincoln's political expertise on most significant issues, including the movement toward emancipation and the use of black soldiers. Grant also deferred to Lincoln on most major military strategic issues—a demonstration that Lincoln indeed was the senior partner in their successful partnership.

Grant and Lincoln were men of the new American West, an area far removed in miles and milieu from the original thirteen colonies of the Eastern Seaboard. Today's Midwest was the West of antebellum America.[6] Lincoln was born in Kentucky, moved to Indiana, and established his permanent home in Illinois. Grant was born in Ohio, married and lived in Missouri, and moved to Illinois. Although Lincoln was a long-term resident of Illinois, Grant had arrived there less than a year before the Civil War erupted—in just enough time to benefit from his Illinois political connections.

Grant's most effective congressional political supporter was Congressman Elihu B. Washburne, a Galena, Illinois, neighbor and the senior Republican in the U.S. House of Representatives. He had been a friend and political associate of Lincoln since the 1840s. Washburne was a loyal supporter of both Lincoln and Grant throughout the war. Most significantly, the congressman had earned Lincoln's trust and used that relationship to protect Grant against vicious attacks from reporters, jealous military competitors, and others seeking to advance their own interests.

Their shared Illinois and Midwestern heritage enhanced Lincoln and Grant's relationship. One astute analyst commented, "A man of the border state, Lincoln could see all sides, could feel the Civil War and all of its issues founded on race and place in his very bones."[7] Lincoln's 1862 annual report to Congress provided insights into his view of the adverse impact of Southern secession on the Upper West, which he described as the "great interior region, bounded east by the Alleghanies [sic], north by the British dominions, west by the Rocky mountains, and south by the line along which the culture of corn and cotton meets...."[8]

After discussing that area's great potential for population growth and agricultural production, he explained the effect of secession: "As part of one nation, its people now find, and may forever find, their way to Europe by New York, to South America and Africa by New Orleans, and to Asia by San Francisco. But separate our common country into two nations, as designed by the present rebellion, and every man of this great interior region is thereby cut off from some one or more of these outlets, not perhaps, by a physical barrier, but by embarrassing and onerous trade regulations.... These outlets, east, west, and south, are indispensable to the well-being of the people inhabiting, and to inhabit, this vast interior region."[9]

The vital importance of the Mississippi River to the Midwest was a clear implication of Lincoln's words. In mid-1863, Union army chaplain John Eaton related Lincoln's mid-war interest in the Mississippi: "He was eager for details of Vicksburg, and his references to the Mississippi River proved that his memories of it had stayed by him, filling his mind with the significance of the commercial influence of the great waterway, and of its effect not only upon the country at large, but particularly upon the Negro population, which, now that the Mississippi was open from the source to its mouth, would swarm to the river as a channel of escape into the North."[10] Clearly, Grant's successful 1862–63 efforts to gain Union control over the Mississippi, Tennessee and Cumberland rivers reflected a Westerner's geographic awareness that meshed perfectly with Lincoln's conception of the significance of those rivers to the nation as a whole.

Grant's increasing value to Lincoln and Lincoln's support and protection of Grant during the Civil War are reflected in two widely reported apocryphal tales. There are many reports that Lincoln, when confronted with rumors and false accounts of Grant's heavy drinking and drunkenness, stated that he wanted to know what whiskey Grant consumed so that he could provide a barrel to each of his generals. In response to recommendations that Grant be removed from command (particularly after the bloody April 1862 Battle of Shiloh), Lincoln is reputed to have said, "I cannot spare this man; he fights." The reason these unverified stories have received such credence is that they appear to reflect Lincoln's actual attitude toward Grant.[11]

McPherson described Lincoln's primary leadership role: "As president and leader of his party as well as commander in chief, Lincoln was principally responsible for shaping and defining policy. From first to last that policy was preservation of the United States as one nation, indivisible, and as a republic based on majority rule.... At all levels of policy, strategy, and operations...Lincoln was a hands-on commander in chief who persisted through a terrible ordeal of defeats and disappointments to final triumph—and tragedy—at the end."[12]

The late Russell F. Weigley, one of America's foremost military historians, proclaimed Grant's uniqueness as a military commander in his willingness to perform under civilian (i.e., Lincoln's) control: "A straightforward man with few pretensions of any kind, Grant certainly did not claim to be a military scholar. His genius for command was a product mainly of clear-eyed native intelligence, even of common sense, not primarily of more specialized professional attainments. He was, therefore, glad to communicate with his civilian superiors with candor and without condescension. But Grant was almost *sui generis*."[13]

Not only was Grant willing to work with Lincoln, but the president also was willing to concede much—though not all—military decision-making to Grant when he became general-in-chief. Lincoln had tried that approach unsuccessfully with Major General George B. McClellan. After McClellan, Lincoln effectively was his own general-in-chief both before he appointed Major General Henry W. Halleck to that position in July 1862 and later when it became clear that Halleck was unwilling or unable to assume the responsibilities of that position. By the time Grant was named general-in-chief in March 1864, Lincoln and Grant both believed "that only the utter military defeat of the Confederacy would suffice to reunite the nation." Their shared non-conciliatory approach and Lincoln's confidence in Grant's military judgment enabled the president to reduce, but not eliminate, his military activity. Lincoln stayed involved as commander-in-chief while Grant effectively performed his role as general-in-chief.[14]

The most significant factor that bound together Lincoln and Grant was their shared belief in the necessity to proactively use appropriate and aggressive force to carry the North's burden of winning the Civil War. Daniel Sutherland concluded that General John Pope's harsh mid-1862 anti-Confederate pronouncements (blessed by Lincoln and Secretary of War Stanton) and concurrent Union confiscation laws cleared the way for Grant's aggressive "total war" campaigns of 1864–65. He stated, "Grant benefitted [*sic*] enormously from the fact that a precedent for waging total war had already been set, the legal machinery erected, and the philosophy accepted. Lincoln knew what had to be done, and ultimately, in the persons of Grant and Sherman, he had the right men to do the job."[15] Although "total war" overstates the hard war practiced by Grant and Sherman, since they did not deliberately kill civilians, Sutherland's point about precedents is valid.

Well before 1864, however, Grant had demonstrated his propensity for aggressively pursuing and taking enemy armies out of action. He had captured enemy armies at Fort Donelson in 1862 (14,000 captured) and Vicksburg in 1863 (almost 30,000 captured). Grant's aggressiveness had paid dividends by repelling a major Confederate attack and saving his army at Shiloh (April 1862) and dealing a crushing blow to Confederate forces at Chattanooga (November 1863).

Beginning with his September 22, 1862, Preliminary Emancipation Proclamation, the president increasingly encouraged utilization of blacks as a vital part of the Union war effort. He pushed for their use in the Union army (about 180,000 served) and navy (about 20,000) and wreaked havoc on the South as blacks abandoned plantations to seek freedom with the advancing Union armies. Unlike George McClellan (who fiercely opposed emancipation) and William T. Sherman (who never outgrew his racism), Grant fully supported Lincoln's emancipation and black soldier policies.

After Lincoln had brought Grant to the East as general-in-chief and before the 1864 Overland Campaign, the president summarized his reaction to Grant in a conversation with his Third Secretary William O. Stoddard: "Well, I hardly know what to think of him, altogether, I never saw him, myself, till he came here to take the command. He's the quietest little fellow you ever saw.... The only evidence you have that he's in any place is that he makes things git! Wherever he is, things move!"[16]

Working in tandem with the president, Grant certainly would "make things git" on a sustained basis for the first time in the Eastern Theater. His unrelenting 1864–65 moves against Lee's army, exactly what Lincoln wanted him to do, almost won the war in two months and did win it in less than a year. Just as significantly, Grant, with Lincoln's blessing, entrusted Sherman with adequate troops and discretion to threaten and capture Atlanta, a significant victory that virtually ensured Lincoln's reelection, and then to march through Georgia in late 1864 and the Carolinas in early 1865—movements that destroyed Confederate morale, caused thousands of Rebel soldiers to desert, and ensured the doom of Robert E. Lee's vaunted Army of Northern Virginia.

In summary, Grant and Lincoln shared a frontier American heritage, as well as common sense and dogged determination. This book describes how each man developed those and other key traits during their childhoods, early lives, the Mexican War (at home and abroad), and their rough-and-tumble economic and political trials of the 1850s. The bulk of this book, however, describes most of the separate, and then later coordinated, activities of Lincoln and Grant during the Civil War. Their exciting successes and dismaying failures in the military and political arenas brought them closer to each other and ultimately evolved into the critical partnership that won the Civil War.

Throughout this chronological study, you should be alert to some underlying themes that are fully summarized in my final chapter. One thread tying these two men together was their critical similar personality traits (specifically humility, decisiveness, clarity of communication, moral courage and perseverance). Beyond those shared characteristics, Lincoln and Grant developed an increasing mutual respect for each other, which then grew into an unshakeable loyalty to each other. Ultimately, their common traits, respect, and loyalty made them victorious.

They developed a working relationship in which each was comfortable with his and the other's role. The critical areas governed by this relationship were national policy, military strategy, military operations and tactics, and military personnel decision-making. As described in some detail in the final chapter, I conclude that:

- As to national policies, Lincoln made the decisions, and Grant accommodated and implemented them.
- As to military strategy, although Lincoln and Grant usually agreed on it, Lincoln was in charge and Grant understood that fact and accepted it.
- As to military tactics, the president generally left Grant free to conduct military operations with tactics of his own choosing.
- As to the murkier area of military operations, particularly in the East, Lincoln did intervene on several occasions, and Grant generally deferred to the president's suggestions and responded to his concerns.
- As to military personnel decisions concerning manpower in the field, their relations were marked by cooperation regarding manpower numbers, recruiting and using black soldiers, and prisoner-of-war exchange policies.

- As to military personnel decisions regarding the appointment and retention of general officers, Grant recognized and deferred to the president's political needs while using face-saving organizational changes to accomplish his military goals, and they successfully cooperated on issues relating to promotion, retention and assignment of generals.

In conclusion, these two Westerners employed their critical shared traits and mutual trust to form an effective partnership that resulted in relentless pursuit and destruction of the enemy, effectively used black soldiers, and ultimately proved decisive in the Civil War. Their successful working relationship reached its peak when Lincoln as commander-in-chief and Grant as general-in-chief brought the war to a successful conclusion within little more than a year after Grant assumed his new position.

CHAPTER 1

MEN OF THE WEST

———•◆•———

Abraham Lincoln and Ulysses S. Grant were men of America's new West—the trans-Appalachia. They also were men of the river—the Ohio and Mississippi Rivers. With their shared roots in frontier poverty, Lincoln and Grant were ordinary Americans who became great Americans.

Steven Woodworth could have been describing Lincoln when he wrote of Grant's "matter-of-fact steadiness," "hard-driving aggressiveness," and "quiet, can-do attitude." Likewise, his conclusion was equally valid for both men: "Nor is it any coincidence that Grant's qualities tended to be those of that up-and-coming region of the country, one day to be called the Midwest, [where people] had approached the challenges of carving farms out of the wilderness."[1] Sharing those traits and similar origins, Lincoln and Grant both came of age in what was then America's frontier region—where diligence and humility trumped pedigree and pretentiousness.

LINCOLN'S FORMATIVE YEARS

Lincoln was born in Hardin, Kentucky, on February 12, 1809. His parents were the barely literate farmer-carpenter Thomas Lincoln and the illiterate Nancy Hanks Lincoln, both of whom came from rural western Virginia. Because of land title problems and competition from large plantations with slave labor, Thomas moved the family to southern Indiana in 1816. By helping his father clear the land and start a new farm, young Abe grew into a muscular youth who excelled at wrestling.[2]

When young Lincoln was only nine, milk sickness killed his mother.[3] After a year of living in squalid conditions, the family morale and living conditions vastly improved when Thomas briefly returned to Kentucky and married Sarah Bush Johnston, a widow with household goods and a pleasant disposition. She immediately came with him to Indiana, created a comfortable home environment and developed a close and loving relationship with Abe. She arranged for his schooling at various informal schools in the area—a total of less than one year of formal education.[4]

Lincoln's initial taste of education whetted his appetite for more, and he embarked on a life-long program of self-education. Among the early books he read were Samuel Kirkham's *English Grammar*, *Aesop's Fables*, *Webster's Spelling Book*, *The Life of Henry Clay*, John Bunyan's *The Pilgrim's Progress*, Daniel Defoe's *Robinson Crusoe*, Parson Mason Weems's *Life of George Washington*, and William Scott's *Lessons of Elocution*. This last tome stimulated Abe to practice public speaking by mimicking sermons and giving political talks to other children.[5]

Perhaps the one trait, other than being a hard worker, that he received from his father was the ability to tell "humorous stories with a rustic, frontier flavor. Abe's skill and confidence in telling these stories in a public forum owed something to his father's convivial and witty nature."[6] While he had a loving relationship with his stepmother, young Abraham had a strained and often hostile relationship with his father. Barely literate himself, Thomas Lincoln did not encourage Abe's quest for knowledge and sometimes beat him for putting his reading ahead of his chores. He even threw out young Abe's books and announced that, "if Abe don't fool away all his time on his books, he may make something yet."[7]

Desiring a broader exposure to the world than his father's small farm, Lincoln spent more and more time in activities elsewhere. He engaged in "house raisings, corn shuckings, timber loggings, hog killings, and fire-wood cuttings for passing steamboats on the Ohio River." The river system provided an eye-opening experience for the nineteen-year-old Lincoln. He traveled with a storekeeper's son down the Ohio and the Mississippi all the way to New Orleans on a flatboat loaded with goods for sale. That trip probably exposed him to the customs of slavery along the river, as well as to the slave market of New Orleans, where thousands of slaves were sold every month. Unlike most of his contemporaries, Lincoln was well-traveled and visited another region—the South—several times.[8]

That first river journey and a later trip to New Orleans definitely revealed to Lincoln the critical importance of the rivers as lifelines of commerce and communication in the infant republic. This realization would be critical to his future national policies and military strategy.

In 1830, Abe helped his parents move the family 200 miles to the fertile plains of south-central Illinois. After helping to clear and fence the land, the twenty-one-year-old Lincoln was free to seek his own fortunes. After having given his labor and wages to his father until he had reached the age of majority, Abraham in 1831 made a clean break from his father and his indolent, ignorant, and backward way of life: "Growing up in the crude and isolated society of frontier agriculture, he escaped from it by force of will. His pioneering experience remained ever visible in the Lincolnian style...."[9]

His temporary hiring by businessman Denton Offutt led to Lincoln's second eye-opening exposure to a world outside his own. In April and May 1831, Offutt, Lincoln and two others took a flatboat of goods down the Sangamon, Illinois and Mississippi rivers all the way (again) to New Orleans. There Lincoln observed and experienced the interaction of a myriad of people and languages. He also had another opportunity to see slavery in action. In disgust, he turned away from the manhandling of a female slave at a slave auction.[10]

After that trip, Offutt hired Lincoln as a clerk in his New Salem, Illinois store. Lincoln quickly proved to be a successful clerk and enjoyed spending his free time reading Shakespeare and numerous other literary and historical authors. His local popularity rose so quickly that he was drafted as a temporary clerk of elections and then elected captain of the local militia company that assembled in 1832 to oppose the Fox and Sac Indians under Chief Black Hawk. As a soldier, he saw the results of a few massacres but did not engage in any fighting. In 1832 he ran unsuccessfully for the state legislature, but in 1834 he ran again and, after intensive English grammar tutoring, was elected to his first political position.

From 1833 to 1836, he also was the postmaster of New Salem, Illinois. There he met and lost the first love of his life, Ann Rutledge, whose death sent Lincoln into deep and almost suicidal depression.

During his early years of independence, as summarized by Jay Winik, "He had his run of bad luck. He set up a store, which failed, then set up as a postmaster, but was unable to make a living at that. When a circuit court issued a judgment against him for overdue notes, the sheriff attached his personal possessions, even his horse." When Lincoln's business partner William Berry died in 1835, their grocery business went broke and thousands of dollars of debt remained. Lincoln not only paid off his share of the debts but Berry's as well. Lincoln spent fifteen years paying off those debts.[11] In addition to his roles as storekeeper and postmaster, he worked hard to become a skilled and respected surveyor who often resolved property disputes.

Young Lincoln found his calling in law and politics. While serving as postmaster, he studied law books and began learning the art of politics as a Whig state legislator from 1834 to 1842. Early in his legislative career, he successfully maneuvered to get the Illinois state capital moved to Springfield. He had obtained passage of a requirement that the capital city being selected provide $50,000 for state public buildings—a provision that eliminated several smaller towns from the competition. When the final one-third payment came due after the Panic of 1837 and resulting economic downturn, Stephen Douglas proposed that Springfield find a way to repudiate the debt. Lincoln, however, found that approach dishonorable ("We have the benefit. Let us stand to our obligation as men," he said), and he and other Springfield leaders paid the debt with borrowed money they subsequently repaid.[12]

As a loyal Whig, Lincoln admired Henry Clay and fought in the legislature for public funding of internal improvements, such as railroads and canals. He became a leader of the Whigs in the legislature and remained an Illinois party leader for them until the party disintegrated in the mid-1850s. William Harris stressed that "Lincoln's western Whig Background enabled him to understand the political, constitutional, and racial realities in the border states"[13]—an understanding that proved valuable during the Civil War.

Disappointed that his various occupations were not resulting in substantial income and stimulated to do so by Indian war acquaintance John Todd Stuart, Lincoln immersed himself in legal treatises and successfully applied for admission to the bar in late 1836. The next year the young lawyer moved to Springfield, where he became Stuart's junior partner. His subsequent legal partners were Stephen T. Logan and William H. Herndon. Between 1837 and 1861 he personally handled about 5,600 cases, all but 194 of them being civil rather than criminal.[14]

GRANT'S FORMATIVE YEARS

Grant was born as Hiram Ulysses Grant in the Ohio River town of Point Pleasant, in Clermont County, Ohio, on April 27, 1822. He was the eldest of six children. Young "Ulysses" or "Ulyss" loved working with horses but detested his father's tannery. By the age of nine or ten, he was earning money breaking horses and driving passengers all over Ohio. In his memoirs, Grant described his childhood as a pleasant one: "I did not like to work; but I did as much of it, while young, as grown men can be hired to do in these days, and attended school at the same time. I had as many privileges as any boy in the village, and probably more than most of them."[15]

His father, however, was a loud, argumentative and litigious bully who excoriated Ulyss for his total failure as a horse-trader. Unknown to Ulysses, his father arranged for his appointment to West Point through their local congressman, Thomas Hamer, who submitted Grant's name as U. S. (Simpson being his mother's maiden name) Grant. Although Grant signed some Academy documents as "Ulysses Hiram Grant," he signed his eight-year enlistment oath as "U. S. Grant" and was on his way to being known to history as Ulysses S. (or U. S.) Grant. William T. Sherman, a cadet three years ahead of Grant, saw his name appearing on a list of new cadets as "U. S. Grant." He and other cadets came up with the names "United States" and "Uncle Sam" to fit the initials and then finally settled on the moniker "Sam," which became Grant's nickname for life.[16]

At West Point from 1839 to 1843, Grant made many lifelong friends, including James Longstreet, who later commanded the First Corps in Lee's Army of Northern Virginia, and Rufus Ingalls, who would serve as Quartermaster of the Army of the Potomac. He knew all of the cadets in the classes that graduated between 1840 and 1846; those classes included over fifty men who were generals in the Civil War.[17] Grant's great horse riding, middling grades, and below-average conduct marks resulted in his graduating twenty-first in his 1843 class of 39.[18] Perhaps the highlight of his West Point years was his graduation ceremony, during which he rode a large, unmanageable horse and jumped a bar higher than a man's head. Grant was the only cadet who could ride that horse well, and their jump astounded the crowd at the ceremony.[19]

During his post-graduation leave of absence in Ohio, Grant twice was mocked about his new military uniform, and the incidents, in Grant's own words, "gave me a distaste for military uniform that I never recovered from." As a result of that experience and the influence of a casually dressed Mexican War mentor, Major General Zachary Taylor, Grant infrequently wore a sword unless ordered to do so, and during the Civil War was notorious for his rumpled, informal, and plain uniforms.[20] He generally wore a private's blouse with his indicia of rank stitched on the shoulders.

As a junior officer, Grant was assigned to Jefferson Barracks outside St. Louis. He visited the nearby home of an Academy roommate, Frederick T. Dent, and met Dent's slaveholder father, Frederick F. Dent, and young Dent's sister, Julia Boggs Dent. Ulysses courted and became engaged to Julia before the Mexican War intervened. Her father, however, gave only lukewarm approval to the match.[21] Grant would have to prove to Frederick Dent, and to himself, that he was a man with great potential.

SHARED EARLY EXPERIENCES
OF LINCOLN AND GRANT

On the threshold of the Mexican-American War (1846–48),[22] Grant was a young and untested military officer, and Lincoln was a successful lawyer and state politician unknown and unproven on the national political scene. They shared common origins and experiences.

Lincoln and Grant were both born in modest circumstances and remained in them for decades. They lived in the rural Ohio River Valley, where Southern and Northern views on social and political issues alternately blended and clashed. Thus, unlike most in the North, South, and East, they were exposed to more than one set of standards and viewpoints.

Both had benefited from loving mothers and experienced uncaring, if not quite hostile, fathers. Neither had much formal education—until Grant went to West Point. From their earliest days, both were hardworking but made little financial headway. Their lives were not easy.

CHAPTER 2

THE MEXICAN WAR: A MILITARY AND POLITICAL TRAINING GROUND

T he Mexican War provided both Lincoln and Grant with their first exposure to the complexities of war. When the fighting ended, Grant was a twenty-six-year-old captain who had been decorated for his bravery; Lincoln was a thirty-eight-year-old freshman congressman. While Grant heroically fought in the war and at least retroactively criticized it, Lincoln's involvement with the war was political. As a new congressman just after the fighting ceased, he faced the difficult task—common in American history—of criticizing the origin of the war without faulting or undermining the troops or appearing unpatriotic. By different paths, both men developed a solid skepticism about the war's purposes combined with support for America's military actions and its soldiers. Grant's military experience and personal contacts would prove invaluable during the Civil War. Lincoln's political experience was less useful and threatened his political future.

LINCOLN'S MEXICAN WAR POLITICAL EXPERIENCES

The most controversial political issue of 1844 was the annexation of Texas, which Democratic President-elect James K. Polk convinced President John Tyler to push through in December 1844. In October 1845 comments to a friend, Lincoln supported the Whig Party indifference to national expansion, said the Texas annexation probably would not affect slavery, and added a telling note of caution: "It is possibly true, to some extent, that with annexation, some slaves may be sent to Texas and continued in slavery, that otherwise might have been liberated. To whatever extent this may be true, I think annexation an evil." He added that free states should not interfere with slavery in slave states, but explained: "I hold it to be equally clear, that we should never knowingly lend ourselves directly or indirectly, to prevent that slavery from dying a natural death...." By 1845, therefore, Lincoln was opposed to the expansion of slavery but believed it was prudent to await a more propitious moment to accomplish anything in regard to its demise.[1]

By 1846 Polk had provoked a war with Mexico in order to expand the nation—and the area available for expansion of slavery. When war broke out and patriotic rallies were held across the country, a reluctant Lincoln was called upon to speak. He unenthusiastically said that since he was not going to war, he would not tell others to do so but rather told them to do what they thought their duty called for.[2] Thus, Lincoln was not an early opponent of the Mexican War and did not make it an issue in his successful congressional election campaign in 1846, when fighting was ongoing in Mexico.

In August 1846 Lincoln was elected to Congress to represent Springfield and its environs. With crossover support from many Democrats, he won impressively: 6,340 votes to 4,829, over his major opponent, Methodist preacher Peter Cartwright—with 56 percent of the total vote. His friend Joshua Speed claimed he gave Lincoln $200 raised by fellow Whigs for his campaign expenses and that Lincoln gave it all back except for seventy-five cents. A former governor commented that the large majority was "the finest compliment personally and the highest political endorsement any man could expect."[3]

Under the strange practice of the day, his term did not begin for another sixteen months—in December 1847. While many Whigs began to criticize the Mexican War as Polk's war of conquest, a frustrated Lincoln remained silent for fear of the usual criticisms about lack of patriotism and failure to support the troops that usually result from anti-war opinions. While in Kentucky in November 1847 on his way to Washington, Lincoln heard Henry Clay, his idol of many years, criticize the origins of the war as he launched his 1848 presidential bid. Lincoln, however, saw that Clay was fading and joined many other Whigs in support of the successful candidacy of General Zachary Taylor, one of the military heroes of the Mexican War.[4]

Lincoln, his wife Mary, and two young sons arrived in Washington in late 1847 and took up residence in a boarding house used by both Whigs and Democrats. Lincoln became the great conciliator when political discussions boiled over. Representative James Pollock of Pennsylvania said that Lincoln "never failed to…restore harmony and smiles, when the peace of our little community was threatened by too earnest or heated controversy on some of the exciting questions of the hour." Slavery and the treatment of slaves in Washington were some of the acrimonious issues that divided the congressmen. After four months, Mary tired of the boarding-house lifestyle and moved temporarily with the boys to her family home in Lexington, Kentucky.[5]

In December 1847, as a Whig representative in Congress, Lincoln criticized Polk's justification for the war. Polk had argued that Mexico had started the war by invading the U.S. and "shedding American blood on American Soil." In his first month in Washington, Lincoln introduced his famous "spot" resolutions demanding to be shown the spot on American soil where fighting had first occurred. He argued that the blood shed was that of American soldiers invading a disputed area to which Mexico had a legitimate claim and in which the residents had no allegiance to the U.S. The next month Lincoln further criticized Polk for "the sheerest deception" as to the war's origin and for the open-ended approach to the war's termination (apparently to maximize U.S. territorial gains).[6]

Lincoln's votes reflected his criticism of Polk and the origins of the war. He voted against a resolution calling the war just and necessary. In January 1848, he provided a crucial vote in supporting the Ashmun Amendment, which declared the Mexican War "unnecessarily and unconstitutionally begun by the President" and was passed 82 to 81.[7]

Lincoln's criticisms of the manner in which Polk had provoked the war raised immediate concerns among Lincoln's political allies, including his law partner William Herndon. In fact, his allegedly "unpatriotic" comments and votes provided grist for Illinois Democrats to use in the 1848 congressional elections against Lincoln's would-be Whig successor (who lost), against Lincoln himself throughout the 1850s (including the Lincoln-Douglas Debates of 1858),[8] and even in the 1860 presidential campaign.

In 1848 Lincoln abandoned his long-time support for Henry Clay and instead worked for the nomination of Zachary Taylor as the most electable Whig candidate for president. After Taylor's nomination, Lincoln actively campaigned for him and gained Eastern exposure with speeches in Maryland, Massachusetts, and Washington, D.C. After Taylor's election, Lincoln was offered but declined the governorship of the Oregon Territory. Honoring an informal agreement with other Whigs to serve only a single term in Congress, Lincoln did not seek reelection. He returned to Springfield in March 1849 after his single congressional term. In fact, "After fifteen years in politics, Lincoln enjoyed no one's endorsement, held no worthwhile political office, and had discovered that the drudgery of work in Congress was 'exceedingly tasteless to me.'" He decided to return to the law and seek advancement elsewhere.[9]

GRANT'S MEXICAN WAR EXPERIENCES

Meanwhile the Mexican War provided West Point graduate Ulysses Grant with the opportunity to gain military experience and possibly fame. It was the highlight of Grant's pre–Civil War career. Grant went to the war early (he even was pre-positioned in Louisiana in expectation of war) and fought in two theaters of that war under two very different commanding officers. He remained in Mexico until the signing of the Treaty of Guadalupe Hidalgo in February 1848.

After proposing to Julia Dent in 1844, Grant left almost immediately for Louisiana and four years of separation because of the growing dispute and ultimate war with Mexico.[10] Pre-positioned in Louisiana for Polk's preemptive war of aggression, Grant later wrote in his memoirs that he had no romantic illusions about the nature of his country's conduct that led to the annexation of Texas and war with Mexico:

> For myself, I was bitterly opposed to the [annexation of Texas], and to this day regard the war, which resulted, as one of the most unjust ever waged by a stronger against a weaker nation.... Even if the annexation itself could be justified, the manner in which the subsequent war was forced upon Mexico cannot. The fact is, annexationists wanted more territory than they could possibly lay any claim to.... The Southern rebellion was largely the outgrowth of the Mexican war. Nations, like individuals, are punished for their transgressions. We got our punishment in the most sanguinary and expensive war of modern times.[11]

Even at the time, then, Grant was skeptical of his nation's motives. He commented, "We were sent to provoke a fight, but it was essential that Mexico commence it." He noted with dismay that many of his peers longed to fight in order to win glory and promotion. On May 6, 1844, he wrote to Julia, "The officers are all collected in little parties discussing affairs of the nation.... Some of them expect and seem to contemplate with a great deal of pleasure some difficulty where they may be able to gain laurels and advance a little in rank." While others were glad to head south for a fight with the Mexicans, Grant viewed such a fight quite differently—as a necessary pre-condition to returning to Julia.[12]

On his way to the war, Lieutenant Grant and his Fourth Infantry regiment took a boat down the Mississippi to New Orleans. As part of the Regular Army, Grant stayed in the Jackson Barracks—quarters more comfortable than those of the volunteer militiamen, who camped on the fields where Andrew Jackson had defeated the British in 1815.[13]

During that war, Grant served under both Winfield Scott ("Old Fuss and Feathers") and Zachary Taylor ("Old Rough-and-Ready"). He clearly preferred Taylor. Grady McWhiney and Perry Jamieson concluded that Grant and Taylor shared several characteristics: opposition to plundering, willingness to work with available resources, informality of uniform, attention to detail on the battlefield, reticence in conversation, ability to quickly compose clear and concise written orders, and calmness in the face of danger and responsibility.[14] Grant retrospectively praised the quality of Taylor's army: "A more efficient army for its number and armament, I do not believe ever fought a battle than the one commanded by General Taylor in his first two engagements on Mexican—or Texan soil."[15]

Perhaps in part because of a famous incident in which Grant rode a wild horse for three hours and thereby tamed it—though probably more because of his ability with horses and mules—Grant was selected as regimental quartermaster and commissary officer. Grant unsuccessfully protested the appointment because he feared it would remove him from combat. However, the military logistics experience (procuring and organizing such essentials as transportation, tents, uniforms, saddles and supplies) proved invaluable: "During the Civil War Grant's armies might occasionally have straggled, discipline might sometimes have been lax, but food and ammunition trains were always expertly handled. [Grant's victories] depended in no small measure on his skill as a quartermaster."[16] The skills Grant learned as a Mexican War quartermaster may have enhanced his willingness and ability to efficiently use railroads and rivers for supply and maneuver in the Civil War.

Grant's 1846 service with Taylor's high-quality army gave Grant an opportunity to perform well, in battles at Palo Alto and Resaca de la Palma, and even heroically, as the Americans captured Monterrey. After the first two battles, he wrote to Julia, "There is no great sport in having bullets flying about one in every direction but I find they have less horror when among them than when in anticipation."[17] In the latter battle, he volunteered to ride through the city streets under enemy fire to carry a message requesting a resupply of ammunition.[18]

In his memoirs, Grant described his admiration for Zachary Taylor in words that may just as well have applied to Grant himself:[19]

> General Taylor was not an officer to trouble the administration much with his demands, but was inclined to do the best he could with the means given him. He felt his responsibility as going no further. If he had thought that he was sent to perform an impossibility with the means given him, he would probably have informed the authorities of his opinion and left them to determine what should be done. If the judgment was against him he would have gone on and done the best he could with the means at hand without parading his grievance before the public. No soldier could face either danger or responsibility more calmly than he. These are qualities more rarely found than genius or physical courage. General Taylor never made any great show or parade, either of uniform or retinue. In dress he was possibly too plain... but he was known to every soldier in his army, and was respected by all.[20]

Brian John Murphy concluded that the no-nonsense leadership style of the "direct, aggressive, methodical, and unflappable" Taylor deeply impressed the young Grant.[21]

Because President Polk feared that Taylor would capitalize on his battlefield victories to win the presidency as a Whig candidate in 1848, Polk decided to spread out the laurels and shifted most of Taylor's force, including Grant's regiment, to another Whig general, Major General Scott.[22] Early in 1847, therefore, Grant's Fourth Infantry Regiment joined Scott's famous campaign from Vera Cruz, on the coast, to Mexico City. After Vera Cruz surrendered, Grant fought in the major campaign battles of Cerro Gordo, Churubusco, Molino del Rey, Chapultepec, and Mexico City. Just outside Mexico City, Grant outflanked causeway-blocking Mexican artillery with a small detachment, hauled a disassembled mountain howitzer to the top of a church, enfiladed the Mexican position, and thereby opened the way into the city.[23]

His heroism, about which he wrote nothing in his correspondence to Julia, earned him two brevet (temporary) promotions.

His duty in Texas and the Mexican War compelled the previously sheltered Grant to live outdoors for a couple of years, a way of life that Grant believed saved his life and restored his health. His extensive correspondence with Julia between 1845 and 1847 is filled with almost desperate pleas that her father approve their marriage. Finally, in the midst of the Mexico City campaign, Grant learned that Julia's father had given his consent. After Mexico City surrendered, Grant did a great deal of sightseeing in Mexico in 1847 and 1848 while attempting to get permission to return to Julia.[24]

During periods of boredom in Mexico when there were lulls in the fighting, Grant and many of his peers engaged in drinking. Grant himself wrote, "Soldiers are a class of people who will drink and gamble let them be where they may, and they can always find houses to visit for these purposes."[25]

An incident occurred during the Fourth Infantry's return to the United States that created a black mark on Grant's military record. Someone stole $1,000 in quartermaster's funds from the trunk of a friend of Grant's, and Grant, as quartermaster, was held accountable. Although a board of inquiry convened at his request cleared Grant, he was still legally required to reimburse the government for the loss—a requirement that would prove difficult to meet. Grant would spend the next several years trying to get that debt invalidated.[26]

What military lessons did Grant learn from his experiences in the Mexican War? From both Taylor and Scott, he learned that aggressiveness on the offensive could lead to victory. This was a useful lesson for Grant, whose side in the Civil War would have the same offensive strategic burden as the United States had in the Mexican War. According to Jean Edward Smith, Grant "saw how time and again Taylor and Scott moved against a numerically superior foe occupying a fortified position, and how important it was to maintain the momentum of the attack."[27] Particularly from Taylor, he learned that speed and maneuver were real assets. From both, he learned the value of being cunning and deceptive about planned offensives.

From Scott's abandoning his supply line midway through his march on Mexico City, Grant learned that an army could live off the countryside—a lesson that he applied during his 1863 Vicksburg Campaign.[28] Grant also learned that death was a normal occurrence among soldiers at war. Of the 78,718 American soldiers engaged in the Mexican War, 13,283 (16.8 percent) perished—10.4 percent from disease alone.[29] This was the highest death percentage of any war the United States Army has fought (including the Civil War and both World Wars). Grant's personal experience with death was quite real; only four of the twenty-one officers originally assigned to his regiment survived the war.[30]

Overall, the Mexican War proved to be an invaluable experience for the young and impressionable Grant. His observation of his fellow officers and his participation in the logistics and fighting components of war would serve him well in the Civil War.

CHAPTER 3

THE TUMULTUOUS 1850s: APPROACH OF THE CIVIL WAR

———— ·•◆•· ————

T he 1850s were a tumultuous time for America and for both Lincoln and Grant. Although he encountered political defeats in Illinois, Lincoln nevertheless ascended to national prominence and the presidency. Grant, on the other hand, met nothing but failure in that decade. Separated from his wife and affected by alcohol, he resigned from the army in disgrace in 1854 and then proceeded to fail at every civilian occupation he undertook for the next six years. Yet, this turbulent decade proved to be a crucial one in the effect it had on the two men who together would shape their nation's future.

LINCOLN'S RISE TO PROMINENCE AND THE PRESIDENCY

In 1849, his last year as a congressman, Lincoln had developed a complex bill calling for the gradual, compensated abolition of slavery by referendum in the District of Columbia—coupled with strong fugitive slave provisions. After he had obtained support from the city's mayor and other key public officials, Southern congressmen convinced them to reverse their positions. Therefore, Lincoln never introduced his bill. But his proposal to abolish D.C. slavery eventually became a reality when as president he signed such a bill on April 16, 1862—almost exactly a year after the firing on Fort Sumter.[1]

After his frustrating experience as a one-term congressman in the minority Whig Party, Lincoln declined the Oregon governorship and a Chicago law partnership. Instead, he began the 1850s by re-immersing himself in his increasingly remunerative law practice in Springfield. While he plied his profession there, he kept an eye on national political developments.

The Compromise of 1850, engineered by a dying Henry Clay with assistance from Stephen Douglas, was the last major action taken by Congress to avert a national clash over the divisive issue of slavery. A series of separate laws provided for a free California to become a state, greatly strengthened enforcement of fugitive slave laws, provided for popular sovereignty in New Mexico and Utah, abolished the slave trade (but not slavery) in the District of Columbia, and resolved a Texas/New Mexico territorial dispute.

By 1854, however, a Democratic-dominated Congress, catering to its Southern element, passed the divisive, Stephen Douglas–inspired Kansas-Nebraska Act. That law repealed the Missouri Compromise of 1820 (which forbid slavery in territories north of Missouri's southern border), authorized slavery in previously off-limits territories under the banner of "popular sovereignty," and propelled the nation toward Civil War. Lincoln was angered by the substantive effect of the new law on slavery in the territories and was no doubt upset that it was the creation of Douglas, a long-standing Illinois political and social nemesis. These factors were sufficient to cause Lincoln to reenter the political arena.

In the fall of 1854, therefore, Lincoln aggressively campaigned for the U.S. Senate seat held by Douglas's ally from Illinois, James Shields. He attacked the Kansas-Nebraska Act for undercutting the Founding Fathers' intent to ultimately eliminate slavery and for depriving blacks of their right, espoused in the Declaration of Independence, to life, liberty, and the pursuit of happiness. Whigs and anti-Douglas Democrats seized control of the state legislature, which was responsible for electing a U.S. senator. Lincoln had the support of all the Whigs but was essentially betrayed by a friend, Democrat Lyman Trumbull, who refused to support Lincoln and leveraged the few anti-Douglas Democrats' votes to gain the senate seat for himself. Trumbull's small group deadlocked the proceedings by refusing to provide either Lincoln or his primary foe with the votes necessary for a majority. Trumbull wanted the office for himself.[2] Lincoln, but never his wife Mary, eventually forgave Trumbull for his political ploy.

Lincoln continuously and fiercely opposed and denounced the Kansas-Nebraska Act but believed he was bound by the Constitution to support Southern states' right to slavery and enforcement of fugitive slave laws. His opposition to that Act's territorial provisions and his advocacy against the extension of slavery to U.S. territories became hallmarks of his political position and led him down the path to the presidency.

In 1856 he took his first practical step in that direction by joining the new Republican Party, which was attracting Northern Whigs and Democrats to its no-slavery-in-the-territories position. His May 29, 1856, adjournment speech at the first Illinois Republican Party convention provided him with an opportunity to lambaste slavery and thereby achieve national fame and notoriety. There is little record left of what may have been one of his finest speeches ever—one that so mesmerized reporters that they stopped taking notes.[3]

The Republicans were shocked and then motivated to action by the Supreme Court's notorious *Dred Scott* decision in 1857. That decision, apparently cleared with new President James Buchanan, held that American blacks, free or slave, were not citizens of the United States or any of the states and thus could not bring a federal lawsuit. But Chief Justice Roger B. Taney and his colleagues did not stop there. They also gratuitously stated that taking a slave into a free state or territory did not result in the slave's emancipation and that Congress had no power to prohibit slavery in U.S. territories. This logic meant that the Missouri Compromise of 1820 had been unconstitutional and raised the specter of a future decision that states themselves could not prohibit slavery.

Lincoln's Republican Party activities led to his 1858 candidacy for an Illinois seat in the United States Senate. His opponent was Stephen A. Douglas, who supported popular sovereignty on the slavery issue and had engineered passage of the divisive Kansas-Nebraska Act. That Senate campaign included the most famous political debates in American history—the Lincoln-Douglas Debates. In this series of seven debates, Lincoln forced Douglas to take a position on the slavery issue that would result in Douglas's obtaining the Senate seat but undercutting his Southern political base for a possible 1860 presidential candidacy.

Specifically, at the Freeport debate, Lincoln asked Douglas how popular sovereignty could be implemented and how a territory could ban slavery prior to statehood in light of the *Dred Scott* decision. Douglas responded that local enforcement laws would be necessary to protect the existence of slavery in each jurisdiction and that failure to pass such local laws would *de facto* exclude slavery. That answer preserved his popular sovereignty position critical to an 1858 victory in Illinois but doomed his 1860 presidential prospects. Southern Democratic politicians, after their huge *Dred Scott* victory, would not countenance any legal or political theory that would prohibit slavery in any of the territories.

Lincoln earned national fame from the 1858 debates—a fame that would lead to the Republican nomination for president in 1860. Lincoln's Republicans actually outpolled the Douglas Democrats in the 1858 Illinois popular vote, 190,468 to 166,374 in the state house and 53,784 to 44,750 in the state senate. But Lincoln was not elected to the U.S. Senate by the unrepresentative, Democrat-controlled Illinois General Assembly in its January 1859 vote.[4] Nevertheless, Republican politicians and newspaper editors began promoting Lincoln for president immediately after the Illinois election. In the words of William C. Harris, Lincoln emerged as the "Republican Champion of the Great West." One Illinoisan wrote from Washington that "many of the leading papers of the country" were proclaiming Lincoln "the leading spirit of the great west." In the fall of 1859, Lincoln burnished his Western presidential credentials by speaking on behalf of Republican candidates in Iowa, Ohio, Indiana, and Wisconsin. Lincoln arranged for the 1860 printing of the Lincoln-Douglas

Debates of 1858; this popular publication probably aided in his nomination and election.[5]

In fact, "It was primarily his mobilization of language that lifted him into contention for the presidency even though he had held no public office for a dozen years and been defeated twice as a senatorial candidate."[6] Although he had suffered in-state political defeats in 1855 and 1859, Lincoln, primarily through his 1858 debates with Douglas, had achieved such national renown by the end of the 1850s that he was a respected dark-horse candidate for the 1860 Republican presidential nomination.

In February 1860, the *Chicago Herald and Tribune*, in the course of endorsing Lincoln for the Republican nomination, perceptively noted that Lincoln was a man of "great breadth and great acuteness of intellect. Not learned, in a bookish sense, but master of great fundamental principles, and of that kind of ability which applies them to crises and events."[7]

At the 1860 Republican National Convention, Lincoln's managers deftly assembled a coalition against front-runner William Seward of New York and then amazingly succeeded in defeating not only Seward, but also Salmon P. Chase of Ohio, Edward Bates of Missouri, and Simon Cameron of Pennsylvania. As the outcome became clear, B. Gratz Brown of Missouri announced the anti-climactic change of that state's votes: "I am instructed to cast the entire vote of Missouri—eighteen votes for that gallant son of the West, Abraham Lincoln."[8]

Lincoln's nomination stirred a sense of pride throughout the West. Indiana's *LaPorte Herald* praised Lincoln as a man of the West who had risen from poverty and obscurity "by the most intense labor and application" to become a "tower of strength" in the region. Iowa's *Davenport Gazette* raved that "the people of the West will feel in voting for him as though they were elevating from their own ranks one who thoroughly understands their interests and will faithfully represent them." St. Louis congressional candidate Frank Blair praised the "Rail Splitter's" Western virtues to a crowd celebrating Lincoln's nomination. His Western roots even received a backhanded compliment in the *Richmond Daily Dispatch*, which credited Horace Greeley with throwing William Seward "underfoot by the backwoodsman of the West, a flat boatman, a mauler of rails, and, worse than all, a man suspected of being 'honest.'"[9]

Lincoln's humble Western roots, however, posed a threat to his credibility as president. His background, gangly appearance, and Western twang made him an easy target for criticism by the Eastern elite. The name-calling included "gorilla," "third-rate lawyer," "nullity," "duffer," "rough farmer," "the original baboon," "a western hick," and "a man in the habit of making coarse and clumsy jokes." Jay Winik summarized his credibility problems: "His high-pitched twang was an oddity in the genteel salons and artful councils of official Washington. The real Lincoln, a curious amalgam of candor and obfuscation, country boy and learned lawyer, was—and would remain—alien to the city's elite."[10]

The 1850s were a disappointing yet glorious time for Lincoln. While beginning the decade as an ignored ex-congressman and suffering political defeats along the way, he had latched onto a new political party and a potent political issue (prohibiting slavery in the territories) that propelled him to the threshold of the presidency of the United States.

GRANT'S DISASTROUS DECADE

Grant, on the other hand, started the decade as a heroic Mexican War officer with a bright military future, yet experienced personal embarrassment and failure again and again, and finished the decade with virtually no prospects for a successful life.

Grant had married Julia Dent on August 22, 1848, with West Point friend James Longstreet at the ceremony as his best man. Grant and his wife visited his family in Ohio and then moved on to duty stations in Sackets Harbor, New York (on Lake Ontario) and Detroit, Michigan. They lived together until mid-1852 except when one or the other went to visit family, such as Julia's giving birth to their first child back in Missouri. Their togetherness ended when he received orders to the Pacific Northwest and decided against taking his pregnant wife and infant son on the dangerous journey to frontier country.

At Sackets Harbor, Grant realized he had a drinking problem, joined the Sons of Temperance, and apparently benefited from their support until he was transferred. He may have had drinking problems in Detroit. That at least was the impression generated when he fell on an icy sidewalk in January 1851 and sued the merchant who owned the sidewalk. The merchant said of Grant, "If you soldiers would keep sober, perhaps you would not fall on people's pavement and hurt your legs." Grant won the case but came under suspicion in the military community.[11]

Before sailing for the West from New York in July 1852, Grant visited Washington in an unsuccessful effort to resolve the quartermaster funds issue. He was stymied by the fact that the entire city was closed for the funeral of Senator Henry Clay for much of the time Grant was there.

Crossing Panama during the journey to the Pacific, Grant heroically helped fight a cholera epidemic, took extraordinary steps to hasten his group's trip and was saddened by the death of a hundred persons, including friends and their children. After staying at the Presidio in San Francisco, he traveled north and assumed his duties as quartermaster at Columbia Barracks (Fort Vancouver), where he invested in a store, cattle, hogs and a farm. These investments, a common practice among officers in those days, brought only losses to Grant. He sold firewood to steamers and rented horses, but the farm was flooded by the Columbia River. Separated from his family, Grant joined many of his fellow officers in excessive drinking. His small size and apparent sensitivity to alcohol made him more likely to become intoxicated, and his behavior was observed by visiting officers such as future general George B. McClellan.[12]

His September and October 1853 requests to go to Washington to settle the old $1,000 claim were denied. Instead he received orders that took him to Fort Humboldt in northern California, where he reported on January 5, 1854. As a company commander there in 1854, Grant served under an officer with whom he had feuded in Missouri. That officer, Lieutenant Colonel Robert Buchanan, made life miserable for Grant. Receiving little mail and anxious to return home, Grant was lonely and depressed, and reportedly often drank heavily.[13]

Separated from his wife and family, Grant reflected his depression in his letters to Julia. He sorely missed the "highly intelligent, lively, affectionate woman who adored him as he adored her."[14] On February 2, he wrote to her, "You do not know how forsaken I feel here.... I got one letter from you since I have been here but it was some three months old."[15] Four days later he voiced greater concern and frustration:

> A mail come in this evening but brought me no news from you nor nothing in reply to my application for orders to go home. I cannot conceive what is the cause of the delay. The state of suspense that I am in is scarsely [sic] bearable. I think I have been from my family quite long enough and sometimes I feel as though I could almost go home "nolens volens [whether willing or not]." I presume, under ordinary circumstances, Humboldt would be a good enough place but the suspense I am in would make paradice [sic] form a bad picture.[16]

In a March 6 letter, he said he was "almost tempted to resign," and on March 25 he wrote that he had received only one letter from Julia at Fort Humboldt (written the prior October) and added, "How very anxious I am to get home once again. I do not feel as if it was possible to endure this separation much longer."[17]

By April 11 Grant had reached his breaking point. Upon receiving notice of his promotion to captain and possibly a threat from Buchanan of a court-martial for being intoxicated while on duty, Grant acknowledged receipt of his new commission, resigned his Army commission (effective July 31, 1854), and requested a leave of absence.[18] He then returned to New York via Nicaragua with funds raised for him in California. Grant's public drinking throughout much of his fifteen-year army career and the circumstances surrounding his resignation had tarred him with a reputation as a heavy drinker.[19] His financial situation deteriorated as he was unable to collect a $1,750 debt owed him in San Francisco and $800 owed to him by an Army sutler. He ended up borrowing $500 from a friend, Captain Simon Bolivar Buckner, to get home from New York.[20]

Joan Waugh perceptively observed, "One can only speculate about the humiliation that Grant endured during this period. He had enjoyed an elite education, proved himself an able and brave soldier in a major war, and compiled a solid record in the peacetime army, at least until the end. Now, at age thirty-two, he returned home in the eyes of many a poverty-stricken failure."[21]

After reentering civilian life, Grant endured the most trying and frustrating years of his life. For several years his primary source of income came from sales of firewood in St. Louis. The firewood had been cut by Grant on land that had been given to Julia by her father, Frederick Dent. Grant was unsuccessful as a farmer and rent collector. He built a ram-shackle house—appropriately named Hardscrabble—that Julia despised. He tried to borrow money from his father. A particularly low point occurred in the midst of the 1857 depression when he pawned his gold watch for $22. Between 1854 and 1860 Grant was quite dependent upon Julia's father, with whom he had an acrimonious relationship. After giving up farming in 1858, Grant dabbled in real estate sales until 1860. Due to the lack of political connections, Grant twice was unsuccessful in obtaining the position of St. Louis County engineer. All in all, these were depressing times.[22]

Although it was difficult for him to do so, Grant went to his own father for help and finally escaped the clutches of Frederick Dent. In May 1860, Ulysses began working under his younger brothers, Simpson and Orvil, in the Grant family's successful leather-goods store in Galena, Illinois. He moved his family into a rented house, led a sober life, and apparently began rebuilding his self-respect.[23] Although he became friends with attorney John A. Rawlins, a Federal elector pledged to the Democrat Stephen A. Douglas, Grant did not meet the Illinois residency requirement for voting in the November 6, 1860, presidential election.

On the eve of the Civil War, therefore, Grant had a less-than-successful record as a peacetime Army officer, a distant history of Mexican War heroism, and a well-known drinking problem when separated from his wife and children. He had proven his dogged determination and persistence, but there was no indication of the military greatness he would demonstrate during the nation's greatest war.

However, Grant's less-than-a-year residency in Galena proved fortunate because there he became acquainted with not only Rawlins, his future chief of staff, but also with Elihu B. Washburne, Galena's Republican congressman and a former Whig who was a long-time political associate of Lincoln. Washburne would become Grant's Washington, D.C. political advocate, protector, and liaison to Lincoln.

LINCOLN AND GRANT ON THE EVE OF THE CIVIL WAR

Joan Waugh compared Lincoln's and Grant's pre–Civil War experiences: "Like Lincoln, Grant was an uncommon common 'western' man who had known both hard times and hard labor. Unlike Lincoln, Grant endured a decade in his middle years soured with abject public failure."[24] Indeed, both these Westerners had worked diligently all their lives, had failed in business ventures, and suffered from depression during challenging times.

By early 1860, however, Lincoln had rebounded from his earlier failures and defeats and had bright national political prospects. The younger Grant had not escaped his troubles and was desperately seeking some way to make a decent living to support his family. Prospects for Grant to resume his military career, which had been terminated in disgrace, seemed nonexistent.

CHAPTER 4

OUTBREAK OF
THE CIVIL WAR

———————◆———————

The 1860 four-candidate presidential election resulted in a victory for Lincoln and set the nation on course for civil war. Unsatisfied with the official Democratic nomination of "Popular Sovereignty" Douglas, Southern Democrats held a rump convention and nominated Kentuckian John C. Breckinridge, who stood for the unfettered right to extend slavery into the territories. Republican Lincoln, of course, opposed such extension, and a compromise candidate John Bell (Constitutional Union Party), who took no position on slavery in the territories, merely siphoned off votes from the major candidates.

These are the election results:

Candidates	Popular Votes	Electoral Votes
Lincoln	1,865,908	180
Douglas	1,380,202	12
Breckinridge	848,019	72
Bell	590,901	39[1]

Lincoln's election is often criticized as unimpressive because he received "only" 39.9 percent of the popular vote. Actually, that number is quite impressive since he was in an unparalleled four-way race and his name was not even on the ballot in nine Southern states.[2] Even if all of Lincoln's opponents' votes had gone to one candidate, he would have won the election because he had a majority of votes in states that controlled a majority of electoral votes.

Lincoln's November 1860 election as the first Republican president moved South Carolina and six other Southern states to secede before he was sworn in as president on March 4, 1861. Grant accurately perceived the Republican Party's opposition to extension of slavery to the territories as the primary cause of secession.[3]

Lincoln's pre-inauguration actions confirmed the significance of that issue. When informed of efforts to compromise on the extension of slavery to avoid possible war, Lincoln advised Illinois Senator Lyman Trumbull to stand fast for Republican Party principles: "Let there be no compromise on the question of *extending* slavery. If there be, all our labor is lost, and, ere long, must be done again. The dangerous ground—that into which some of our friends have a hankering to run—is Pop[ular]. Sov[ereignty]. Have none of it. Stand firm. The tug has to come, & better now, than any time hereafter."[4]

After the Confederates initiated hostilities by firing on Fort Sumter on April 12, 1861, Grant, like many Midwesterners, was anxious to enter the fray in response to Lincoln's call for 75,000 volunteers. He attended and was called upon to preside over a public meeting in Galena and chaired a recruiting rally there two days later. After refusing to become a mere captain of the company of Galena volunteers, he nevertheless conducted their training drills in Galena and at Camp Yates near Springfield. Although Grant initially declined to seek political intervention in order to obtain a senior military position, he did not refuse an offer of assistance from Congressman Washburne, the senior Republican in the House of Representatives. With Washburne's help, Grant became a military aide to Illinois Governor Richard Yates on April 29. That position had high promotion potential. Grant took charge of training raw recruits and mustering ten regiments of them into Illinois service.[5]

When that assignment was completed, Grant still had no military command or position, but he hoped that his fifteen years of Army service would quickly earn him a position of leadership and responsibility in the United States Army. His hopes were soon dashed. First, he wrote a May 24 letter to the Adjutant General in Washington, offering his services for the duration of the war and stating his competence to command a regiment. Next, he personally applied in Cincinnati for a position with Major General George McClellan, who commanded Ohio's militia and was within months to become commander of the Eastern Army of the Potomac. Hearing nothing from McClellan, Grant next applied to Brigadier General Nathaniel Lyon in St. Louis. Again, he heard nothing.[6]

Grant resigned himself to returning home and somehow creating his own opportunity. However, his mustering-in work had caught the attention of Washburne. He had seen Grant's performance, realized his possible military potential, and helped convince Governor Yates to name Grant a colonel and regimental militia commander. Perhaps even more significant was the request to Yates from the officers of the 21st Illinois Volunteers that Grant himself replace their commander. Their colonel had lost control of the volunteers; the men had become notorious for their drunken rowdiness, petty thefts, and lack of any military discipline. Yates consulted his aides, who had been impressed by Grant's professional direction of that and other regiments, and then offered the command to Grant.

After his June 15 appointment, Grant quickly brought discipline to the previously unruly regiment, which was then mustered into national service on June 28. To convince his troops to extend their ninety-day enlistments to three years as a condition of undertaking national service, Grant had them addressed by Democratic congressmen (and later generals) John A. McClernand and John A. ("Black Jack") Logan.[7] Both of them had long records of political involvement with Lincoln in Illinois politics.

In taking command of his regiment, Grant recognized that lack of leadership was its fundamental problem. He addressed that issue in his first order of the war: "In accepting this command, your Commander will require the co-operation of all the commissioned and non-commissioned Officers in instructing the command, and in maintaining discipline, and hopes to receive also the hearty support of every enlisted man."[8] Jean Edward Smith perceptively analyzed the significance of this order and what it represented in Grant's approach to commanding units primarily consisting of volunteers:

> The phraseology is vintage Grant. The cooperation of officers and noncommissioned officers was required; the support of the enlisted men was something to be hoped for. That distinction became a hallmark of Grant's leadership. No West Point-trained officer understood the nature of the Union's volunteer army better than Grant. Having survived a number of years on the bottom rung in civil life, he had developed an instinctive feel for how civilians behaved. He recognized that volunteer soldiers were not regulars and never tried to impose the Spartan discipline of the old army.[9]

Grant used his experience and common sense to establish his credibility in numerous ways. When ordered to move his men one hundred and sixteen miles to the Mississippi River, Grant declined rail transportation and had his men march the distance. He told Yates, "The men are going to do a lot of marching before the war is over and I prefer to train them in friendly company, not in the enemy's." Based on his Mexican War experience, his supply requisitions were complete and required no changes. One day, when his men were unprepared for an early morning march, he started without many of them and the laggards hurriedly dressed and ran to catch up; the next morning they were ready on schedule.[10]

In early July, Grant's regiment was ordered to Quincy, Illinois, then to Ironton, Missouri, and finally to Florida, Missouri. Grant was to move on the latter two locations to dislodge Confederate forces reportedly there. During those two movements, Grant first experienced the pre-battle anxiety of a Civil War commander. In his memoirs, he described these emotional experiences:

> My sensations as we approached what I supposed might be "a field of battle" were anything but agreeable. I had been in all the engagements in Mexico that it was possible for one

person to be in; but not in command. If some one else had been colonel and I had been lieutenant-colonel I do not think I would have felt any trepidation.... As we approached the brow of the hill from which it was expected we could see Harris' camp, and possibly find his men ready formed to meet us, my heart kept getting higher and higher until it felt to me it was in my throat. [After finding the enemy camp abandoned,] [m]y heart resumed its place. It occurred to me at once that Harris had been as much afraid of me as I had been of him. This was a view of the question I had never taken before; but it was one I never forgot afterwards. From that event to the close of the war, I never experienced trepidation upon confronting an enemy, though I always felt more or less anxiety.[11]

This incident is a key to understanding Grant the man; it was the moment he stopped worrying about what the enemy was going to do and started concentrating on what *he* was going to do (a trait he still demonstrated two and a half years later when he advised a subordinate on the first evening of the Battle of the Wilderness to stop worrying about what Lee was going to do next).

During the summer and early autumn, Grant commanded several regiments in Missouri, was appointed brigadier general of volunteers on August 5 (based on Washburne's recommendation), and named his Galena friend, John Rawlins, his adjutant.[12] While in Missouri, Grant told his headquarters he was, contrary to orders, not building fortifications for his troops. He wrote, "I am not fortifying here at all.... Drill and discipline is more necessary for the men than fortifications.... I have...very little disposition to gain a 'Pillow notoriety' for a branch of service that I have forgotten all about."[13] As Jean Edward Smith noted, "Fortifications reflected a defensive mentality alien to his nature."[14]

Major General John C. Frémont, Union theater commander in the West, passed over more senior generals and appointed Grant commander of the District of Southeast Missouri. This appointment put Grant in charge of the critical Mississippi River region between Missouri on the west and Kentucky and Illinois on the east. He established his headquarters in Cairo, Illinois, where the Mississippi and Ohio rivers meet.[15]

Grant immediately faced a crisis and converted it into a strategic success. He learned that Confederate soldiers, under the command of Lieutenant General Leonidas Polk, had breached Kentucky's neutrality and had occupied and were fortifying Columbus, a strong position on the Mississippi a mere twenty miles south of Cairo. More critically, Grant heard from a supposedly reliable spy that Confederates were marching on Paducah, a key Kentucky town at the junction of the Ohio and Tennessee rivers. As soon as he learned of the Confederate occupation of Columbus and the apparent threat to Paducah, Grant wired Frémont of the developments and his intent to move on Paducah unless instructed otherwise.

Within a day, Grant organized an expedition and on September 6, 1861, took possession of Paducah with troops and gunboats. Grant seized Paducah, "a masterful countermeasure to the Confederate occupation of Columbus," in the words of Donald J. Roberts II, without any orders to do so.[16] Grant did not wait for an answer to his wire to Frémont; Frémont's orders to take Paducah were awaiting Grant at Cairo when he returned from Paducah.[17] Although Confederate troops had not actually been marching on Paducah, Grant's initiative in quickly seizing the town reflected not only its vulnerability, but also Grant's concern about the damage its loss could impose and his belief in its utility to the Union.[18]

Lincoln, a Kentucky native, was constantly concerned about developments in that crucial border state and strove to keep it in the Union. According to Lincoln's secretaries, John Nicolay and John Hay, the "culmination of affairs in Kentucky [Polk's invasion and Grant's quick response] had been carefully watched in Washington."[19]

Just as Grant took military advantage of Polk's foolish invasion of Kentucky, Lincoln took political advantage of it. When resolutions were introduced in the Kentucky General Assembly condemning Polk's violation of Kentucky's peace and neutrality, demanding expulsion of the invaders, and seeking Federal aid to do so, Lincoln took a critical step to ensure both the passing of the resolutions and Kentucky's remaining in the Union. He provided assurances to the legislators that he would be undoing Frémont's premature emancipation proclamation in the Western Theater. This *quid pro quo* ensured Kentucky's loyalty for the time being and reinforced the calamitous effect (for the Confederacy) of Polk's ill-considered invasion.[20]

Frémont transferred Grant back to Cairo and replaced him at Paducah with Brigadier General Charles F. Smith (Grant's commandant at West Point and his early Civil War mentor). Although Smith was Grant's subordinate (because of Grant's Illinois-related promotion), Grant greatly respected him and used him as a key advisor. Shortly thereafter, Smith's troops occupied Smithland, where the Cumberland meets the Ohio. Thus, the scene was set for Grant's early 1862 thrust into Kentucky and Tennessee via the two riverine highways, the Tennessee and the Cumberland.

Grant's prompt occupation of Paducah brought him, apparently for the first time, to the attention of his fellow Illinoisan, Lincoln, for something he had accomplished. Being intimately familiar with the multi-river geography in the Illinois/Kentucky area, the president must have appreciated the significance of Grant's unhesitating seizure of Paducah at the crucial juncture of the Ohio and Tennessee rivers. During the first two years of the war, Lincoln greatly feared the loss of critically situated Kentucky and thus must have been greatly relieved by Grant's initiative in occupying the two vital Kentucky towns.

Grant's first battle was his November 7, 1861, attack on a Confederate camp at Belmont, Missouri, slightly upstream from Major General (and Episcopal bishop) Leonidas Polk's Columbus, Kentucky stronghold. Grant kept Polk from reinforcing the camp by operating in a deceptive manner that led Polk to suspect that Grant intended to attack Columbus. After hard fighting, Grant's men broke the Rebel line at Belmont, lost discipline looting the camp, were effectively reorganized by Grant for a counterattack through a newly formed Rebel line, and then barely escaped to Union transports as Polk's additional belated reinforcements arrived too late.

On the down side, Grant had underestimated the Rebels' ability to counterattack his men; this tendency to overlook the potential for enemy attacks would create problems for him again at Fort Donelson and Shiloh—as well as during Jubal Early's 1864 raid on Washington. But Grant's deceptive hit-and-run attack kept Polk from effectively using his superior numbers and amazingly resulted in slightly more casualties for the defenders than the attackers—an unusual occurrence in the Civil War. Of the 3,100 men led by Grant, only about 500 were killed, wounded, or missing. The Confederate force of 7,000, including reinforcements from Columbus, reported about 640 men killed, wounded, or missing.[21] Grant was pleased with the results: his soldiers gained self-confidence, the Rebel forces at Columbus were at least disconcerted, and the Confederates canceled any plans to move troops across the Mississippi to assist their comrades in Missouri.

Even more importantly for the North, Belmont once again brought Ulysses Grant's name to the attention of President Lincoln, who was desperate for any kind of action by a Union general.[22] Charles B. Flood concluded, "The Battle of Belmont was the foundation of Grant's reputation for taking the war to the enemy.... [I]n him the Union had a man of the West, a man who had spent years near the Mississippi and viscerally understood the strategic importance of that river and its tributaries."[23] Paducah and Belmont were a modest beginning to a series of positive and aggressive actions by Grant that appealed to Lincoln, who from the start of the war understood that the North had the affirmative burden of winning the war and thus had to go on the offensive as often as possible.

Lincoln learned of this skirmish at the very least from a letter sent to him by Brigadier General John A. McClernand, a self-promoting Illinois political general who had been an associate of Lincoln's before the war and had been under Grant's command at Belmont. In response to McClernand's letter to his pre-war associate, Lincoln sent him a social, unofficial response assuring him that he had just conferred with Congressman Washburne and that the Illinois troops were not being forgotten. Lincoln and Grant had not heard the last of McClernand.[24]

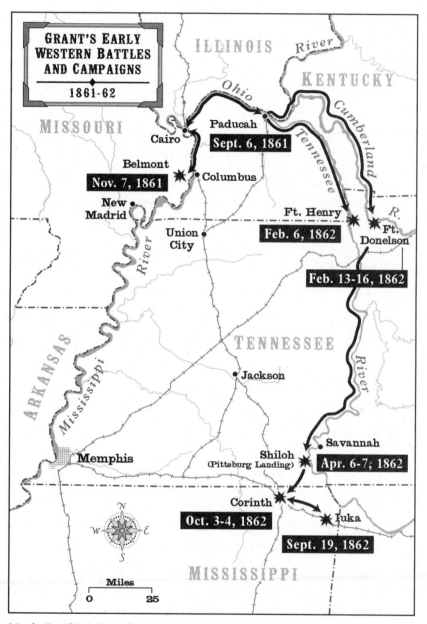

GRANT'S EARLY WESTERN BATTLES AND CAMPAIGNS

1861-62

ILLINOIS

River

KENTUCKY

Ohio

MISSOURI

Paducah

Cairo

Sept. 6, 1861

Cumberland

Tennessee

Belmont

Nov. 7, 1861

Columbus

New Madrid

Ft. Henry

Feb. 6, 1862

Ft. Donelson

R.

Union City

Feb. 13-16, 1862

River

TENNESSEE

Mississippi

Jackson

River

ARKANSAS

Savannah

Shiloh
(Pittsburg Landing)

Apr. 6-7, 1862

Memphis

Corinth

Oct. 3-4, 1862

Iuka

Sept. 19, 1862

N

W   E

S

MISSISSIPPI

Miles

0   25

Map by David Deis, Dreamline Cartography, Northridge, California

CHAPTER 5

LINCOLN PROTECTS GRANT

A s 1862 began, Lincoln was growing increasingly frustrated by the inertia of his theater commanders George McClellan in the East, Don Carlos Buell in eastern Kentucky, and Henry Halleck, who had replaced Frémont in the upper Mississippi valley. Despite constant prodding by the president, Union forces under their command remained relatively inert. One minor exception was a Halleck-authorized demonstration in force by Grant in western Kentucky. When Grant received January 6 orders to make threatening moves with his troops, he (unlike McClellan and others) saw the bad weather and road conditions as an opportunity and not a hindrance: "The continuous rains for the last week or more has [*sic*] rendered the roads extremely bad and will necessarily make our movements slow. This however will operate worse upon the enemy, if he should come out to meet us, than upon us."[1]

Grant's analysis typified his positive and practical approach to his duties, and in early 1862 his name "begins to acquire a special prominence and value," according to Lincoln's former secretaries. Looking

back two decades later, they evaluated Grant's usefulness at this stage of
the war:

> [Grant's] usefulness and superiority were evinced by the clear-
> ness and brevity of his correspondence, the correctness of
> routine reports and promptness of their transmission, the
> pertinence and practical quality of his suggestions, the readi-
> ness and fertility of expedient with which he executed orders.
> Any one reading over his letters of this first period of his
> military service is struck by the fact that through him some-
> thing was always accomplished. There was absence of excuse,
> complaint, or delay; always the report of a task performed. If
> his means or supplies were imperfect, he found or improvised
> the best available substitute; if he could not execute the full
> requirement, he performed so much of it as was possible. He
> always had an opinion, and that opinion was positive, intel-
> ligible, practical.[2]

At the time, however, Lincoln may have had some doubts. Having
received reports about Grant's alleged drinking, the president submitted
those reports to Washburne for comment. The Illinois mutual protective
association apparently worked in Grant's favor.[3]

According to his secretaries, "[t]he President's patience was well-nigh
exhausted" by the continuing lack of aggressiveness by Halleck and Buell
in Kentucky. Lincoln's frustration led him to deliver a military lecture to
them in identical messages of January 13: "... I state my general idea of
this war to be that we have the greater numbers and the enemy has the
greater facility of concentrating forces upon points of collision; that we
must fail unless we can find some way of making our advantage an over-
match for his; and that this can only be done by menacing him with
superior forces at different points at the same time, so that we can safely
attack one or both if he makes no change; and if he weakens one to
strengthen the other, forbear to attack the strengthened one, but seize
and hold the weakened one, gaining so much."[4]

While Lincoln was pushing Halleck from above, Grant was incurring Halleck's wrath when he went to St. Louis to advocate aggressive southward movements from the Ohio River up two rivers in Kentucky. Shortly after Grant had begun his presentation, Halleck rudely dismissed him. Halleck's rudeness to Grant may have been the result of his dissatisfaction with Grant's unkempt appearance, his belief that Grant was gullible and might be drinking again, his own discomfort from a case of measles, or a combination of these factors.[5]

Although Halleck at first rejected Grant's recommendation to send troops and gunboats up the Tennessee and Cumberland Rivers to capture Forts Henry and Donelson, Lincoln provided a boost for Grant's plans. Lincoln had been urging the War Department to hastily complete and ship mortar boats from Pittsburgh, Pennsylvania, to Cairo, Illinois, for use on the internal rivers. In fact, Lincoln communicated about them with Secretary of War Stanton and Navy Flag Officer Andrew H. Foote, who, along with Grant, was pushing Halleck for the upriver move.[6] Frustrated by McClellan's "slows" in the East, the president issued President's General War Order No. 1 on January 27, 1862. That order directed a general movement against insurgent forces on February 22, 1862, and specifically directed that "The Army and Flotilla at Cairo," among others, "be ready for a movement on that day."[7] Although somewhat simplistic and born of frustration, the president's order proved effective at least in Grant's area of responsibility. At this early stage of the war, both Lincoln and Grant were anxious to take the fight to the enemy.[8]

Within the next three weeks, Grant carried out the president's aggressive intent. With his discretion nullified by the president, Halleck had no choice but to approve Grant's move (along with Foote) against Fort Henry on the Tennessee River. After a two-hour artillery duel, Foote took the surrender of that poorly situated fort. Without authority to do so, Grant advised Halleck that he was next moving overland fifteen miles east against Fort Donelson.[9]

Reinforcing Grant's success, Halleck sent more troops to aid Grant against a Confederate buildup of 16,000 or more troops at Donelson.

Foote's gunboats were decimated by the well-located Rebel guns at
Donelson, and they careened downstream carrying dead sailors and the
wounded Foote. Although Grant meanwhile had pinned the Rebels inside
the fort, they forcefully opened an escape route to Nashville while Grant
was a few miles down river conferring with the injured Foote. Grant
returned to find chaos on the battlefield, ordered a counterattack all along
his lines, closed the Confederate escape route, and compelled the February 16 unconditional surrender of the enemy. The nation's press was soon
praising "Unconditional Surrender" Grant for his dual victories.

That same day Lincoln wrote to Halleck that Donelson was safe
"unless Grant shall be overwhelmed from outside" and urged Halleck
and Buell to cooperate in preserving Grant's victory. Recognizing the
significance of what Grant had done, the president concluded, "Our success or failure at Donnelson [sic] is vastly important; and I beg you to put
your soul in the effort." Meanwhile McClellan and his friend Buell had
provided no assistance to Grant despite pleas for help from Halleck.
Donelson thus had become Grant's to win or lose on his own.[10]

As Lincoln wrote to Halleck, Grant completed his Fort Donelson
victory and wired Halleck: "We have taken Fort Donelson and from
12,000 to 15,000 prisoners, including Generals Buckner and Bushrod
Johnson; also about 20,000 stand of arms, 48 pieces of artillery, 17 heavy
guns, from 2,000 to 4,000 horses, and large quantities of commissary
stores."[11] Grant sent a similar but more detailed report of the victory to
Halleck's chief of staff.[12]

Halleck pounced on this opportunity for self-promotion and
requested, in addition to promotions for Buell, Grant and Pope, command in the West for himself "in return for Forts Henry and Donelson."[13]
The previous evening Secretary Stanton had brought to Lincoln for his
signature a nomination of Grant as a major general of volunteers. As he
signed the document, Lincoln is reported to have said, "If the Southern-
ers think that man for man they are better than our Illinois men, or
Western men generally, they will discover themselves in a grievous mistake."[14]

On February 19 the Senate confirmed Grant's nomination retroactive
to February 16. Washburne immediately telegraphed the news to Grant.[15]

Pope and Buell were promoted a month later, and promotions of officers serving under Grant followed in due course. As Nicolay and Hay later explained, "By this brilliant and important victory Grant's fame sprang suddenly into full and universal recognition."[16] Although the president did not send personal congratulations to Grant,[17] Grant's additional successes further enhanced his good standing with the president—a relationship Grant would need in the coming months.

In the days immediately following the fall of Fort Donelson, Halleck, Buell and McClellan communicated about who should move on Nashville with what forces. While they dithered, Grant simply suggested that some of Buell's troops, who finally had arrived at Donelson under the command of Brigadier General William "Bull" Nelson, proceed upstream and occupy Nashville. To the consternation of Buell and Halleck, that is exactly what occurred.[18] Grant further aggravated them by going to Nashville to coordinate activities there. While they dallied, he acted.

Halleck proceeded to treat the victorious Grant as a pariah rather than a hero. Not only did Halleck fail to send a congratulatory message to Grant, but he also took the trouble to wire his thanks to Major General David Hunter, Union commander in Kansas, merely for sending reinforcements to Grant.[19] After Grant's victories at Forts Henry and Donelson, the first major Union victories of the war, the possibly jealous theater commander astoundingly ordered Grant to stay at Fort Henry while his troops proceeded southward up the Tennessee under the field command of Brigadier General Charles F. Smith. Although Grant later claimed he had been placed under arrest, Carl R. Schenker, Jr. asserted that was not the case because Grant continued organizing the southward expedition and "Smith looked to him for orders."[20]

While placing Grant at least "on hold," Halleck launched attacks on Grant in messages to Grant and General-in-Chief George McClellan. On March 3 he wrote to McClellan: "I have had no communication with General Grant for more than a week. He left his command without my authority and went to Nashville. His army seems to be as much demoralized by the victory of Fort Donelson as was that of the Potomac by the defeat of Bull Run. It is hard to censure a successful general immediately after a victory, but I think he richly deserves it. I can get no returns, no reports, no information of any kind from him. Satisfied with his victory, he sits down and enjoys it without any regard to the future. I am worn-out and tired with this neglect and inefficiency."[21] On March 4 Halleck wrote Grant: "You will place Major Genl C.F. Smith in command of expedition, & remain yourself at Fort Henry. Why do you not obey my orders to report strength & positions of your command?"[22]

After McClellan then authorized Halleck to arrest Grant and place Smith in command,[23] Halleck sent the following response on March 4: "A rumor has just reached me that since the taking of Fort Donelson General Grant has resumed his former bad habits. If so, it will account for his neglect of my often-repeated orders. I do not deem it advisable to arrest him at present, but have placed General Smith in command of the expedition up the Tennessee. I think Smith will restore order and discipline."[24] It is unclear what motivated Halleck to launch his generally unsupported attacks on Grant; there are no records to support his accusations, such as copies of any of the allegedly disobeyed orders requesting troop reports.[25] Possibilities include jealousy, anger about Grant's alleged administrative sloppiness,[26] eliminating a potential rival, and deflecting blame for Halleck's own failures to keep McClellan informed about the status of troops in the field.

In fairness to Halleck, the record indicates that he refused Grant's three requests to be relieved from duty and told Grant to be ready to assume command in the field.[27] Their standoff came to a conclusion after Halleck heard from Washington. On March 10, Adjutant General Lorenzo Thomas wrote Halleck about a report that Grant had been AWOL and inquired: "By direction of the President the Secretary of War desires you to ascertain and report whether General Grant left his command at any time without proper authority, and, if so, for how long; whether he has made to you proper reports and returns of his force; whether he has committed any acts which were unauthorized or not in accordance with military subordination or propriety, and, if so, what."[28] In other words, Halleck was being told—probably by the president—to put up or shut up.[29]

Now realizing that Congressman Washburne likely had taken the Halleck-Grant dispute to Lincoln, Halleck quickly backed off. On March

13, he wired Grant: "You cannot be relieved from your command. There is no good reason for it. I am certain that all which the authorities at Washington ask is that you enforce discipline and punish the disorderly.... Instead of relieving you, I wish you as soon as your new army is in the field to assume the immediate command and lead it on to new victories."[30]

Halleck still owed Adjutant General Thomas some answers. So, on March 15, he explained that Grant's trip to Nashville was with good intentions and a desire to serve public interest, that probably avoidable "irregularities...said to have occurred at Fort Donelson" in Grant's absence violated Grant's own orders, and his failures to report troop status resulted from subordinates' failures and telegraph problems. "All these irregularities have now been remedied," concluded Halleck, who advised that Grant had "been directed to resume his command in the field."[31]

Although Halleck, in backing down, may have been motivated in part by a sense of relief that the March 11 President's War Order No. 3 had relieved McClellan as general-in-chief (when he left Washington for his Peninsula Campaign in southeastern Virginia), expanded Halleck's command and made him superior to Buell, it is likely that Lincoln's probable intervention and Thomas's inquiry were key factors in Halleck's change of attitude. Thus, the relationship of Illinoisans Lincoln, Washburne, and Grant likely saved Grant's career—for the first time.[32]

After Halleck allowed Grant to leave Fort Henry, Grant headed southward up the Tennessee to join his troops near Pittsburg Landing, close to the small Shiloh Methodist Church. His assignment was to await the arrival of Buell's Army of the Ohio for a joint attack on the northeastern Mississippi rail crossroads town of Corinth. Grant became so focused on the planned attack that he gave little consideration to what the Confederates were doing. In fact, they were assembling a 40,000-plus-man army from the Mississippi Valley and Deep South in order to attack Grant before Buell arrived.

The overconfident Grant and Brigadier General William T. Sherman, one of his division commanders, ignored indications of a Confederate attack, and Grant assured Halleck there would be none. Under the command of General Albert Sidney Johnston, however, the Confederates

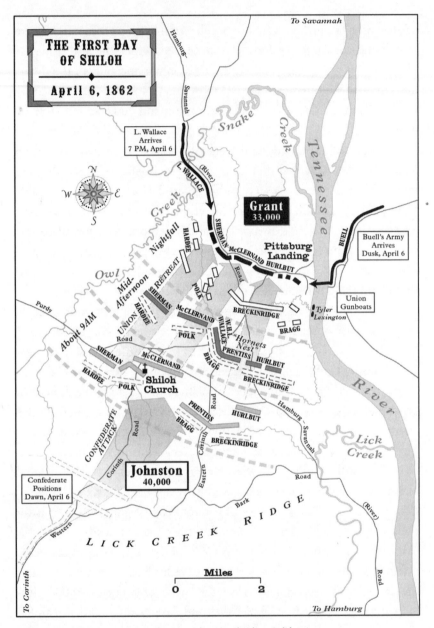

THE FIRST DAY
OF SHILOH
◆
April 6, 1862

Map by David Deis, Dreamline Cartography, Northridge, California

launched their surprise assault at Shiloh early on Sunday, April 6. Grant took hands-on control of the battlefield, visited throughout the day with his division chiefs while under fire, rallied them and their troops to keep his army from being driven into the Tennessee, and truly saved his army that day.[33]

Despite his subordinates' advice to retreat across the river that night, Grant instead ordered a massive counterattack early the next morning. To those recommendations of retreat across the Tennessee, he responded, "Tomorrow we shall attack them with fresh troops and drive them, of course."[34] That unexpected and successful assault drove the Rebels off the field and back toward Corinth. The result was a significant, but costly, Union victory. Grant paid a high price for his lack of preparedness. He took the brunt of the blame for the unprecedented casualties that resulted from Shiloh. His 13,100 casualties exceeded the Confederates' 10,700. The cumulative casualties in the ferocious two-day battle not only exceeded the American casualties suffered in all prior American wars but also resulted in the first claims that Grant was a "butcher" and the revival of drunkenness allegations against him.

The outcry against Grant led Lincoln to inquire of Halleck "whether any neglect or misconduct of General Grant or any other officer contributed to the sad casualties that befell our forces on Sunday [April 6]." Halleck responded that, while some subordinates had performed badly, Grant had performed well and rumors to the contrary were false.[35] Halleck may have defended Grant to avoid embarrassment to Halleck's theater command or he may have done so because he had recently learned that Grant had a friend in a very high place—the president himself. An early indication that Lincoln would support Grant's performance at Shiloh came when just days later the president issued an April 10 Proclamation of Thanksgiving for Victories, in which he spoke of "signal victories" and "casualties and calamities of sedition and civil war."[36]

The criticism of Grant rose to an outcry in many quarters for his dismissal. It is unclear when and whether the president said of Grant, "I can't spare this man; he fights," but he clearly did defend Grant against the charges.[37] Pennsylvania politician and publisher Alexander McClure was one of those who claimed Lincoln used those words when McClure suggested Grant should be removed because of public outcries. McClure later wrote, "The only man in all the nation who had the power to save Grant was Lincoln, and he decided to do it."[38] In 1865, Lincoln himself explained, "If I had done as my Washington friends, who fight battles with their tongues instead of swords far from the enemy, demanded of me, Grant, who has proved himself so great a military captain, would never have been heard of again."[39]

Confirmation of Lincoln's strong protection of Grant came from Washburne, who later wrote to Grant: "No man can feel more kindly and more grateful to you than the President.... But most of all, and for which he will have my everlasting gratitude, when the torent [sic] of obloquy and detraction was rolling over you, and your friends, after the battle of Shiloh, Mr. Lincoln stood like a wall of fire between you and it, uninfluenced by the threats of Congressmen and the demands of insolent cowardice."[40]

An April 9, 1862, letter from John Hay to Nicolay sheds some light on the positive views of Grant the president was receiving from his secretaries. Hay wrote, "Glorious news come borne on every wind but the South Wind [McClellan's front]. While [Major General John] Pope is crossing the turbid and broad torrent of the Mississippi in a blaze of enemy's fire [Island Number Ten] and Grant is fighting the overwhelming legions of [General P.G.T.] Beauregard at Pittsburgh [Pittsburg Landing; Shiloh], the Little Napoleon [McClellan] sits trembling before the handful of men at Yorktown afraid either to fight or run."[41]

The significance of Lincoln's protection of Grant was critical. As Brooks D. Simpson concluded, "The value of Lincoln's retention of Grant cannot be [over]estimated. Had the president sacked the general, Grant would have been lost to history—something that might also have happened to a Lincoln stripped of his greatest general."[42]

James M. McPherson likewise concurred: "Perhaps the greatest contribution Lincoln made to the successful strategy of Union forces in the Western theater, and eventually in the war as a whole, was to stick with Grant through thick and thin when others wanted to get rid of him."[43] Elsewhere, McPherson argued, "Had it not been for Lincoln's support at this time, the Grant of history would not have existed—and perhaps neither would the Lincoln of history."[44]

In the field, as Allen Guelzo commented, "Grant's army was blended with a second federal force under the West's own version of George McClellan, Don Carlos Buell, and to Grant's frustration, all federal campaigning in the West slowed to the point of lethargy."[45] Probably the harshest result of Shiloh for Grant was the deterioration of his relationship with Halleck—an ironic development in light of Halleck's assurances to Lincoln about Grant's performance at Shiloh. Halleck came to Shiloh and assumed command of a massive combination of the Army of the Tennessee, Buell's Army of the Cumberland, and John Pope's Army of the Mississippi. Grant was replaced by George Thomas as commander of the Army of the Tennessee and of Halleck's right wing and was placed in a powerless position as Halleck's deputy. Halleck denied Grant any authority and ignored his advice for a two-month period during which Grant asked to be relieved several times. In frustration, Grant moved his headquarters away from the main army camp while Halleck proceeded to conduct his plodding Corinth Campaign.[46] Halleck biographer John Marszalek contends that Halleck's treatment of Grant resulted from Halleck's disdain for Grant because of his lack of discipline, organization and temperance—things that mattered to Halleck.[47]

Halleck's 120,000 to 130,000 troops constituted perhaps the largest single force assembled during the war (challenged only by Joseph Hooker's Army of the Potomac at Chancellorsville). But he proceeded to waste this tremendous resource in a pathetic campaign against Corinth. Because the commanding general insisted on entrenching every night and reined in any unit that moved too quickly, the twenty-mile "march" to Corinth took an unbelievable thirty days. Grant and other competent officers were disgusted. Although Halleck greatly outnumbered his foe, Indiana Governor Oliver P. Morton curiously telegraphed Lincoln from Halleck's camp that Halleck was outnumbered and desperately needed reinforcements; Lincoln replied there were none to spare.[48]

Halleck capped off this campaign by allowing Beauregard to escape on May 29–30 from Corinth with 50,000 Rebel troops and all their weapons.

Instead of pursuing them fifty miles south to Tupelo, Halleck declared the capture of Corinth a victory and began to disperse his armies. As Nicolay and Hay observed, "The achievement was the triumph of a strategist, not the success of a general."[49] The evacuated Rebel troops would form the bulk of Braxton Bragg's army that invaded eastern Tennessee and eastern Kentucky in the autumn of 1862. Grant had stood by helplessly while Halleck disappointed Lincoln's hope for a meaningful victory at Corinth. The president may have compared Halleck's Pyrrhic victory at Corinth with Grant's significant successes (with fewer troops) at Donelson and Shiloh.

Meanwhile, another futile campaign was being conducted by McClellan on the Virginia Peninsula between the James and York rivers. Forsaking his preference for an overland route to Richmond that simultaneously covered Washington, Lincoln had reluctantly acquiesced to McClellan's effort to launch a waterborne campaign. When McClellan finally took to the field, Lincoln relieved him as general-in-chief. But "Little Mac" wasted two months getting to Richmond and allowed the Confederates to take the initiative there. In early May, with McClellan up the peninsula, Lincoln and Secretaries Stanton and Chase went to Fort Monroe, scouted the shores of Hampton Roads, and found a safe landing area that provided a foothold for the successful capture of Norfolk and the consequent Confederate destruction of the ironclad CSS *Virginia* (known to many as the *Merrimac*).[50]

Just after Halleck occupied abandoned Corinth, McClellan saw an opportunity to discourage reinforcements from being brought against his stalled army on the Virginia Peninsula. On June 5 he wrote to Lincoln about the great importance of occupying Chattanooga, Tennessee, and Dalton, Georgia. He helpfully added, "The evacuation of Corinth would appear to render this very easy." Lincoln forwarded the request to Halleck, who responded that troops had moved in the direction of Chattanooga.[51] Halleck had chosen the slow-moving Buell, instead of the fast-moving Grant, to march eastward across the length of Tennessee. Buell's campaign went quite slowly and was terminated when Bragg brought his troops the long way around via Mobile, Atlanta, and Chattanooga to invade eastern Tennessee and Kentucky in early autumn of 1862.

By June 28, as McClellan's unsuccessful Peninsula Campaign was collapsing in Virginia, Stanton ordered Halleck to send 25,000 infantrymen to Richmond. Halleck said sending troops to the East would necessitate cancelling the Chattanooga expedition. Stanton told him to keep his troops because the president thought it was "one of the most important movements of the war." Lincoln reassured Halleck by saying, "Please do not send a man if it endangers any place you deem important to hold, or if it forces you to give up, or weaken, or delay the expedition against Chattanooga," and repeated the same admonition more than once in the next few days. The president focused on the critical strategic importance of the railroad connecting Chattanooga and Atlanta and stated that occupation around Cleveland, Tennessee—east of Chattanooga on that railroad—would be "fully as important as the taking and holding of Richmond." Halleck responded that Lincoln's decision "saves Western Tennessee."[52] Typically, Halleck did not express any confidence or urgency about capturing Chattanooga.

At this juncture, Lincoln was trying to bring order out of chaos as he dealt with McClellan's Peninsula defeat and continuous calls for reinforcements. During the slow and unsuccessful Peninsula Campaign, McClellan bombarded Lincoln and Stanton with complaints and demands for reinforcements. These outbursts "greatly wounded," "sorrow[ed]," "pain[ed]," and "dismay[ed]" the president.[53] Unfortunately, their deletion by an officer at the War Department telegraph office deprived Stanton and Lincoln of seeing McClellan's following mutinous words written to Stanton just after McClellan's defeat at Gaines' Mill in the Seven Days' Campaign: "If I save this army now, I tell you plainly that I owe no thanks to you or to any other persons in Washington. You have done your best to sacrifice this army."[54] Had they seen those words, Lincoln and Stanton likely would have removed McClellan before he could have done more damage. When Lincoln visited McClellan to seek military advice after the Seven Days' defeat, the general presented him with his notorious and presumptuous July 7 Harrison's Landing Letter containing political advice urging a gentlemen's war and avoidance of emancipation.[55] McClellan's behavior made other generals, like Halleck and Grant, look good by comparison.

Lincoln also was dealing with Halleck's not-fully-understood inaction and calls for reinforcements, as well as Buell's ineffective expedition against Chattanooga. Halleck's error in allowing 50,000 Rebel troops to escape from Corinth fed into McClellan's erroneous contention that Richmond was being reinforced by at least some of those troops. Unfortunately, Lincoln appears to have accepted McClellan's argument. In a July 3, 1862, letter to Union governors, for example, the president commented, "The enemy having given up Corinth, it is not wonderful that he is thereby enabled to check us for a time at Richmond."[56]

More Union troops seemed at least a partial answer to Lincoln's difficulties. One problem obtaining troops was that Stanton foolishly had cancelled military recruiting only a couple of months earlier. Lincoln and Seward deftly avoided an embarrassing about-face by encouraging the Northern governors to publicly ask the president to call for volunteers. To encourage the governors to act, Lincoln wrote a June 28 letter to Seward setting forth his views on "the present condition of the War." He included prescient words that described what Grant would accomplish in the next year and a half: "What should be done is to hold what we have in the West, open the Mississippi, and, take Chatanooga [sic] & East Tennessee...." The governors' circular of June 28 provided the basis for Lincoln's July 1 call for 300,000 volunteers.[57]

That summer Lincoln personally encouraged massive recruitment efforts. When he received a question about recruiting new Illinois regiments, he asked Stanton on August 9 to respond and added, "I think we better take while we can get." Three days later he urgently pleaded with Pennsylvania Governor Andrew G. Curtin: "It is very important for some regiments to arrive here at once. What lack you from us? What can we do to expedite matters? Answer."[58]

The president's elevating Halleck to general-in-chief ended Grant's in-theater problems with Halleck. Exasperated by McClellan's failures on the Virginia Peninsula and specifically at the Seven Days' Battle outside Richmond, Lincoln looked hopefully, and unsuccessfully as events transpired, to Halleck for a professional, successful, and aggressive general-in-chief. An early sign of Lincoln's interest was his July 2 cipher wire to

Halleck inquiring, "Please tell me, could you make a flying visit, for consultation, without endangering the service in your Department?" Because of fighting in his theater, Halleck responded that he could not "safely be absent from my Army."[59] After a disheartening visit with McClellan, his corps commanders, and his army on July 8 and 9, Lincoln returned to Washington and promptly issued an order elevating Halleck to general-in-chief of all Union land forces and directing him to report expeditiously to Washington.[60]

Halleck, whose major Western successes were those of Grant at Henry and Donelson and Pope at Island No. 10 on the Mississippi, was being elevated beyond his level of competence (as Second Manassas would demonstrate), but the president was desperate. Lincoln and Grant were both desperate for someone to be an effective general-in-chief. In the words of John Marszalek, "Lincoln's administration and the nation as a whole looked to [Halleck] for answers, for leadership, for decisiveness, for results. There was widespread public belief that he was up to the difficult task. He would prove otherwise."[61]

Lincoln's July 11 order to Halleck directed him to report to Washington "as soon as he can with safety to the positions and operations within the Department now under his special charge." Halleck responded, "Genl Grant next in command is at Memphis. I have telegraphed to him to immediately repair to this place [Corinth]. I will start for Washington the moment I can have a personal interview with Genl. Grant." A frustrated Lincoln wired Halleck on July 14 that he was "very anxious—almost impatient" to have Halleck in Washington. Halleck responded that Grant had just arrived from Memphis and that Halleck planned to leave for Washington on July 17.[62] Reporting directly to Halleck, Grant was now one step away from dealing directly with the president (or at least with Stanton).

With Halleck transferred out of his theater, Grant was free once again to go on the offensive to the extent his resources permitted. According to Lance Janda, "While McClellan clung tenaciously to the past, U. S. Grant waged the war of the future in Tennessee and Mississippi, quickly abandoning archaic notions of warfare which seemed at variance with reality." After Shiloh, said Janda, Grant saw that Southern resolve demanded an approach that would force millions of people into submission and decided to "wage war on resources." Thus, Janda contends that Grant and his protégés Sherman and Phil Sheridan became "fervent and eloquent advocates of total war."[63] "War on resources" is much more accurate than "total war" to describe the Civil War strategy of Grant and his subordinates. They sought to destroy Southern resources but not Southern people. There was considerable destruction inflicted on civilians during the Civil War, but much less than people often think, and almost all of it within the boundaries of the law of nations as understood in the 1860s.

In the East, Lee's September 17 strategic defeat at Antietam in Maryland and McClellan's failure to destroy or pursue Lee's army caused Lincoln to move in a direction similar to Grant's. On September 22 the president changed the entire nature of the war by issuing his Preliminary Emancipation Proclamation declaring slaves in Confederate-held territory as of January 1, 1863, to be free.[64]

Reinforcing his determination to seriously pursue all courses of action necessary for victory, Lincoln two days later ordered that "all rebels and Insurgents, their aiders and abettors…and all persons discouraging volunteer enlistments, resisting militia drafts, or guilty of any disloyal practice" would be subject to trial by courts-martial or military commissions. Further, he suspended the writ of habeas corpus for any person confined by the military or sentenced by a court-martial or military commission.[65] Those actions provided for military, rather than civilian court, control over conduct perceived to be detrimental to the war effort.

At that same time, to send a message to his soldiers (especially those under McClellan), Lincoln took swift and firm action against a Union field grade officer, Major John J. Key, the brother of McClellan's acting judge advocate, Colonel Thomas M. Key. On September 26, the president took the unusual step of writing directly to Major Key asking whether he had explained the failure to "bag" Lee's army after the Battle of Antietam with the words, "That is not the game. The object is that neither army shall get much advantage of the other; that both shall be kept in the field till they are exhausted, when we will make a compromise and save slavery." The next day Lincoln interviewed Key and a witness, learned that Key did not deny making the statement, and immediately ordered him dismissed from military service. Lincoln's intent to send a message became crystal clear two months later when he denied Key's request for reconsideration by explaining, "I had been brought to fear that there was a class of officers in the army...who were playing a game to not beat the enemy when they could, on some peculiar notion as to the proper way of saving the Union.... I dismissed you as an example and a warning to that supposed class."[66]

A few days after dismissing Key, Lincoln visited McClellan from October 1 to 3, 1862, near the Antietam battlefield to try convincing him to pursue Lee's army. While there, Lincoln tallied the number of McClellan's soldiers as 88,095. Back in Washington, the president on October 6 had Halleck send McClellan an order that began, "The President directs that you cross the Potomac and give battle to the enemy or drive him south. Your army must move now while the roads are good." But it would be another three weeks before McClellan began crossing the Potomac—a crossing that took eight days. A totally frustrated Lincoln waited for the completion of congressional elections and removed McClellan from command on November 5.[67]

During that November, the president reduced to writing his frustrations about the major Eastern army:

> The Army is constantly depleted by company officers who give their men leave of absence in the very face of the enemy, and on the eve of an engagement, which is almost as bad as desertion. This very moment there are between seventy and one hundred thousand men absent on furlough from the Army of the Potomac. The army, like the nation, is demoralized by the idea that the war is to be ended, the nation united, and peace restored, by strategy, and not by hard desperate fighting. Why, then, should not the soldiers have furloughs?[68]

Lincoln would have to look elsewhere for meaningful progress and a general who practiced "hard desperate fighting."

CHAPTER 6

EMANCIPATION AND MILITARY USE OF FORMER SLAVES

———◆•◆•◆———

After a cautious start in 1861 and early 1862, the president began moving toward use of the slavery issue to weaken the Confederacy. His caution was due to fears of losing the border states, especially Kentucky, to the Confederacy. On April 16, 1862, however, he signed into law a bill abolishing slavery in the District of Columbia.[1] After taking unsuccessful soundings among border state leaders on some kind of gradual emancipation compromise,[2] Lincoln moved toward more direct emancipation. Following weeks of drafting, he unveiled his first official draft of an emancipation proclamation to his cabinet on July 22. It proposed the January 1, 1863, emancipation of all slaves in Rebel-controlled areas. Only Postmaster General Montgomery Blair opposed the proposal, but Lincoln concurred with Seward's recommendation that its issuance be postponed until some military success occurred that would help avoid the appearance that the proclamation was a measure of desperation.[3]

Exactly a month later Lincoln wrote a famous letter to editor Horace Greeley responding to a pro-emancipation editorial and explaining his wartime priorities and his position on slavery. He proclaimed that Union preservation superseded slavery as the most important official issue for the president although he personally desired the end of slavery:

> I would save the Union. I would save it the shortest way under the Constitution.... If there be those who would not save the Union, unless they could at the same time save slavery, I do not agree with them. If there be those who would not save the Union unless at the same time they could destroy slavery, I do not agree with them. My paramount object in this struggle is to save the Union, and is not either to save or destroy slavery. If I could save the Union without freeing any slave I would do it, and if I could save it by freeing all the slaves I would do it; and if I could save it by freeing some and leaving others alone I would also do that.... I have here stated my purpose according to my view of official duty; and I intend no modification of my oft-expressed personal wish that all men everywhere could be free.[4]

Lincoln historian Harold Holzer, however, said that Lincoln, knowing that he had a drafted emancipation proclamation ready to issue when a Union victory occurred, was taking advantage of a Greeley-provided "opportunity to couch his forthcoming order as a matter of military necessity, rather than a humanitarian gesture, which would have elicited far more opposition."[5]

Lincoln and Grant, meanwhile, were developing a common interest in providing blacks with an opportunity to actively participate in the war.

LINCOLN FREES THE SLAVES

Lincoln appears to have taken an early step when, apparently in July 1862, he authored a memo supporting the military recruiting of free blacks, slaves of disloyal owners, and slaves of loyal owners if the loyal owners consented. He even consented to recruiting the latter slaves without their owners' consent if "the necessity is urgent." It is possible he wrote this document in conjunction with the July 22 cabinet discussion of emancipation and recruiting of blacks. Recruiting of blacks began that month under the authority of the Confiscation Act and an act amending the Force Bill of 1795, both pushed through Congress by Republican Radicals and then approved by Lincoln on July 17.[6]

When a Louisianan complained that the Union army's presence in Louisiana was disturbing master-slave relationships, Lincoln, on July 28, explained, "The truth is, that what is done, and omitted, about slaves, is done and omitted on the same military necessity. It is a military necessity to have men and money; and we can get neither, in sufficient numbers, or amounts, if we keep from, or drive from, our lines, slaves coming to them."[7]

Grant, commanding in western Tennessee and northern Mississippi, received from General-in-Chief Halleck August 2, 1862, orders taking an aggressive position on the issue of unfriendly, slave-owning locals. Halleck ordered Grant to "take up all active sympathizers, and either hold them as prisoners or put them beyond our lines. Handle that class without gloves, and take their property for public use.... It is time that they should begin to feel the presence of the war."[8]

However, Lincoln had *not* concluded that the time was ripe for use of blacks as actual Union soldiers. The *New York Tribune* reported that on August 4 Lincoln met with a delegation offering the services of "two colored regiments from the State of Indiana" but "stated to them that he was not prepared to go the length of enlisting negroes as soldiers." Lincoln supposedly stated that he would employ blacks as laborers but not necessarily as soldiers. The article concluded that he would only arm blacks if a more pressing emergency arose because he did not want to lose Kentucky and "turn 50,000 bayonets from the loyal Border States against" the North.[9]

Lincoln was more philosophical than the down-to-earth Grant. In September 1862, as he anticipated issuing his Preliminary Emancipation Proclamation, Lincoln wrote, "The will of God prevails. In great contests each party claims to act in accordance with the will of God. Both *may* be, and one *must* be wrong. God cannot be *for*, and *against* the same thing at the same time. In the present civil war it is quite possible that God's purpose is something different from the purpose of either party...."[10] But while "Lincoln undoubtedly believed that [emancipation] was God's will...he also believed in the adage that God helps those who help themselves." Therefore, he issued his Emancipation Proclamation. It was the culmination of his pragmatic evolution from free-soiler to emancipationist.[11]

Exactly one month later, on September 22, Lincoln finally went public with his Preliminary Emancipation Proclamation. Seward's pre-condition of military success had been barely met by the September 17 bloodbath at Sharpsburg, Maryland, the Battle of Antietam, where McClellan missed several chances to destroy Lee's army but Lee was compelled to retreat to Virginia. Lincoln put the South on notice that continuation of the war would result in termination of its major social institution by declaring:

> That on the first day of January in the year of our Lord, one thousand eight hundred and sixty-three, all persons held as slaves within any state, or designated part of a state, the people whereof shall then be in rebellion against the United States shall be then, thenceforward, and forever free; and the executive government of the United States, including the military and naval authority thereof, will recognize and maintain the freedom of such persons, and will do no act or acts to repress such persons, or any of them, in any efforts they may make for their actual freedom.[12]

In his proclamation, Lincoln also quoted recent statutes in which Congress had prohibited military officers and men from returning fugitive slaves, made the fugitive slave retrieval process more difficult, and freed slaves of persons "engaged in rebellion against the government" or those giving aid or comfort to such persons once those slaves reached Union lines or came under Union control.[13]

This proclamation changed the purpose of the war from preserving the Union to both preserving the Union and terminating slavery. It was a brilliant step because it precluded European intervention (the British and French not wanting to support slavery), undermined the Southern economy by encouraging slave desertions, and eventually provided about half of the 200,000 blacks who joined the Union army and navy. The major negative impact of Lincoln's action was a decline in Northern Democratic (especially Irish) support for a conflict that could lead to black competition for whites' jobs on the bottom economic rung. Lincoln was willing to pay that political price.

Following up on his Preliminary Emancipation Proclamation, Lincoln wrote to Grant and others in October urging them to cooperate with certain persons in Louisiana and Tennessee in seeking the return of those states to the Union under the "old" Constitution of the United States. In hopes that the threat of emancipation would stimulate their return to the Union, the president encouraged congressional elections in those states.[14]

By mid-November, the president declared, "Do you not know that I may as well surrender this contest, directly, as to make any order, the obvious purpose of which would be to return fugitive slaves?" The next day, in the same vein, he told Kentucky Unionists "that he would rather die than take back a word of the Proclamation of Freedom...."[15]

In his December 1, 1862 annual message to Congress, Lincoln thoroughly addressed the issue of emancipation. He described his efforts to find a foreign location to which free blacks could emigrate and regretfully reported that the only countries willing to accept them were Liberia and Haiti, countries to which free black Americans did not wish to emigrate. He proceeded to propose constitutional amendments that would require states to end slavery by 1900, permanently free all slaves who had been free at any time during the war, and provide compensation for those emancipations.[16]

GRANT EMPLOYS THE CONTRABANDS

Unlike McClellan, Grant immediately understood and agreed with the direction in which the president desired to take the nation on the issue of slavery and black rights. Therefore, Grant responded sympathetically

to the needs of thousands of former slaves who fled into his lines in the
closing months of 1862. One step he took was the designation of Chaplain
John Eaton of the 27th Ohio Infantry Volunteers "to take charge of the
contrabands [Union Major General Benjamin F. Butler's term] that come
into camp in the vicinity of the post, organizing them into suitable com-
panies for working, see that they are properly cared for, and set them
to work picking, ginning and baling all cotton now out and ungath-
ered in field. Suitable guards will be detailed...to protect them from
molestation."[17]

Overwhelmed by this unique assignment, Eaton quickly went to visit
Grant at his La Grange, Tennessee, headquarters. After unsuccessfully
trying to escape the assignment, which involved taking blacks away from
providing personal services to Union soldiers and dealing with the complexities of cotton speculation, Eaton settled into a long and "earnest
conversation" with Grant on "the Negro problem, with which thus early
we had been brought face to face." In the absence of specific direction
from Washington, Grant was determined, for reasons of military necessity
and humanity, to exercise "some form of guardianship" over the blacks—
particularly "as winter was coming on and the Negroes were incapable
of making any provision for their own safety and comfort."[18]

According to Eaton, on about November 12, 1862, Grant outlined
how he would convert the blacks "from a menace into a positive assistance to the Union forces." They could perform soldierly duties in the
surgeon-general, quartermaster and commissary departments and build
bridges, roads and earthworks. The women could work in camp kitchens
and hospitals. Grant explained that performing these duties well would
show that blacks were capable of being fighting soldiers and ultimately
citizens.[19]

Grant was probably relieved a few days later when his initial plans
were confirmed by General-in-Chief Halleck. In a November 16 response
to his November 15 request for guidance on what to do with the blacks
("...Negroes coming in by wagon loads. What do I do with them? I am
now having all the cotton still standing out picked by them."), Grant was
advised, "The sectry of war directs that you employ the refugee negroes

as teamsters, laborers, &c, so far as you have use for them in the Quartermasters Dept, in forts rail roads, &c; also in picking & removing cotton on account of the Government."[20] Based on the reasonable assumption that Halleck and Stanton were reflecting Lincoln's views, it appears that Lincoln and Grant were of the same mind about increasing use of blacks for the Union cause as early as the latter part of 1862.

In late November and again in December, Grant issued a series of orders strengthening Eaton's ability to assist fugitive blacks. A November 14 order directed him to take charge of all fugitive slaves; open a camp for them at Grand Junction, Tennessee, and put them to work picking, ginning and baling cotton. The order provided rations, medical care and protection for the fugitives and directed all commanding officers to "send all fugitives that come within the lines, together with teams, cooking utensils, and other baggage as they may bring with them" to Eaton. In a November 17 order, the Department Quartermaster was directed to furnish Eaton with tools, implements, cotton-baling materials, and clothing for men, women and children.[21]

Eaton encountered problems because, as he put it, "The soldiers of our army were a good deal opposed to serving the negro in any manner," and "To undertake any form of work for the contrabands, at that time, was to be forsaken by one's friends and to pass under a cloud." In at least one instance, Grant had to personally intervene to keep a colonel from obstructing Eaton's effort to direct a band of fugitives to his camp. When Chaplain Eaton found "contempt in which all service on behalf of the blacks was held by the army," and Grant realized the tenuous nature of Eaton's position, Grant reinforced Eaton's powers.

On December 17, therefore, Grant issued an order designating Eaton as General Superintendent of Contrabands for the Department with the power to designate assistant superintendents. The blacks' work was greatly expanded to include "working parties in saving cotton, as pioneers on railroads and steamboats, and in any way where their service can be made available." Earnings from sales of cotton were to be provided to Eaton for the workers' benefit. In conclusion, the order gave labor assignment control to Eaton while protecting blacks' rights: "All applications for the service of contrabands will be made on the General Superintendent, who will furnish such labor from negroes who voluntarily come within the lines of the army. In no case will negroes be forced into the service of the Government, or be enticed away from their homes except when it becomes a military necessity."[22]

AFRICAN AMERICANS JOIN THE MILITARY

In his January 1, 1863, Emancipation Proclamation, Lincoln permanently freed all slaves in all areas then in rebellion against the United States. Often overlooked is an additional provision in that proclamation by which Lincoln specifically authorized the use of freed slaves in Union military service: "And I further declare and make known, that such persons [declared to be free] of suitable condition, will be received into the armed service of the United States to garrison forts, positions, stations, and other places, and to man vessels of all sorts in said service."[23] Thus, the way was formally cleared for the blacks' direct participation in the war.

A step in that direction was taken with the March 25, 1863, War Department issuance of orders to Brigadier General Lorenzo Thomas, the Army's adjutant general, to proceed to Grant's theater and confer with him about maximum use of the black fugitives. That use was to extend to "Labors incident to military operations, and also in performing the duties of soldiers under proper organization." Thomas went to Grant's theater in the early stages of Grant's Vicksburg Campaign, visited twelve camps with Chaplain Eaton, and explained to the troops that the use of blacks as Union soldiers was a mandatory Army policy. Ultimately seventy thousand black soldiers were recruited for the United States Colored Troops (USCT) in the Mississippi Valley Theater.[24]

On August 1, 1863, Lincoln praised Major General David Hunter for his use of black soldiers in Florida. The president noted that Confederates were attacking them fiercely and cautioned, "It is important to the enemy that such a force shall not take shape, and grow, and thrive, in the South; and in precisely the same proportion, it is important to us that it shall. Hence the utmost caution and vigilance is necessary on our part."[25]

But it was in his Mississippi Valley Theater that Grant proved to be the most dedicated and effective military supporter of Lincoln's emancipation and black soldier policies. In an August 1863 letter to Washburne, Grant demonstrated the strength of his conversion to this position. He admitted that he had never been an abolitionist or even anti-slavery but that it had become "patent to my mind early in the rebellion that the North & South could never live at peace with each other except as one nation, and that without Slavery.... I would not therefore be willing to see any settlemen[t] until this question is forever settled."[26]

CHAPTER 7

GRANT IMPRESSES LINCOLN WITH VICTORY AT VICKSBURG

lthough Halleck's departure from the Western scene left Grant with a freer hand in the Mississippi Valley, Beauregard's escape with 50,000 Rebel troops from Halleck at Corinth would hamper Grant's ability to go on the offensive. The fifty thousand Confederates Halleck had allowed to escape were placed under the command of General Braxton Bragg and transported via Mobile and Atlanta for an autumn invasion of eastern Tennessee and Kentucky. Buell was sent north to head off the incursion and required large numbers of reinforcements from Grant's command.

The end of Buell's dilatory expedition toward Chattanooga came after Lincoln, on July 13, wired Halleck (then still at Corinth), "They are having a stampede in Kentucky. Please look to it." Lincoln was referring to reports he had received of Kentucky raids by Confederate Brigadier General John H. Morgan—a prelude to the Bragg invasion. Halleck reacted by issuing a July 14 order directing Buell to "Do all in your power to put down the Morgan raid even if the Chattanooga expedition should be delayed."[1]

That campaign would not just be delayed; it would be cancelled. Instead Buell and his troops were forced to scamper northward through Tennessee and into Kentucky to intercept the uncoordinated Confederate invasion led by Bragg and Major General Edmund Kirby Smith. The Union forces arrived in time to prevent the Rebels from reaching the Ohio River. The decisive fight of the campaign was the October 8, 1862, Battle of Perryville (Kentucky)—a tactical draw that was followed by Bragg's withdrawal to eastern Tennessee.

After Bragg retreated from Kentucky, Buell failed to pursue from his Nashville base in north-central Tennessee. Lincoln was concerned that Bragg was moving east into the Shenandoah Valley of Virginia. On September 10 Buell assured Lincoln that such was not the case, but he was less than reassuring about his ability to pursue Bragg. Buell wrote: "[Bragg's] movements will probably depend on mine. I expect that for the want of supplies I can neither follow him nor remain here. Think I must withdraw from Tennessee."[2]

Grant meanwhile had been successful in preventing Rebel major generals Sterling Price and Earl Van Dorn from sending more troops north in support of Bragg. He did so by pressuring them into fighting at Iuka and Corinth, Mississippi, where Grant added two more victories to his record. Those victories led to the first direct exchange of wires between Lincoln and Grant. On October 8, the president, into his third week of trying to get McClellan to pursue Lee after Antietam, wired Grant, "I congratulate you and all concerned on your recent battles and victories. How does it all sum up?" Two days later, Grant responded with an optimistic but incomplete report of the Iuka and Corinth casualty figures. As to Corinth, he said, "Cannot tell the number of dead yet. About Eight hundred Rebels already buried. Their loss in Killed about Nine to one of ours."[3]

Grant's dissatisfaction with what he perceived to be Major General William Rosecrans's mistakes at Iuka and Corinth probably caused him to consider replacing Rosecrans.[4] Before he could act, however, Washington decision-makers (particularly Lincoln) once again came to Grant's rescue. "Old Rosey" was named to replace the dilatory Buell as commander of the Army of the Ohio in eastern Tennessee; after taking command on October 27, he promptly renamed it the Army of the Cumberland. This step resulted from Lincoln's and Stanton's dissatisfaction with Buell's failure to aggressively pursue Bragg southward after the Battle of Perryville. Lincoln was well aware of Tennessee Governor Andrew Johnson's long-standing lack of confidence in Buell.[5] In fact, on September 29 Buell had received an order replacing him with George Thomas, who shocked everyone by declining the appointment—on the grounds Buell was ready to move against the enemy and Thomas was not as well informed as he should have been. Thomas's declination opened the door for Rosecrans's appointment less than a month later.[6]

Thus, as fall turned to winter in 1862, Lincoln replaced his leading generals in the Eastern and Middle theaters (McClellan and Buell, respectively) because of their lack of aggressiveness. But in the Mississippi Valley he left in place the one commanding general who had consistently pursued the enemy and produced victories: Ulysses Grant. As Halleck's inadequacies became clear in Washington, Lincoln may have begun to realize the handicaps Grant had operated under in Halleck's theater. With his troops being returned to him from the Buell/Rosecrans forces, Grant would be able to return to the strategic offensive.

Grant assumed command of the Department of the Tennessee on October 24, 1862. According to Steven Woodworth, Grant then built the Army of Tennessee in his own image—steady, hard-driving, can-do, and aggressive. He explained, "Nor is it any coincidence that Grant's qualities tended to be those of the...Midwest, from which the army was almost exclusively recruited. The men were quick to adopt Grant's approach to war, because it was the way their own fathers had approached the challenges of carving farms out of the wilderness."[7]

McCLERNAND TRIES TO REPLACE GRANT

Grant, however, did face a threat—from within the Union military establishment. During the fall of 1862, self-promoting Major General

John A. McClernand went to Washington to round up support for an independent mission he envisioned against Vicksburg, Mississippi, the last major Confederate bastion on the Mississippi River. He convinced his fellow Illinoisan Lincoln to lend him assistance contingent on massive recruiting by McClernand in Indiana, Illinois and Iowa. Lincoln had known McClernand, a southern Illinois Democratic politician, for many years; he knew of McClernand's prior successful recruiting efforts, and was eager to ensure his continued political support for the war effort. McClernand, however, represented a threat to Grant's command in the Mississippi Valley.

At the president's direction, Stanton issued an order to McClernand that had been carefully crafted by General-in-Chief Halleck to encourage McClernand's recruiting by appearing to give him command of an expedition against Vicksburg. The order, however, kept the forces subject to Halleck's control and, for Grant's protection, provided that McClernand's independent force would consist only of forces "not required by the operations of General Grant's command."[8]

Lincoln wrote an endorsement to McClernand on the order authorizing him to show it to others and stressing his interest in a Vicksburg expedition ("I add that I feel deep interest in the success of the expedition, and desire it to be pushed forward with all possible dispatch....").[9]

It is clear that Lincoln wanted to stimulate a campaign against the vital Vicksburg stronghold. He was so anxious to do so that he encouraged McClernand, a proven recruiter, to flood the Mississippi Valley with additional Union soldiers. It is unclear how Lincoln envisaged Grant and McClernand working out the command arrangements for such an effort, and in this instance the president's actions could have jeopardized Grant's command. However, Stanton and Halleck ensured Grant's control by their wording of the order issued to McClernand.

Evidence that Lincoln was not privy to Stanton and Halleck's maneuver is contained in a November 17, 1862, cipher communication from Lincoln to the politically connected General Francis P. Blair, Jr. Lincoln assured Blair that, as he desired, he was being ordered "to form part of McClernand's expedition, as it moves down the river; and he—McC.— is so informed." A telegram from Stanton to McClernand two days earlier had stated, "General Frank Blair will be attached to your expedition...."[10] For the time being, Stanton continued to imply that McClernand would be in charge on the Mississippi although steps already had been taken to ensure that Grant would control the newly recruited forces. Without that protection of Grant's prerogatives, Lincoln might have badly undermined him on the eve of his greatest campaign.

LINCOLN MAKES CHANGES

Although Lincoln was focused on the Mississippi, he maintained a comprehensive view of the nationwide situation. To a correspondent who evidently stressed the great importance of the Mississippi, Lincoln, on November 19, 1862, wrote, "... You do not estimate the value of the object you press [the Mississippi River], more highly than it is estimated here. It is now the object of particular attention. It has not been neglected, as you seem to think, because the West was divided into different military Departments. The cause is much deeper. The country will not allow us to send the whole Western force down the Mississippi, while the enemy sacks Louisville and Cincinnati...."[11]

To his south, Grant faced additional competition for Union resources. On November 9, 1862, Major General Nathaniel P. Banks, a Massachusetts Democrat and political general, was appointed commander of the Department of the Gulf. He assumed command in New Orleans on December 17. Meanwhile the president had paved the way for naval cooperation with Banks by sending a November 11 communication urging Commodore David G. Farragut to cooperate with and assist Banks.[12] Lincoln apparently envisioned Banks moving north to capture Port Hudson, Louisiana, and then Vicksburg, Mississippi, the last two Confederate bastions on the Mississippi River.

While trying to stimulate offensive action in the Mississippi Valley, Lincoln was doing the same thing in the East. He relieved McClellan from command of the Army of the Potomac on November 5 and later that month proposed a plan for attacking and trapping Lee's army at Fredericksburg.[13] A month later, after the slaughter of Union soldiers resulting from an ill-advised assault at Fredericksburg, Lincoln praised the Army of the Potomac for its courage.[14] Consistently the president was seeking to generate Union attacks, offensive campaigns, and victories.

As 1863 dawned, however, Lincoln was having no success in finding competent military leadership in the East. Pope and McClellan had failed him at Second Manassas and Antietam. The Fredericksburg debacle had led to many calls for Burnside's removal as commander of the Army of the Potomac—many from Burnside's subordinates. When Burnside proposed to again cross the Rappahannock and his primary subordinates objected, Lincoln, on January 1, 1863, tried unsuccessfully to encourage Halleck to act as a real general-in-chief. Lincoln requested him to observe the ground with Burnside and either approve or disapprove his proposed movement. The president wrote to Halleck, "Your military skill is useless to me if you will not do this." After Halleck submitted his resignation to Stanton, Lincoln withdrew his letter to Halleck "because [it was] considered harsh by Gen. Halleck." Halleck then withdrew his resignation.[15]

Problems with Burnside continued unabated. Aware of the clamor for his resignation and frustrated by Lincoln and Halleck's disapproval of his plans for another offensive at Fredericksburg, Burnside submitted a letter of resignation on January 5. On January 7 Halleck responded, advised that he had recommended a crossing at upstream fords on the Rappahannock, and broadly stated, "In all our interviews I have urged that our first object was, not Richmond, but the defeat or scattering of Lee's army, which threatened Washington and the line of the Upper Potomac." It appears that Halleck, under Lincoln's tutelage, had come to understand that Confederate armies, not points and places, were to be the strategic targets of Union armies if victory was to be obtained. A day later, Lincoln advised Burnside that he approved Halleck's letter and that he would not accept Burnside's resignation of his commission.[16] With neither Halleck nor Burnside performing their missions effectively, Lincoln still yearned for military leadership in the East.

Things were no better in the West.[17] As early as November 22, Lincoln expressed dissatisfaction with Banks's apparent delay in moving on the enemy from his Louisiana base while requisitioning an inordinate quantity of supplies. Lincoln's continuing frustration with delays was apparent: "My dear General, this expanding, and piling up of impedimenta, has been, so far, almost our ruin, and will be our ruin if it is not abandoned."[18] Two days later he complained about the absence of aggressive generals: "I certainly have been dissatisfied with the slowness of Buell and McClellan; but before I relieved them I had great fears I should not find successors to them, who would do better; and I am sorry to add, that I have seen little since then to relieve those fears. I do not clearly see the prospect of any more rapid movements."[19]

GRANT MOVES AGAINST VICKSBURG

Meanwhile, in November 1862, Grant had launched a two-pronged campaign against Vicksburg from his Tennessee base. While Grant commanded a campaign southward into the heart of Mississippi, he sent Sherman down the Mississippi toward Vicksburg. Grant planned to simultaneously attack that city from the landside and the river. His scheme was foiled by a successful Confederate attack on his northern Mississippi supply base at Holly Springs. After an ineffective subordinate unnecessarily surrendered that base, Grant felt compelled to retreat to Tennessee because his supply line had been severed. His retreat left Sherman, unaware of Grant's setback, to attack Vicksburg with his troops alone. Also, the Rebel troops facing Grant were free to move to Vicksburg to bolster its defenses. The result was disastrous as the united Confederates easily repelled Sherman at the late December Battle of Chickasaw Bluffs near Vicksburg and inflicted almost 1,800 casualties while suffering less than two hundred.

Sherman's initiation of his separate campaign on the Mississippi enraged McClernand, who was senior to Sherman and still believed he should be in command of all operations against Vicksburg. On December 17, 1862, McClernand asked Lincoln and Stanton if he had been superseded. Three days before, Grant had advised Halleck that McClernand was "unmanageable and incompetent." After discussions with the president, Stanton advised the disappointed McClernand that Grant was in command of all operations in his department. On December 18, Grant reorganized his department into four corps, with McClernand joining Sherman, Stephen Hurlbut and James B. McPherson as a (mere) corps commander.[20] This order clearly told McClernand where he stood. According to Chester Hearn, "When the president tried to create a face-saving compromise for McClernand, Halleck disagreed and ignored the president's suggestion."[21] Lincoln's strong desire to please and retain the support of McClernand had come close to jeopardizing Grant's command of his vital army.

On the day after the Holly Springs fiasco that undid Grant's dual campaign, Chaplain Eaton was impressed by the calm demeanor of Grant upon his receipt of the bad news. Eaton wrote that Grant "quietly and dispassionately" told him he had forewarned the Holly Springs commander of the impending Rebel raid but that commander had failed to heed the warning. Eaton summarized the scope of the disaster and Grant's concern about how others might view his role: "The loss of the supplies was then considered a great blow to the army, and necessitated an immediate withdrawal and reorganization of all General Grant's plans. In spite of his calmness, he felt it acutely, and remarked to me, 'Many people will believe that I was taken unawares and did nothing to protect my supplies, whereas I did all that was possible.'"[22]

GRANT AND LINCOLN STYMIE McCLERNAND

Grant returned to Holly Springs by December 23 and, after railroad repairs had been made, moved his command to Memphis on January 10. From then on he would stay on or near the Mississippi until he succeeded in capturing Vicksburg. Meanwhile McClernand had gone downriver, assumed command of Sherman's and his own troops, and led a successful expedition up the Arkansas River to capture Fort Hindman at Arkansas Post, along with about 5,000 prisoners. When Grant somewhat ironically complained to Halleck that McClernand had been on "a wild goose chase" while achieving such a success, Halleck authorized Grant to remove McClernand from command; Grant wrote an order doing so but did not issue it. He may have hesitated to do so out of deference to

Lincoln, who obviously had hoped that some meaningful role could be found for his Illinois compatriot. McClernand would remain a thorn in Grant's side for several more months.[23]

When McClernand finally realized that Halleck fully intended that Grant, not McClernand, command the campaign against Vicksburg, McClernand complained to Lincoln in an intemperate letter on January 7, 1863. He charged Halleck with "wilful contempt of superior authority" and "utter incompetency." The heart of his complaint was that Halleck had violated the cleverly drafted Mississippi River Expedition order of the prior October by setting McClernand aside for Grant as commander of the expedition. Obviously angry about the fine print in the order, McClernand spelled out the reasons he believed Halleck was incompetent to serve as general-in-chief.[24]

Lincoln, already frustrated by the contemporaneous in-fighting among Army of the Potomac generals following the Fredericksburg slaughter, bluntly refused to intervene. He wrote to McClernand, "I have too many family controversies (so to speak) already on my hands, to voluntarily...take up another. You are now doing well—well for the country, and well for yourself—much better than you could possibly be, if engaged in open war with Gen. Halleck. Allow me to beg, that for your sake, for my sake, & for the country's sake, you give your whole attention to the better work."[25] Thus, Lincoln somewhat belatedly realized the problem he had created and backed Grant against McClernand's maneuvering to replace him in the Mississippi Valley.

GRANT TAKES CHARGE

After McClernand returned to the mouth of the Arkansas River, both Sherman and Admiral David Dixon Porter sent messages to Grant urging him to join them and take personal command because of their doubts about McClernand's competence. On January 17 Grant journeyed downriver, met with McClernand and others, and realized he would have to assume personal command. Grant could not put Sherman in command of the planned expedition against Vicksburg because he was junior to

McClernand, and Grant chose not to exercise the authority recently given to him by Halleck to relieve McClernand. Even when McClernand responded disrespectfully upon Grant's assuming personal command on January 29 at Young's Point near Vicksburg, Grant chose not to relieve him because of his political value as a strong, pro-Union Democrat from President Lincoln's home state.[26]

Grant's confidence had been boosted a few days earlier when Halleck advised him that the president had directed that as much of Arkansas as Grant desired would be temporarily attached to his department to give him control of both banks of the Mississippi. Halleck also advised Grant not to count on Banks's command being able to pass or defeat Port Hudson in order to join with Grant. Being junior to the incompetent Banks, Grant probably was not upset by this cautionary warning.[27]

Lincoln was following Vicksburg-related developments. On January 7 and 29, 1863, he wrote to Major General John A. Dix at Fort Monroe in Virginia to inquire whether the Richmond papers had any news about Vicksburg.[28] He made this inquiry because developments south of Memphis, and sometimes all those south of Cairo, Illinois, were beyond the direct telegraphic communication reach of Washington.

Months earlier, in August 1862, Lincoln had taken an extraordinary step that would prove extremely helpful to Grant's Vicksburg Campaign. Navy Commander David Dixon Porter met with the president to request an active field assignment instead of the backwater administrative post to which he had just been assigned. When Lincoln inquired about the difficulty of capturing Vicksburg, Porter explained the geographic problems and the necessity for army/navy cooperation. An impressed Lincoln soon thereafter had Porter promoted directly to acting rear admiral and Commander of the Mississippi River Squadron—over the heads of all the disappointed captains in the navy.[29]

Craig L. Symonds contended that this experience with Porter reflected three Lincoln traits: eagerness to solicit advice from experts, ability to forgive past errors (particularly those of commission, not omission),[30] and reluctance to intervene in the details of military and naval operations. He concluded, "[Lincoln] defined the objective and allowed his subordinates to define the means they would employ to achieve it. Men like Porter and [David G.] Farragut, or, for that matter, men like Grant and Sherman, grasped the essence of Lincoln's directions, and applied their professional expertise toward the accomplishment of those goals, and they did so without whining, or complaining, or asking constantly for reinforcement."[31]

It was during this same period of time, specifically December 17, 1862, that Grant issued his ignominious General Orders No. 11, which provided:

1. The Jews, as a class, violating every regulation of trade established by the Treasury Department, and also Department orders, are hereby expelled from the Department.
2. Within twenty-four hours from the receipt of this order by Post Commanders, they will see that all of this class of people are furnished with passes and required to leave, and any one returning after such notification, will be arrested and held in confinement until an opportunity occurs of sending them out as prisoners unless furnished with permits from these Head Quarters.
3. No permits will be given these people to visit Head Quarters for the purpose of making personal application for trade permits.

Grant apparently issued this order in an angry reaction to his own father's appearance at his Holly Springs, Mississippi camp with three Jewish merchant partners and a scheme to participate in the cotton speculation that was flourishing through Grant's lines.[32]

The president promptly countermanded Grant's order and then had Halleck soften the blow. Halleck explained to Grant, "It may be proper to give you some explanation of the revocation of your order expelling all Jews from your department. The President has no objection to your expelling traitors and Jew peddlers, which, I suppose, was the object of your order; but, as it in terms proscribed an entire religious class, some of whom are fighting in our ranks, the President deemed it necessary to revoke it."[33] Lincoln did what he had to do but also acted in a manner that maintained his critical working relationship with Grant.

In March 1863 Lincoln further supported Grant when Rosecrans embarrassed himself with a self-serving plea to Lincoln. He cited a promise from Stanton after the Battle of Stone's River that "Anything you and your command want you can have," and then complained that his request that his major general's commission be backdated to December 1861 had been denied. As matters stood, Rosecrans's promotion was effective March 21, 1862—more than a month later than Grant's February 16, 1862, date of rank. The president proceeded to reject Rosecrans's not-so-subtle effort to outrank Grant and to skewer Rosecrans for his audacity:

> Now, as to your request that your Commission should date from December 1861. Of course you expected to gain something by this; but you should remember that precisely so much as you should gain by it others would lose by it. If the thing you sought had been exclusively ours, we would have given it cheerfully; but being the right of other men, we having a merely arbitrary power over it, the taking it from them and giving it to you, became a more delicate matter, and more deserving of consideration. Truth to speak, I do not appreciate this matter of rank on paper, as you officers do. The world will not forget that you fought the battle of "Stone River" and it will never care a fig whether you rank Gen. Grant on paper, or he so, ranks you.[34]

GRANT TRIES AGAIN AND AGAIN

Although the safe thing for Grant to do in early 1863 would have been, as Sherman advised, to return to Memphis and Holly Springs and launch another overland campaign against Vicksburg, Grant was concerned that doing so would demoralize the North:

It was my judgment at the time that to make a backward movement as long as that from Vicksburg to Memphis, would be interpreted, by many of those yet full of hope for the preservation of the Union, as a defeat, and that the draft would be resisted, desertions ensue and the power to capture and punish deserters lost. There was nothing left to be done but to go forward to a decisive victory. This was in my mind from the moment I took command in person at Young's Point.[35]

The politically astute Grant probably realized that a "retreat" to Memphis was likely to increase the tremendous pressure on Lincoln to relieve Grant of command.[36]

Rather than be seen as retreating northward, Grant initiated a series of experiments intended to secure a base on the east bank of the Mississippi for an attack on Vicksburg. Geography made the chore difficult. The city was protected on the north by the Yazoo River and associated swamps, as well as heavily-fortified Haines' Bluff. Its western edge consisted of high bluffs overlooking the Mississippi. Grant saw the experiments as diverting the attention of his troops, the enemy, and the public; he had doubts about their success but was prepared to take advantage if any succeeded.[37]

The first of these experiments was the digging of a canal that was intended to divert the river in a straight north-south path across a peninsula and away from the bend below Vicksburg. Four thousand men— mostly blacks—struggled to dig this canal between late January and March 8, when the river broke through a dam that had been built on the north end of the canal to protect the excavation. Even had the canal been completed, its effectiveness would have been reduced by the fact that it was within range of Confederate guns about a mile away.[38] Slightly farther to the west, Grant ordered General McPherson and his troops to flood Lake Providence and attempt to clear a waterway through bayous and rivers all the way back to the Mississippi south of Port Hudson. This project began January 30 and was discontinued at the same time as the failed canal project.[39]

Those two projects west of the Mississippi were matched in futility by two others on the east side of the river. First, Grant sought backdoor access to the Yazoo River by destroying a levee on the Mississippi across from Helena, Arkansas, far north of Vicksburg. The plan was to restore a previously navigable waterway through the bayous to the Yazoo River. A Union expedition of 4,500 troops on transports made it all the way to Confederate Fort Pemberton at the juncture where the Tallahatchie and Yalobusha rivers formed the Yazoo. The expedition, however, was repelled by Confederate fire from the fort. After destroying another levee on the Mississippi in an unsuccessful effort to flood Fort Pemberton, the Union fleet retreated.[40]

Grant's second effort on the east side of the Mississippi consisted of an Admiral Porter-led fleet of five gunboats, four mortar-boats, and troop-carrying river steamers trying to wend their way through another series of waterways to the Yazoo River about ten air miles above Haines' Bluff. Grant himself accompanied the fleet at the start of the mission but went back to hurry up reinforcements under Sherman. The smaller gunboats got too far ahead of the steamers, which were impeded by the heavy, overhanging swamp trees and the sharp turns in the bayous. Just as the lead vessels were about to break into open water, they ran into more obstructions and a 4,000-man contingent of Confederates. The gunboats were no match for the Rebel sharpshooters, Sherman's infantry left their hung-up ships and marched along the riverbanks to rescue the gunboats and their crews, and the Union vessels were lucky to be able to back out of the hazardous waterways. As Edwin Bearss concluded, "thus ended in failure the fourth attempt to get in rear of Vicksburg."[41]

In fact, Grant made one final effort—back on the west bank—to use waterways to bypass Vicksburg. He had his men dredging and widening natural bayou channels from Milliken's Bend, northwest of Vicksburg, through Richmond, Louisiana, and back to the Mississippi at Carthage, a few miles below Vicksburg. He halted the work when it became clear that a usable channel could not be developed. Deteriorating levees and abnormally high water in the river caused excessive water everywhere and made dry land a rarity. As a result, Union soldiers were afflicted with malaria—in addition to the usual measles and chickenpox.[42] Lincoln was closely following Grant's projects and rejected as "humbuggery" a *New York Mercury* report that this canal project had succeeded. He told Stanton, "Now, it is not past belief that such news would be at Cairo that length of time, and not be sent directly to us—especially as [Navy Captain Alexander M.] Pennock is under strict orders to send every thing promptly. Besides there are no[t] six iron-clads, nor 15000 men at Vicksburg to pass through the canal, even if the Mississippi River had risen fifteen feet in as many minutes."[43]

Reports of these abysmal conditions—and the several failed projects—caused grumbling back home and new calls for Grant's replacement. Many Northern newspapers called for Grant's removal and suggested that he be replaced with McClernand, Frémont, McClellan, or Brigadier General David Hunter. The *New York Times* reported on March 12 that "There is no symptom of any plan of attack on Vicksburgh [*sic*]" and later that month that "Nothing visible...has been done lately toward the reduction of Vicksburgh [*sic*]."[44] On March 15 McClernand launched a personal campaign against Grant by writing to Lincoln. McClernand told the President that Grant had been "gloriously drunk" on March 13 and sick in bed all the next day. If the president had decided to remove Grant, McClernand, the next senior officer, likely would have succeeded him.[45] Lincoln had other ideas.

Others were critical, too. Congressman Washburne's brother, Cadwallader C. Washburn,[46] a brigadier general in McPherson's Corps in Grant's army, wrote that "All Grant's schemes [against Vicksburg] have failed. He is frittering away time and strength to no purpose. The truth must be told even if it hurts. You cannot make a silk purse out of a sow's ear." The *Chicago Tribune* editor—upset that Grant was allowing competing Copperhead (anti-war Democratic) newspapers to be distributed to his troops—wrote to Congressman Washburne:

> Your man Grant has shown his cloven foot and proves himself to be little better than a secesh [secessionist].... No man's military career in the army is more open to destructive criticism than Grant's. We have kept off of him on your account.

We could have made him stink in the nostrils of the public like an old fish had we properly criticized his military blunders. Look at that miserable and costly campaign into northern Miss. when he sent crazy Sherman to Vicksburg and agreed to meet him there by land. Was there ever a more weak and imbecile campaign. But we forbore exposing him to the excruciation of the people.[47]

Similarly, a Cincinnati newspaper editor, Murat Halstead, wrote to Secretary of the Treasury Salmon P. Chase that Grant was "a jackass in the original package. He is a poor drunken imbecile. He is a poor stick sober, and he is most of the time more than half drunk, and much of the time idiotically drunk." Chase passed the letter to Lincoln with the warning that "Reports concerning General Grant similar to the statements made by Mr. Halstead are too common to be safely or even prudently disregarded."[48]

But Lincoln had the final word and stood by Grant once again. He is alleged to have said, "I think Grant has hardly a friend left, except myself. What I want, and what the people want, is generals who will fight battles and win victories. Grant has done this and I propose to stand by him."[49] At about this time, Lincoln may have uttered the oft-cited statement that he wanted to determine what kind of whiskey Grant drank so he could send some of it to other Union generals.[50]

Regardless of what his critics had to say, Grant had a purpose in having his men undertake the series of winter operations against Vicksburg—in addition to the possibility they just might succeed. As British military historian General J. F. C. Fuller explained, "All were extremely difficult, entailed immense labor on the part of the army and the fleet; and though all failed in their object, they undoubtedly formed admirable training for Grant's army, hardening and disciplining the men, in fact turning them into salted soldiers."[51]

As a result of Grant's lack of success and the continuing complaints against him, Lincoln expressed some concern. In a March 1863 off-the-record conversation with a *New York Tribune* reporter, the president said that he was not sanguine about Vicksburg and thought the side expeditions were hopeless but did hope that the on-the-ground military commanders knew prospects and possibilities better than he. On April 2 Halleck warned Grant that the president had become impatient with Grant's unsuccessful efforts, which Halleck described as "several eccentric operations." The general-in-chief "astutely" advised Grant that "The division of your army into small expeditions destroys your strength, and, when in the presence of an enemy, is very dangerous," urged him to try coordinating with Banks against either Vicksburg or Port Hudson, and concluded with the hope that Grant "will push matters with all possible dispatch."[52]

The president also took the precautionary step of having Stanton send Charles A. Dana from the War Department to Grant's headquarters to determine the truth about Grant, his behavior, his operations, and his command. Although Dana was allegedly coming to check on a paymaster problem, Grant knew his real purpose, advised his staff to treat Dana cooperatively and respectfully, and actually established a friendship with Dana. As a result, Dana's secret reports to Stanton were positive and reinforced Lincoln's determination to keep his most aggressive general in command.[53] Similar positive reports about Grant and his army reached Washington from Adjutant General Lorenzo Thomas and a medical officer sent by Stanton, both of whom had been sent, in part, to make those assessments.[54]

While Grant moved toward momentous success at Vicksburg, Lincoln's problems in the East continued unabated. In January 1863, Burnside sought the president's permission to sack Hooker and seven other generals. Burnside's timing, immediately after his army's disastrous "Mud March,"[55] was not propitious. At a January 25 meeting at the White House, Lincoln instead announced his decision to replace Burnside with Hooker as commander of the Army of the Potomac.[56]

In a January 26 letter to Hooker, Lincoln criticized him for thwarting Burnside and warned him, "I much fear that the spirit which you have aided to infuse into the Army, of criticising their Commander, and withholding confidence from him, will now turn upon you. I shall assist you as far as I can, to put it down. Neither you, nor Napoleon, if he were alive again, could get any good out of any army, while such a spirit prevails in it."[57]

During April 1863 Lincoln was micromanaging Hooker's plans and efforts in the Fredericksburg area. Lincoln visited Hooker's army, approved his campaign plans, and criticized their execution.[58] Lincoln's worst fears about Hooker became a reality in early May. After assembling a huge army of 130,000 men and surprising Lee by crossing the Rappahannock and Rapidan rivers at fords west of Fredericksburg, Hooker froze and panicked once Lee and Jackson moved against him in the Battle of Chancellorsville. In the midst of this multi-day battle, Hooker was knocked unconscious for a few hours by a Confederate shell, and no one else took charge. With half of Hooker's numbers, Lee drove Hooker's army back across the rivers—at a high cost of casualties for both sides.

Lee then convinced President Davis to keep Lee's army intact in the East to facilitate an offensive campaign into Pennsylvania. That decision precluded any reinforcements from Lee's army to Confederates facing Rosecrans's Army of the Cumberland in eastern Tennessee or to Rebels attempting to thwart Grant's invasion of Mississippi. As Lee moved north into Pennsylvania, a squabble between Hooker and Halleck about whether to evacuate Harpers Ferry provided Lincoln with an opportunity to accept Hooker's resignation as commander of the Army of the Potomac. Lincoln turned to George Meade as that army's new commander. Meade's army occupied and held the high ground at the Battle of Gettysburg (Pennsylvania), where his troops inflicted 28,000 casualties on Lee's army on July 1–3, 1863.

While Lincoln had to micromanage and then relieve Hooker in the East, he also had to deal with Rosecrans's immobility and insecurity in eastern Tennessee. On April 23, 1863, for example, Lincoln had to reassure Rosecrans that he had heard no complaints against that general, who had written to Lincoln requesting that rumored complaints against Rosecrans be sent directly to him.[59] In fact, the myriad problems Lincoln was having with Eastern and Middle theater generals differed sharply from his knowledge of and experience with Grant—especially as reinforced by Dana's reports.

GRANT BEGINS HIS DECISIVE VICKSBURG CAMPAIGN

As Grant was closing out his unsuccessful cold-weather attempts to reach and conquer Vicksburg and beginning to execute his brilliant, gambling, and successful game plan to do so, Halleck advised him of the significance of his operation. On March 20 he wrote that "The eyes and hopes of the whole country are now directed to your army.... the opening of the Mississippi River will be to us of more advantage than the capture of forty Richmonds." Only four days later, however, the vacillating general-in-chief was calling to Grant's attention "the importance of your not retaining so many steamers on the Mississippi. It is absolutely necessary that a part of these boats be returned."[60]

Grant's grand plan for the capture of Vicksburg—and possibly its defenders—involved marching his army down the west bank (Louisiana side) of the Mississippi River, crossing the river below Vicksburg on transports the navy would have moved south past Vicksburg, and advancing on the city from the south (possibly from Grand Gulf). He outlined that plan as part of a long communication to Halleck on April 4.[61]

An April 9 wire from Halleck to Grant seemed to reflect the impatience and anxiety of Lincoln, Stanton, and Halleck. He wrote, "You are too well advised of the anxiety of the Government for your success, and its disappointment at the delay, to render it necessary to urge upon you the importance of early action. I am confident that you will do everything possible to open the Mississippi River. In my opinion this is the most important operation of the war, and nothing must be neglected to insure success."[62]

Before implementing his master plan, Grant utilized several diversions to keep Confederate Lieutenant General John Pemberton in Vicksburg guessing as to his intentions. He created four diversions to the north and east of Vicksburg to deflect Confederate attention from his campaign plans to its west and south. First, he sent Major General Frederick Steele's troops in transports one hundred miles northward up the Mississippi River toward Greenville, Mississippi. This movement led General Pemberton in Vicksburg to conclude that Grant was retreating (to reinforce Rosecrans in eastern Tennessee) and to allow about 8,000 Rebel troops to be transferred from Mississippi back to Bragg in Tennessee.[63]

Second, Grant initiated a cavalry raid from Tennessee to Louisiana through the length of central and eastern Mississippi. Incurring a mere handful of casualties, Colonel Benjamin H. Grierson conducted the most strategically effective Union cavalry raid of the entire war with just 1,700 cavalrymen. They tore up railroads and destroyed trains and other Rebel infrastructure throughout eastern and central Mississippi.[64]

The raid's effect on Pemberton is reflected in the fact that on April 27 he sent seventeen messages to Mississippi commands about Grierson's raiders and not a single one about Grant's build-up on the west bank of the Mississippi River. By the twenty-ninth, Pemberton had further played into Grant's hands by sending all his cavalry in pursuit of Grierson. He advised his superiors: "The telegraph wires are down. The enemy has, therefore, either landed on this side of the Mississippi River, or they have been cut by Grierson's cavalry.... All the cavalry I can raise is close on their rear."[65]

Sixteen days and six hundred miles after starting their dangerous venture, Grierson's men rode south out of Mississippi and reached the safety of Union lines at Baton Rouge, Louisiana, on May 2—two days after Grant's amphibious landing at Bruinsburg on the Mississippi. They had survived several close calls, created havoc in their wake, and performed their primary mission of diverting attention from Grant's movements west and south of Vicksburg. They had inflicted one hundred casualties and captured over five hundred prisoners. Miraculously, all this had been accomplished with fewer than twenty-five casualties. There was good reason for Sherman to call it the "most brilliant expedition of the Civil War."[66]

Grant's third diversion involved another cavalry foray. At the same time as Grierson traveled the length of Mississippi, other Union forces went on the offensive far to the east. Colonel Abel D. Streight led a "poorly

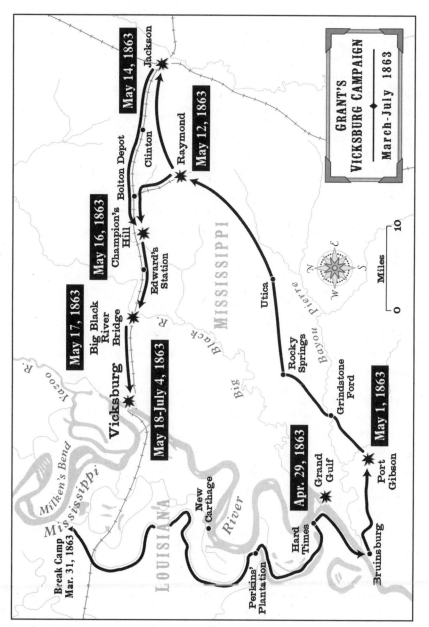

Map by David Deis, Dreamline Cartography, Northridge, California

mounted horse and mule brigade" across northern Alabama into Georgia to attack railroads and draw the ever-dangerous cavalry of Nathan Bedford Forrest away from Grierson's raiders.[67] Streight's party of 1,600 was captured by Forrest. By May 13 Lincoln had learned of the capture but commented, "Whether [the expedition] had paid for itself,...I do not know."[68] He seems to have realized the raid's diversionary purpose.

To completely confuse Pemberton, Grant used a fourth diversion. While he was moving south with McClernand and McPherson on the west bank (Louisiana shore), Grant had Sherman's 15th Corps stay in the Vicksburg vicinity and threaten that city from the north. On April 27 Grant directed Sherman to proceed up the Yazoo River and threaten the bluffs northeast of Vicksburg. On April 29 Sherman debarked ten regiments of troops and appeared to be preparing an assault while eight naval gunboats bombarded the Confederate forts at Haines' Bluff. Having suffered no casualties, Sherman withdrew on May 1 to hastily follow McPherson down the west bank of the Mississippi. His troops were ferried across the river on May 6 and 7 to rejoin Grant's two other corps in downstate Mississippi.[69]

After moving two-thirds of his army down the west bank of the Mississippi to get below Vicksburg, Grant undertook a challenging amphibious crossing to Bruinsburg, Mississippi, on April 30, 1863. As Grant did so, Congressman Washburne, accompanying Grant's army, wrote a tongue-in-cheek endorsement of Grant to Lincoln: "I am afraid Grant will have to be reproved for want of style. On this whole march for five days he has had neither a horse nor an orderly or servant, a blanket or overcoat or clean shirt, or even a sword.... His entire baggage consists of a toothbrush."[70] This humorous communication from the field demonstrates the strength of the Lincoln-Washburne-Grant relationship as the Vicksburg Campaign began in earnest.

THE BATTLE OF PORT GIBSON

The next day, May 1, brought conflict and the first of Grant's five victories in battles leading to the siege of Vicksburg: the Battle of Port Gibson.[71] Two Confederate brigades, which had belatedly marched as many as forty-four miles from positions near Vicksburg, and the garrison from Grand Gulf had crossed the bridge over the North Fork of Bayou Pierre at Port Gibson. They confronted McClernand's troops about three miles west of Port Gibson. The Confederate left fell back under intense attack from three of McClernand's divisions as Union sharpshooters picked off the brave and effective Rebel gunners manning the defenders' artillery. Following the initial Rebel retreat, McClernand and visiting Illinois Governor Richard Yates delivered victory remarks and did some politicking with the troops. Grant put an end to those proceedings and ordered the advance to resume. Meanwhile, Grant had reinforced McClernand's left wing with two of McPherson's brigades, and that wing drove the Confederate right wing back toward Port Gibson. Victory was confirmed the next morning (May 2), when Grant's soldiers found Port Gibson abandoned by the Confederates, who had crossed and burned the bridges across Big Bayou Pierre (to Grand Gulf) and Little Bayou Pierre.[72] Although Grant's troops were on the offensive all day at Port Gibson, the two sides' casualties were surprisingly comparable— almost nine hundred each.[73]

Despite narrow roads, hilly terrain, and dense vegetation that aided the defenders, Grant's superior force had gained the inland foothold it needed and access to the interior. The battle set the tone for those that followed in the campaign and affected the morale of the winners and losers. Through deception and celerity, Grant would consistently outnumber his foes on five battlefields in eighteen days although his troops were outnumbered by the Confederates scattered around western Mississippi. That concentration of force proved decisive. From Vicksburg, Pemberton accurately and somewhat desperately telegraphed Richmond: "A furious battle has been going on since daylight just below Port Gibson.... Enemy's movement threatens Jackson, and, if successful, cuts off Vicksburg and Port Hudson from the east...." With minimal losses, Grant was moving inland. Meanwhile, a rattled Pemberton sent an urgent message to his field commanders directing them to proceed at once—but neglecting to say to where.[74]

By winning the Battle of Port Gibson on May 1, Grant established a firm beachhead and prepared to move into the heart of Mississippi. After his troops had quickly built a bridge across Little Bayou Pierre, Grant accompanied McPherson northeast to Grindstone Ford, the site of the next bridge across Big Bayou Pierre. Fortunately, they found the bridge still burning and only partially destroyed. They made rapid repairs and crossed Big Bayou Pierre. Because Grant was now in a position to cut off Grand Gulf, the Confederates abandoned that river town and retreated north toward Vicksburg. At Hankinson's Ferry, north of Grand Gulf, the Confederates retreated across a raft bridge over the Big Black River, the only remaining geographical barrier between Grant and Vicksburg.[75]

By May 8 the good news about Grand Gulf had reached Lincoln, who wired it to Hooker. Lincoln began his telegram, "The news is here, of the capture, by our forces of Grand Gulf—a large & very important thing."[76] Three days later Lincoln inquired of General Dix whether the Richmond papers had any news about Grand Gulf or Vicksburg.[77]

GRANT MOVES INLAND

On May 3 Grant rode into the abandoned and ruined town of Grand Gulf, boarded the *Louisville*, took his first bath in a week, caught up on his correspondence, and rethought his mission. He had learned of the successful completion of Grierson's diversionary mission[78] and also of the time-consuming campaign of General Nathaniel P. Banks up the Red River. He decided to deviate radically from his orders, which called for him to send McPherson's Corps south to Port Hudson to await the return of Banks and cooperate with Banks in the capture of Port Hudson—all of this before a decisive move on Vicksburg. Grant realized that he would lose about a month waiting to cooperate with Banks in taking Port Hudson, he would gain only about 12,000 troops from Banks, and the intervening time would give Confederates the opportunity to gather reinforcements from all over the South to save Vicksburg. Instead, Grant decided to move inland with McPherson's and McClernand's Corps, and he ordered Sherman to continue moving south from Vicksburg, cross the Mississippi, and join him with two of his three divisions.[79]

Therefore, before leaving Grand Gulf at midnight on May 3, Grant wrote to Halleck:

The country will supply all the forage required for anything like an active campaign and the necessary fresh beef. Other supplies will have to be drawn from [the west bank]. This is a long and precarious route but I have every confidance [*sic*] in succeeding in doing it.

I shall not bring my troops into this place [Grand Gulf] but immediately follow the enemy, and if all promises as favorably hereafter as it does now, not stop until Vicksburg is in our possession.[80]

Grant was going for Vicksburg—now! Until Sherman's troops arrived, Grant had only 25,000 troops across the river to face 50,000 Confederates in Mississippi with as many as another 20,000 on the way.[81]

When he moved inland to Hankinson's Ferry at daybreak on May 4, Grant learned that McPherson's men had captured intact the bridge across the Big Black River and established a bridgehead on the opposite shore. While awaiting the arrival of Sherman's corps, Grant ordered McPherson and McClernand to probe the countryside, and the former's patrols discovered that the Confederates were fortifying a defensive line south of Vicksburg. Their patrols also were designed to create the impression that Grant would directly attack Vicksburg from the south. With the arrival of Sherman and the bulk of his corps on May 6 and 7, Grant was ready to move in force.[82]

Realizing that Vicksburg by now was well defended on the south and that its defenders could flee to the northeast if he attacked from the south, Grant decided on a more promising—but riskier—course of action. In the words of T. Harry Williams, "Then the general called dull and unimaginative and a mere hammerer executed one of the fastest and boldest moves in the records of war."[83] He cut loose from his base at Grand Gulf, withdrew McPherson from north of the Big Black River, and ordered all three of his corps to head northeast between the Big Black on the left and Big Bayou Pierre on the right. His goal was to follow the Big Black, cut the east/west railroad between Vicksburg and the state capital of Jackson, and then move west along the railroad to Vicksburg. In what Thomas Buell called "the most brilliant decision of his career,"

Grant "would attack first [Joseph] Johnston [who was bringing in reinforcements from east of Mississippi] and then Pemberton before they
could unite and thereby outnumber him, the classic example of defeating
an enemy army in detail."[84]

On May 9 Grant wrote to Sherman: "I do not calculate upon the
possibility of supplying the Army with full rations from Grand Gulf. I
know it will be impossible without constructing additional roads. What
I do expect however is to get up what rations of hard bread, coffee & salt
we can and make the country furnish the balance.... A delay would give
the enemy time to reinforce and fortify."[85] Given the poor condition of
the dirt roads, the tenuous supply situation, and the threat of Confederate interference from many directions, according to Vicksburg Campaign
expert Ed Bearss, Grant's "decision to move northeast along the Big
Black–Big Bayou Pierre watershed was boldness personified, and Napo-
leonic in its concept."[86]

William B. Feis concluded: "From the outset, Grant designed his
movements to sow uncertainty in Pemberton's mind as to the true Federal
objective. The key to success, especially deep in Confederate territory,
was to maintain the initiative and make the enemy guess at his objec-
tives."[87] Noteworthy is Grant's determination to not only occupy Vicksburg but to trap Pemberton's army rather than allow it to escape to fight
again. As he would do later in Virginia, Grant stayed focused on defeating, capturing, or destroying the opposing army—not simply occupying
geographic positions. J. F. C. Fuller pointed out that Grant's plan not
only was daring and contrary to his instructions from Halleck, but that,
just as importantly, he insisted that his commanders move with haste to
execute it. He clearly wanted to move quickly inland to negate any forces
other than Pemberton's, destroy Vicksburg's supply line, and then quickly
turn on Vicksburg with his own rear protected.[88]

As Grant moved inland, he planned to live off the previously unsacked
countryside. His troops slaughtered livestock and harvested crops and
gardens to obtain food and fodder. They also gathered an eclectic collection of buggies and carriages to assemble a small, heavily guarded wagon
train that would carry salt, sugar, hard bread, ammunition, and other
crucial supplies from Grand Gulf to Grant's army. Grant would depend

on those intermittent and vulnerable wagon trains to meet some of his needs for two weeks until a regular supply line was opened on the Yazoo River north of Vicksburg on May 21.[89]

From May 8 to 12, Grant's army moved out of its Grand Gulf beachhead and up this corridor with McClernand hugging the Big Black on the left and guarding all the ferries, Sherman in the center, and McPherson on the right. They gradually swung in a more northerly direction and moved within a few miles of the critical Vicksburg and Jackson Railroad without serious opposition. Then, on May 12, McPherson ran into stiff opposition south of the town of Raymond.[90]

BATTLES OF RAYMOND AND JACKSON

Aggressive assaults ordered by Confederate Brigadier General John Gregg, who believed he was facing a single brigade, threw McPherson's soldiers into disarray. Strong counterattacks led by Major General "Black Jack" Logan drove the outnumbered Confederates back into and through Raymond. Gregg's aggressiveness cost him eight hundred twenty casualties. McPherson reported four hundred forty-two casualties. Grant's campaign of maneuver and concentration of force was resulting in progress at the cost of moderate casualties.[91]

Even more significantly, Grant's daring crossing of the Mississippi and inland thrust were wreaking havoc at the highest levels of the Confederacy. Pemberton, in command at Vicksburg, was caught between conflicting orders from President Jefferson Davis and General Joseph Johnston, his theater commander. Davis told Pemberton that holding Vicksburg and Port Hudson was critical to connecting the eastern Confederacy to the Trans-Mississippi. The Northern-born Pemberton, who had been eased out of his Charleston, South Carolina command for suggesting evacuation of that city, decided to obey President Davis and defend Vicksburg at all costs. He did this despite May 1 and 2 orders from Johnston that, if Grant crossed the Mississippi, Pemberton should unite all his troops to defeat him. Grant was the beneficiary of Pemberton's decision because Pemberton kept his fifteen brigades in scattered defensive positions behind the Big Black River while Grant moved away from them toward Jackson. Meanwhile, Johnston belatedly moved from Tennessee to Pemberton's aid.[92]

The battle at Raymond caused Grant to realize the seriousness of the Confederate threat to his right flank—and then to his rear—if he simply continued north to the railroad and then turned west toward Vicksburg. He had received reports that Johnston had arrived in Jackson and reinforcements from the east and south were headed for that town. Jackson was the obvious rail junction for Confederate troops and supplies headed for Vicksburg. Thus, Grant decided to attack Jackson and eliminate it and the troops there as a threat to his Vicksburg campaign. On the evening of May 12, therefore, he issued orders for McPherson and Sherman to move on Jackson. They threatened Jackson by nightfall on May 13.[93]

That very evening, Johnston arrived at Jackson. Advised by Gregg that Union troops were astride the railroad to Vicksburg, that only 6,000 Confederate troops were in the Jackson vicinity, and that Confederate reinforcements were on the way, Johnston hoped to assemble 12,000 troops at Jackson within a day and trap Grant between Pemberton's force and his. To accomplish this, he sent three couriers with messages directing Pemberton to organize a converging attack and, if practicable, attack the Federal troops at Clinton. He stressed that "Time is all important." In a concurrent telegram to Confederate Secretary of War James Seddon, Johnston concluded by saying, "I am too late."[94] In light of Grant's initiative and Pemberton's hesitance to carry out Johnston's order or abandon Vicksburg, Johnston was indeed too late.[95] Partly because Grant's spy network had advised him of Johnston's arrival and plans for reinforcement, Grant did not hesitate to continue his expedited offensive.[96]

Because of Grant's concentration of force at Jackson, and despite torrential downpours, his troops were able to drive the Confederates from Jackson in less than a day of battle on May 14.[97] McPherson fought his way in from the west and Sherman from the southwest; they occupied the city by mid-afternoon. Jackson cost the Union about three hundred casualties while the Confederates suffered an estimated five hundred casualties and the loss of seventeen cannon. Confederate industrial losses in Jackson were significant. Johnston himself burned all the city's cotton and railroad rolling stock worth five million dollars, and Sherman followed that up by burning an arsenal, foundries, machine shops, and cotton factories and warehouses. During the assault, Pemberton spent the day probing southeast of Vicksburg for Grant's virtually non-existent line of communication with Grand Gulf, and Johnston retreated from Jackson to the north away from Pemberton's movement. Even worse for the Rebels, a pessimistic and passive Johnston turned back reinforcements that were moving toward Jackson by rail.[98]

Grant then learned from McPherson that one of Johnston's three couriers carrying his May 12 "attack" message to Pemberton was a Union spy. Thus, Grant learned of Johnston's order and immediately turned his army westward to deal with Pemberton. He ordered McClernand to Bolton Station (Bolton Depot), about twenty miles west of Jackson on the Vicksburg and Jackson Railroad and the nearest point to Jackson on the railroad where Johnston might merge his and Pemberton's forces. He also ordered McPherson to swiftly move west along the railroad and Sherman to destroy the railroads[99] and enemy property in and around Jackson. These actions were all accomplished without delay on May 15, and Grant at last was prepared to march directly toward Vicksburg.

THE BATTLE OF CHAMPION'S HILL

At five in the morning on May 16, Grant learned from two railroad workers that Pemberton was supposedly moving toward him with about 25,000 troops. Grant immediately sent Sherman orders to cease his destructive work at Jackson and move hastily west to join Grant, McClernand, and McPherson. Meanwhile, Pemberton, having wasted his time on the southward movement to cut off Grant from his nonexistent base, had finally decided to obey his orders from Johnston and move east toward Jackson to confront Grant. Pemberton occupied a strong defensive position at Champion's Hill, astride the Vicksburg and Jackson Railroad and two parallel roads. Pemberton's men, however, were exhausted from their confused handling on the 15th, while Grant's troops had been efficiently moved into a threatening position.[100]

At the May 16 Battle of Champion's Hill, Grant's 32,000 troops in both McPherson's and McClernand's Corps moved against 23,000 Confederate defenders. An aura of uncertainty hung over the Confederate troops as word spread of General Pemberton's belated decision, made that morning, to disengage from the enemy and move northeast to join Johnston. His decision (his third different strategic decision in three days as he tried to figure out what Grant was doing) came too late because the armies were soon locked in battle.[101] After an initial blocking action, Pemberton gave orders for some infantry to disengage by moving west and then northeast. His efforts were foiled by Grant's rapid movement, and the Rebels could not escape battle.[102]

Under Grant's oversight and McPherson's control, Union soldiers launched a late-morning assault on the north side of the battlefield. By early afternoon, they not only had carried Champion's Hill, but they also had gained control of Jackson Road west of the crossroads, thereby cutting off one of Pemberton's only two escape routes back toward Vicksburg. In the process, they had shattered one Confederate division and captured sixteen precious guns.[103] Seeing the north end of his line collapsing, Pemberton ordered reinforcements from his right. At 2:30 that afternoon veteran Arkansas and Missouri brigades launched a furious assault on the Union soldiers who only recently had taken control at the crossroads. The two Rebel brigades not only drove the Yankees out of the key crossroads but all the way back beyond the crest of Champion's Hill.[104]

Grant and McPherson organized yet another attack to regain the lost ground. As at Belmont, Donelson, and Shiloh, Grant took personal charge at a critical moment to turn adversity into victory. He said, "[Brigadier General Alvin P.] Hovey's division and [Colonel George] Boomer's brigade are good troops. If the enemy has driven them he is not in good plight himself. If we can go in here and make a little showing, I think he will give way." Led by a newly arrived division of McPherson's Corps, the Federals made that "little showing" and drove the stubborn Rebels off Champion's Hill and out of the crossroads.[105] With Union forces pressing them all along the front and only one retreat route open, most of the Confederates fled across the Big Black River toward Vicksburg.

One 7,000-man Rebel division was cut off, abandoned its twelve guns, and headed toward Jackson. By the time it reached Jackson, it had melted away to 4,000.[106]

The Battle of Champion's Hill involved about three hours of skirmishing and four hours of fierce fighting on Grant's center and right. Although Grant was on the offensive throughout the battle and attained his goal of pushing the enemy toward Vicksburg, the numbers of his dead and wounded were remarkably similar to his enemy's. Both sides had about four hundred killed and 1,800 wounded, but Grant's two hundred missing paled alongside the Confederates' 1,700 missing. In addition, Grant captured thirty pieces of artillery and cut Major General W. W. Loring's 7,000-man division off from the rest of Pemberton's army.[107]

This battle closed the door on possible escape by Pemberton's army and cleared the way for the siege of Vicksburg. It has been described by James R. Arnold as "arguably the decisive encounter of the war." While Pemberton had kept forty percent of his troops behind the Big Black River, Grant had pressed forward with all available troops and thereby gained a crucial and decisive 3:2 manpower advantage. Grant later described the military significance of the victory: "We were now assured of our position between Johnston and Pemberton, without a possibility of a junction of their forces."[108]

ATTACKS NEAR AND ON VICKSBURG

With the demoralized Confederates having moved back to the Big Black River, Grant sent word to the trailing Sherman to head northwest to cross that river at Bridgeport with his 15th Corps and thereby flank Pemberton's troops. Yet, before Sherman arrived on their flank, the Confederates had been beaten. At the Big Black River, the Confederates again had a respectable defensive position from which to confront Grant's assault. Inexplicably, however, they built a parapet of cotton bales and dirt on the east side of the river instead of on the higher ground west of the river. Thus they failed to fully utilize the river's defensive potential during the brief battle that ensued. Pemberton's over-commitment to the east bank was accompanied by his withdrawal of all the artillery horses to the west bank, thereby making withdrawal of those guns east of the river difficult or impossible.[109]

On the morning of May 17, Grant's troops arrived near the river and came under fire as the Battle of the Big Black River began.[110] A brigade of Iowa and Wisconsin troops scurried under fire to an old river meander scar (an oxbow) near the center of the battlefield. From there they launched a dramatic three-minute charge through a swamp and abatis (an obstacle of cut trees with sharp points aimed at attackers) and entered the Confederate lines—to the shock of everyone on the field. They captured many startled defenders while the rest of the Rebels east of the deep river started a major "skedaddle." A few of them tried to swim across the river while most scrambled back across two "bridges" (one a converted steamboat), which the Confederates then burned behind them as they fled to Vicksburg. Although the bridge-burning prevented Grant's immediate pursuit across the high river, fast-moving Union troops and the river trapped at least a thousand Confederates on the east side of the river. Thus, Grant captured those soldiers, eighteen guns, and the last obstacle between his army and Vicksburg—at the small cost of two hundred eighty casualties.[111]

As the Battle of the Big Black River was about to begin, an officer from General Banks's staff arrived with a May 11 letter to Grant from Halleck ordering Grant to return to Grand Gulf and cooperate with General Banks in capturing Port Hudson. Grant told the startled officer he was too late and that Halleck would not have given the order if he had known of Grant's position. The next day, May 18, Grant crossed the Big Black and met Sherman, who had crossed miles above as planned. They rode together hastily toward their long-sought position on the Yazoo River northeast of Vicksburg, where they could establish a base for supplies from the Mississippi.[112] In his memoirs, Grant remembered the moment of elation he shared with Sherman:

> In a few minutes Sherman had the pleasure of looking down from the spot coveted so much by him the December before on the ground where his command had lain so helpless for offensive action. He turned to me, saying that up to this minute

he had felt no positive assurance of success. This, however, he said was the end of one of the greatest campaigns in history and I ought to make a report of it at once. Vicksburg was not yet captured, and there was no telling what might happen before it was taken; but whether captured or not, this was a complete and successful campaign.[113]

As Grant approached Vicksburg, he could look back on the past eighteen successful days with satisfaction. He had entered enemy territory against a superior force and with no secure supply-line, fought and won five battles, severely damaged the Mississippi capital, driven away Johnston's relief force, driven Pemberton's army back into Vicksburg, inflicted over 7,000 losses on the enemy, separated 7,000 troops from the main enemy army, and thus had reduced Pemberton's Army by 14,000 troops. Grant's own casualties were between 3,500 and 4,500. In 1882, Francis Vinton Greene succinctly summarized the greatness of Grant's campaign on that point: "We must go back to the campaigns of Napoleon to find equally brilliant results accomplished in the same space of time with such a small loss."[114]

Shortly after Grant had reached Vicksburg, Lincoln emphasized the need for his continuing support of Grant and praised the general's campaign: "I have had stronger influence brought against Grant, praying for his removal, since the battle of Pittsburg Landing, than for any other object, coming too from good men; and now look at his campaign since May 1. Where is anything in the Old World that equals it? It stamps him as the greatest general of the age, if not of the world."[115]

Back in Richmond, Lee had convinced Davis not to expend resources opposing Grant's supposedly doomed campaign.[116] Therefore, Grant could focus on Vicksburg without having his rear threatened by significant Rebel reinforcements until it was too late. In any event, Grant wasted no time and immediately moved on Vicksburg with all three of his corps and ordered the first assault at 2 p.m. on May 19. Riding the momentum of his string of successes, Grant wanted to catch the defenders before they had an opportunity to fully organize. Although that assault tightened the noose around the town and resulted in Grant's troops achieving covered and advanced positions, it also demonstrated that capture of the town by assault would be difficult. It cost Grant nine hundred casualties to the Rebels' two hundred. Nevertheless, Grant decided on a second assault. Therefore, on May 22, all three corps launched simultaneous attacks, bravely approached the enemy fortifications and were repulsed. In response to dubious claims of success by McClernand, Grant sent him reinforcements and continued attacks elsewhere—causing additional casualties. Grant had 3,200 casualties while the defenders incurred about five hundred. With that final assault having failed, Grant settled in for a siege.[117]

In his memoirs, Grant expressed his regrets for the May 22 assault but explained his reasons for that attack:

> We were in a Southern climate, at the beginning of the hot season. The Army of the Tennessee had won five successive victories over the garrison of Vicksburg in the three preceding weeks.... The Army of the Tennessee had come to believe that they could beat their antagonist under any circumstances. There was no telling how long a regular siege might last. As I have stated, it was the beginning of the hot season in a Southern climate. There was no telling what the casualties might be among Northern troops working and living in trenches, drinking surface water filtered through rich vegetation, under a tropical sun. If Vicksburg would have been carried in May, it would not only have saved the army the risk it ran of a greater danger than from the bullets of the enemy, but it would have given us a splendid army, well equipped and officered, to operate elsewhere with.[118]

British General Fuller pointed out that Grant had seven reasons to attack rather than simply besiege Vicksburg: (1) Johnston was gathering an army in his rear, (2) a quick victory would allow Grant to attack Johnston, (3) Union reinforcements would be required to perfect the siege, (4) the troops were impatient to take Vicksburg, (5) the weather was getting hotter, (6) water was scarce, and (7) the men were not anxious to dig entrenchments. Although he has been criticized in hindsight for initiating the May 22 assault, Grant had sufficient reasons to justify his attempt to take the town by assault. Even though his casualties that day were five hundred killed and 2,550 wounded, Grant's casualties in the three prior weeks of fighting had been a mere seven hundred killed and 3,400 wounded. Cumulatively, these casualties were a fair price to pay for having struck at the heart of the western Confederacy and trapping a 30,000-man army in the citadel on the Mississippi whose capture would culminate in an extraordinarily significant Union victory.[119]

Shortly after the second assault, Grant finally relieved McClernand of his corps command after McClernand foolishly issued and sent to newspapers, without Grant's required approval, an order praising his own corps' performance and reflecting negatively on Sherman's and McPherson's Corps. When Colonel James H. Wilson happily delivered the relief order to McClernand, the latter astutely commented, "Well, sir! I am relieved! By God, sir, we are both relieved."[120]

In a June 19 message, Grant advised Halleck that he had relieved McClernand "for his publication of a congratulatory address calculated to create dissension and ill-feeling in the army. I should have relieved him long since for general unfitness for his position." Within a few days, Lincoln himself acknowledged seeing Grant's dispatch.[121]

In a fuller explanation of the dismissal, Grant demonstrated his respect for presidential prerogatives: "A disposition and earnest desire on my part to do the most I could with the means at my command, without interference with the assignments to command which the President alone was authorized to make, made me tolerate General McClernand long after I thought the good of the service demanded his removal. It was only when almost the entire army under my command seemed to demand it that he was relieved."[122] Grant's contemporaneous statement to the U.S. Army's adjutant general clearly shows his recognition of the president's rights and needs concerning military appointments. This attitude—a far cry from that of McClellan and some other generals—constituted a firm foundation for the productive Lincoln-Grant relationship.

Subsequently, Lincoln supported Grant's action when McClernand appealed his dismissal to his fellow Illinoisan. In early August, prominent Illinois politicians advised Lincoln of a "deep and general feeling" of dissatisfaction with McClernand's dismissal. On August 12 Lincoln wrote to McClernand, "I doubt whether your present position is more painful to you than to myself" and expressed his gratitude for the Democratic general's early support for the war. He went on to deny having seen Grant's reasons for his dismissal and concluded, "...I could do nothing without doing harm.... For me to force you back upon Gen. Grant, would be forcing him to resign." Subsequently, McClernand asked for, and was denied, a court of inquiry; he resigned in January 1864 and complained of his inability to defend himself against "the proscription and calumnies of...Maj. Gen. U. S. Grant." McClernand had defied Grant once too often, and he was gone—with the president's approval.[123] Grant's patience in dealing with McClernand made it easier—and almost imperative—for Lincoln to support Grant's dismissal of the trouble-making Illinois Democrat.

SIEGE AND VICTORY AT VICKSBURG

During the siege of Vicksburg, Grant may have over-indulged in alcohol on one occasion.[124] There are many reports of Lincoln humor-ously rebuffing complaints about Grant's alleged drinking problem. In the midst of the Vicksburg campaign, Colonel T. Lyle Dickey of Grant's cavalry was sent to Washington with dispatches for the president and secretary of war. When meeting with the president, Colonel Dickey, an old political associate of Lincoln, assured him that rumors about Grant's drinking were false. According to Dickey, the president responded, "...if those accusing General Grant of getting drunk will tell me where he gets his whiskey, I will get a lot of it and send it around to some of the other generals...."[125]

Grant's alleged drinking episode, if it ever occurred, did not interfere with the business at hand. After the May 22 attack on Vicksburg, Grant had his troops dig in for a sustained siege. They dug trenches and protected them with sandbags and logs while Union sharpshooters kept the besieged defenders from interfering with the construction. With only four engineering officers in his army, Grant directed every West Point graduate to actively supervise the siege-line construction. With Johnston assembling an "Army of Relief" consisting of 31,000 troops from all over the South to trap him, Grant received reinforcements of his own from Missouri, Tennessee, and Kentucky. His army grew from 51,000 to 77,000. As reinforcements arrived, Grant used them to cut off all communication out of Vicksburg south along the Mississippi, secure the countryside back to the Big Black River, destroy bridges across that river, and thereby protect his army from being attacked by Johnston's force from the east.[126]

Grant's risky campaign left him somewhat vulnerable to a Confederate counterattack between May 22 and June 8, when the first division of Union reinforcements arrived. During that time Grant had about 51,000 troops caught between Pemberton, with 29,500 men, and Johnston, with a force of 22,000 that increased to 30,000 by June 3. But Lee's persuasive arguments against more reinforcements, together with Johnston's temerity and the lack of Confederate coordination, kept Grant from being attacked.

As the Confederate surrender at Vicksburg grew imminent, as indicated earlier, Lincoln exclaimed, "Grant is my man and I am his the rest of the war!"[127] On June 22 Grant learned that some of Johnston's Rebel cavalry had crossed the Big Black River to threaten his rear. Immediately Grant put Sherman in charge of the half of his army protecting against such an attack and readied other forces to reinforce Sherman if needed. With 30,000 men and seventy-two guns, Sherman's "Army of Observation" guarded all of the Big Black River crossings. Johnston backed off.[128]

On June 25 and July 1, Union troops exploded mines in tunnels they had dug under the Confederate lines. Although these explosions did not afford the besiegers an opportunity to enter the city, they did force the defenders to further constrict their lines. For forty-seven days, the Confederate forces and Vicksburg residents were subjected to continuous Union fire from ships and shore that may have totaled 88,000 shells and killed perhaps twenty civilians. With deserters reporting that morale and food supplies were running low in Vicksburg and with his trenches having been advanced as far as possible, Grant planned an all-out assault for July 6. Coincidently, Johnston had chosen that same date for his own long-delayed assault on Grant.[129]

Lincoln's consultation of Richmond newspapers finally reaped dividends when he learned from them of Grant's Vicksburg Campaign successes. Seeking confirmation of the good news, Lincoln wrote to Major General Stephen A. Hurlbut in Memphis. In his May 22 telegram, the president said the Richmond papers of the prior two days carried a dispatch from Joe Johnston and other news about Grant's nine-hour victory over Pemberton and Loring near Edwards' Station (Champion's Hill). On May 23 Hurlbut replied with details he had just received from Rawlins. Rawlins reported the Bruinsburg landing; victories (with Rebel casualty numbers) at Port Gibson, Raymond, Jackson, Baker's Creek (Champion's Hill), and Big Black (River) Bridge; and the investment of Vicksburg. Hurlbut incorrectly added that 15,000 to 20,000 Confederates were in Vicksburg and erroneously speculated that "Grant has probably captured nearly all."[130]

A few days later Lincoln paid tribute to Grant and his subordinates in a letter rejecting a recommendation that he dismiss Halleck. He wrote:

> Whether Gen. Grant shall or shall not consummate the capture of Vicksburg, his campaign from the beginning of this month up to the twenty second day of it, is one of the most brilliant in the world. His corps commanders, & Division commanders, in part, are McClernand, McPherson, Sherman, Steele, Hovey, Blair, & Logan. And yet taking Gen. Grant & these seven of his generals, and you can scarcely name one of them that has not been constantly denounced and opposed by the same men who are now so anxious to get Halleck out....[131]

The oft-vilified Grant had now earned such respect from Lincoln that the president cited his campaign as "one of the most brilliant in the world."

Because communications from Vicksburg remained slow, Lincoln on May 27 sought information about Grant from Hooker in Virginia and Rosecrans in eastern Tennessee. Rosecrans responded that a Rebel dispatch said Johnston had crossed the Big Black north of Grant with 20,000 troops.[132] That news must have concerned the president because the next day he wired Rosecrans: "I would not push you to any rashness; but I am very anxious that you do your utmost, short of rashness, to keep Bragg from getting off to help Johnston against Grant."[133]

With Lincoln looking over his shoulder, Halleck tried to pressure Rosecrans into taking some action to assist Grant. Halleck told Rosecrans that, since some of Bragg's troops (facing Rosecrans) were being detached and sent to oppose Grant, "a portion of your troops must be sent to Grant's relief." After Rosecrans promised to send relief but did nothing, Halleck asked him to explain his inactivity. After conferring with his seventeen generals, Rosecrans advised Halleck that none of them wanted to send troops to assist Grant until the Vicksburg Campaign was completed! He added that a "great military maxim" forbids fighting two great battles at once. Halleck, famous as a military strategist, replied that the maxim applied to one army, not two; explained that it was in the Confederates' interest (since they were acting on interior lines) to fight Rosecrans and Grant at different times, and added a droll comment that "councils of war never fight." It was not until early July that Rosecrans finally maneuvered Bragg out of middle Tennessee and back across the Tennessee River.[134] Halleck thus was unsuccessful in convincing Rosecrans to comply with one of Lincoln's major strategic principles: overcome the Rebels' interior lines advantage by attacking them at two places at the same time (a strategy Lincoln had unsuccessfully urged upon Halleck and Buell in early 1862).

On June 2 Lincoln asked Grant whether he was in communication with Banks and whether Banks was moving toward or away from Grant. Because the communications to and from Vicksburg had to go through Memphis by water transport, it was June 8 before Grant replied that Banks had closely invested Port Hudson and that Grant would forward a letter he had received from Banks.[135]

On June 6 and 8 Lincoln assured General Dix, who had reported a dearth of Vicksburg information in the Richmond papers, that dispatches to Washington indicated the Vicksburg siege was progressing without further general fighting and that "things looked reasonably well for us" at Port Hudson.[136]

On June 11, midway through the Vicksburg siege, Chaplain John Eaton visited Grant at his headquarters outside Vicksburg. Eaton described the general's down-to-earth appearance:

> As I spoke, my eye noted the peculiarly unassuming appearance of the General. Unassuming indeed he always was, and now his very clothes, as well as the crows' feet on his brow, bore testimony to the strenuousness of the life he was leading. Later on he told me jocosely that a toothbrush and a comb had been his outfit in the campaign just closing. He was dressed when I first saw him in an old brown linen duster surmounted by an old slouch hat; his trousers showed holes worn by the boot-straps, where they had rubbed against the saddle.[137]

Eaton's visit was to provide Grant with a report on the treatment and use of blacks under Eaton's direction. Included in the report were details of the Government's savings from black labor and a recommendation for black-only regiments commanded by high-quality white officers. After discussing the report, Grant wrote a cover letter to Lincoln. Grant praised Eaton's efforts in providing for blacks and finding useful employment for them. He commended the entire report to Lincoln, especially its recommendation of nationwide orders concerning "the contraband subject."[138]

In Virginia, meanwhile, Lee was moving his troops toward and then down the Shenandoah Valley as they embarked on the fateful Gettysburg Campaign. This movement provided Lincoln with a chance to advise Hooker on what to do and not to do. He told him not to cross the Rappahannock: "In one word, I would not take any risk of being entangled upon the river, like an ox jumped half over a fence, and liable to be torn by dogs, front and rear, without a fair chance to gore one way or kick the other." A few days later he advised Hooker, "I think Lee's Army, and not Richmond, is your true objective point. Fight him when opportunity offers. If he stays where he is, fret him, and fret him."[139] As Grant's Fort Donelson victory showed and his Vicksburg Campaign was demonstrating, Grant already understood that enemy armies were his primary goal. By mid-war, Lincoln and Grant firmly agreed on this critical principle.

On July 4 Pemberton surrendered Vicksburg and his 28,000-man army to Grant, who once again was proclaimed a national hero. After word of this huge victory reached Lincoln via Admiral Porter and Secretary of the Navy Welles, a disgruntled Stanton advised Grant that future military successes were to be reported to the War Department, not the navy.[140]

Because of concerns about the transportation and other resources that would have been used to send his prisoners off to Northern prison camps, Grant paroled Pemberton's army. Chester Hearn provided some insights on that action:

> Some northerners wanted Grant censured for not forwarding the rebels to Northern prisons, but the general's parole agreement hastened capitulation. Those who complained did not know that half the garrison was sick or wounded, the other half was starving, and the North had no facilities for incarcerating so great an infusion of prisoners. Grant later reversed his position on paroles because Jefferson Davis dishonored the rules and unlawfully released parolees from their pledges. A few months later...[Grant] found the very same men paroled at Vicksburg occupying the heights at Chattanooga.[141]

Following Meade's victory over Lee at Gettysburg, Lincoln was quite dismayed by Meade's failure to aggressively pursue and destroy Lee's retreating army. On July 6 he told Halleck that Union generals' actions "... appear to me to be connected with a purpose to cover Baltimore and Washington, and to get the enemy across the river again without further collision, and they do not appear connected with a purpose to prevent his crossing and to destroy him."[142] (Perhaps Lincoln was not aware that Halleck typically instructed Eastern generals to cover Washington and Baltimore—which was consistent with Lincoln's own war-long concerns about the capital.) On July 7 the president wrote, "We have certain information that Vicksburg surrendered to General Grant on the 4th of

July. Now, if General Meade can complete his work, so gloriously pros-
ecuted thus far, by the lieteral [sic] or substantial destruction of Lee's
army, the rebellion will be over."[143] Poor Meade. Less than ten days after
assuming command of the Eastern Union army, he was being compared
by Lincoln to Grant, who had just compelled the surrender of a second
Confederate army, on the crucial issue of pursuing, capturing or destroying Rebel armies.

By July 8 Meade was continuing to make Grant look even better to
Lincoln. Lincoln advised the Republican candidate for governor of California that it was "entirely certain that Vicksburg surrendered to Gen.
Grant on the glorious old 4th" and that Lee was being "closely pressed
by Meade" while crossing the Potomac after Gettysburg. Later that same
day, the president had lost his patience and remarked that forces being
gathered near Carlisle "will, in my unprofessional opinion, be quite as
likely to capture the Man-in-the-Moon as any part of Lee's army."[144]

About that same time, Chaplain Eaton arrived in Washington from
Memphis to provide his freedmen's report and Grant's cover letter to the
president. Lincoln took the opportunity to grill Eaton about his "fighting
general," his subordinate officers, the Vicksburg Campaign, and Eaton's
experiences with blacks. Eaton later commented, "During the whole of
my acquaintance with the President, he seemed to me to be doing all in
his power to measure the personal character of prominent men. He
gauged the strength of his armies by their leaders. He seemed constantly
to be taking these measurements, and when he had taken them, to lay
them aside in that wonderful brain of his for future use." Specifically with
regard to Lincoln's probing about Grant, Eaton said, "[H]is close questioning in regard to Grant was the most remarkable feature of the interview. From that day to this there has been a growing conviction in my
mind that the President meant to find out what his 'fighting General'
thought of his policy. What Lincoln thought of Grant was pretty well
determined, but true to his habit he let slip no opportunity by which he
might gain a clearer view of the character of the man he was dealing
with...."[145]

The real breakthrough in the Lincoln-Grant relationship came when
Lincoln wrote to Grant on July 13 about the Vicksburg Campaign:

My dear General

I do not remember that you and I ever met personally. I write this now as a grateful acknowledgment for the almost inestimable service you have done the country. I wish to say a word further. When you first reached the vicinity of Vicksburg, I thought you should do, what you finally did—march the troops across the neck, run the batteries with the transports, and thus go below; and I never had any faith, except a general hope that you knew better than I, that the Yazoo Pass expedition, and the like, could succeed. When you got below, and took Port-Gibson, Grand Gulf, and vicinity, I thought you should go down the river and join Gen. Banks; and when you turned Northward East of the Big Black, I feared it was a mistake. I now wish to make the personal acknowledgment that you were right, and I was wrong.

Yours very truly

A. Lincoln[146]

Not only did the president send Grant the most praise-filled letter of any he sent to any general during the war,[147] but he also voluntarily apologized for a belief of which no one else had any knowledge. Lincoln was opening up to Grant. He trusted his general. Interestingly, Grant did not respond to the letter; perhaps he believed there was little he could say that would not embarrass the president. In an August 9 letter, Lincoln, who may not have realized Grant's awkward situation, asked Grant if he had received the July 13 letter; Grant simply acknowledged that the letter had been "duly received." Grant did, however, thank Lincoln "very kindly for the great favors you have ever shown me...."[148] Their relationship was now secure.

In contrast, Lincoln was most disappointed by Meade's failure to bring Lee to battle after Gettysburg. He had Halleck tell Meade, "I need hardly say to you that the escape of Lee's army without another battle has created great dissatisfaction in the mind of the President, and it will require an active and energetic pursuit on your part to remove the impression that it has not been sufficiently active heretofore." In light of this censure by the president, Meade submitted his resignation, which Halleck promptly declined with an assurance that the words he used were intended as a stimulus and not a censure.[149] Lincoln's thoughts at that time were reflected in a letter he drafted—but never sent—to Meade. At its heart, the letter stated, "Again, my dear general, I do not believe you appreciate the magnitude of the misfortune involved in Lee's escape. He was within your easy grasp, and to have closed upon him would, *in connection with other late successes*, have ended the war."[150] The reference to "other late successes" revealed the continuing East/West comparisons occupying the president's mind.

Not surprisingly, when Eaton returned to the West from Washington, he found that Grant shared Lincoln's views about Meade's reticence. According to Eaton, "Grant was particularly anxious to know what reasons were understood to have influenced General Meade not to pursue General Lee across the Potomac—or rather, what induced him not to prevent Lee from crossing the Potomac at all. Grant seemed never to be altogether persuaded that Meade was justified in not following up his advantage at that point."[151]

Lincoln and Grant also shared a growing enthusiasm for the use of black troops in battle. During the siege of Vicksburg, on June 7, an outnumbered force of recently recruited and barely trained former slaves repelled an attack by 2,000 Confederates at nearby Milliken's Bend.[152] Their success in brutal hand-to-hand fighting earned them respect among their white comrades; even the Confederate commander admitted that "this charge was resisted by the negro portion of the enemy's force with considerable obstinacy."[153] Charles Dana later wrote, "The bravery of the blacks...completely revolutionized the sentiment of the army with regard to the employment of negro troops. I heard prominent officers who formerly in private had sneered at the idea of negroes fighting express themselves after that as heartily in favor of it. Among the Confederates, however, the feeling was very different. All the reports which came to us showed that both citizens and soldiers on the Confederate side manifested great dismay at the idea of our arming negroes."[154] Reports of black soldiers' bravery at Milliken's Bend confirmed similar ones resulting from a May 27 Federal assault at Port Hudson, Louisiana.[155]

Late that July Lincoln turned his attention to recruiting additional black troops in Grant's theater. On July 21 he told Stanton, "I desire that a renewed and vigorous effort be made to raise colored forces along the shores of the Missi[ssi]ppi," and referred to General Lorenzo Thomas as "one of the best, if not the very best, instruments for this service."[156] In a July 30 order, the president responded to reports of mistreatment of black prisoners of war by declaring that a Rebel soldier would be executed for each Union prisoner killed and that a Rebel soldier would be placed at hard labor for each Union prisoner who was enslaved.[157] Because its implementation would have resulted in a series of successive slaughters, this declaration was never carried out.

On August 9 Lincoln followed up with Grant on the black recruiting issue. He said he had "no reason to doubt that you are doing what you reasonably can" to assist Thomas's recruiting efforts and explained that this effort weakened the enemy and strengthened the Union. He added, "Mr. Dana understands you as believing that the emancipation proclamation has helped some in your military operations. I am very glad if this is so."[158] On August 23 Grant responded to Lincoln, "I have given the subject of arming the negro my hearty support. This, with the emancipation...is the heavyest [sic] blow[159] yet given the Confederacy." A non-abolitionist, Grant was expressing his views as a military commander. After describing efforts he was launching to recruit even more blacks, Grant continued with words that must have warmed the president's heart:

> Gen. Thomas is now with me and you may rely on it I will give him all the aid in my power. I would do this whether the arming the negro seemed to me a wise policy or not, because it is an order that I am bound to obey and do not feel that in my position I have a right to question any policy of the Government. In this particular instance there is no objection

however to my expressing an honest conviction. That is, by arming the negro we have added a powerful ally. They will make good soldiers and taking them from the enemy weaken him in the same proportion they strengthen us. I am therefore most decidedly in favor of pushing this policy to the enlistment of a force sufficient to hold all the South falling into our hands and to aid in capturing more.[160]

It is clear that Lincoln and Grant were seeing eye-to-eye on the benefits of recruiting blacks into the Union military and that Grant had astutely communicated his support for the president on emancipation and use of black soldiers to the president both directly and through Dana. Unlike McClellan, who likely would have resented and insulted Dana, Grant had converted a would-be spy on his operations into a powerful ally. Grant not only deferred to the president as the policymaker, but he enthusiastically adopted and implemented Lincoln's policies on this politically sensitive issue.

Late July issues about disposition of the Ninth Corps provided Lincoln with an opportunity to discuss his view of Grant's personal attributes. General Ambrose Burnside, commanding in Cincinnati, had inquired about when the Ninth Corps, which had been sent to reinforce Grant at Vicksburg on June 4, would be returned to him. On July 27 Lincoln explained that Grant had indicated in early July that he would do so and added, "For some reason, never mentioned to us by Gen. Grant, they have not been sent, though we have seen out-side intimations that they took part in the [post–July 4] expedition against Jackson. [They had.] Gen. Grant is a copious worker, and fighter, but a very meagre writer, or telegrapher. No doubt he changed his purpose in regard to the Ninth Corps, for some sufficient reason, but has forgotten to notify us of it."[161] Clearly the president was giving maximum discretion to the general he believed was a hard worker and aggressive fighter.

Grant's brilliant Vicksburg Campaign cemented his relationship with the president, who now recognized him as the general who would lead the Union to victory. Lincoln saw that Grant was an aggressive risk-taker who used whatever resources he had to achieve whatever victory was within his grasp. The president also perceived that Grant was a brilliant military strategist who could achieve success even when outnumbered in hostile country. When difficulties or opportunities arose in the future, Lincoln knew that Grant was his man.

CHAPTER 8

LINCOLN CALLS ON GRANT TO SAVE A UNION ARMY

———————◆———————

fter Vicksburg fell, Grant advocated a campaign against Mobile, Alabama, to bring the Union closer to victory. He realized that seizing Mobile would close the Rebels' last major port on the Gulf of Mexico. Before July had ended, Grant wrote to Halleck: "My troops are very much exhausted, and entirely unfit for any present duty requiring much marching. But, by selecting, any duty of immediate pressing importance could be done. It seems to me that Mobile is the point deserving the most immediate attention...."[1]

On August 9 the president rejected Grant's Mobile proposal: "[That proposal] would appear tempting to me also, were it not that in view of recent events in Mexico [French installation of Maximilian as Mexico's emperor], I am greatly impressed with the importance of re-establishing the national authority in Western Texas as soon as possible."[2] Lincoln made the same points in a discussion that same day with his secretary John Hay, who recorded in his diary: "[Lincoln] is very anxious that

Texas should be occupied and firmly held in view of French possibilities. He thinks it just now more important than Mobile. He would prefer that Grant should not throw his army onto the Mobile business before the Texas matter is safe. He wrote in that sense, I believe, to Grant today."[3]

While acquiescing to the president's priorities, Grant managed to reiterate the importance of moving on Mobile: "After the fall of Vicksburg I did incline very much to an immediate move on Mobile. I believed then the place could be taken with but little effort, and with the rivers debouching there, in our possession, we would have such a base to opperate [sic] from on the very center of the Confederacy as would make them abandon entirely the states bound west by the Miss. I see however the importance of a movement into Texas just at this time."[4] Lincoln must have been pleasantly surprised that one of his generals understood that his political and diplomatic priorities sometimes would trump military considerations.[5]

As a result of Lincoln's priorities, Banks launched an autumn 1863 invasion of south Texas. He landed troops at Brownsville and marched them up the coast to Port Lavaca—only to turn around when General John B. Magruder sent troops to confront him. Not for the last time, Banks's effort gained nothing for the Union cause and delayed any offensive movement against Mobile.

As Grant continued to push for Banks to attack Mobile, Halleck, in a January 8, 1864, communication to Grant, repeated the president's rationale for sending Banks into Texas:

> In regard to General Banks's campaign against Texas, it is proper to remark that it was undertaken less for military reasons than as a matter of State policy. As a military measure, simply, it perhaps presented less advantages than a movement on Mobile and the Alabama River, so as to threaten the enemy's interior lines and effect a diversion in favor of our armies at Chattanooga and East Tennessee. But, however this may have been, it was deemed necessary as a matter of political or State policy, connected with our foreign

relations, and especially with France and Mexico, that our troops should occupy and hold at least a portion of Texas. The President so ordered, for reasons satisfactory to himself and his cabinet, and it was, therefore, unnecessary for us to inquire whether or not the troops could have been employed elsewhere with greater military advantage.[6]

This explanation reinforced the knowledge Grant already had that the president faced broader concerns than did Grant and that those could preempt sound military decisions and recommendations.

Simultaneously, Rosecrans and his Army of the Cumberland were making slow progress in eastern Tennessee—much to the consternation of Lincoln and Halleck. On July 24, 1863, Halleck urged Rosecrans to move on Chattanooga before his opponent, Confederate General Braxton Bragg, could be reinforced by Joseph Johnston, who had been involved in opposing Grant's Vicksburg Campaign. Halleck told Rosecrans that he had fought to prevent his removal for inactivity and that "It has been said that you are as inactive as was General Buell, and the pressure for your removal has been almost as strong...." Rosecrans's responses to Halleck and Lincoln blamed supply and terrain problems for his lack of movement and told Lincoln, "Genl. Hallecks [*sic*] dispatches imply that you not only feel solicitude for the advance of this Army but dissatisfaction at its supposed inactivity."[7]

Lincoln responded to Rosecrans that he had been concerned that, when Grant invested Vicksburg, Johnston would attack him from the rear. He added that he and Halleck believed Rosecrans's attacking Bragg in Johnston's absence or sending Grant reinforcements would have been appropriate. The president then slowly turned the knife: "When...I saw a despatch [*sic*] of yours arguing that the right time for you to attack Bragg was not before but after the fall of Vicksburg, it impressed me very strangely.... It seemed no other than the proposition that you could better fight Bragg when Johnston should be at liberty to return and assist him, than you could before he could so return to his assistance."[8] Rosecrans's continued whining elicited another response from Lincoln on

August 31.[9] Grant's active campaigning and Rosecrans's concurrent inactivity and excuse-making enhanced the president's respect for Grant and declining confidence in Rosecrans.

Lincoln continued to be frustrated by the lack of significant progress in the East. On September 19, he inquired of Halleck whether, since Lee could protect Richmond with 60,000 troops to Meade's 90,000, it would be possible to use 50,000 Eastern troops elsewhere while Meade protected Washington with 40,000 against Lee's 60,000. Lincoln once again stressed to Halleck that he "desired the Army of the Potomac, to make Lee's army, and not Richmond, it's [sic] objective point"[10] —an approach on which Lincoln and Grant agreed. Unbeknownst to Lincoln and Halleck, the Confederates, on September 7, had started sending 15,000 of Longstreet's troops from Lee to Bragg. As a result, the Union leaders shortly would be sending Union troops from Virginia to Chattanooga.

In his summer 1863 Tullahoma Campaign, Rosecrans had moved south toward Chattanooga, crossed the Tennessee River, occupied Chattanooga and pushed Bragg's Army of Tennessee southward into Georgia. The overconfident Rosecrans next split his forces in early September and barely escaped having some of them destroyed in detail before he hurriedly gathered them together at a place called Chickamauga. There, on September 19 and 20, Bragg (with 5,000 or more of Longstreet's reinforcements from Virginia) attacked Rosecrans's line. On the morning of the 20th, an erroneous order issued by Rosecrans left a gap in his line through which the Rebels poured. Rosecrans and much of his army fled toward Chattanooga while Major General George Thomas earned the sobriquet "Rock of Chickamauga" by holding off the attacking Confederates until evening and thus saving Rosecrans's army from destruction.[11]

The Confederates pursued Rosecrans to Chattanooga and trapped his army there by occupying the high ground to the southwest (Lookout Mountain), east (Missionary Ridge), and northeast (Tunnel Hill) of the town. Union forces depended on an inadequate 60-mile-long supply line across the mountains north and west of town. Chattanooga, a critical railroad junction on the Tennessee River, would become either the

Confederate gateway again to eastern Tennessee and Kentucky or the Union gateway to Atlanta and the rest of Georgia. Lincoln recognized its importance; on September 21 he wrote to Halleck, "I think it very important for Gen. Rosecrans to hold his position, at or about Chattanooga, because, if held from that place to Cleveland [a nearby point], both inclusive, it keeps all Tennessee clear of the enemy, and also breaks one of his most important Railroad lines." [12] The president was urging Burnside, who had occupied Knoxville northeast of Chattanooga on September 2, to come to Rosecrans's assistance. [13]

In early October, Rosecrans's soldiers in Chattanooga went on half rations, devoured their animals, and were on the verge of starvation. Fortunately for them, Lincoln and Stanton realized the gravity of their situation and the significance of Chattanooga. Unlike their Confederate counterparts, they responded by sending massive reinforcements to Chattanooga and assigning a Union commander there capable of meeting the crisis: Ulysses S. Grant.

After having to micromanage them, Lincoln had lost confidence in Meade, Rosecrans, and Burnside, and so he unsurprisingly turned to Grant in this time of crisis. The president had closely followed Grant's successes at Fort Donelson, Shiloh, Iuka, Corinth, and Vicksburg. [14] In an October 3 dispatch to Lieutenant Colonel James H. Wilson at Cairo, Halleck requested that the following message be conveyed to Grant, "General, it is the wish of the Secretary of War, that as soon as Gen Grant is able to take the field [following a fall from a horse in New Orleans] he will come to Cairo and report by telegraph." That message did not reach Grant until October 10. [15]

While moving to place Grant in command over Rosecrans and offering him the opportunity to relieve "Old Rosey" from command, Lincoln continued to push Rosecrans. In an October 4 wire, the president said, "If we can hold Chattanooga, and east Tennessee, I think the rebellion must dwindle and die. I think you and Burnside can do this; and hence doing so is your main object." He went on to unrealistically suggest that the besieged general could "menace or attack" the enemy. [16] Later, in the same vein, Lincoln wishfully told Rosecrans, "You and Burnside now have [the enemy] by the throat, and he must break your hold, or perish."[17] Because the president, in fact, did not think Rosecrans and Burnside were up to the task of holding Chattanooga and eastern Tennessee, he was turning to Grant.

Stanton convinced Lincoln during a midnight crisis meeting to move the 20,000 troops of the 11th and 12th corps, under Hooker's command, by rail from Virginia, through the Western states, and all the way to Stevenson, Alabama, from which they marched to Chattanooga. Before they arrived, Stanton had personally met with Grant as the general traveled to Chattanooga. Stanton advised Grant he was authorized to relieve Rosecrans, which he did.[18] Grant, now a theater commander (Military Division of the Mississippi) of three armies (Armies of the Ohio, the Cumberland, and the Tennessee), named Thomas to command the Army of the Cumberland in Chattanooga. Sherman succeeded Grant as commander of the Army of the Tennessee.

Military necessity was tempered by political concerns. Although Lincoln was anxious to place Grant in command at Chattanooga, the president delayed the appointment until October 16—three days after a critical October 13 gubernatorial election in Ohio, where Rosecrans remained popular among pro-war Democrats. The delay proved to have been unnecessary since anti-war Clement L. Vallandingham, the nation's most notorious Copperhead, was crushed in the Ohio race.[19]

Within five days of Grant's October 23 arrival in the nearly besieged city, he approved a previously devised nighttime amphibious operation that opened a workable supply line (the "Cracker Line") into the town. Union troop morale soared. The Cracker Line was solidified when the 11th and 12th corps marched into the Chattanooga environs and rebuffed a Confederate counterattack at Wauhatchie on the night of October 28–29. Dana telegraphed the good news to Stanton, and Lincoln advised Seward that the 11th and 12th corps fought well.[20]

Lincoln's recognition of the critical significance of Chattanooga was reflected in his appointment of Grant to command there, his movement of two corps from the East, and his approval of Sherman and the bulk of his

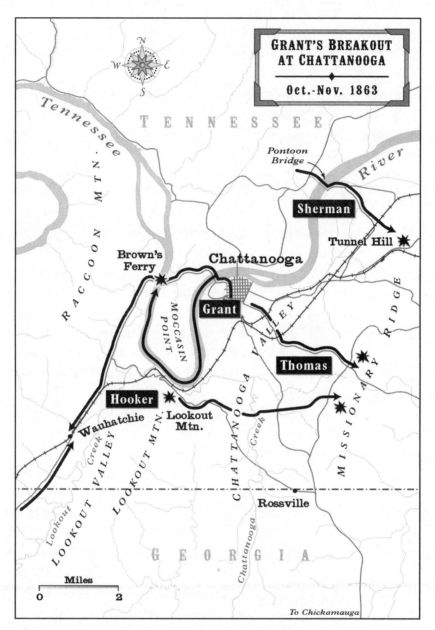

Map by David Deis, Dreamline Cartography, Northridge, California

corps being ordered to march from the Mississippi Valley to Chattanooga. Lee stymied Rebel plans to send more reinforcements to Chattanooga by refusing to part with any more troops,[21] and Lee, Davis, Bragg, and Longstreet agreed to reduce Confederate strength at Chattanooga by moving Longstreet and 15,000 troops from there to Knoxville.[22] Thus, as Grant was building his strength in the critical river town to nearly 80,000, the Confederate leadership reduced Rebel strength there to a mere 35,000.[23] Peter Cozzens called this Lee-inspired transfer "the most egregious error of [Bragg's] checkered career," one that left him with no mobile reserve at Chattanooga.[24]

On the manpower front, Lincoln recognized the need to replace volunteers whose terms were expiring and to increase the strength of Union armies. Therefore, he issued an October 17, 1863, proclamation calling for 300,000 volunteers for the shorter of the duration of the war or three years.[25] By early 1864 the need for soldiers was even greater, and Lincoln issued a call for a 500,000-man draft and then one for another 200,000.[26]

In response to Lincoln's inquiry ("What is the news?"), Burnside was pleased to report on November 17 that he had held off Longstreet's 15,000 troops the prior day at Campbell's Station, between Knoxville and Chattanooga, and had retreated in good order to Knoxville.[27]

As Grant moved the Chattanooga crisis toward resolution, the president journeyed to Gettysburg, where he delivered brief remarks at the dedication of a national cemetery on the famous battlefield. Looking ahead to the fighting that remained to be done, Lincoln concluded with the words, "It is rather for us to be here dedicated to the great task remaining before us—that from these honored dead we take increased devotion to that cause for which they gave the last full measure of devotion—that we here highly resolve that these dead shall not have died in vain—that this nation, under God, shall have a new birth of freedom—and that government of the people, by the people, for the people, shall not perish from the earth."[28]

Within a week thereafter, Grant had received sufficient reinforcements, the Confederates remained at their reduced strength, and Grant went on the offensive. On November 23 Thomas's men moved toward

Missionary Ridge and occupied Orchard Knob. That day's success brought relief to Lincoln; that night Hay noted, "Got news tonight of Grant's advance on the enemy at Chattanooga & Thomas success. The President who had been a little despondent abt Grant took heart again."[29] The next day Sherman crossed the Tennessee and attacked the Rebel right flank while Hooker captured Lookout Mountain on the Confederate left. Grant reported these developments to Lincoln, who responded, "Your despatches [*sic*] as to fighting on Monday & Tuesday are here. Well done. Many thanks to all. Remember Burnside."[30] The president was pleased but obviously remained concerned about Longstreet's threat to Burnside at Knoxville.

On November 25 Grant continued his all-out assault on the Confederates, who still occupied high ground on the east side of Chattanooga and the Tennessee River Valley. The battle did not go as Grant had planned, but his use of all his troops broke the Rebel line. He expected Sherman to break through on the Union left at Tunnel Hill, but Sherman was stymied by unfavorable terrain and the best Confederate troops under Major General Patrick Cleburne. His secondary hope was that Hooker would roll up the Confederates on the Union right, but Hooker failed to move swiftly through the valley between Lookout Mountain and Missionary Ridge. To relieve pressure on his flanks, Grant ordered Thomas's troops to advance on Confederate rifle pits at the base of Missionary Ridge. After those rifle pits were easily taken, the attackers found themselves in a deadly no-man's land and, instead of retreating, charged up Missionary Ridge. To the surprise of all involved, the attackers quickly broke the thin Rebel line on top of the ridge. After they attacked to the right and left of the breakthrough area, the Confederate army, except for Cleburne's wing, fled in panic back to Georgia. Cleburne's men retreated in an orderly fashion and saved Bragg's army by forming an effective rearguard at Ringgold Gap.

Aware of Lincoln's concern for Burnside, Grant immediately organized a relief expedition for Knoxville. However, Burnside's rebuff of Longstreet's incompetently planned and executed November 29 attack on Knoxville made Sherman's cautionary trek to Knoxville unnecessary because Longstreet had withdrawn to the east before his arrival. Lincoln, who demonstrated a war-long concern for the safety of Unionists in eastern Tennessee, was so relieved when he learned that Knoxville was safe and that Longstreet had retreated into the mountains[31] that he issued a December 7 glowing press release of thanksgiving:

> Reliable information being received that the insurgent force is retreating from East Tennessee, under circumstances rendering it probable that the Union forces cannot hereafter be dislodged from that important position; and esteeming this to be of high national consequence, I recommend that all loyal people do, on receipt of this, informally assemble at their places of worship and tender special homage and gratitude to Almighty God, for this great advancement of the national cause.[32]

The next day, in his annual message to Congress, Lincoln noted two developments that reflected Grant's major accomplishments of 1863: "The rebel borders are pressed still further back, and by the complete opening of the Mississippi the country dominated by the rebellion is divided into distinct parts, with no practical communication between them. Tennessee and Arkansas have been substantially cleared of insurgent control...."[33]

At the same time, Lincoln thanked Grant and his troops for their Tennessee successes:

> Understanding that your lodgment at Chattanooga and Knoxville is now secure, I wish to tender you, and all under your command, my more than thanks—my profound gratitude— for the skill, courage, and perseverance, with which you and they, over so great difficulties, have effected that important object. God bless you all.[34]

Grant passed the president's praise on to his soldiers in a general order.[35] In late November, Meade attempted to motivate his troops in Virginia by ordering that a telegram announcing Grant's Chattanooga victory be read to them.[36]

The president had become comfortable enough with Grant that he approached him on a delicate personnel matter. On December 19 Lincoln wrote him about Major General Robert H. Milroy, who had suffered a disastrous defeat in June 1863 at Winchester, Virginia, where his troops had been overrun by Confederates on their way to Gettysburg. Lincoln said Milroy was sincere, courageous, not difficult to satisfy, and eager to fight again, and that most of the Indiana congressional delegation wanted him back in action. So he asked Grant, "Could you, without embarrassment, assign him a place, if directed to report to you?" Although there is no record of a response from Grant, Milroy was assigned to General Thomas in May 1864.[37]

By this stage of the war, the president had great confidence in Grant and supported him even when the facts were not available to Lincoln. One example was his handling of a complaint from Governor Thomas E. Bramlette of Kentucky. On January 5, 1864, he complained that Major General John G. Foster, who had succeeded Burnside at Knoxville, had ordered all Union troops in Kentucky to proceed to Knoxville, thereby exposing Kentucky to ruin. Lincoln disclaimed knowledge of the order, but presumed that it came from Grant and that "it has an object which if you understood, you would be loth [sic] to frustrate." The president went on to cloak Grant with the presumption of correctness:

> True, these troops are, in strict law, only to be removed by my order; but Gen. Grant's judgment would be the highest incentive to me to make such an order. Nor can I understand how doing so is bad faith or dishonor; nor yet how it exposes Kentucky to ruin. Military men here do not perceive how it such [sic] exposes Kentucky, and I am sure Grant would not permit it, if it so appeared to him.[38]

Chattanooga cemented the Lincoln-Grant partnership. Recognizing that city's critical importance, the president had called upon Grant to save

Rosecrans's trapped army and had provided him with the necessary resources to achieve one of the most significant victories of the war. Grant, in turn, had justified Lincoln's faith in him, opened the Cracker Line in five days, and then, within a month, thrown all his men into a massive assault that drove Bragg's Rebel army out of Tennessee.

CHAPTER 9

LINCOLN ELEVATES GRANT TO GENERAL-IN-CHIEF

B y the start of 1864, Lincoln had become increasingly frustrated with Meade's failure to bring Lee to battle. When word was received that Longstreet's troops were creeping from Tennessee back into southwestern Virginia without opposition, his frustration grew. Lincoln complained, "If this Army of the Potomac was good for anything—if the officers had anything in them—if the army had any legs, they could move thirty thousand men down to Lynchburg and catch Longstreet. Can anybody doubt if Grant were here in command that he would catch him." However, Lincoln did acknowledge that Grant's successes might have been aided by the lack of administration meddling with his activities.[1] Lincoln realized that he and other Washingtonians had been very deeply involved in Eastern, but not Western, military decisions and operations.

The president nominated Commander David Dixon Porter for promotion to rear admiral in recognition of his Vicksburg Campaign exploits,[2] and similarly promoted Grant to permanent major general in the regular army. Lincoln did not immediately move to promote Grant to lieutenant general. There were at least two reasons for the president's hesitation to do so. First, only George Washington had been a permanent (three-star) lieutenant general in U.S. history, and promotion to that rank would require congressional creation of a lieutenant general's position.[3] Second, Lincoln was concerned that Grant had presidential aspirations.

Lincoln's concerns may have contributed to his appointing Grant to overall command of the Western Theater without creating a single department there for him to command. However, there was a valid alternative explanation for this multi-departmental approach. As Halleck explained to Grant, this arrangement "is to give you the general military control and at the same time to relieve you from the burden of official correspondence and office duty. If the whole were organized into a single department under your immediate command, your time would be mostly taken up with the details of courts-martial, furloughs, discharges, &c., while the present arrangement enables you to give your full attention to military operations."[4]

In any event, Congress, led by Washburne, passed a joint resolution honoring Grant and his command for their accomplishments and requesting the president to have a gold medal struck for him and to have a copy of the congressional resolution engrossed on parchment for transmittal to Grant. Lincoln approved the resolution on December 18 and requested Washburne to oversee preparation of the medal and parchment.[5]

Immediately after his Chattanooga victory, Grant again had proposed a winter offensive against Mobile, still the last significant Confederate port on the Gulf of Mexico. He had proposed a similar effort after capturing Vicksburg. Grant was not satisfied to sit idly by while more Confederate targets beckoned. Thus, on November 29, he proposed the Mobile campaign to Charles Dana, and he repeated the proposal in a December 7 letter to Halleck. In the words of Bruce Catton, "[Grant] had at last reached the point where he could see that final triumph for the Union depended on crowding a beaten foe without respite, permitting no breathing spell in which the weaker antagonist could regain his balance and repair damages—using the superior power of the North, in short, to apply unrelenting pressure of a sort the Confederacy had not the resources to resist."[6] He soon would have an opportunity to implement his national strategy.

In early 1864 Grant repeated his recommendation of an early movement by Banks against Mobile. After its capture, Grant foresaw a movement northeast into Georgia—a campaign that would complement one by Sherman into Georgia from his Chattanooga base. Again because of foreign policy concerns, Lincoln vetoed Grant's military recommendation.

But Lincoln's control of strategy went much further. After his Banks-to-Mobile proposal had been rejected, Grant recommended that he divide his own troops in southeast Tennessee to move separately against Atlanta and Mobile/Montgomery. Once again Halleck explained that Lincoln disapproved. The president did not want to leave open any possibility of Confederate re-conquest of East Tennessee, an area always dear to Lincoln. Thus, Halleck directed that maximum supplies be gathered at Chattanooga and that transportation be strengthened from Nashville to Chattanooga to Knoxville.[7]

Lincoln was not through determining military strategy. Grant was asked for his thoughts on a possible Eastern campaign and responded with a plan for a thrust from Norfolk to Raleigh in order to force Lee out of Virginia to protect his lines of communication and supply. This proposal, however, touched another one of Lincoln's sensitive points; it would involve some risk to Washington by reducing the strength of Union forces between Lee and Washington. The adequacy of troops protecting Washington had been a contentious issue between Lincoln and McClellan (and his successors). Halleck forwarded Grant's proposal to Lincoln but forewarned Grant of its disapproval.

All of this Grant-Halleck correspondence, perhaps the most revealing strategic correspondence of the war, represented an ongoing struggle between a creative Grant, who thought the war was to be won in the West, and Halleck, who favored the same old overland movement to Richmond.

In mid-February 1864 Colonel Eaton, now Superintendent of Freedmen, visited Grant at Chattanooga. The general treated him to the details of the prior autumn's victory there, including creation of the Cracker Line and the breakout at Missionary Ridge. Grant gave credit for the successes to his men and officers, especially Generals George Thomas and "Baldy" Smith. Their discussions then turned to the continuing issue of black fugitives. Although there were fewer fugitives in southeastern Tennessee, an area with few plantations, a significant number of them became Union soldiers.[8]

According to Eaton, Grant had been an effective advocate for black fugitives in western Tennessee at Memphis, in southeastern Tennessee at Chattanooga, and also in central Tennessee at Nashville. Eaton quoted a report of the Western Freedmen's Aid Commission describing Grant's efforts in middle Tennessee: "We received but little cooperation from any officers there till General Grant assumed command of the department. A store-room was then immediately secured at Nashville; an order given for the transportation of all supplies and another for rations for our teachers."[9]

Throughout the first eight months of 1864, there was considerable political maneuvering by a number of government officials and military generals—both active and retired—to replace Lincoln as president. His own Secretary of the Treasury Salmon P. Chase gave his blessing to the organization of a committee (the Pomeroy Committee) and distribution of a circular promoting his candidacy. When that circular was released, Chase immediately wrote to Lincoln, falsely denied knowledge of the circular, and offered to resign. After initially just acknowledging receipt of Chase's letter, Lincoln finally responded to it on February 29. After stating his early awareness of the Pomeroy Committee's activities, the president ironically concluded, "I fully concur with you that neither of us can be justly held responsible for what our respective friends may do without our instigation or countenance; and I assure you, as you have assured me, that no assault has been made upon you by my instigation, or with my countenance." He added that he saw no need to remove Chase from the cabinet at that time.[10]

The Pomeroy imbroglio was occurring at the same time as Grant's congressional supporters were moving to elevate him to lieutenant general—the first permanent American three-star general since George

Washington. Lincoln was looking for some assurance that such a promotion was not a precursor to a Grant presidential movement. The president was concerned because both the *New York Herald* and Democratic and Republican politicians were urging a Grant candidacy.

One of the *Herald*'s pro-Grant editorials sparked a late December 23 conversation between John Hay and Democratic Party kingmaker Samuel S. Cox in which Cox, according to Hay, explained, "Grant belongs to the Republicans. We cant [*sic*] take him after his letter to Washburne. But for that we might have taken him. The Republicans wont [*sic*] take him either. They have got his influence and have no further use for him."[11] Cox was referring to Grant's August 30, 1863, letter to Washburne in which he had made strong anti-slavery statements.[12] Thus, Grant's support of the president's anti-slavery position made him a *persona non grata* to the Democrats.

Grant provided Lincoln with the necessary assurance that he had no presidential ambitions at that time. He did this by writing to several associates that "this is the last thing I desire. I would regard such a consummation unfortunate for myself if not for the country.... Nobody could induce me to think of being a presidential candidate, particularly so long as there is a possibility of having Mr. Lincoln reelected." One of Grant's Illinois friends, J. Russell Jones, carried one of the letters to a meeting with Lincoln at which the letter's contents were disclosed to the president. Lincoln, greatly relieved, explained, "My son, you will never know how gratifying that is to me. No man knows, when the presidential grub gets to gnawing on him, just how deep it will get until he has tried it; and I didn't know but what there was one gnawing at Grant." As early as February 16, Halleck was writing to Sherman that he presumed Grant would be made a lieutenant general. Halleck also expressed his happiness at the prospect of being relieved as general-in-chief, an office "not understood by the country."[13]

The next day Halleck wrote to Grant about Grant's campaign recommendations and frankly stated that he presumed the President would look to Grant for the final decision on the Union's 1864 campaign or campaigns in the East. Halleck, however, did advise Grant the president was likely to disapprove Grant's recommendation of a campaign against

Richmond and Raleigh from the east because Washington would become vulnerable and Lee's army itself should be the Union target. Reflecting Lincoln's priorities, Halleck concluded that "Our main efforts in the next campaign should unquestionably be made against the armies of Lee and Johnston, but by what particular lines we shall operate cannot be positively determined [now].... The final decision of this question will probably depend, under the President, upon yourself."[14]

The bill reviving the rank of lieutenant general was introduced by Washburne in the House and James Doolittle of Wisconsin in the Senate. The senator generously calculated that Grant had won seventeen Civil War battles, captured 100,000 prisoners, and seized five hundred artillery pieces.[15]

Grant had commanded one army at Vicksburg and three armies at Chattanooga. Once selected and promoted, he would serve as general-in-chief of all the armies of the United States. He would be in charge of nineteen departments and seventeen commanders.[16] His major job, working with Chief of Staff Halleck, would be coordinating their actions so that they were synchronized and mutually supporting.

GRANT GOES TO WASHINGTON

Assured that Grant would support his re-nomination and reelection, Lincoln approved Grant's promotion to lieutenant general, which became effective March 2, 1864. As Brooks Simpson observed, Grant had earned his promotion to the top and had overcome Lincoln's concerns to do so: "[Lincoln's] confidence [in Grant] had not always been there; it grew during the war and was far more a product of Grant's accomplishments than of Lincoln's foresight. Grant's slow rise to top command reflected Lincoln's justifiable skepticism about Grant's uneven record from April 1862 to April 1863."[17]

Grant was ordered from Nashville to Washington and proceeded there with his thirteen-year-old son Fred. Upon their arrival in the capital on March 8, Grant and his son initially were offered a small, out-of-the-way room by the unsuspecting desk clerk at the Willard Hotel. After

Grant wrote his name in the register, the clerk snapped to life, apologized, and offered them the best room in the house.

That evening Grant went to the Executive Mansion, where the president was hosting a weekly reception. There, Lincoln and Grant met for the first time. When the six-foot-four president introduced the general to the crowd, he had the five-foot-eight Grant stand on a couch so he could be seen by more of the guests. At Lincoln's request, Grant stayed afterward and met with him privately. Lincoln advised Grant that he had arranged for a formal presentation the next day of his commission as a lieutenant general, would make a short speech, and desired Grant to make a short acceptance speech. According to Lincoln's secretaries, the president provided Grant with a copy of his own speech as a model because he was "perhaps not so much accustomed to public speaking" as Lincoln. He also asked the general to include two points in his remarks: something that would prevent jealousy on the part of other Union generals and something that would enhance his relations with the Army of the Potomac.[18]

At 1 p.m. the next day Lincoln hosted the small ceremony attended by the cabinet, two members of Grant's staff, and Lincoln's private secretary.[19] In addition to words of appreciation, the president's remarks looked to his future expectations of Grant: "The nation's appreciation of what you have done, and it's [sic] reliance upon you for what remains to do, in the existing great struggle, are now presented with this commission, constituting you Lieutenant General in the Army of the United States. With this high honor devolves upon you also, a corresponding responsibility. As the country herein trusts you, so, under God, it will sustain you. I scarcely need to add that with what I here speak for the nation goes my own hearty personal concurrence."[20]

For whatever reason, Grant's responsive remarks barely touched on the two points the president had asked him to make. The general simply said: "I accept this commission with gratitude for the high honor confered [sic]. With the aid of the noble armies that have fought on so many fields for our common country, it will be my earnest endeavor not to disappoint your expectations. I feel the full weight of the responsibilities now devolving on me and know that if they are met it will be due to those armies, and above all to the favor of that Providence which leads both Nations and men."[21]

On Thursday, March 10, Lincoln, on behalf of his wife, invited Grant and Meade to dine with them that Saturday evening. After accepting on behalf of Meade and himself, Grant reconsidered and left town before the dinner, which was attended by most of the Union generals in Washington. In declining the White House dinner, Grant told Lincoln, "I appreciate the honor, but time is very important now, and I have had enough of this show business." Grant had more important things to do. The declination caused the anti-Lincoln *New York Herald* to exclaim, "We have found our hero."[22]

On the same day as the social invitation, Lincoln formally designated Grant general-in-chief of the armies of the United States.[23] On March 12, at Halleck's request and apparently at Lincoln's direction, Secretary Stanton issued an order relieving Halleck as general-in-chief, assigning Grant (again) to command of the armies of the U.S., and flexibly providing that army headquarters would be both in Washington and with Grant in the field. Halleck was designated chief of staff under the direction of Stanton and Grant.[24] "Halleck became the link between the President and his generals," observed Marszalek, "providing ideas and suggestions to both, explaining one side to the other, and freeing Grant from having to deal with administrative details that Halleck had mastered and enjoyed handling."[25] After Lincoln designated Grant as general-in-chief, according to McPherson, the president "maintained a significant degree of strategic oversight" but "did not become directly involved at the tactical level."[26]

About that same time, Lincoln wrote a list of candidates for West Point. First on the list was John D. C. Hoskins; his name was followed by a notation, "Has served in this war—Gen. Grant's boy." Back on January 20 Lincoln had endorsed an appointment of young Hoskins, the son of Charles Hoskins, adjutant of the Fourth Infantry who was killed September 21, 1846, at the Battle of Monterrey. The president's March 10 note indicates that Grant had interceded on behalf of the son of his old Mexican War Fourth Infantry comrade. Grant's memoirs describe his loaning his horse to Lieutenant Hoskins, the regimental adjutant, during the Battle of Monterrey—shortly before Hoskins was killed and Grant succeeded him as adjutant.[27]

Grant had declined the Lincolns' dinner invitation and left Washington to confer extensively with Sherman about a coordinated series of campaigns to bring the war to a close. Grant had appointed Sherman to replace him as commander of the Military Division of the Mississippi. Just before their conferences, Lincoln privately wrote to Grant requesting a corps command in Sherman's army for the politically connected Major General Frank Blair. Grant and Sherman went to some lengths to accommodate the president's request, and Blair had his corps command.[28]

Between then and early May, Grant planned a truly national campaign. Evidence of the broad geographical scope of his deliberations is found in a mid-April dispatch from Grant to Halleck asking the president to authorize unification of the Department of Arkansas by including Fort Smith and the Indian Territory (future Oklahoma) within it. On April 16 Lincoln simply endorsed the request with the words, "Let it be done."[29]

MILITARY PERSONNEL ISSUES

As Grant looked to utilize all available resources, he proposed to use soldiers from non-combat areas like Washington. When Stanton objected, Grant took Stanton and the issue to Lincoln. The president sided with Grant and astutely said, "You and I, Mr. Stanton, have been trying to boss this job, and we have not succeeded very well with it. We have sent across the mountains for Mr. Grant, as Mrs. Grant calls him, to relieve us, and I think we had better leave him alone to do as he pleases."[30]

Grant did not automatically carry out the president's requested military appointments. On March 29, 1864, for example, Lincoln wrote to Grant about a possible appointee to his staff: "Capt. Kinney, of whom I spoke to you as desiring to go on your Staff, is now in your camp in company with Mrs. Senator Dixon. Mrs. Grant and I and some others agreed last night that I should, by this despatch [*sic*], kindly call your attention to Capt. Kinney." Grant's immediate reply was negative: "Your dispatch suggesting Capt. Kinney for a staff appointment just recd. I would be glad to accommodate Capt. Kinney but in the selection of staff I do not want any one whom I do not personally know to be qualified for the position assigned them."[31]

Lincoln did not automatically refer all high-level military personnel-related documents to Grant. For example, when the president received a strong telegraphic protest from Tennessee Governor Andrew Johnson against assignment of General Buell to that state, Lincoln referred the protest to Stanton with a note stating, "I leave to the Sec. of War whether this shall be brought to the notice of Gen. Grant."[32]

However, once Grant made military leadership personnel decisions, Lincoln would give him his full support. An example occurred on the eve of the Overland Campaign when General Stephen A. Hurlbut, another Illinoisan, complained about his transfer from the active theater of Tennessee to the backwater of Cairo, Illinois. Hurlbut had requested a court of inquiry after being advised by Sherman, "There has been marked timidity in the management of affairs since Forrest passed north of Memphis. General Grant orders me to relieve you."[33] After Hurlbut asked Stanton for a court of inquiry, Halleck referred the request to Grant, who rejected it.[34] Lincoln sustained Grant's decision by advising Hurlbut, "I snatch a moment to say that my friendship and confidence for you remains unabated, but that Gen's Grant & [George] Thomas [commanding in Nashville] cannot be held to their just responsibilities, if they are not allowed to control in the class of cases to which yours belongs. From one stand point a court of Inquiry is most just, but if your case were my own, I would not allow Gen's Grant and Sherman [to] be diverted by it just now."[35]

As a result of Lincoln's priorities, General Banks was sent on the disastrous, unsuccessful, and perhaps needless Red River Campaign (March 14–May 20, 1864), from which Banks, his army, and accompanying naval vessels were fortunate to escape. Ten thousand of Grant's troops had augmented Banks, and the conquest of Mobile was delayed for about a year. By mid-April it was clear that Banks's campaign had become a fiasco. He started late, operated ineptly, and began retreating after losing the April 8 Battle of Mansfield. He almost managed to lose all of Admiral David D. Porter's accompanying naval vessels.

Having his hopes for a quick success and freeing Banks's troops for a Mobile campaign demolished, Grant advised Halleck of his desire to sack Banks. Sensitive to the president's political concerns, Halleck advised Grant that Lincoln wanted to defer the matter since "General Banks is a personal friend of the President, and has strong supporters in and out of Congress." Lincoln, said Halleck, needed a military justification from Grant for such a politically harmful move. Grant astutely suggested that Banks keep administrative control of the Department of the Gulf while Major General Edward R. S. Canby was given command of the field troops. Satisfied to retain Banks for political activities related to reconstruction in Louisiana, Lincoln approved Grant's proposal, and Canby began planning his Mobile Campaign.[36]

Historian McPherson commented on the positive effect that resolution of this potential stumbling block had on the relationship between Lincoln and Grant: "The affair actually strengthened the bonds of understanding between Lincoln and Grant. The president deferred to Grant on a military matter that fell within his province as general-in-chief. But Grant learned that Lincoln's responsibilities as commander in chief included important political considerations that could never be fully divorced from questions of military command in a democracy—especially in an election year."[37]

Slavery and its ramifications continued to be vexing issues for Lincoln. On April 4, 1864, he summarized his views on slavery and the actions he had taken concerning it. This summary grew out of a visit to the president by former Kentucky Senator Archibald Dixon and Kentucky's *Frankfort Commonwealth* editor Albert G. Hodges. After Lincoln explained his views on slavery to them in their meeting, he responded to their request to reduce them to writing:

> I am naturally anti-slavery. If slavery is not wrong, nothing is wrong. I can not remember when I did not so think, and feel.

And yet I have never understood that the Presidency conferred upon me an unrestricted right to act officially upon this judgment and feeling.... Was it possible to lose the nation and yet preserve the constitution?...I felt that measures, otherwise unconstitutional, might become lawful, by becoming indispensable to the preservation of the constitution, through the preservation of the nation....

After describing his 1861–62 disapprovals of efforts to emancipate or arm slaves and his unsuccessful 1862 efforts to obtain border state approval of compensated emancipation, Lincoln continued:

[The border states] declined the proposition; and I was, in my best judgment, driven to the alternative of either surrendering the Union, and with it, the Constitution, or of laying strong hand upon the colored element. I chose the latter [emancipation in Confederate-controlled areas and enlistment of black soldiers].... [This approach] shows a gain of quite a hundred and thirty thousand soldiers, seamen, and laborers.[38]

A month later Lincoln faced a difficult situation arising out of an April 12 massacre of surrendering black Union troops and their officers by Confederates commanded by Nathan Bedford Forrest at Fort Pillow, located on the Mississippi River in Tennessee.[39] On May 3 Lincoln advised his cabinet of the massacre and sought their advice about what action the government should take. Four of them recommended retaliatory executions (which would have incited reciprocal Confederate actions), and three recommended execution of those involved if they were captured (unlikely to quickly occur).[40] Thus, Lincoln was on his own to devise an appropriate response.

Demonstrating that no satisfactory resolution was possible, Lincoln drafted ineffective instructions to Stanton on May 17. They would have directed him to set aside a number of Confederate prisoners equivalent to those massacred and to treat them as ordinary prisoners of war if there was assurance that all Union prisoners would be treated "according to the laws of war." Similarly, Lincoln's draft told Stanton to set aside a number of Confederate prisoners equal to Union "colored soldiers supposed to have been captured" by the Confederates and be exchanged for such black soldiers.

The draft instructions ominously concluded that the U.S. government would "take such action as may then appear expedient and just" if the Confederates failed to account for or exchange black Union prisoners, who otherwise would be assumed to have been murdered or enslaved. This draft, with spaces for numbers left blank, apparently never was signed or delivered.[41] It reflected the president's frustrations in responding to the massacre and the fate of captured black soldiers, and it laid the groundwork for a total halt to prisoner exchanges.

Even before initiating his Overland Campaign, Grant cooperated with Stanton, several state governors, and ultimately Lincoln in obtaining additional short-term troops for use in an emergency. The governors of five states (Ohio, Indiana, Illinois, Iowa, and Wisconsin) offered Lincoln a total of 100,000 one-hundred-day soldiers "for the approaching campaign."[42] When consulted by Stanton, Grant succinctly advised:

> As a rule I would oppose receiving men for a short term, but if one hundred thousand (100,000) men can be raised in the time proposed by the Governors of Ohio Indiana Illinois & Iowa, they might come at such a crisis as to be of vast importance
>
> I would not recommend accepting them in lieu of Quotas now due on any previous calls for three years troops. Otherwise I would.[43]

Stanton forwarded the governors' offer and Grant's endorsement to Lincoln. The president accepted the proposition and ordered Stanton to execute it.[44]

Grant's promotion to general-in-chief and relocation to the East formalized his partnership with Lincoln and provided them with an opportunity to see, evaluate, and work with each other on a face-to-face basis. Their physical meeting served to seal the meeting of minds that had begun much earlier. Their newfound ability to address both political and military issues with dispatch set the stage for the final phase of the war.

CHAPTER 10

GRANT GOES ON THE OFFENSIVE WITH LINCOLN'S FULL SUPPORT

———— ⋅◆⋅ ————

The profound impact of Grant's assumption of command of all Union armies has been observed by many, but Gordon Rhea expressed it with elegant succinctness: "The turning point of the entire Civil War would be when Grant took command. He had a completely different way of doing things."[1] In Grant, the Union now had a general with a broad national view of the war, one who could and would coordinate the activities of all theaters, and one who realized that destruction of Lee's army was the primary mission in the Virginia Theater. The Confederacy had no one with a corresponding vision and scope of authority.

Although Grant kept Meade as commander of the Army of the Potomac, he was its *de facto* commander. Never again would Eastern soldiers be the victims of the incompetence or timidity so often demonstrated by their earlier commanders, Irvin McDowell, McClellan (twice), Pope, Burnside, Hooker, and Meade, who cumulatively had suffered

144,000 casualties without moving the war to conclusion. Union soldiers would now be part of a coordinated nationwide assault on Confederate armies, rather than against mere places. As Rhea concluded, "Their objective under Grant was the destruction of Confederate armies, and the days of short battles followed by months of inactivity were over. Henceforth, Union armies were to engage the armed forces of the rebellion and batter them into submission, giving no respite."[2] Michael C. C. Adams has astutely observed that one of the turning points of the war probably was "the decision of Grant to march with the Army of the Potomac, for this ensured that Lee would be hit hard at last."[3]

On the Confederate side, Grant's old friend Longstreet knew what was coming. As renowned historian Bruce Catton told it,

> Over in the Army of Northern Virginia, James Longstreet was quietly warning people not to underestimate this new Yankee commander: "That man will fight us every day and every hour till the end of the war." Nobody in the North heard the remark, but the quality which had called it forth had not gone unnoticed. Here was the man who looked as if he would ram his way through a brick wall, and since other tactics had not worked perhaps that was the thing to try. At Fort Donelson and at Vicksburg he had swallowed two Confederate armies whole, and at Chattanooga he had driven a third army in head-long retreat from what had been thought to be an impregnable stronghold, and all anyone could think of was the hard blow that ended matters. Men seemed ready to call Grant the hammerer before he even began to hammer.[4]

Lincoln wanted an aggressive, proven winner to challenge and defeat Lee. Grant was his man. Troops in the Army of the Potomac agreed. Among them was soldier-artist Charles Ellington Reed, who welcomed Grant's appointment even though he foresaw tough fighting ahead: "placeing [sic] Grant in command is the grandest coup yet. It has inspired all with that confidence that insures success. I have not the slightest doubt but that we shall be gloriously successful this comeing [*sic*] campaign. There will be hard fighting without doubt. Many assert that our next battle will eclipse all others in magnitude and slaughter, but that remains to be seen."[5] Needing Grant to make substantial early progress to ensure his own reelection, Lincoln demonstrated his complete confidence in the general by telling Stanton to "leave him alone to do as he pleases."[6]

On the eve of the Overland Campaign, Lincoln and Grant exchanged letters that reflected their working relationship and epitomized their mutual trust and respect. The president first wrote to Grant:

> Not expecting to see you again before the Spring campaign opens, I wish to express, in this way, my entire satisfaction with what you have done up to this time, so far as I understand it. The particulars of your plans I neither know, or seek to know. You are vigilant and self-reliant; and, pleased with this, I wish not to obtrude any constraints or restraints upon you. While I am very anxious that any great disaster, or the capture of our men in great numbers, shall be avoided, I know these points are less likely to escape your attention than they would be mine. If there is anything wanting which is within my power to give, do not fail to let me know it.[7]

What emerges from this letter is Lincoln's supreme confidence in Grant on military issues. Although he certainly was aware of Grant's general campaign plans, the president denied any interest in knowing their details and promised Grant whatever possible additional support he requested. No other general received, or had earned, such presidential trust.

The next day Grant responded in kind. He wrote:

> Your very kind letter of yesterday is just received. The confidence you express for the future, and satisfaction with the past, in my Military administration is acknowledged with pride. It will be my earnest endeavor that you, and the country, shall not be disappointed.

From my first entrance into the volunteer service of the country, to the present day, I have never had cause of complaint,
have never expressed or implied a complaint, against the
Administration, or the Sec. of War, for throwing any
embarassment [*sic*] in the way of my vigerously prossecuting
[*sic*] what appeared to me my duty. Indeed since the promotion that placed me in command of all the Armies, and in view
of the great responsibility, and importance of success, I have
been astonished at the readiness with which every thi[n]g
asked for has been yielded without even an explaination [*sic*]
being asked. Should my success be less than I desire, and
expect, the least I can say is, the fault is not with you.[8]

Grant's grateful response is notable for characteristics that were lacking
in Eastern commanders who preceded him (such as McClellan, Burnside
and Hooker): humility, gratitude, and acceptance of responsibility. His
closing words—"the fault is not with you"—must have been particularly
satisfying to Lincoln.

In fact, before Grant opened his campaign, Lincoln had formed an
extremely positive view of him. In a discussion with his secretary Stoddard, the president raved about his new general-in-chief:

Grant is the first general I've had! He's a general!... You
know how it's been with all the rest. As soon as I put a man in
command of the army, he'd come to me with a plan of campaign
and about as much as say, "Now, I don't believe I can do it, but
if you say so I'll try it on"; and so put the responsibility of success
or failure on me. They all wanted me to be the general. Now it
isn't so with Grant. He hasn't told me what his plans are. I don't
know, and I don't want to know. I'm glad to find a man who
can go ahead without me.... You see, when any of the rest set
out on a campaign, they'd look over matters and pick out some
one thing they were short of and they knew I couldn't give them,
and tell me they couldn't hope to win unless they had it, and it
was most generally cavalry. Now, when General Grant took

hold, I was waiting to see what his pet impossibility would be, and I reckoned it would be cavalry, as a matter of course, for we hadn't horses enough to mount even what men we had. There were 15,000 or thereabouts, up near Harpers Ferry, and no horses to put them on. Well, the other day, just as I expected, Grant sent to me about those very men; but what he wanted to know was whether he should disband 'em or turn 'em into infantry. He doesn't ask me to do impossibilities for him, and he's the first general I've had that didn't.[9]

GRANT TAKES THE REINS

On March 10, the day after receiving his three-star commission, Grant visited Meade at the Army of the Potomac's headquarters in Brandy Station, Virginia. Meade graciously offered to step aside as army commander so that Grant could name someone of his own choosing. Meade's gracious gesture so surprised Grant that if he had any plans of making such a change of command (he may at one time have planned to appoint William "Baldy" Smith),[10] Meade's offer ended them. Grant assured him that he would retain the command. Although Grant avoided the politics of Washington by keeping his command in the field with Meade's army, Grant generally issued orders to the Army of the Potomac through Meade.[11]

Keeping Meade, instead of commanding the army himself, may have been a mistake because of the ambiguity their relationship created about who really was in charge. Bruce Catton observed, "At the very least it must be said that the dual command arrangement was a handicap,"[12] and Robert N. Thompson concluded that, as a result of Grant's intention to issue instructions through Meade, "the Army of the Potomac appeared to have two heads."[13]

Having decided to retain Meade in place and to accompany him in the field, Grant quickly made other important decisions. Sherman would command a three-army march on Atlanta, James B. McPherson would replace him as commander of the Army of the Tennessee, and John "Black Jack" Logan would replace McPherson as a corps commander.[14]

In an early interview with Lincoln, Grant expressed his dissatisfaction with the Eastern Union cavalry and secured the president's consent to bring Phil Sheridan east to command the Army of the Potomac's cavalry corps.[15] Grant's senior team was now in place. By April 6, Grant also had assembled an experienced and professional personal staff. Unlike Lee, Grant had a large, competent staff and used it.[16]

Grant also took care of another important piece of business in Washington. His former superior, Halleck, requested to be relieved as general-in-chief in light of Grant's promotion. Grant and Lincoln astutely arranged for Halleck to be chief of staff. Through this deft separation of administration from strategic command, "a crucial innovation in modern warfare," Grant had Halleck handle the political and hand-holding chores in Washington while Grant was free to command in the field.[17] Halleck proved adept at translating between civilians Lincoln and Stanton on one hand and military leaders like Grant and Sherman on the other.

This new arrangement appears to have pleased the president. On March 24, John Hay observed:

> I suppose Halleck is badly bilious about Grant. Grant the Prest. says is Commander in Chief & Halleck is now nothing but a staff officer. In fact says the President "when McClellan seemed incompetent to the work of handling an army & we sent for Halleck to take command he stipulated that it should be with the full power and responsibility of Commander in Chief. He ran it on that basis till Pope's defeat [at Second Manassas]; but ever since that event, He [sic] has shrunk from responsibility whenever possible."[18]

About a month later, Hay similarly wrote, "We appointed [Halleck] & all went well enough until after Pope's defeat when he broke down—nerve and pluck all gone—and has ever since evaded all possible responsibility—little more since that than a first-rate clerk."[19] Nevertheless, Grant was pleased that Halleck was willing and able to undertake the

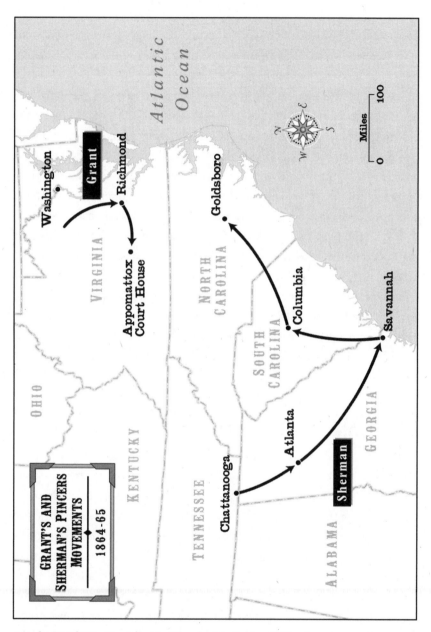

Map by David Deis, Dreamline Cartography, Northridge, California

necessary administrative chores that otherwise might have been his, and, after a period of testing, Grant was satisfied that Halleck would carry out his orders and protect him in Washington.[20]

Although Meade was left in command of the Army of the Potomac, it quickly became known as "Grant's army." One reason for that designation may be that changes immediately began to take place. Inspectors general suddenly took an interest in what units were and were not doing, unit commanders had to reduce the discrepancy between "numbers present for duty" and "numbers present for duty, equipped," discipline became tighter, infantrymen were drilled on how to fire a rifle (since so many abandoned weapons on battlefields had contained multiple Minie balls—indicating they had never been fired), artillerymen were drilled on assembling and disassembling their guns, cavalrymen received new Spencer seven-shot repeater rifles, and the entire army benefited from trainloads of supplies and equipment that arrived at Brandy Station.[21] These improvements probably resulted from Grant's Mexican War quartermaster experience and his excellent use of staff.[22]

GRANT PLANS A COORDINATED CAMPAIGN

In March and April 1864, Grant devised a grand strategy that would put all Union troops on the offensive against their Confederate counterparts and thereby keep the latter from using their interior lines to transfer troops among theaters. This plan envisioned Sherman's three armies (the Cumberland, the Tennessee, and the Ohio) pushing Joseph Johnston's Army of Tennessee southeastward back toward Atlanta, Nathaniel Banks joining Sherman after capturing Mobile, Major General Franz Sigel clearing Confederates out of the Shenandoah Valley, Major General Benjamin F. Butler directly attacking Petersburg-Richmond via the James River, and the Army of the Potomac going after Lee's Army of Northern Virginia until it was defeated or destroyed.[23] Every Union army had a role. As Lincoln told Grant and Grant told Sherman (without attribution), "Those not skinning can hold a leg."[24] Consistent with Lincoln's views,

Grant told Meade: "Lee's army will be your objective point. Wherever Lee's army goes, you will go also."[25]

This strategy would not only advance the offensive goals of the Union, but it also would preclude the Confederates from having the flexibility to converge their forces in a meaningful counterattack. Remembering earlier Confederate convergences at Shiloh and Chickamauga, Grant and Sherman were determined to prevent a repetition of them.[26] The primary reason Grant had declined to attend the White House banquet in his honor was so he could quickly head west to meet with Sherman. Coordination with Sherman was so important to Grant that he spent March 11 to 23 on a trip to visit him in Nashville, including extended consultations on Grant's return train ride from Nashville to Cincinnati. Grant made it clear that Sherman's primary objective was Johnston's Army of Tennessee and that his secondary objective was Atlanta. Grant's hope was that a successful campaign there would divide the remaining Confederacy in half.[27]

On his return trip, Grant was accompanied to Cincinnati by his friends and confidants, Sherman and Grenville Dodge. There they laid out maps and planned their end-the-war campaigns. Sherman later said that Grant's plan was simple: Grant would go for Lee, and Sherman would go for Joe Johnston.[28] Grant's primary concern then and later was to ensure that Sherman's thrust in Georgia and Meade's in Virginia would keep the Confederates so occupied that they could not reinforce each other. To protect against the possibility of Confederate inter-theater transfers, he wrote to Sherman:

> What I now want more particularly to say is, that if the two main attacks, yours and the one from here, should promise great success, the enemy may, in a fit of desperation, abandon one part of their line of defense, and throw their whole strength upon the other, believing a single defeat without any victory to sustain them better than a defeat all along their line, and hoping too, at the same time, that the army meeting with no resistance, will rest perfectly satisfied with their laurels,

having penetrated to a given point south, thereby enabling them to throw their force first upon one and then on the other.

   With the majority of military commanders they might do this. But you have had too much experience in traveling light, and subsisting upon the country, to be caught by any such ruse. I hope my experience has not been thrown away. My directions, then, would be, if the enemy in your front shows signs of joining Lee, follow him up to the full extent of your ability. I will prevent the concentration of Lee upon your front, if it is in the power of this army to do it.[29]

Sherman promised Grant that he would "ever bear in mind that Johnston is at all times to be kept so busy that he cannot, in any event, send no [sic] part of his command against you or Banks."[30]

   As Grant planned his campaign against Lee, at least he was moderately free of presidential interference. In Grant's first interview with Lincoln, the president told him he was not a military man and would not interfere but that he was opposed to procrastination.[31] That was not a problem he would have with Grant. Lincoln was confident that he finally had a forceful and effective general in the East, where Union commanders had little to show for all their losses—except the casualties Lee's frequently attacking army had suffered.[32] Grant, however, was to be handicapped in 1864 by incompetent political generals (Sigel, Banks, and Butler) commanding many of his ancillary campaigns and by the waste of resources on the Red River Campaign, which Lincoln had mandated.[33]

   Union intelligence confirmed the springtime arrival of Longstreet's First Corps back in the Virginia Theater and pinpointed its location at Gordonsville, about a day's march from Lee's other two corps near the Rapidan River.[34] As late as March 25, Lee remained doubtful that Grant, the Westerner, would direct the primary Union assault against his army in Virginia rather than one against Johnston's army in Georgia. Lee reminded Davis of the ruses Grant had used at Vicksburg, told him he doubted the first Union effort would be against Richmond, and concluded that Grant's first efforts would be against Johnston in Georgia or Longstreet in Tennessee. Lee seems not to have contemplated Grant directing simultaneous assaults by two Union armies of 100,000 or more apiece.[35]

Grant's primary decision concerning his advance in Virginia was whether to move to the east or west of Lee. An advance to the west was more likely to force Lee to fight in the open west of the dense Wilderness and thereby enhance the value of Grant's supremacy in overall numbers and especially in artillery. That course of action, however, would compel Grant to rely on tenuous overland lines of supply via questionable roads and a single rail line. Grant decided to move east of Lee so that he could utilize Union waterborne transportation to supply his troops via rivers that fed into the Potomac River and Chesapeake Bay. That route also would facilitate coordination with the movements on the James River by Butler, in whom Grant had little or no confidence. In addition, the fords across the Rapidan were more accessible by the eastern route, Longstreet's Corps was farther away from that route, and the previous November Lee had taken thirty hours to defend his right flank in the same area.[36]

William Feis captured the gist of Grant's strategy as he began the Overland Campaign:

> In any event, the endgame for Grant was not the capture of strategic points but the destruction of Lee's army, and he could achieve this in one of two ways. He could fight him on open ground or in the Wilderness, or perhaps force him to retreat. Even if Lee withdrew, Grant understood that it would only delay the inevitable. To prevail in this war, the military might of the Confederacy had to be destroyed. At some point, therefore, Grant would have to stand toe to toe with Lee and beat him, regardless of the circumstances. Nothing short of this would guarantee the death of the rebellion.[37]

In the same letter in which Grant told Meade that his objective was Lee's army, Grant also advised that Burnside's independent 9th Corps would be brought east to add another 25,000 men to the Union forces in Virginia.[38]

With the addition of Burnside's Corps, the Army of the Potomac had 120,000 soldiers against Lee's 66,000.[39] Although Grant would move toward Richmond, he would do so because Lee had to defend the Confederate capital and major rail hub and manufacturing center. In the words of Jean Edward Smith, "Richmond was to be attacked because it was defended by Lee, not Lee because he defended Richmond."[40] Grant also realized that an army's communications and supply were vital to its survival and went after Lee's communications and supply routes whenever possible.[41]

Taking the initiative and clinging to Lee's army, however, would be costly. According to Rhea, "The very nature of Grant's assignment guaranteed hard fighting and severe casualties. Mistakes there were. The facts, however, do not support the caricature of Grant as a general who eschewed maneuver in favor of headlong assaults and needlessly sacrificed his men. Quite the opposite is true."[42] Grant was prepared to pay the price to end the war, produce early results, and get Lincoln reelected. This time, unlike earlier Eastern efforts, the price would buy results.

In just two months Grant took control of all Union armies and worked out his grand strategy to end the war. Grant realized that Lee had seriously weakened his and other Confederate armies through the massive casualties of 1862 and 1863. Therefore, Union armies would continuously pressure the Confederates everywhere and continue to do so until the war was won.[43] Grant decided to use all of the Union's military forces to keep the Confederates on the defensive everywhere and thereby preclude their sending reinforcements to each other.[44] This strategy generally deprived the Rebels of the advantage they possessed by virtue of their inner, shorter lines of communication and reflected Grant's determination to take advantage of the Union's manpower superiority. Grant's strategy resulted in Union victory in about a year.

GRANT STARTS THE OVERLAND CAMPAIGN

On May 4 Grant launched his Overland Campaign toward Richmond as Meade's Army of the Potomac crossed the Rapidan River west of Fredericksburg to draw Lee's Army of Northern Virginia into battle. The

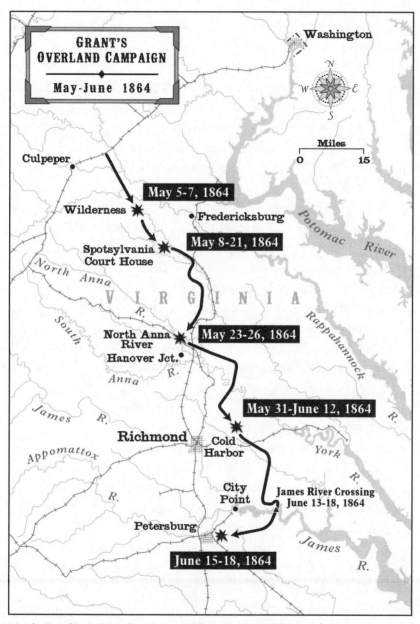

GRANT'S
OVERLAND CAMPAIGN
May-June 1864

Washington

N
W · E
S

Miles
0   15

Culpeper

May 5-7, 1864

Wilderness

Fredericksburg

Potomac River

May 8-21, 1864

Spotsylvania
Court House

North Anna
R.

V I R G I N I A

South
Anna
R.

North Anna
River
Hanover Jct.

May 23-26, 1864

Rappahannock
R.

James R.

May 31-June 12, 1864

Richmond

Cold
Harbor

York
R.

Appomattox
R.

City
Point

James River Crossing
June 13-18, 1864

Petersburg

June 15-18, 1864

James
R.

Map by David Deis, Dreamline Cartography, Northridge, California

result was the bloody two-day Battle of the Wilderness on May 5 and 6.[45] Grant and Lee each attacked the other's army for both days. They made little offensive progress in the thick woods, deaths and woundings occurred at a horrendous pace, and some of the wounded were burned to death as fires broke out between the moving lines. Leading a Rebel counter-attack across the Confederate front on the second day, Longstreet was seriously wounded when accidentally shot by Confederate soldiers. Union troops suffered almost 18,000 casualties while imposing over 11,000 on the Confederates.

After such bloody fighting and heavy losses, Grant's Eastern predecessors would have retreated across the Rapidan and Rappahannock perhaps to fight again—at a much later date. But Grant, in a major turning point for the Eastern Union army, had other plans. He ordered his troops to march toward the southeast away from the stench and smoke of the burning Wilderness. As the troops approached an intersection, they realized that they were either turning back or advancing toward Richmond depending upon which road they were ordered to take. When it became clear they were advancing around Lee's right flank, they threw their hats into the air and cheered. Grant ordered them to maintain silence but must have been heartened by their enthusiasm for moving ahead and finally trying to bring the war to a close.

At that same time, the Marine Band was serenading the president in Washington. When the crowd cried for a speech, Lincoln responded, "In lieu of a speech, I propose that we give three cheers for Major [sic] General Grant and all the armies under his command."[46] That day Lincoln had told Gideon Welles that he had not slept the prior night. In fact, Francis Carpenter, the famous artist who painted Lincoln presenting the preliminary Emancipation Proclamation to his cabinet, wrote that Lincoln "scarcely slept at all" during the first week of Grant's campaign.[47] Grant, aware of the president's concerns, was sending word that evening from the Wilderness with a young *New York Tribune* reporter that whatever happened "there is to be no turning back"; Lincoln reportedly hugged and kissed the astounded reporter when he delivered that message. Four days later, on May 11, from Spotsylvania Court House Grant wired Halleck, "I propose to fight it out on this line if it takes all summer."[48]

As the Overland Campaign proceeded, Lincoln and Grant were each focusing on the other. Grant was uppermost in Lincoln's mind. Evidence of Lincoln's appreciation of and trust in Grant was provided in private and public endorsements on May 9. That day he explained to John Hay and Francis Carpenter that Grant was quite unlike his predecessors:

> How near we have been to this thing before and failed. I believe if any other General had been at the head of that army it would now have been on this side of the Rapidan.... The great thing about Grant...is his perfect coolness and persistency of purpose.... He has the grit of a bull-dog! Once let him get his "teeth" in, and nothing can shake him off.... It is the dogged pertinacity of Grant that wins.[49]

That night Lincoln responded to a serenade by the Twenty-seventh Michigan Volunteers band and an accompanying crowd. On the White House lawn they were celebrating news of Grant's apparent victory at the Wilderness[50] and his movement to Spotsylvania Court House. After expressing his gratitude to brave Union soldiers, their "noble commanders," and "our Maker," Lincoln focused on Grant:

> I think, without knowing the particulars of the plans of Gen. Grant, that what has been accomplished is of more importance than at first appears. I believe I know, (and am especially grateful to know) that Gen. Grant has not been jostled in his purposes; that he has made all his points, and today he is on his line as he purposed [sic] before he moved his armies.... There is enough yet before us requiring all loyal men and patriots to perform their share of the labor and follow the example of the modest General at the head of our armies, and sink all personal considerations for the sake of the country.[51]

Clearly, the president had come to regard Grant as successful, steadfast, and humble.

Earlier that day, after receiving reports on the Battle of the Wilderness, Lincoln had issued a press release, which began, "Enough is known of Army operations within the last five days to claim our especial gratitude to God" and then recommended prayers to help accomplish "what remains undone."[52] That same day he wrote to a Pennsylvania woman who had inquired about his health and welfare in "this trying period." He told her, "I have been very anxious for some days in regard to our armies in the field, but am considerably cheered, just now, by favorable news from them."[53]

Lincoln continued to be pleased with the news from Grant's front. On May 13, in a wire to Major General Lew Wallace in Baltimore, he closed by saying, "The good news this morning I hope will have a good effect all around." He was referring to full-page newspaper coverage of the Wilderness battle.[54] By May 14 Northern newspapers were raving about the "glorious" Union success at the Mule Shoe at Spotsylvania Court House. Lincoln was concerned that overstatements of success would prove harmful over time. He complained to his unofficial spokesman Noah Brooks, "The people are too sanguine. They expect too much at once.... I wish when you write and speak to people you would do all you can to correct the impression that the war in Virginia will end right off victoriously."[55]

Soon news from other Union fronts turned sour. Franz Sigel reinforced his record of incompetence by being rebuffed in the Shenandoah Valley by an inferior Rebel force at the May 15 Battle of New Market. The next day Benjamin Butler's Army of the James was repelled at the Battle of Drewry's Bluff near Petersburg, and he backed his army into a non-threatening defensive position between the James and Appomattox rivers. In Grant's words, Butler's army had "hermetically sealed itself up at Bermuda Hundred" and "was as completely shut off from further operations directly against Richmond as if it had been in a bottle strongly corked."[56] Lincoln told Hay that Butler was "like Jim Jett's brother[.] Jim used to say his brother was the biggest scoundrel that ever lived but in the infinite mercy of Providence he was also the biggest fool."[57] In any event, thousands of Confederate troops facing political generals Sigel and Butler became available to reinforce Lee against Meade and Grant; in addition, Grant was deprived "of an opportunity to crush Lee in a campaign of maneuver." Grant accepted these political limitations and hindrances without complaint.[58]

But the commanding general did take corrective action when he could. Sigel's failure led Grant to fire him. The general-in-chief minced no words as he directed Halleck: "All of General Sigel's operations from the beginning of the war have been so unsuccessful that I think it advisable to relieve him from all duty, at least until present troubles are over. I do not feel certain at any time that he will not after abandoning stores, artillery, and trains, make a successful retreat to some place." Sigel was relieved on July 7. He later asked for a court of inquiry, which fortunately for him was never held.[59]

It soon became obvious that heavy losses in Virginia and the expiration of many three-year enlistments would create the need for additional military manpower. On May 17, therefore, the president signed the draft of an order calling for the involuntary induction of 300,000 men to occur as soon as practicable after July 1. Perhaps because a hoax proclamation calling for a 400,000-man draft was published in two New York papers on May 18, Lincoln's draft was not issued.[60] Congress and Lincoln would return to this issue in July.

Meanwhile, the president continued to safeguard Grant's prerogatives. On May 16 Butler, the ineffective commander of Union troops unsuccessfully "attacking" near Petersburg and Richmond, wrote to Lincoln that he had heard that his commission as a major general of U.S. Volunteers was expiring and inquired whether he might be given a vacant regular army commission. Lincoln coolly responded, "As to the Major Generalships in the Regular Army I think I shall not dispose of another, at least until the combined operations now in progress under direction of Gen. Grant...shall be terminated."[61]

Secretary Stanton was even more protective of Grant against press incursions than was the president. On May 23, E. A. Paul of the *New York Times* bureau in Washington sent Lincoln a pass to the Army of the Potomac that Stanton had declined to approve. Lincoln's endorsement to Stanton said, "The *Times* I believe is always true to the Union, and therefore should be treated at least as well as any." Stanton, however, returned the letter to Lincoln, stated that all newspapers were treated alike, and refused to give special treatment to the *Times* reporter because, "No pass is granted by the Department to any paper except upon the permission of General Grant or General Meade. Repeated applications by Mr. Forney and by other editors have been refused on the same ground as the Times until the correspondent is approved by the Commanding General."[62] Press access to the Army of the Potomac was often denied because of Meade's running feud with the press; after the press had criticized his post-Gettysburg failure to effectively pursue Lee's army, Meade tried to hinder reporters' access to his army, and they responded by declining to give him credit for any of his army's positive accomplishments.

As Grant and the Army proceeded south, he painted a favorable picture for the president. On the night of May 23 from the North Anna River, he concluded, "Every thing looks exceedingly favorable for us." Lincoln quoted those words in a May 24 letter to Ohio Governor John Brough, who had sought Stanton's assurance that the campaign was going well.[63] About ten days later, as the campaign was reaching its one-month mark, Lincoln remained very supportive of Grant but seemed to recognize the difficulties facing the general. The president's attitude was reflected in his June 3 declination of an invitation to a New York City demonstration in support of General Grant and the Union cause. He wrote:

> I approve…whatever may tend to strengthen and sustain Gen. Grant and the noble armies now under his direction. My previous high estimate of Gen. Grant has been maintained and heightened by what has occurred in the remarkable campaign he is now conducting; while the magnitude and difficulty of the task before him does not prove less than I expected. He and his brave soldiers are now in the midst of their great trial, and I trust that at your meeting you will so shape your good words that they may turn to men and guns moving to his and their support.[64]

As usual, Lincoln created an apt phrase—"their great trial"—to describe what was happening to the Army of the Potomac under Grant's tutelage. Although the New York event had been planned to promote Grant at Lincoln's expense just before the Union Party presidential convention, Lincoln's pro-Grant letter undercut that effort and ironically turned the rally into "a mass movement in support of Lincoln."[65] Meanwhile, despite heavy casualties, Grant's soldiers were pushing closer and closer to Richmond while imposing irreplaceable casualties on Lee's troops.

In the weeks leading up to the June 7–8 convention, opponents of Lincoln advocated the nomination of Grant. While the president appeared nonchalant about that prospect, Grant was having nothing to do with it. Lincoln (probably believing his own re-nomination now was secure) said, "If Grant could be more useful than I in putting down the rebellion, I would be quite content. He is fully committed to the policy of emancipation and employing Negro soldiers and with this policy faithfully carried out, it will not make much difference who is president." He often remarked, "If [Grant] takes Richmond, let him have [the nomination]." For his part, Grant told reporters, "Lincoln is just the man of all others whom the country needs, and his defeat would be a great national calamity."[66] These were the words of men who trusted and respected each other.

Meanwhile, Horace Greeley had unsuccessfully argued for a two-month delay of the convention to stall and possibly kill Lincoln's nomination. When that gambit failed, an assortment of Lincoln opponents—particularly members of the anti-Lincoln Grand Council of the Union League—gathered on June 5, two days before the convention, in an effort to derail Lincoln's nomination. Their plan was to nominate Grant and start a groundswell of approval for drafting him. Chester Hearn described how a surprise speech by Kansas Senator Jim Lane squelched their plans:

> The audience gave a shudder because Lane, always an unpredictable and fiery orator, had lately been seen at the White House. He warmed up quickly, soon had his audience on the

edge of their seats, and said any nomination other than Lincoln's would be tantamount to nominating McClellan, and to nominate anyone other than Lincoln would destroy the Republican Party and the Union, reinstate the Confederacy, repudiate emancipation, and dishonor the men who had given their lives for freedom. Lane kicked the traces from under the Union League and killed the movement to draft Grant.[67]

On June 7 the Union Party (the Republican Party plus pro-war allies) began its presidential nominating convention at Baltimore's Front Street Theatre. John G. Nicolay, Lincoln's personal secretary, was the president's eyes and ears at the convention. After Nicolay advised John Hay, Lincoln's other secretary, about vice presidential, platform, and other maneuverings in Baltimore, Lincoln wrote an endorsement on a letter disclaiming any desire to interfere with the convention's deliberations on either the vice presidential selection or the platform writing. Hay conveyed Lincoln's views to Nicolay.[68]

The convention proceeded to unanimously nominate Lincoln on the first ballot—but only after 22 Missouri radicals were convinced to change their votes from Grant to Lincoln. The delegates next proceeded to nominate Democrat Andrew Johnson of Tennessee as Lincoln's running-mate in an effort to appeal to Northern pro-war Democrats. According to Pennsylvania political operative Alexander McClure, Lincoln secretly promoted Johnson's nomination. Pennsylvania's Simon Cameron, who had been replaced by Stanton as Lincoln's secretary of war in early 1862, swung that state's 52 votes and ultimately the convention to Johnson after initially casting those votes for Hannibal Hamlin, the incumbent vice president.[69]

On June 9 a committee representing the National Union Convention came to Washington to formally advise Lincoln of their re-nomination of him as president. In his presentation to the president, convention president William Dennison said, "I need not say to you, sir, that the Convention, in thus unanimously nominating you for reelection, but gave utterance to the almost universal voice of the loyal people of the country. To doubt of your triumphant election, would be little short of abandoning the hope of a final suppression of the Rebellion and the restoration of the Government over the insurgent states." In his informal acceptance remarks, Lincoln focused on the Union Party's platform provision calling for a constitutional amendment to end slavery. He called it "a fitting, and necessary conclusion to the final success of the Union cause."[70]

That same day Lincoln was presented with resolutions of support from the previously unsupportive National Union League. He thanked their delegation and the convention for determining that "I am not entirely unworthy to be intrusted [sic] with the place I have occupied for the last three years." His concluding words were: "I have not permitted myself, gentlemen, to conclude that I am the best man in the country; but I am reminded, in this connection, of a story of an old Dutch farmer, who remarked to a companion once that 'it was not best to swap horses when crossing streams.'" That evening, when serenaded by the Ohio delegation and a brass band, Lincoln showed that his thoughts were elsewhere when, in his brief remarks, he called for "success under General Grant" and concluded by asking for "three rousing cheers for General Grant and the officers and soldiers under his command."[71]

Manpower concerns continued to occupy the president. On June 6 he wrote a negative endorsement on a letter written by an attorney contending that certain New York soldiers who had enlisted in June 1862 were only obligated to serve until May 9, 1864, three years from the date of enlistment of men whose ranks they filled. The attorney assured Lincoln that only one hundred eighty-six men would be affected. In his endorsement, however, the president stated, "The Secretary of War says this attempt, if successful, would reach forty thousand of the army."[72] A mere two days later, Lincoln forwarded to Congress a letter from Stanton calling for repeal of the law allowing a man to pay $300 in lieu of military service. With Stanton's letter was a report showing that one-half of drafted men were paying the $300 and not serving in the military. Lincoln concurred in Stanton's recommendation.[73]

Meanwhile, the president faced the problem of overly aggressive Union recruiting of black soldiers. On June 13, he wrote to Major General Lorenzo Thomas at Louisville, Kentucky, about a complaint that blacks were being involuntarily impressed by Union soldiers. Lincoln asked Thomas to investigate and to "see that the making soldiers of

negroes is done according to the rules you are acting upon, so that unnecessary provocation and irratation [*sic*] be avoided." Thomas responded
that the complaint seemed well-founded and assured the president that
he would "take immediate measures to prevent a recurrence of any acts
of violence on the person of officers engaged in recruiting colored troops
in Ky [Kentucky]."[74]

Grant's Overland Campaign was making slow but bloody progress.
At the North Anna River between May 23 and 26, Lee lured Grant's
army into a trap with an inverted "V" formation; the Federals escaped
when they realized their vulnerable position and a bedridden Lee failed
to attack. Grant's awkward command relationship with Meade played
a role in the delayed and disastrous Union attack at Cold Harbor on June
3. Grant and Lee's armies faced off there from May 31 to June 12.
Grant's attacking army incurred 12,737 casualties while Lee's army suffered only 4,595. About ten days after that disaster, Grant secretly dis-
engaged his entire army and began moving it south of the James River.[75]

On June 14, he advised Lincoln of the movement and his plans: "Our
forces will commence crossing the James to-day. The enemy show no
signs yet of having brought troops to the south side of Richmond. I will
have Petersburg secured, if possible, before they get there in much force.
Our movement from Cold Harbor to the James River has been made
with great celerity and so far without loss or accident." The president
responded, "Have just read your despatch [*sic*] of 1 p.m. yesterday. I
begin to see it. You will succeed. God bless you all."[76] Unfortunately for
the Union, Grant's plans did not succeed. His subordinates, primarily
Winfield Hancock and "Baldy" Smith, failed to use their 50,000 troops
to capture Petersburg, which was defended by a mere 3,500 Confederates
for two and a half days before Lee belatedly sent reinforcements from
north of Richmond.[77] Thereafter, Grant ceased his offensive and partially
besieged Richmond and Petersburg.

While the battle for Petersburg raged from June 15 to 18, Lincoln
went to Philadelphia to attend the Great Central Sanitary Fair. It was
sponsored by the Sanitary Commission and the Christian Commission,
which provided care and support for wounded and sick soldiers. The
president addressed the Fair on June 16. In the midst of his speech, he

referred to Grant's earlier assurance to him and built upon it: "Speaking of the present campaign, General Grant is reported to have said, I am going through on this line if it takes all summer. This war has taken three years; it was begun or accepted upon the line of restoring the national authority over the whole national domain, and for the American people, as far as my knowledge enables me to speak, I say we are going through on this line if it takes three years more."[78]

In concluding his address, Lincoln evoked an image of Grant: "If I were to hazard [a prediction], it is this: That Grant is this evening, with General Meade and General Hancock, of Pennsylvania, and the brave officers and soldiers with him, in a position from whence he will never be dislodged until Richmond is taken [loud cheering], and I have but one single proposition to put now, and, perhaps, I can best put it in form of an interrogative. If I shall discover that General Grant and the noble officers and men under him can be greatly facilitated in their work by a sudden pouring forward of men and assistance, will you give them to me? [Cries of "yes."] Then, I say, stand ready, for I am watching for the chance. [Laughter and cheers.]"[79] Aware that Grant was in the Petersburg area, Lincoln correctly predicted that Grant's perseverance would compel him to remain there until Richmond fell the following year.

Lincoln's belief was reinforced when he, along with son Tad, left Washington on June 21 for a brief visit with Grant and his troops outside Petersburg. According to Orville Browning, Grant had reassured Lincoln with the following parting words: "You, Mr. President, need be under no apprehension. You will never hear of me farther from Richmond than now, till I have taken it. I am just as sure of going into Richmond as I am of any future event. It may take a long summer day, but I will go in." Attorney General Bates reported that the president was encouraged by Grant's "persistent confidence" and was convinced he would press ahead until the job was completed.[80]

In mid-1864 Lincoln encountered a problem involving discriminatory payment of black soldiers. When black troops complained about unequal pay, Lincoln asked Attorney General Edward Bates to resolve the issue. On June 24 the president formally solicited an opinion as to what pay, bounty and clothing were owed to free blacks who had been enlisted and mustered into military service between December 1862 and June 1864. Bates found that an 1862 law that allowed the procurement of blacks' services for specified low pay rates did not apply to blacks who had voluntarily enlisted, been mustered into military service, and were performing the duties of U.S. soldiers. He concluded firmly: "I give it to you unhesitatingly as my opinion that the same pay, bounty, and clothing are allowed by law to the persons of color referred to in your communication...as are, by the laws existing at the times of the enlistments of said persons, authorized and provided for and allowed to other soldiers in the volunteer services of the United States of like arms of the service...." Lincoln referred this opinion to Stanton, who forwarded it to the adjutant general with instructions to pay black soldiers in accordance with it.[81] Lincoln's intervention thus secured equal pay for black soldiers.

As Grant's army settled into a partial siege of Richmond and Petersburg, Lincoln continued to protect Grant from outside nuisances. When a certain J. Rutherford Worster sent Lincoln a sample of his wash-leather sandal-socks to be worn over ordinary socks and asked for access to Grant, the president in late June wrote Grant: "Dr. Worster wishes to visit you with a view of getting your permission to introduce in the Army 'Harmon's Sandal Sock.' Shall I give him a pass for that object?" No reply from Grant has been found.[82] Two months later the president asked Grant if a pass should be issued to a Colonel Thomas Worthington of Ohio to come see Grant. A grateful Grant replied that "I should be very sorry to see the Col. He has nearly worried the life out of me at times when I could not prevent an interview." Worthington had been dismissed from service by Grant's friend Sherman.[83] Lincoln also deferred to Grant on matters with potential military implications; when he issued a pass to two individual would-be peace negotiators, he only authorized them to pass to Grant's headquarters and asked Grant whether he wanted to allow them to proceed through his lines.[84]

Grant's movement across the James and partial siege of Richmond and Petersburg merged Meade's and Butler's troops and thereby created a politically sensitive senior personnel problem. The incompetent and previously "bottled-up" Butler, a well-connected Democratic politician, was senior to all generals in the theater except Grant. Butler also engaged in a series of disputes with major generals Quincy Gillmore and "Baldy" Smith, his subordinates, as well as Major General Horatio Wright. These West Pointers all hated Butler, and the feeling was mutual. The acrimony destroyed Grant's plan to bolster the militarily incompetent Butler with capable subordinates.[85]

So Grant was still left with the problem that, in Grant's absence, Butler would command all Union forces there. To avoid such a calamity, Grant could have relieved Butler of command; Grant knew, however, that such an action would be politically harmful to the president. Therefore, he instead recommended to Halleck that Butler be reassigned elsewhere. Halleck presented such a transfer order to Lincoln, who approved it and then, because of the potential political fallout, directed Grant to sign it. After Butler confronted Grant and threatened to turn the Republican convention against Lincoln, Grant decided to protect Lincoln and did not sign the order. This episode is an excellent example of Grant modifying his military behavior in order to support the competing political interests of the president.[86]

Eventually Grant accepted Halleck's recommendation to "kick Butler upstairs" to a non-operational department administrator position (as Grant had previously done with Nathaniel Banks). With Grant's concurrence, Lincoln appointed William F. "Baldy" Smith commander of the Army of the James on July 7. That appointment did not last long because Smith could not get along with his fellow generals and criticized most of them, including Grant and Meade. Therefore, Grant had Smith transferred out of the Virginia Theater.

So Butler retained his army command—much to the political satisfaction of Lincoln, who at the end of July said Butler "has my confidence in his ability and fidelity to the country and to me. And I wish him sustained in all his efforts in our great common cause." Lincoln was at his political nadir in the summer of 1864 and could not afford to dismiss such a powerful Democratic politician.[87] An officer on Meade's staff observed, "Thus did Smith the Bald try the Machiavelli against Butler the cross-eyed, and got floored in the first round."[88]

During the second half of 1864, Grant kept Lee pinned down in Petersburg and Richmond, encouraged Sherman's success in Georgia, and finally drove the Confederates out of the Shenandoah Valley. Taking minimal casualties, Grant tightened the noose around Lee's Army and readied the way for victory in 1865. One of Grant's constant efforts was to threaten Lee's supply lines by extending his own left flank and making cavalry raids beyond the lines.[89]

Grant's first significant problem after the siege began was that Confederate General Jubal Early and his Second Corps were on the loose—and Grant did not know it. His intelligence system broke down, and Grant was not aware of Early's position until Early neared Frederick, Maryland, on an ill-conceived approach to Washington. At the same time Grant was moving his army to and across the James River, Lee had sent Early's Corps west to defend Lynchburg against Union Major General David Hunter's attack out of the Shenandoah Valley. Outnumbering Hunter 14,000 to 11,000, Early scared Hunter away from Lynchburg and back into the Kanawha Valley of West Virginia.[90]

At that point, Lee could have ordered Early to return to Richmond, to reinforce Johnston at Atlanta, or to do something else. The brilliant strategic move would have been to reinforce Johnston, who was being overwhelmed by Sherman's numerical superiority but needed to hold Atlanta if Lincoln was to be defeated in the November presidential election. That was the move most feared by Grant and Sherman. Instead, on June 27, Lee authorized Early to proceed north down the Shenandoah Valley to threaten Washington. Early's orders contained a quixotic authorization for him to go around Washington and free Confederate prisoners at the isolated Point Lookout prison camp far southeast of Washington.[91]

Although the fortifications and forts surrounding Washington made it unlikely that Early would accomplish much, he created a stir. Early's 18,000 troops made their way north down the Shenandoah and entered Maryland. Early demanded and received ransoms of $20,000, $1,500, and $200,000, respectively, from the citizens of Hagerstown, tiny Middletown, and Frederick. At first Grant refused to believe reports that Early was in Maryland. He reported from the Richmond area on July 3 that "Early's corps is now here." Two days later, Grant, apparently concerned about continuing reports of Early's possible movement, told Stanton and

Halleck that he would send a full corps to Washington if the city was threatened; they declined. After Meade reported to Grant that deserters claimed Early was heading for Maryland and Washington, Grant sent Brigadier General James B. Ricketts' Third Division of the Sixth Corps north by vessel to Baltimore as an insurance policy.[92]

By July 5, Lincoln was wiring John W. Garrett, the astute president of the Baltimore & Ohio Railroad, to ascertain Early's whereabouts after his troops had taken Martinsburg and Harpers Ferry. Lincoln directed Stanton to ask Governors Andrew G. Curtin of Pennsylvania and Horatio Seymour of New York for 12,000 militiamen from each of their states as 100-day soldiers to defend Washington.[93]

Finally realizing where Early was, Grant ordered the rest of the Sixth and all of the 19th Corps north to defend Washington. Ricketts' 5,000-man division greatly strengthened the force that was cobbled together by General Lew Wallace at Monocacy Creek, south of Frederick, to oppose Early's advance. During the July 9 Battle of Monocacy, Wallace's makeshift force fiercely held the three bridges at those crossings. After hours of fighting at the bridges, Early, however, had his cavalry cross the river at a ford a mile downstream from the fighting and then attack the Union left flank. Overwhelming numbers of Rebel cavalry and infantry finally drove Wallace's men back toward Baltimore after seven hours of fighting.[94]

On July 9 Lincoln asked Garrett what he had heard of that day's Battle of Monocacy. That evening Garrett responded that his telegraph operator eight miles east of the Monocacy reported that an aide to Major General Lew Wallace had arrived and reported that Union troops had been badly defeated and given way at Monocacy. Late that night Halleck wired Wallace, "I am directed by the President to say that you will rally your forces and make every possible effort to retard the enemy's march on Baltimore."[95] While Wallace's troops were an obstacle to an eastern movement by Early, the road south to Washington was open.

Grant, at 6 p.m. on July 9, had advised Halleck somewhat unrealistically, "Forces enough to defeat all that Early has with him should get in his rear south of him, and follow him up sharply, leaving him to go north, defending depots, towns, &c., with small garrisons and the militia." The reality was that Early was moving south from Frederick, Maryland, across the Monocacy and toward Washington. There were no forces in his rear or between him and Washington. Sensing that his assurance might not be adequate, Grant added, "If the President thinks it advisable that I should go to Washington in person I can start in an hour after receiving notice, leaving everything here on the defensive."[96]

It was 2 p.m. the next afternoon when Lincoln told Grant that Halleck said, "we have absolutely no force here fit to go to the field," and that Halleck thought 100-day men and invalids could defend Washington and "scarcely Baltimore." After describing other Union troops that would be of little use (including Hunter's wasted troops belatedly coming out of West Virginia), the president painted an ominous picture and asked Grant to head for Washington:

> Wallace with some odds and ends, and part of what came up with [Brigadier General James B.] Ricketts [Third Division of the 19th Corps previously sent to Baltimore by Grant], was so badly beaten yesterday at Monocacy, that what is left can attempt no more than to defend Baltimore. What we shall get in from Penn. & N.Y. will scarcely [be] worth counting, I fear. Now what I think is that you should provide to retain your hold where you are certainly, and bring the rest with you personally, and make a vigorous effort to destroy the enemie's [sic] force in this vicinity. I think there is really a fair chance to do this if the movement is prompt. This is what I think, upon your suggestion, and is not an order[.][97]

That morning Lincoln had given some weak assurances to Baltimore residents who had complained to him that their city was imperiled and "large re-enforcements" were needed. The president responded, "I have not a single soldier but whom is being disposed by the Military for the best protection of all. By latest account the enemy is moving on Washington. They cannot fly to either place. Let us be vigilant but keep cool. I hope neither Baltimore nor Washington will be sacked."[98]

The worried president could not have been fully reassured by Grant's response to his plea for Grant to come personally and bring troops to Washington. Instead Grant just sent troops. He was sending the entire 19th Corps and 3,000 additional troops from the Sixth Corps. Grant told Lincoln that the reinforcements, under Major General Horatio G. Wright, could join with Hunter's 10,000 against the Confederates. In closing, Grant declined to come to Washington and expressed excessive optimism about the fate of those invaders: "I think on reflection it would have a bad effect for me to leave here [Richmond-Petersburg area], and with Genl [Edward O.C.] Ord at Baltimore and Hunter and Wright with the forces following the enemy up, could do no good[.] I have great faith that the enemy will never be able to get back with much of his force."[99]

Lincoln graciously accepted Grant's decision as "very satisfactory" but expressed well-founded concern about trapping Early's troops. He cautioned, "The enemy will learn of Wright's arrival, and then the difficulty will be to unite Wright and Hunter, South of the enemy before he will recross the Potomac."[100] As Lincoln had feared, the Union forces did not converge to trap and destroy Early's raiders. Instead, Early and his troops retreated to the safety of the Shenandoah Valley.

The Battle of Monocacy cost Early a day, and two divisions of seasoned Sixth Corps troops had arrived from Grant and were waiting for him in Washington by the time he arrived at midday on July 11. Early then undertook a retreat into the lower Shenandoah Valley; he constituted a continuing offensive threat, which was demonstrated by his burning of Chambersburg, Pennsylvania, on July 30 when the residents were unable to raise sufficient tribute money.[101] The net result of Early's raid was that Lee had used one of his three corps to cause Grant to send two of his seven corps away from Richmond. In addition, the Washington garrison would not provide additional troops to Grant.

Even after Early's departure from the Washington environs, the president's concerns about Rebel invaders continued on July 12. He wired Grant about vague rumors that Longstreet's Corps was on its way to the Washington area and asked Grant to "look out for it's [sic] absence from your front." The next day Grant answered that evidence from deserters, scouts and cavalry confirmed that none of A. P. Hill's Third or Longstreet's First Corps had left his front.[102]

Following the Jubal Early scare, Lincoln found time to respond to Pennsylvania Governor Curtin's mid-June eleven-page letter complaining about the poor condition of the Second Pennsylvania Heavy Artillery and its commander, Colonel Augustus A. Gibson. On July 17 the president asked Curtin to come to Washington to deal with the issue. The governor declined to come to Washington and instead offered to send his military agent to see Lincoln. On July 22 Colonel Gibson was mustered out of the army.[103] In this instance, Lincoln appears to have resolved a politically sensitive military command issue.

When Grant warned Sherman on July 16, 1864, that Early with possibly 25,000 troops had departed Maryland and could be heading to Georgia, he was reflecting his continuing concern that Lee eventually would send reinforcements to protect Atlanta. He wrote, "… It is not improbable, therefore, that you will find in the next fortnight [25,000] re-enforcements in your front.… I advise, therefore, that if you can get to Atlanta you set about destroying the railroads as far to the east and south of you as possible; collect all the stores of the country for your own use, and select a point that you can hold until help can be had. I shall make a desperate effort to get a position here which will hold the enemy without the necessity of so many men. If successful, I can detach from here for other enterprises, looking as much to your assistance as anything else." Lincoln, forever reading originals and copies of military telegrams at the War Department, conditionally complimented Grant on his stance: "Pressed as we are by lapse of time, I am glad to hear you say this; and yet I do hope you may find a way that the effort shall not be desperate [sic] in the sense of great loss of life."[104] The president's words reflected his awareness that timely progress was necessary in his reelection year and that Grant's heavy casualties were causing concern.

Setting himself up for his imminent departure, Major General Hunter (whose incompetence had opened the way for Early's escapade), requested that Lincoln relieve him of command because he had been "selected as the scapegoat" in an order from Halleck to pursue the retreating Early. Lincoln denied there was any attempt to make him a scapegoat and assured Hunter that Grant wished him to remain in command and "I do not wish to order otherwise."[105] Hunter continued to disappoint the president. When Lincoln, on July 23, asked Hunter whether he could "take care of the enemy [Early] when he turns back on you, as he probably will," Hunter replied, "My force is not strong enough to hold the enemy should he return upon us with his whole force."[106] Thus, the fiasco continued in the northern Shenandoah Valley.

After Early's escape from Washington to the Shenandoah, Grant was unhappy about Halleck's unwillingness to coordinate the four Union departments in Maryland in opposing Early. Most of Washington was disgusted with Halleck's feeble performance during the Jubal Early scare. Attorney General Bates complained to Lincoln about "the ignorant imbecility of the late military operations, and my contempt for Genl. Halleck." Postmaster General Blair joined Stanton in urging Lincoln to remove Halleck. Lincoln declined to do so and deferred to Grant on the issue.[107]

Dissatisfied with Halleck's failure to take charge in the Washington area during and after Early's raid, Grant proposed to change the command structure in that area. On July 18 he proposed to Halleck that Major General William Franklin be placed in command of the four involved departments. Halleck warned Grant that Lincoln would not approve Franklin because of the latter's disloyalty to Burnside after the Battle of Fredericksburg, his poor performance during that battle and his persistent criticism of the Lincoln administration. Grant raised the stakes by suggesting Meade as an alternative to Franklin, but Lincoln did not want to appear to be caving in to critics of Meade by downgrading him months before the presidential election.[108]

Grant was relieved that Early was wasting time burning Chambersburg instead of reinforcing Johnston at Atlanta. In early July, Grant had written Sherman about his concern that Early's Corps would be sent to Atlanta, and on July 15 Grant wrote Halleck that his greatest fear was such a movement.[109] Fortunately for Grant and Sherman, Lee kept Early's 14,000 to 18,000 troops in his own theater. Confederate General Porter Alexander later criticized Lee for his use of Early to try to bluff Grant, whom he said could not be bluffed, and for not sending Early's

Corps to Georgia, "the very strongest play on the military board. Then every man sent might have counted for his full weight in a decisive struggle with Sherman &, if it proved successful, then Early might return bringing a large part of Johnston's army with him to reinforce Lee."[110]

Grant's friend Sherman also was being helped unwittingly by President Jefferson Davis. On July 17, with the reluctant concurrence of Lee,[111] Davis replaced Joseph Johnston, who had retreated to Atlanta, with Lieutenant General John Bell Hood. Davis was dissatisfied with what he perceived to be Johnston's lack of aggressiveness. Hood, who suffered a serious arm injury at Gettysburg and lost a leg at Chickamauga, was notorious for his aggressiveness (some said recklessness) on the battlefield. That aggressiveness explains why his appointment was unwelcome in the Confederate Army of Tennessee but greeted with optimism among the Union officers who knew Hood.[112]

Their hopes were rewarded as Hood, who was temporarily promoted to full general, went on the offensive three times in his first twelve days of command. Although his strategic mission was defensive and his soldiers were not expendable, Hood attacked—as he usually did. Those three attacks (Peach Tree Creek on July 20, Decatur on July 22, and Ezra Church on July 28) cost Hood 14,000 casualties to Sherman's 4,000, earned him an ironic rebuke from Davis for attacking the enemy in entrenchments, and made his army likely to lose Atlanta.[113] As Sherman had expected, Hood had immediately gone on the offensive, and, as Sherman had hoped, Hood had so weakened his army that Atlanta was vulnerable.

Back in Virginia, Grant was successful in establishing and maintaining control of the James River north of his City Point base at the intersection of the James and Appomattox Rivers. From June 20 onward, his forces held a fortified bridgehead on the northwest bank of the James at the narrow horseshoe curve called Deep Bottom (because the James River was very deep at that point). For the next two months, they cleared Confederate mines from the river and blocked the creeks flowing into it. Lee declined Early's request for artillery and infantry that were necessary to dislodge Grant's forces, and the Union troops thus prevented a Rebel blockade of the river, safeguarded their City Point base of operations, and kept viable their ability to transfer troops between the Petersburg and Richmond fronts.[114]

In late July, Grant sent Hancock and Sheridan on a mission to challenge the northern end of Lee's lines, divert Lee's attention from a planned mine explosion in Petersburg, widen the Union bridgehead on the north side of the James River, and thus more effectively threaten Lee's Richmond lines. At what became known as the First Battle of Deep Bottom, aggressive Rebel defenders caused Hancock to hesitate and not use his overwhelming numerical advantage. Although Hancock failed to achieve his mission (except to divert Lee's attention), he inflicted more casualties than he incurred.[115]

To compensate for Grant's casualties and bring the war to an end, Lincoln issued a July 18 proclamation calling for 500,000 volunteers. The proclamation also mandated, beginning September 5, a draft of one-year soldiers to fill the local quotas unmet by volunteers. Proving that their thoughts were running in the same direction, Grant wired Lincoln on July 19 an independent recommendation for "an immediate call for, say, 300,000 men to be put in the field in the shortest possible time." He reasoned, "With the prospect of large additions to our force [Rebel] desertions would increase. The greater number of men we have the shorter and less sanguinary will be the war. I give this entirely as my views and not in any spirit of dictation, always holding myself in readiness to use the material given me to the best advantage I know how." Lincoln graciously answered, "... I suppose you had not seen the call for 500,000 made the day before, and which I suppose covers the case. Always glad to have your suggestions."[116] Lincoln continued to encourage their operating in tandem.

Not all of Lincoln's generals cooperated with his policies. Sherman's racist attitudes, not atypical for his time, led him to oppose recruitment of black soldiers near his camps. On July 14 he complained to Halleck about the folly of sending civilian recruiting agents into Southern states, and said, "I will not have a set of fellows here hanging about on any such pretenses." Lincoln noticed his telegraphic complaints and wrote to him about it. After explaining that the law, which he favored, called for such recruitment activity, Lincoln told Sherman he would try to "save you from difficulties arising out of it," and asked, "May I ask therefore that you will give your hearty co-operation?" Sherman weakly replied, "I have the highest veneration for the law, and will respect it always, however it conflicts with my opinion as to its propriety. I only telegraphed to General Halleck because I had seen no copy of the law, and supposed the War department might have some control over its operations."[117]

Grant meanwhile recommended to Lincoln that Major John H. Hammond be appointed as brigadier in command of "colored troops"—a recommendation that Lincoln forwarded to Stanton and that resulted in Hammond's brevet promotion to brigadier later that year.[118] Unlike many other Union generals, Grant continued to fully support Lincoln's encouragement of the use of black soldiers.

Having been burned by Early's embarrassing raid that reached Washington's outskirts, Grant decided to provide a better defense for the capital by eliminating the Confederate threat from the Shenandoah. On July 25 Grant proposed to Lincoln a combination of four departments (Susquehanna, Washington, Middle Virginia, and West Virginia) under Meade's command—with Hancock then assuming command of the Army of the Potomac. Grant had General Rawlins deliver the letter to Stanton, who instead placed Halleck in command of those departments with responsibility for defending against attack and "capture and destruction" of the enemy.[119] This temporary fix relying on the ineffective Halleck would not last long.

The president was determined to put an end to any threats to Washington and decided to press the issue with Grant. Lincoln had Stanton request Grant to meet the president at Fortress Monroe on July 28. In an exchange of telegrams, the meeting was pushed back to July 31. On the back of Grant's last telegram, Lincoln wrote "Meade & Franklin/McClellan/Md. & Penna."[120] This notation appears to reflect Lincoln's agitation about prior Union failures to capitalize on opportunities to capture Rebel armies and terminate threats to Washington. The Lincoln/Grant meeting was delayed because Grant was planning for the July 30 Battle of the Crater at Petersburg.

Toward the end of June, Grant had authorized Pennsylvania Volunteer miners under Burnside's command to dig a five-hundred-foot tunnel under the Confederate fortifications at Petersburg. By July 23 they had finished their digging and were ready to detonate eight tons of explosives under the Confederate lines. In the latter days of July, Grant transferred troops north from Petersburg toward Richmond. By doing so, he caused Lee to move four of seven infantry divisions from Petersburg to Richmond and thereby weaken that sector of Lee's line. Then on the night of July 29–30, Grant surreptitiously brought most of his troops back to the Petersburg front in an effort to exploit the expected breakthrough from the planned explosion. Early on the morning of July 30, Union troops set off a massive explosion under the Confederate lines, thereby creating a huge opening and an opportunity for a breakthrough.[121]

However, Meade, fearing criticism for heavy casualties they might incur, had ordered a last-minute replacement of the black troops who had been trained to lead the assault. Brigadier General James Ledlie, the division commander of the replacement troops, cowered in a bunker behind the lines—drunk again (as he had been at the North Anna River a few weeks before). Therefore, contrary to Grant's orders stressing "the absolute necessity of pushing entirely beyond the enemy's present line," Ledlie's men entered "The Crater" but then hesitated to move farther. The belated and ineffective Union advance provided the initially shocked Confederates with time to reorganize and counterattack. The Rebel response resulted in a slaughter of Union troops in the crater and execution of surrendered black troops. What Grant later called "this stupendous failure" resulted in 4,000 Union casualties while the Confederates suffered only 1,500. Ledlie at last was removed from command.[122]

Lincoln's concern about the situation in the lower Shenandoah must have been heightened when he saw a panic-filled July 30 telegram from Hunter at Harpers Ferry. Hunter apparently was responding to Lincoln's inquiry to him earlier that morning ("What news this morning?"). Hunter reported that Horatio Wright's Corps was fatigued, scattered and unable to move. He then bemoaned his situation and pleaded for help: "… my information is so unreliable and contradictory that I am at a loss to know in which direction to pursue the enemy. If I go toward the fords over which he has passed to cut off his retreat by the Valley, he turns to the right, pushes toward Baltimore and Washington, and escapes by the lower fords of the Potomac. If I push on toward Frederick and Gettysburg, I give him a chance to turn down the Valley unmolested. Please with your superior chances for information…direct me what is best to be done…."[123]

In the immediate aftermath of Hunter's demonstration of his incompetence, Early's July 30 burning of Chambersburg, Pennsylvania, and Grant's disaster at "The Crater," the president and his general-in-chief finally met at Hampton Roads on July 31. Lincoln, frustrated by Early's escape and the continuing turmoil in the northern Shenandoah on Washington's doorstep, most likely pushed Grant for decisive corrective action. They apparently agreed on the desirability of placing Grant's protégé, Major General Phil Sheridan, in operational command of the Shenandoah troops. The next day Grant sent Sheridan and another division of cavalry to the Shenandoah and wired Halleck, "I am sending General Sheridan for temporary duty whilst the enemy is being expelled from the border. Unless Gen. Hunter is in the field in person I want Sheridan put in command of all the troops in the field with instructions to put himself south of the enemy and follow him to the death. Wherever the enemy goes let our troops go also…."[124]

Lincoln may have decided to let Grant deal with the delicate issue of Hunter's seniority over Sheridan. When it became clear that Halleck was delaying Sheridan's assignment, Lincoln jumped into the fray in what was perhaps the war's best-documented example of Lincoln's aggressive oversight of Grant when Lincoln thought it necessary. Lincoln sent Grant an August 3 wire quoting Grant's August 1 wire to Halleck and then prodding Grant to do more:

> This, I think, is exactly right, as to how our forces should move. But please look over the despatches [sic] you may have receved [sic] from here, even since you made that order, and discover, if you can, that there is any idea in the head of any one here, of "putting our army South of the enemy" or of ["] following him to the death" in any direction. I repeat to you it will neither be done nor attempted unless you watch it every day, and hour, and force it.[125]

Lincoln had Grant's attention. On August 4 Grant responded, "Your dispatch of 6 p.m. just received. I will start in two hours for Washington & will spend a day with the Army under Genl Hunter."[126] Taking the president's not-so-subtle hint, Grant immediately left his City Point headquarters and headed north to resolve this situation. After visiting in Washington with Stanton and Lincoln,[127] he went to Monocacy, Maryland, where he met General Hunter. Since Hunter was unable to tell Grant where the enemy was, Grant decided to smoke out the enemy troops by sending a trainload of soldiers four miles west of Harpers Ferry to draw them out. After Grant also ordered Hunter's cavalry and wagons to move west in search of Confederates and explained that Sheridan would command in the field, Hunter requested that he be relieved of command.[128]

Grant gladly complied and thus had Sheridan where he wanted him—in charge of 30,000 troops tasked with clearing the Valley of Confederates. When Grant returned to Washington on August 7, he rescinded Halleck's control over the four Maryland/Washington departments and placed them under the command of Sheridan, whom Lincoln had temporarily approved as commander of the Middle Military Division.[129] Neither Lincoln nor Grant would be disappointed in Sheridan. Between August 13 and 20, Grant assisted Sheridan by moving troops north of the James to keep Lee from reinforcing the Shenandoah.

During August, Grant dealt with manpower issues. In mid-August, he wrote to his friend and political advocate, Congressman Elihu Washburne:

> The rebels have now in their ranks their last man. The little boys and old men are guarding prisoners, guarding rail-road bridges and forming a good part of their garrisons for intrenched [sic] positions. A man lost by them can not be replaced. They have robbed the cradle and the grave equally to get their present force. Besides what they lose in frequent skirmishes and battles they are now loosing [sic] from desertions and other causes at least one regiment per day.[130]

Grant told Washburne that he foresaw a Union victory if the North was true to itself and rejected Southern hopes for the election of a peace candidate.[131]

Grant recognized that prisoner exchanges benefited the Confederates, who had limited manpower. On August 18, he wrote, "If we commence a system of exchanges which liberates all prisoners taken we will have to fight on until the whole South is exterminated. If we hold those caught they amount to no more than dead men. At this particular time to release all rebel prisoners [in the] North would insure Sherman's defeat and would compromise our safety here."[132] The next day he wrote, "We ought not to make a single exchange nor release a prisoner on any pretext whatever until the war closes. We have got to fight until the military power of the South is exhausted and if we release or exchange prisoners captured it simply becomes a War of extermination."[133]

At the very same time, Lincoln was using the same rationale to defend emancipation as necessary to winning the war. He did so during an August 19 interview with Alexander W. Randall and Joseph T. Mills. The president criticized George McClellan, the likely Democratic presidential candidate, and the Democrats for unrealistically believing that the war could be won through conciliation and without black troops. His comments included the following analysis of the need for black soldiers and a defense of emancipation:

> There are now between 1 & 200 thousand black men now in the service of the Union. These men will be disbanded [under Democratic strategy], returned to slavery & we will have to fight two nations instead of one. I have tried it. You cannot concilliate [sic] the South, when the master & control of millions of blacks makes them sure of ultimate success.... Abandon all the posts now possessed by black men[,] surrender all these advantages to the enemy, & we would be compelled to abandon the war in 3 weeks. We have to hold territory. Where are the war democrats to do it[?]...My enemies say I am now carrying on this war for the sole purpose of abolition. It is & will be carried on so long as I am President for the sole purpose

of restoring the union. But no human power can subdue this rebellion without using the Emancipation lever as I have done. Freedom has given us the control of 200,000 able bodied men, born & raised on southern soil.... My enemies condemn my emancipation policy. Let them prove by the history of this war, that we can restore the Union without it.[134]

Less than three weeks later, Lincoln was presented a Bible by "the loyal colored people of Baltimore" and, in the course of acknowledging the gift, said, "I can only now say, as I have often before said, it has always been a sentiment with me that all mankind should be free."[135]

Lincoln was so anxious to enhance the army's strength that he, without Grant's knowledge, on September 1 approved the enlistment at Rock Island, Illinois, of Confederate prisoners who were unwilling to be exchanged and sent to the South. Most of them had been born in the North or in a foreign country. Stanton twice refused to execute the plan until Lincoln personally explained it to him and made the order peremptory. One problem that had occurred with a similar program to obtain naval recruits was that prisoners had taken an oath of allegiance, failed their physical examinations, and then been placed back among the Rebel prisoners. When Lincoln apparently learned from Stanton that Grant had opposed this prisoner recruiting, the president wrote an apology to Grant: "... I did not know...that you had protested against that class of thing being done; and I now say that while this particular job must be completed, no other of the sort, will be authorized without an understanding with you, if at all. The Secretary of War is wholly free of any part in this blunder." Grant advised Stanton that the ex-prisoners should be placed in one regiment and sent to either Minnesota or New Mexico— far from the North-South conflict.[136]

In early October, Lincoln acted as he had indicated he would and deferred to Grant on an unusual prisoner-exchange issue. On October 4 Lincoln, Halleck and Stanton learned of a Navy Department plan for a small exchange of naval prisoners and, together with Seward, agreed to defer to Grant in a letter from the president. The president sent Grant the relevant letters about the exchange proposed to occur near him—even though Seward and Stanton interestingly wanted him to write to Butler. After stating that the plan "gives us some uneasiness," Lincoln continued, "I therefore send [relevant correspondence] to you with the statement that as the numbers to be exchanged under it are small, and so much has already been done to effect the exchange, I hope you may find it consistent to let it go forward under the general supervision of Gen Butler, and particularly in reference to the points he holds vital in exchanges. Still you are at liberty to arrest the whole operation, if in your judgment the public good requires it." Grant turned the whole matter over to Butler.[137] Lincoln's handling of this matter showed his sensitivity to Grant's concerns about prisoner-of-war exchanges.

By mid-August Grant, informed by the Bureau of Military Intelligence (BMI), was aware that Lee had sent reinforcements to the Shenandoah and believed he could take advantage of their absence. By threatening Richmond on the north end of the battle-lines, Grant thought Lee would have to so weaken Petersburg in response that Petersburg could be taken. Thus he had Hancock, with 29,000 troops, move on Richmond, which was defended by a well-entrenched force of 7,700. Due to serious bungling and lack of coordination, this Second Battle of Deep Bottom, from August 14 to 20, resulted in little progress (other than overrunning and capturing eight large guns that threatened Union control of the James) being made by the Union forces, which incurred 2,900 casualties while imposing about 1,500 on the defenders.[138] But Grant was keeping the pressure on Lee.

That approach was consistent with a Grant-Lincoln-Halleck exchange of views that occurred that same month. On August 11, Halleck initiated the communications by writing that possible Northern draft riots would necessitate the withdrawal of troops from the Army of the Potomac to deal with the insurrections. Grant strongly disagreed, contended that state militias would have to deal with any riots, and said, "If we are to draw troops from the field to keep the loyal states in the harness it will prove difficult to suppress the rebellion in the disloyal states. My withdrawel [sic] now from the James River would insure the defeat of Sherman." Lincoln then chimed in and wired Grant, "I have seen your despatch [sic] expressing your unwillingness to break your hold where you are. Neither am I willing. Hold on with a bull-dog gripe [sic], and chew & choke, as much as possible." An amused Grant laughed when he read Lincoln's homespun response and told some of his staff, "The president has more nerve than any of his advisors."[139]

Although the Union casualties of July and August were far less than those of May and June, they continued without any assurance that Richmond, Petersburg, or Atlanta was about to fall into Union hands. The result was a continuing decline in Northern morale that threatened Lincoln's reelection prospects. Virtually all the political kingmakers and self-proclaimed experts were recommending that Lincoln step aside and allow someone to run who had a chance of winning.

Many of Lincoln's detractors were Radical Republicans. These included Maryland Congressman Henry Winter Davis, long embittered by Lincoln's failure to include him in his cabinet, and Ohio Senator Benjamin Wade. In the spring and summer of 1864, they collaborated to produce the Wade-Davis Bill, which proposed to punish the South and produce a harsh congressionally controlled reconstruction after the war. It represented a direct challenge to Lincoln's Proclamation of Amnesty and Reconstruction of December 9, 1863. Therefore, the president pocket-vetoed the bill after Congress adjourned at noon on July 4.[140]

But that was not the end of the matter. Davis, Wade and their fellow radicals fumed over this presidential put-down for a month and finally went public with their objections. They enlisted the support of the mercurial Horace Greeley, who published their Wade-Davis Manifesto in his *New York Tribune* on August 5. Using bombastic and intemperate language, they attacked Lincoln for his "studied outrage on the legislative authority of the people" and accused him of "grave Executive usurpation." They continued, "The whole body of Union men of Congress will not submit to be impeached by him of rash and unconstitutional legislation; and if he wishes our support he must confine himself to his executive duties—to obey and execute, not make the laws—to suppress by arms the rebellion, and leave political reorganization to Congress." This attack was a fitting introduction to August 1864—the nadir of Lincoln's presidential life as his prospects for reelection moved toward an apparent collapse.[141]

Once again Radical Republicans focused on Grant as a possible presidential candidate. Lincoln was intrigued or concerned enough about this possibility that he again inquired into Grant's intentions. In an August 12 meeting at the White House, Lincoln asked Colonel Eaton what Grant thought about efforts being made to nominate him. After Eaton pleaded ignorance, Lincoln continued,

> Well, the disaffected are trying to get him to run, but I don't think they can do it. If he is the great General we think he is, he must have some consciousness of it, and know that he cannot be satisfied with himself and secure the credit due for his great generalship if he does not finish his job. I do not believe that they can get him to run.[142]

The president asked Eaton to visit Grant to ascertain his views on the campaign and issued a pass to him to visit Grant at City Point, his siege headquarters. Eaton later reported that Lincoln was concerned about Grant concluding his military mission and not about rivalry for the nomination. Eaton said Lincoln's "confidence in Grant was one of the finest things I have ever witnessed," and quoted the president's explanation about his generals failing him until Grant arrived:

> Before Grant took command of the Eastern forces, we did not sleep at night here in Washington. We began to fear the rebels would take the Capitol [sic], and once in possession of that, we feared that foreign countries might acknowledge the Confederacy. Nobody could foresee the evil that might come from the destruction of records and property. But since Grant has assumed command on the Potomac, I have made up my mind that whatever is possible to have done, Grant will do, and whatever he does n't [sic] do, I don't believe is to be done. And now we sleep at night.[143]

Eaton then proceeded to City Point to visit Grant. After discussing other issues, Eaton told Grant he had been asked on a train whether he thought Grant could be induced to run as a citizens' candidate for president. Grant, according to Eaton, responded fiercely: "Grant's reply came in an instant and with a violence for which I was not prepared. He brought his clenched fists down hard on the strap arms of the camp-chair. 'They can't do it! They can't compel me to do it!'" Grant continued, "I consider it as important for the cause that [Lincoln] should be elected as that the army should be successful in the field." Eaton quickly returned to Washington and relayed Grant's reaction to Lincoln, who "fairly glowed with satisfaction" and said, "I told you they could not get him to run until he had closed out the rebellion."[144] Here then was the essence of their mature relationship: Lincoln was delighted to have Grant as his commanding general, and Grant was delighted to have Lincoln as his president.

The end of August brought favorable developments near Atlanta. On August 31 at Jonesboro, south of Atlanta, Hood lost 4,000 more troops unsuccessfully trying to drive Union troops away from the last open railroad serving Atlanta. Hood afterward criticized his subordinate Lieutenant General William J. Hardee's assault as feeble because of the low percentage of his casualties (15 percent). Because Sherman's armies now controlled all railroads into and out of Atlanta, Hood was compelled to abandon the city on September 1. Sherman occupied it the next day, the North went wild in celebration, and Lincoln's reelection was virtually assured.[145] It is difficult to overstate the significance of Atlanta's fall in causing a sweeping change in public opinion and virtually ensuring Lincoln's reelection. Overnight his prospects went from very negative to quite positive.

The Democrats had simultaneously nominated George McClellan as Lincoln's opponent on August 31 at their Chicago convention; his candidacy was virtually doomed before the campaign began. On September 3 the president demonstrated his joy by issuing an order of celebration calling for numerous one hundred-gun salutes for the captures of Atlanta and Mobile Harbor; orders of thanks to Sherman, Admiral David Farragut, and Major General Edward Canby for those successes, and a proclamation of thanksgiving and prayer.[146]

As in Virginia, the Atlanta Campaign had not been a bloodless one for either side. Sherman incurred casualties of 31,687, while his Confederate opponents lost 34,979—almost 20,000 of those after Hood replaced Johnston.[147] On September 12 Grant sent a personal letter to Sherman that was delivered by Colonel James McPherson of Grant's staff. He closed by congratulating Sherman on his Atlanta campaign: "In conclution [*sic*] it is hardly necessary for me to say that I feel you have accomplished the most gigantic undertak[ing] given to any General in this War and with a skill and ability that will be acknowledged in history as unsurpassed if not unequalled." Grant told Sherman that he was sending McPherson to get Sherman's views on future actions, but Grant did suggest the possibility of moves on Mobile and Savannah.[148] Grant was thinking ahead on a national scale.

From June 22 to August 21, Grant had intermittently focused on extending his south-of-Petersburg lines westward to block the north/south Weldon Railroad, over which Lee's army was receiving many of its supplies from Weldon, North Carolina. After unsuccessfully moving on that railroad in late June with a loss of 3,000 troops, Grant's forces tried again in August. Major General Gouverneur K. Warren's Fifth Corps extended its line three miles to the west, took and fortified a position on the railroad, and then held on against a Confederate counterattack at the Battle of Globe Tavern (or Weldon Railroad) on August 18–21. Thereafter the Confederates had to bypass the section of that railroad held by Grant's troops via a thirty-mile detour by wagon, and thus Richmond, Petersburg and Lee's army were more difficult to supply.[149]

In the Deep South, meanwhile, Admiral David G. Farragut had taken major actions against Mobile, Alabama, a key port and rail center that had long been on Grant's list of primary targets. Not only was it the last major open port on the Gulf, but Mobile was also the only extant rail connection point between the remaining eastern and western segments of the Confederacy. Lincoln's reelection prospects were enhanced by Farragut's "Damn the torpedoes—full speed ahead" charge into Mobile Bay on August 5 and the August 23 capture of Fort Morgan, which controlled that bay. Although the city itself was not occupied until April 1865, its use as a Confederate port was ended by Farragut's actions.[150]

The morale-boosting impact of the Mobile Bay and Atlanta victories was captured by Secretary of State William H. Seward, who said, "Sherman and Farragut have knocked the bottom out of the [Democrats'] Chicago platform."[151] Lincoln exchanged telegrams with Grant about whether the Richmond papers had covered the fall of Fort Morgan. Grant's final response included the following dispatch in the *Richmond Sentinel*: "The report of the surrender of Fort Morgan was most unexpected & we await some explanation of so unfortunate an occurrence."[152]

After the fall of Atlanta and Mobile harbor, Northern Democratic newspapers switched their defeatist criticisms to Sheridan's Shenandoah Theater. In response, Lincoln prodded Grant in a September 12 telegram: "Sheridan and Early are facing each other in a dead lock. Could we not pick up a regiment here and there, to the number of say ten thousand men, and quietly, but suddenly concentrate them at Sheridan's camp and enable him to make a strike? This is but a suggestion." Despite the final disclaimer, Lincoln was involving himself militarily at the operational level. Grant took the advice in stride and replied, "It has been my intention for a week back to start to-morrow, or the day following, to see Sheridan and arrange what was necessary to enable him to start Early out of the Valley. It seems to me it can be successfully done."[153]

On September 15, therefore, Grant left City Point for another visit with Sheridan. In his memoirs, Grant said he went to Harpers Ferry to discuss an offensive greater than Stanton or Halleck would have authorized if he had tried to communicate by telegraph. Grant brought a campaign plan with him but kept it in his pocket when Sheridan produced a plan of his own—an indicator of Grant's willingness to delegate authority. Grant shared Lincoln's interest in ending years of "pussyfooting" by Union generals in the Valley, and he was now more certain than ever that Sheridan was the man to do it. Thus began Sheridan's successful 1864 Shenandoah Valley campaign.[154]

On September 19, at Opequon Creek (Winchester), Sheridan took 5,000 casualties while imposing 4,000 casualties on Early and driving his troops south with a two-division cavalry charge. Lincoln wired his congratulations on "your great victory." Now convinced that Grant had been right about Sheridan, the president promoted "Little Phil" to brigadier general in the regular army and made him permanent commander of the Middle Military Division. Three days later, at Fisher's

Hill, Sheridan repeated his assault and, at a cost of only 500 casualties, inflicted 1,200 casualties on Early and drove him farther south.[155]

Sheridan chased Early so far south up the Valley that Sheridan lost contact with Washington. To allay Lincoln's fears that Lee would successfully reinforce Early against Sheridan, Grant told him he would attack Lee to keep him from doing so. To do that, Grant issued September 28 orders to Ord's 18th and Major General David B. Birney's Tenth corps and Brigadier General August V. Kautz's cavalry to threaten the Richmond end of Lee's lines.[156] In doing so, Grant this time was one day ahead of Lincoln's concerns. On September 29, the concerned, election-conscious but deferential president wired Grant, "I hope it will lay no constraint on you, nor do harm any way, for me to say that I am a little afraid lest Lee sends re-enforcements to Early, and thus enables him to turn upon Sheridan." Grant immediately replied that he was precluding that possibility: "I am taking steps to prevent Lee sending reenforcements [sic] to Early by attacking him here. Our advance is now within six miles of Richmond and have [sic] captured some very strong enclosed forts, some fifteen or more pieces of artillery and several hundred prisoners."[157]

Between September 29 and October 2, Grant launched simultaneous offensives on both ends of the Petersburg/Richmond siege lines, captured important Fort Harrison outside Richmond, induced Lee to launch a costly and unsuccessful counterattack against that fort, and compelled Lee to extend his lines three miles farther west of Petersburg, thereby thinning and weakening Lee's defensive perimeter. Utilizing excellent BMI intelligence, Grant and Sheridan caught Major General Joseph B. Kershaw's Division in transition between Richmond and the Shenandoah Valley while Grant was conducting his successful dual assaults against Lee's weakened army. A few days later, Grant's troops used Spencer repeating rifles to repulse a Lee-directed assault along Darbytown Road.[158]

A month later, on October 19, Early surprised Sheridan's troops at Cedar Creek and drove them in retreat several miles north of their camps toward Winchester. Sheridan had been in Washington conferring with Stanton, at the latter's request, and had arrived back at Winchester the prior evening. That morning he rode toward the sound of the fighting just in time to stop the panicked retreat of many of his troops, turn around thousands of fleeing Union soldiers and organize a counterattack. In one of the war's greatest demonstrations of a commander's battlefield leadership, Sheridan reassembled his troops and launched an all-out attack that routed and drove Early's soldiers from the Lower Shenandoah Valley for the final time. Both sides withdrew most of their remaining troops to the Richmond/Petersburg front, and significant fighting in the Shenandoah was over. Although Sheridan had suffered 5,900 casualties to Early's 2,900, his third and final major victory in the Valley in about 35 days provided more grist for the Lincoln reelection mill.[159]

Now fully sharing Grant's trust in Sheridan, Lincoln promoted Sheridan to permanent major general in the regular army and wired him, "I tender you and your brave army, the thanks of the Nation, and my own personal admiration and gratitude, for the month's operations in the Shenandoah Valley." A few weeks later, at City Point, the lanky president encountered the diminutive, mud-splattered general and told him, "General Sheridan, when this peculiar war began I thought a cavalryman should be at least six feet four high, but I have changed my mind—five feet four will do in a pinch."[160]

Two days before Cedar Creek, the president had deflected a panicky governor's concerns. On October 17, Pennsylvania Governor Curtin alerted Lincoln that he had information about an enemy raid into his state by the end of the month because of transfers away from Sheridan. Lincoln reassured Curtin, "Your information is erroneous. No part of Sheridan's force has left him, except by expiration of terms of service. I think there is not much danger of a raid into Pennsylvania."[161] That same night, Lincoln urged participants in a torchlight parade at the Executive Mansion to give three hearty cheers for Sheridan and "three cheers for General Grant, who knew to what use to put Sheridan...."[162] Three days after the battle, Lincoln again acknowledged his gratitude for Sheridan's accomplishments by wiring "my own personal admiration and gratitude, for the month's operations in the Shenandoah Valley; and especially for the splendid work of October 19, 1864."[163] Lincoln was grateful that his reelection prospects had been enhanced by Sheridan's successful Shenandoah Campaign.

After all the September fighting, Lee the next month proposed to Grant that prisoner exchanges be resumed. Grant responded that exchanges could be resumed if Lee agreed that black prisoners would be exchanged "the same as white soldiers." Lee, in turn, replied that "… negroes belonging to our citizens are not considered subjects of exchange and were not included in my proposition." Grant, therefore, declined resumption of exchanges, in accordance with Lincoln's policy on the matter—a policy that cost Lincoln votes in the November election. Some voters were not pleased that white soldiers' imprisonments were being extended in order to protect blacks.[164]

While 1864 saw Union military and naval forces moving toward victory, political issues still loomed large.

CHAPTER 11

LINCOLN WINS REELECTION WITH GRANT'S FULL SUPPORT

I n 1864 Lincoln once again demonstrated a political aggressiveness that matched Grant's military aggressiveness. In that year's political campaign, he, along with Republican Radicals, insisted that the Republican platform contain a plank advocating a constitutional amendment abolishing slavery. He encouraged his secretary of war to work with his generals to allow as many soldiers from non-absentee-ballot states as possible to return home to vote for president.[1]

But the election results, especially before the fall of Atlanta, were not pre-ordained. Lincoln was vulnerable because the North was divided on the issues of war, the draft, and slavery. There had been draft riots in New York City, anti-war "Copperhead" sentiment flourished in the Midwest, and the Democrats adopted a peace platform at their convention. Just after McClellan's nomination, Secretary of the Navy Welles worried that "McClellan will be supported by War Democrats and Peace Democrats, by men of every shade and opinion; all discordant elements will be made to harmonize, and all differences will be suppressed." The next day, however, he took a contrary position: "Notwithstanding the factious and petty intrigues of some professed friends...and much mismanagement and much feeble management, I think the President will be reelected, and I shall be surprised if he does not have a large majority."[2]

As Archer Jones observed, "Increasingly, Confederate leaders and people, including the soldiers, looked to the Union presidential election of 1864 as the crucial time when the North could have a referendum on whether or not to continue the war."[3] As early as May 1863, Confederate Chief of Ordnance Josiah Gorgas noted in his diary the vulnerability of the North to political defeat: "No doubt that the war will go on until at least the close of [Lincoln's] administration. How many more lives must be sacrificed to the vindictiveness of a few unprincipled men! For there is no doubt that with the division of sentiment existing at the North the administration could shape its policy either for peace or for war."[4]

As the armies looked ahead to the crucial campaigns of 1864, Confederate Lieutenant General Longstreet on March 27 prophetically wrote, "Lincoln's re-election seems to depend upon the result of our efforts during the present year. If he is re-elected, the war must continue, and I see no way of defeating his re-election except by military success."[5] Longstreet also saw the connection between Grant's progress, or lack thereof, in the 1864 campaigns and the election: "If we can break up the enemy's arrangements early, and throw him back, he will not be able to recover his position or his morale until the Presidential election is over, and then we shall have a new President to treat with."[6]

During the summer of 1864, many Northerners were upset by the Army of the Potomac's numerous casualties, as its soldiers carried out their Overland Campaign from the Rappahannock River across the James River. Ever attacking, they suffered mounting losses at the Wilderness, Spotsylvania Court House, the North Anna River, Cold Harbor, and Petersburg.

Union casualty names and statistics were being published daily in Northern newspapers. In addition, many Northerners were frustrated by the failure of Union armies to capture either Richmond or Atlanta— which were perceived to be the respective targets of Grant and Sherman.

Newspaper editors and Republican Party leaders urged Lincoln not to run again—to step aside for someone who could win. New York editor Horace Greeley wrote, "Mr. Lincoln is already beaten. He cannot be elected."[7] In July he asked Lincoln to open peace negotiations with the Confederacy because "our bleeding, bankrupt, almost dying country longs for peace." Then in August, shrewd and powerful New York politico Thurlow Weed said, "The people are wild for peace.... Lincoln's reelection an impossibility."[8]

Lincoln himself was doubtful about his election prospects. That August he told a friend, "You think I don't know I am going to be beaten, but I do and unless some great change takes place, badly beaten."[9] In fact, on August 23 Lincoln reduced his pessimism to writing. At a cabinet meeting, he produced a piece of paper on which he had written: "This morning, as for some days past, it seems exceedingly probable that this administration will not be re-elected. Then it will be my duty to so co-operate with the President elect, as to save the Union between the election and the inauguration; as he will have secured his election on such ground that he can not possibly save it afterwards."[10] Without disclosing those words to his cabinet members, he had seven of them sign the document on the reverse side as evidence of the date of his words.

On November 11, a few days after the presidential election, Lincoln at last read those words to his cabinet after John Hay had cut the sealed document open. He then went on, according to Hay's diary, to explain his mindset at that time:

> [Y]ou will remember that this was written at a time [6 days before the Chicago nominating convention] when as yet we had no adversary, and seemed to have no friends. I then solemnly resolved on the course of action indicated above. I resolved, in case of the election of General McClellan being certain that he would be the Candidate, that I would see him and talk matters over with him. I would say, "General, the election has demonstrated that you are stronger, have more influence with the American people than I. Now let us together, you with your influence and I with all the executive

power of the Government, try to save the country. You raise
as many troops as you possibly can for this final trial, and I
will devote all my energies to assisting and finishing the war."

In response, Secretary Seward said, "And the General would answer you
'Yes, Yes'; and the next day when you saw him again & pressed these
views upon him he would say 'Yes—yes' & so forever and would have
done nothing at all." And Lincoln concluded, "At least I should have
done my duty and have stood clear before my own conscience."[11]

Back in August, Lincoln's prospects looked dim. On August 22
Weed wrote to Seward, "When, ten or eleven days since, I told Mr.
Lincoln that his re-election was an impossibility, I also told him that
the information would soon come to him through other channels. It
has doubtless, ere this, reached him. At any rate, nobody here doubts
it; nor do I see any body from other States who authorises the slightest
hope of success."[12]

Probably in coordination with Weed, Henry J. Raymond, Republican
National Chairman and *New York Times* editor and owner, wrote to
Lincoln about his reelection prospects. He painted a gloomy nationwide
picture:

> I feel compelled to drop you a line concerning the political
> condition of the country as it strikes me. I am in active cor-
> respondence with your staunchest friends in every state and
> from them all I hear but one report. The tide is setting strongly
> against us. Hon. E. B. Washburne writes that 'were there an
> election to be held now in Illinois we should be beaten.' Mr.
> Cameron writes that Pennsylvania is against us. Gov. Morton
> writes that nothing but the most strenuous efforts can carry
> Indiana. This state [New York], according to the best informa-
> tion I can get, would go 50,000 against us to-morrow. And so
> of the rest. Nothing but the most resolute and decided action
> on the part of the government and its friends, can save the
> country from falling into hostile hands.[13]

As late as September 2, Greeley and two other New York newspaper editors appealed to Northern governors to support a movement to replace Lincoln with another candidate.[14] John Waugh noted, "The cantankerous James Gordon Bennett at the...*New York Herald* incessantly beat the drum for General Grant, who incessantly denied that he was a candidate."[15] Perhaps affected by all these negative reports, the president was working with black leader Frederick Douglass in an effort to inform as many slaves as possible of the Emancipation Proclamation and the possible need to seek freedom before McClellan could be elected president and cancel the proclamation.[16]

Lincoln's dim reelection prospects brought hope to Confederates. For example, on August 26, Jedediah Hotchkiss, Stonewall Jackson's famed cartographer, wrote to his wife, "The signs are brightening, and I still confidently look for a conclusion of hostilities with the ending of 'Old Abe's' reign."[17] McPherson concluded: "If the election had been held in August 1864 instead of November, Lincoln would have lost. He would thus have gone down in history as an also ran, a loser unequal to the challenge of the greatest crisis in the American experience."[18]

At their Chicago convention, the Democrats adopted a peace platform that spoke of "four years of failure" and called for a halt of fighting "with a view to an ultimate convention" to resolve the major issues dividing the nation. Especially after the fall of Atlanta, McClellan was compelled to back off from what too many would deem an unacceptable surrender to the South. Thus he issued a September 9 letter setting forth his position; he rejected the "four years of failure" language, but he conceded that, when the Southern states were interested in returning to the Union on any terms, he would negotiate with them.[19]

Democrats emphasized the issue of race. One of their campaign posters read: "ELECT LINCOLN and the BLACK REPUBLICAN TICKET. You will bring on NEGRO EQUALITY, more DEBT, HARDER TIMES, and another DRAFT! Universal Anarchy, and Ultimate RUIN! ELECT McCLELLAN and the whole Democratic Ticket. You will defeat NEGRO EQUALITY, restore Prosperity, re-establish the UNION! In an Honorable, Permanent and Happy PEACE." Two Democratic editors published a spurious pamphlet, supposedly a Republican document, that supported interracial marriage.[20]

Late August was Lincoln's nadir, but three military developments changed everyone's perspective. The first was the fall of Mobile Bay, which was completed with the capture of Fort Morgan on August 26. The second was Phil Sheridan's September and October defeats of Jubal Early and his destruction of the Confederate "breadbasket" in the Shenandoah Valley. Grant deserves much of the credit for the Shenandoah successes because he forcefully pushed Lincoln to approve Sheridan's role and command there and he kept Lee occupied in order to prevent him from sending more troops to Early.

Finally, the third major event changing people's attitudes and minds— the "great change" Lincoln needed for reelection—was the fall of Atlanta. Atlanta's capture instantly changed Northern public opinion and suddenly made Lincoln a favorite to win reelection. Meanwhile the Democrats had committed a major strategic error; they had postponed their own convention until the end of August in hopes of capitalizing on the high casualties and lack of success by Grant and Sherman. Instead, no sooner did they nominate McClellan on September 1 than Sherman took Atlanta and derailed McClellan's campaign before it could start, let alone gain any momentum. Grant had contributed to Atlanta's fall by maintaining pressure on Lee to keep him from reinforcing the Confederates defending Atlanta. General Fuller emphasized the importance of these three military victories: "These battles were not only of great value to Grant in furthering the war, but of immense importance to Lincoln in gaining his election, without which the war would in all probability have collapsed."[21]

Lincoln's reelection was a critical, war-saving event. The Democratic platform called for a cease-fire prior to a convention of the states in order to restore the Union with all states' rights, including slavery, guaranteed. Davis would have shunned a convention without a guarantee of Southern states' independence, Washington would have been in a state of confusion, and the Thirteenth Amendment would have been in jeopardy. A "temporary" cease-fire likely would have become a permanent cessation of hostilities.

Even after the September 2 fall of Atlanta, some skepticism about Lincoln's prospects continued. On September 10, the *London Daily News* correspondent wrote, "I think of Lincoln's chances at this moment as five to three."[22] As late as October 17, his fellow Illinoisan, Congressman Washburne, wrote to Lincoln, "It is no use to deceive ourselves.... There is imminent danger of our losing the State."[23]

Most of the post-Atlanta news and views, however, were quite positive. Atlanta had fallen just before the state and congressional elections that preceded November's presidential election. On September 13, Lincoln received word from Maine Republican chairman James G. Blaine of a great victory—embellished with a confident prediction: "The Union majority in Maine will reach 20,000. We will give you thirty thousand (30,000) in November."[24] About that same time, the president scribbled an electoral vote calculation that he would receive 172 votes, McClellan 66, and Frémont 7.[25] It is unclear whether that prediction was his or someone else's.

Taking no chances, Lincoln pressured military commanders to provide adequate leave for soldiers from Indiana and other states that did not allow absentee balloting so that they could presumably vote for their commander-in-chief.[26] Three-quarters of the more than 250,000 troops who voted cast their ballots for Lincoln.[27] On September 19, Lincoln urged Sherman to do anything he could "safely do" to allow Indiana soldiers to return home to vote in the October 11 state elections because of the effect those elections would have on the November election. He was responding to a petition from Indiana Governor Morton and others that he delay the draft and return 15,000 soldiers to Indiana before the state election. Lincoln refused to suspend the draft but told Sherman of the importance of the Indiana election: "... the loss of it...would go far towards losing the whole Union cause. The bad effect upon the November election, and especially giving the State Government to those who oppose the war in every possible way, are too much to risk, if it can possibly be avoided.... Indiana is the only important State, voting in October, whose soldiers cannot vote in the field. Any thing you can safely do to let her soldiers, or any part of them, go home and vote at the State election, will be greatly in point. They need not remain for the Presidential election, but may return to you at once."[28] On September 26, Lincoln wrote to Rosecrans, then commanding in Missouri, to ensure that soldiers would be allowed to vote in Missouri and said, "Wherever the law allows soldiers to vote, their officers must allow it."[29]

Governor Morton was not the only politico who was recommending suspension of the 500,000-man draft of September 5 until after the election. These included Cameron of Pennsylvania and Chase of Ohio. Grant and Sherman provided rebuttals. Grant wrote, "A draft is soon over, and ceases to hurt after it is made. The agony of suspense is worse upon the public than the measure itself." Sherman added, "If the President modifies [the draft] to the extent of one man, or wavers in its execution, he is gone forever; the army will vote against him." Lincoln finally concluded, "What is the Presidency worth to me if I have no country?" and allowed the draft to proceed on schedule.[30]

On October 10 and 11 Lincoln, personally and in writing, urged Secretary of the Navy Welles to facilitate vote-gathering visits to "Seamen and sailors" by Charles Jones, Chairman of the Union State Central Committee for the State of New York. Welles described in his diary a visit from Lincoln and Seward "relative to New York voters in the Navy. Wanted one of our boats to be placed at the disposal of the New York commission to gather votes in the Mississippi Squadron." With Lincoln's blessing, the request and cooperation were extended to the Union blockading squadrons. On October 11 and 12 the president asked for and received a report from Simon Cameron on the Pennsylvania congressional and state legislative voting of October 11.[31]

Demonstrating the importance of election results to both of them, Lincoln shared information on state elections with Grant in an October 12 telegram: "Sec. Of War not being in, I answer yours about election. Pennsylvania very close, and still in doubt on home vote. Ohio largely for us, with all the members of congress but two or three. Indiana largely for us. Governor, it is said by 15,000, and 8 [o]f the eleven members of congress. Send us what you may know of your army vote."[32]

Indiana's reelected Governor Morton immediately urged Lincoln and Stanton to retain his state's sick and wounded soldiers in Indiana until after the presidential election. Lincoln responded cautiously on October 13. He reminded the governor that Lincoln's September 19 letter to Sherman had "said that any soldiers he could spare for October need not remain for November." Although Lincoln said he thus could not press Sherman on the point, "All that the Sec. of War and Gen. Sherman feel they can safely do, I however, shall be glad of." Morton's final plea stated, "It is my opinion that the vote of every soldier in Indiana will be required to carry this state for Mr. Lincoln in November. The most of them are sick and wounded and in no condition to render service and it is better to let them remain while they are here."[33]

On October 13, Lincoln himself created a two-column list of possible state-by-state results in the coming presidential election. By including New York, Pennsylvania, Illinois, and Maryland on the "Supposed Copperhead Vote" side of his equation, he calculated that the Union/Republican electoral vote could be 117 (not counting the yet-to-be-admitted State of Nevada with its three electoral votes) and the Democratic/Copperhead vote a scary 114.[34] It appears that Lincoln may have been creating and analyzing a "worst-case" scenario for the next month's election.

Although risking his relationship with the press during the sensitive election season, he deferred to Grant on the issue of reporters' access to "his" army. During the Overland Campaign, Grant, apparently at Meade's request, had revoked passes for reporters, including those of William Swinton of the *New York Times* and William H. Kent of the *New York Tribune*. After Swinton's pass had been restored by Meade, Kent applied to Lincoln on September 27 for similar treatment. The president referred the letter to Grant "for his consideration and decision." After receiving negative endorsements from Meade and Hancock indicating that Kent had filed false and damaging reports about Hancock's command, Grant denied the request: "The most liberal facilities are afforded to newspaper correspondents, but they cannot be permitted to misrepresent facts to the injury of the service. When they so offend their pass...is withdrawn.... In this case there appears to have been a deliberate attempt to injure one of the best Generals [Hancock] and Corps in the service. I cannot therefore consent to Mr. Kent's return to this army."[35]

While Lincoln was having no easy time getting reelected, Sherman reported that Lincoln's Confederate counterpart was creating his own difficulties by conducting himself in an un-Lincolnesque manner. After Sherman reported Jeff Davis's presence in Georgia on September 26, Lincoln speculated that "I judge that [Georgia Governor Joseph E.] Brown and [Confederate Vice President Alexander] Stephens are the objects of his visit." There was no love lost between Davis and either of them. On September 28, Sherman responded, "I have positive knowledge that Jeff Davis made a speech at Macon on the 22nd.... It was bitter against [Joseph E.] Johnston & Govr Brown. The [Georgia] militia is now on furlough."[36] Unlike Lincoln, Davis was publicly criticizing both a general and a governor who were critical to his cause.

Even on electoral issues, Lincoln retained his sense of humor. Secretary Seward provided him with an October 15 letter from a "P. J. J." in New York stating, "On the point of leaving I am told by a gentleman to whose statements I attach Credit, that the opposition Policy for the Presidential Campaign will be to 'abstain from voting.'" Lincoln's October 16 endorsement on the letter snapped, "More likely to abstain from stopping once they get at it, until they shall have voted several times each."[37]

Three days later Lincoln addressed a more serious problem. In responding to a crowd celebrating adoption of a new no-slavery Maryland constitution, he talked about speculation that he might try to ruin the government if not reelected or that the Democrats would seize the government if their candidate won. The president reassured the crowd:

> I hope the good people will permit themselves to suffer no uneasiness on either point. I am struggling to maintain government, not to overthrow it. I am struggling especially to prevent others from overthrowing it. I therefore say, that if I shall live, I shall remain President until the fourth of next March; and that whoever shall be constitutionally elected therefor in November, shall be duly installed as President on the fourth of March; and that in the interval I shall do my utmost that

whoever is to hold the helm for the next voyage, shall start with the best possible chance to save the ship. This is due to the people both on principle, and under the constitution. Their will, constitutionally expressed, is the ultimate law for all. If they should deliberately resolve to have immediate peace even at the loss of their country, and their liberty, I know not the power or the right to resist them.... I may add that in this purpose to save the country and it's [sic] liberties, no class of people seem so nearly unanamous [sic] as the soldiers in the field and the seamen afloat. Do they not have the hardest of it? Who should quail while they do not?[38]

Not only was Lincoln confident of the military vote, he was not above using it to shame others into voting for him.

Even his October 20 Proclamation of Thanksgiving served the president's political purposes. In it, he praised Almighty God for "many and signal victories over the enemy" and for "augment[ing] our free population by emancipation and by immigration."[39]

Lincoln stayed in touch with political operatives around the country, such as Alexander K. McClure of Pennsylvania. On November 5, three days before the election, McClure advised the president that he would carry the Pennsylvania "home [non-soldier] vote" by 5,000 to 10,000 or more. McClure added that he was "greatly encouraged by the conviction that your Election will be by a decisive vote, & give you all the moral power necessary for your high & holy trust."[40]

Meanwhile, on October 31 the president, in hopes of acquiring three more electoral votes, proclaimed Nevada a state.[41] Not only was every electoral vote important to Lincoln, but so was every individual vote. Thus, on November 3, he wrote to Stanton, "This man wants to go home to vote. Sec. of War please see him."[42] As late as November 7, Lincoln personally issued a five-day pass to one Lieutenant A. W. White to visit Philadelphia and return to Washington.[43]

To ensure an orderly election in Democrat-controlled New York, the scene of draft riots the prior year, the president sent Butler and Federal troops there. When the commander of the state militia challenged Federal authority relating to the election in New York in an October 29 order, Butler proposed to trump him with an equally bombastic order asserting Federal authority. After consultations with Stanton, Lincoln decided to forestall issuance of Butler's order until its necessity was more apparent: "I think this might lie over till morning. The tendency of the order, it seems to me, is to bring on a collision with the State authority, which I would rather avoid, at least until the necessity for it is more apparent than it yet is."[44] Lincoln also sent Seward back to his home state of New York to keep an eye on election matters.[45]

Riding the wave of the Atlanta, Mobile Bay, and Shenandoah military victories, Lincoln convincingly won reelection. Out of slightly more than four million votes, Lincoln received 2,218,388 (55 percent) while McClellan garnered 1,812,807 (45 percent). These votes resulted in a smashing 212–21 electoral vote victory for Lincoln. Although these statistics seem to reflect a landslide, the election was much closer than it appeared. The switch of a mere three-quarters of one percent of the votes (29,935 out of 4,031,195) in specific states would have given McClellan the ninety-seven additional electoral votes he needed to barely win with one hundred eighteen electoral votes. He could have picked up the huge states of Pennsylvania and New York—and their fifty-nine electoral votes—with a swing of fewer than 13,000 voters. The additional thirty-eight electoral votes he would have needed could have been found in any number of smaller states where he had significant percentages of the vote.[46] Lincoln was right to have been concerned about his reelection prospects and would not have won without the positive military events that preceded the election.

In the twelve states where military ballots were counted separately, Lincoln received 78 percent of them (119,754 to 34,291)—compared with his 53 percent of the civilian vote in those states.[47] The soldiers' decision was a striking endorsement of the Lincoln/Grant approach to war—in sharp contrast to that of McClellan, under whose command many of them had served. Chester Hearn asserted that the military vote was decisive in Connecticut, New York, and Maryland (where that vote also was responsible for passage of a new state constitution that banned slavery).[48]

Aware of Lincoln's great interest in the soldiers' votes, Grant sent Stanton a November 9 telegram giving the following vote totals in the Army of the Potomac:

State	Total Votes	Lincoln's Majority	(Lincoln/ McClellan)
Maine	1,677	1,143	1,410/267
New Hampshire	515	279	397/118
Vermont	102	42	72/30
Rhode Island	190	134	162/28
Pennsylvania (partial)	11,122	3,494	7,308/3,814
West Virginia	82	70	76/6
Ohio	684	306	495/189
Wisconsin	1,065	633	849/216
Michigan	1,917	745	1,331/586
Maryland	1,428	1,160	1,294/134
U.S. Sharpshooters (Multi-state)	124	89	106/18
New York	305	113	209/96
	19,211	8,208	13,709/5,502[49]

These numbers reflect the Eastern soldiers' support for Lincoln, Grant and their aggressive efforts to bring the war to a successful close.

The next day (November 10) Grant sent his congratulations to Lincoln via Stanton: "Enough now seems to be known to say who is to hold the reins of Government for the next four years. Congratulate the President for me for the double victory. The election having passed off quietly, no bloodshed or rioit [sic] throughout the land, is a victory worth more to the country than a battle won. Rebeldom and Europe will so construe it."[50] A few days later, Grant told John Hay that he was impressed most by "the quiet and orderly character of the whole affair."[51]

Defeating Lincoln in 1864 had been the Confederacy's best opportunity for victory. McClellan's well-documented respect for Southern "property rights" could have led to some sort of settlement short of a total Union victory that included abolition of slavery—and perhaps to a ceasefire and *de facto* Southern independence while the peace terms were being negotiated. In a study of the war, David Donald, Jean Baker, and Michael Holt concluded that "Lincoln's reelection ensured that the conflict would not be interrupted by a cease-fire followed by negotiations, and in that sense was as important a Union victory as any on the battle-field...."[52]

The closeness of that election demonstrates how important it had been for Grant to launch an aggressive nationwide offensive only two months after he became the Union general-in-chief. Without the capture of Atlanta, victory in the Shenandoah Valley and the capture of Mobile Bay, Lincoln's chances of reelection would have been slim to none.

In the wake of the election, Lincoln addressed two serenading groups on November 8 and 10 at the Executive Mansion. In the latter response, he proclaimed, "We cannot have free government without elections; and if the rebellion could force us to forego, or postpone a national election, it might fairly claim to have already conquered and ruined us.... [The election] has demonstrated that a people's government can sustain a national election, in the midst of a great civil war. Until now it has not been known to the world that this was a possibility." Lincoln was making the same points Grant did in his wire of the same day. The president then spoke of the need to "re-unite in a common effort, to save our country...."[53]

CHAPTER 12

LINCOLN AND GRANT WIN THE WAR

———◄•◆•►———

A s the crucial election approached and Lincoln then secured a close victory, it receded in the public consciousness as Lincoln and Grant successfully brought closure to the war on the battlefield.

After occupying Atlanta and allowing Hood's army to escape (for which Grant did not criticize him), Sherman deliberated on what to do next. As early as September 10, Grant talked about sending Union troops to Savannah. Sherman's response mentioned several possible Georgia targets and the possibility that he could "sweep the whole State of Georgia." On September 12 Grant sent Lieutenant Colonel Porter to visit Sherman and get his views on future operations.[1]

Sherman watched and then followed as Hood moved north and then west toward and eventually into Alabama. Initially Hood went after Sherman's supply line, the Western and Atlantic Railroad, from Chattanooga to Atlanta. Finally, Sherman decided that pursuing Hood and protecting his own extended supply line was getting him nowhere.

Instead, on October 9, Sherman made a radical proposal to Grant: Sherman should break loose from his supply line, destroy the railroad between Chattanooga and Atlanta (his supposed lifeline), and "move through Georgia smashing things to the sea." Sherman told Grant, "I can make Savannah, Charleston or the mouth of the Chattahoochee," and asked for quick approval.[2]

That same evening, Grant succinctly indicated his approval: "Your dispatch of to-day received. If you are satisfied the trip to the sea coast can be made holding the line of the Tennessee River firmly you may make it destroying all the rail-road South of Dalton or Chattanooga, as you think best."[3] Of Sherman's proposal for his famous march, Grant later wrote: "His suggestions were finally approved, although they did not immediately find favor in Washington. Even when it came to the time of starting, the greatest apprehension, as to the propriety of the campaign he was about to commence, filled the mind of the President, induced no doubt by his advisers. This went so far as to move the President to ask me to suspend Sherman's march for a day or two until I could think the matter over.... I was in favor of Sherman's plan from the time it was first submitted to me. My chief of staff [Brigadier General John Rawlins], however, was very bitterly opposed to it and, as I learned subsequently, finding that he could not move me, he appealed to the authorities at Washington to stop it."[4]

The president had concerns about Sherman heading toward the Atlantic while Hood posed a threat to Tennessee, the Ohio River line, and thus Indiana and Ohio. Therefore Lincoln and Grant gave final approval to Sherman's proposal only after Sherman sent George Thomas and John Schofield (with the 12,000-man Army of the Ohio) to defend Tennessee against a likely incursion by Hood.[5] Sherman, however, only parted with his smallest army (his two weakest corps) and provided Thomas with virtually no horses for his cavalry, no supply train and no bridging equipment. In other words, Sherman kept the best and the bulk of his army to march almost unmolested against inferior opposition while sending an undermanned and undersupplied Thomas to oppose Hood and the only significant Rebel army in the theater.[6]

It was on November 2 that Grant officially approved Sherman's proposed campaign through Georgia. Only two weeks later, on November

16, Sherman left Atlanta with about 60,000 troops, deftly feinted moves toward different destinations, and wreaked a path of destruction as wide as sixty miles from Atlanta to Savannah. They destroyed railroads, factories, and Confederate arsenals. They seized anything that could be eaten by men, horses or mules. Despite orders to the contrary, they liberally burned and pillaged. In general, they burned unoccupied dwellings but not those where families remained. When Lincoln grew concerned about Southern press reports that Sherman's men were demoralized and starving, Grant told Lincoln not to worry.[7]

Confederate Lieutenant General William Hardee, a Georgia native, came back to his home state, raised some troops, and harassed Sherman's unstoppable force as it continued toward Savannah. Sherman arrived at Savannah's outskirts and began his siege of that city on December 10. In order to establish contact with the Federal fleet that had arrived off the coast of Savannah, Union Brigadier General William B. Hazen's Division had to assault and capture Fort McAllister—Sherman's first hard fighting since Atlanta. Once he had access to the shipboard mails, Sherman was able to read a December 3 letter from Grant. In that letter, Grant expressed his confidence in Sherman and his awareness of the relationship of their mutual activities:

> Not liking to rejoice before the victory is assured I abstain from congratulating you and those under your command until bottom has been struck. I have never had a fear however for the result.
>
> Since you left Atlanta no very great progress has been made here. The enemy has been closely watched though and prevented from detaching against you.[8]

Although Hardee's 11,000 defenders inexcusably[9] were allowed to escape the city into South Carolina to fight again the next year, Sherman occupied Savannah in time to make it a Christmas present to the president. He informed the president: "I beg to present to you as a Christmas-gift the city of Savannah, with one-hundred and fifty heavy guns and plenty of ammunition, also about twenty-five thousand bales of cotton." The greatest significance of the capture of Savannah was that it gave Sherman an ocean base for supplies. For the balance of the war, his army could be supplied with ammunition and other essentials by sea and rail through Atlantic Ocean ports.[10]

Sherman's march from Atlanta to Savannah had a devastating effect on the Georgia countryside and towns, as well as a demoralizing effect on the inhabitants, their soldier relatives serving with Lee and elsewhere, and the entire South. In his memoirs, Grant gave full credit to Sherman for the conception and execution of this critical march:

> ... the question of who devised the plan of march from Atlanta to Savannah is easily answered: it was clearly Sherman, and to him also belongs the credit of its brilliant execution. It was hardly possible that any one else than those on the spot could have devised a new plan of campaign to supersede one that did not promise success.[11]

On December 26 Lincoln sent Sherman a letter congratulating him for completing his successful campaign and for sending Thomas off to Tennessee to successfully repel a Rebel invasion. The self-effacing president admitted his own reticence and gave full credit to Sherman: "When you were about leaving Atlanta for the Atlantic coast, I was anxious, if not fearful; but feeling that you were the better judge, and remembering that 'nothing risked, nothing gained' I did not interfere. Now, the undertaking being a success, the honor is all yours; for I believe none of us went farther than to acquiesce."[12]

In Tennessee, Thomas had the good fortune to be facing an overly aggressive commander in John Bell Hood. After Schofield's two Union corps escaped a trap set by Hood's army of 25,000 at Spring Hill, Tennessee, on November 29, a furious Hood ordered a suicidal assault the next day at Franklin, Tennessee. He was not convinced that his soldiers were willing to fight other than behind fortifications. They were. The results were devastating: the Confederates lost thirteen generals (including six killed or mortally wounded), more than sixty of their one hundred regimental commanders were killed or wounded, 1,750 Confederate soldiers were killed, and another 5,500 were wounded or captured. Hood's 32 percent casualty rate at Franklin made this perhaps the most foolish attack of the war and exceeded Cold Harbor and Pickett's Charge at Gettysburg in its self-inflicted damage.[13]

Still not satisfied, Hood ordered his battered army to proceed toward Nashville. With his inadequate force, Hood fortified in front of Nashville while Thomas consolidated his forces and received reinforcements, horses, supplies and equipment. Sherman had undercut Thomas by sending him to Tennessee with his weaker troops, cavalry without mounts, and no bridging equipment. For the next two weeks, Grant (under some prodding from Lincoln and with little knowledge of a devastating ice storm and other on-the-spot conditions) repeatedly urged Thomas to attack.[14]

A frustrated Grant finally wired Halleck to replace Thomas with Schofield. Lincoln and Halleck delayed those orders to give Thomas more time to act. As the ice-storm delay continued, Grant decided to go to Washington and then on to Nashville to personally remove Thomas. In Washington, on December 15, Grant met with Lincoln, Stanton, and Halleck. Lincoln advised against a change of command on the eve of battle and pointed out that Thomas knew more than they did about on-the-spot conditions at Nashville. Grant insisted on Thomas's removal, and the president yielded. Grant wrote a removal order and ordered it telegraphed to Thomas. Before that was done, however, a wire from Thomas arrived and reported a great battlefield success. Grant's attempted micro-management of Thomas demonstrates that he had less confidence in Thomas than he did in Sherman and that he had no friendship with Thomas. Their dysfunctional relationship had begun when Halleck replaced Grant with Thomas as an army commander in the Corinth Campaign and deteriorated further during their joint activities at Chattanooga (where Thomas's success destroyed Grant's plan for a heroic victory by Sherman).[15]

On December 15 and 16, Thomas had launched a massive assault on Hood's forces and inflicted another 6,600 casualties—26 percent of the remainder of the Army of Tennessee. Between the two days of fighting at Nashville, Lincoln wired his congratulations—accompanied by the usual Lincolnesque plea for elimination of the enemy army: "Please accept for yourself, officers, and men, the nation's thanks for your good work of yesterday. You made a magnificent beginning. A grand consummation is within your easy reach. Do not let it slip." After the second day's fighting, the broken remnants of Hood's army headed back to Alabama in frigid winter conditions. Aided by two major rivers and the horrid weather, Hood and the remnants of his beaten troops escaped to Tupelo, Mississippi—much to Lincoln and Grant's chagrin. They held Thomas to a higher standard than they held Sherman. In five months, however, Hood had reduced his own army from 50,000 to 18,000 or less.[16]

The two-day Battle of Nashville was as close to a perfect offensive victory as occurred during the war. Thomas's plans to hold Hood's right in place while storming his left flank and rear worked to perfection. He made the most effective combat use of black troops in a major Civil War battle, used the cavalry he had taken the time to assemble (over Grant's objections about the time consumed) as a rapid infantry force to outflank and pursue the Confederates, and suffered a moderate number of casualties while obliterating Hood's army.[17] T. Harry Williams concluded, "The victory at Nashville was the only one in the war so complete that the defeated army practically lost its existence. It was also a complete vindication of Lincoln's faith in Thomas. Again the President had been more right than Grant."[18] Grant compounded his mistreatment of Thomas by deferring his immediate promotion to major general in the regular army; Lincoln, on the advice of Stanton, overruled Grant and approved the immediate promotion.[19]

After the Battle of Nashville, Grant began shifting Thomas's soldiers to the East while leaving Thomas in what had become a backwater theater. In 1865 Thomas played no role in closing out the war. Unlike Sherman and Sheridan, he was not one of Grant's favorites. While Grant failed to criticize Sherman for allowing Hood's army to escape from Atlanta and for inexcusably allowing Hardee's troops to escape from a trap at Savannah, he blamed Thomas for permitting the flight of what was left of Hood's army under extreme winter conditions. The bottom line was that Grant did not like Thomas, and Lincoln was not about to intervene in this military personnel matter while Grant was in the process of finally winning the war. Furthermore, Lincoln may have somewhat unfairly put Thomas in a category along with McClellan and Meade: victorious generals who allowed the enemy to escape to fight another day. Grant himself had set the standard high and met the president's expectations by capturing Rebel armies at Fort Donelson and Vicksburg; no other general on either side had captured an army.

During the second half of 1864, therefore, Grant had tightened the noose around Richmond and Petersburg and overseen successful operations in other theaters. Nowhere did Union forces suffer significant casualties compared with those they inflicted on the enemy—especially when considered in light of their offensive missions and significant accomplishments. By the end of 1864, Grant's multi-front campaign had succeeded in capturing Atlanta, Savannah, Mobile, and the Shenandoah Valley, reelecting President Lincoln, virtually destroying the Army of Tennessee, and laying the groundwork for the final defeat of Lee and the Confederacy. Congress recognized his achievements on December 17 by passing a joint resolution thanking Grant, his officers, and his soldiers and authorizing a gold medal to be struck and presented to him.

While all this military progress was occurring, Lincoln was busy on the domestic front trying in myriad ways to bring the war closer to a conclusion. In apparent desperation for anything that might work, Lincoln, on November 17, forwarded to Seward for his thoughts a suggestion from one Mr. Livingston that the government or private supporters purchase controlling interests in the allegedly thirty-six remaining newspapers in the Confederacy. Seward surprisingly thought the idea "very judicious and wise" and suggested that Stanton or Thurlow Weed might be able to provide funding.[20] Nothing came of this idea. Two days later Lincoln declared the Union-controlled ports of Norfolk, Virginia, and Fernandina and Pensacola, Florida, exempt from the Union blockade.[21]

Emancipation remained on Lincoln's agenda. In his December 6 annual message to Congress, the president urged approval of a constitutional amendment abolishing slavery despite its earlier rejection by the House of Representatives. He stated that the just-elected Congress was certain to pass it when it convened late the following year and asked,

"May we not agree the sooner the better?"[22] He succeeded in obtaining narrow House approval in January 1865, and the Thirteenth Amendment was ratified by the states exactly one year after Lincoln's message to Congress. Lincoln was so anxious for passage of that amendment that he took the constitutionally unnecessary step of approving the Congressional Resolution and submitting it to the states on February 1, 1865.[23]

In late December 1864 the president issued his final call for volunteers and draftees. Calculating that his July 18 call for 500,000 volunteers had fallen short by 260,000 and that additional casualty replacements were needed, Lincoln called for 300,000 volunteers—or draftees sufficient to reach the desired number. On February 15, 1865, the call for volunteers became a draft.[24] Lincoln wanted to ensure that Grant had sufficient troops to finish the war in short order.

In a December 26 letter to Sherman, Lincoln deferred to his generals as to Sherman's next mission: "But what next? I suppose it would be safer if I leave Gen. Grant and yourself to decide."[25] Grant originally planned to bring Sherman's troops to Virginia by vessel, but Sherman objected when he learned how long that would take. Instead he proposed that his troops march through the Carolinas to continue his devastation of the South and its will to fight while closing the vise on Lee's army in Virginia. Grant agreed.

As early as January 21, Grant was making arrangements for up to 30,000 Western troops to be brought east to the ports of Wilmington and New Bern, North Carolina, from which they could move inland to reinforce Sherman.[26]

Sherman later explained the importance of his intended march through the Carolinas: "Were I to express my measure of the relative importance of the march to the sea and of that from Savannah northward, I would place the former at one, and the latter at ten, or the maximum."[27] The plan had multiple purposes: it would allow Sherman to destroy the railroads supplying Lee from the Carolinas, discourage a southward retreat by Lee, and ultimately link up Sherman's and Grant's armies.[28]

Late in December, with Sherman outside Savannah, Grant had analyzed Lee's vulnerability to Sherman's actions. On December 18, Grant wrote to Sherman about Lee's focus on Richmond: "If you capture the garrison of Savannah it certainly will compel Lee to detach from Richmond or give us nearly the whole South. My own opinion is that Lee is averse to going out of Virginia, and if the cause of the South is lost he wants Richmond to be the last place surrendered. If he has such views it may be well to indulge him until everything else is in our hands."[29]

In the first months of 1865, Grant would concentrate virtually all his forces in the Carolina/Virginia Theater to bring the war to a decisive end. As the year opened, Grant had Lee pinned down in Richmond and Petersburg, Sherman was poised to march through the Carolinas from Savannah, and George Thomas was prepared to send tens of thousands of troops eastward after his rout of Hood at Franklin and Nashville.

Ignoring the wishes of President Davis, the Confederate Congress passed a January 19 law effectively making Lee the Confederate general-in-chief. He, however, had dwindling forces to command since forty percent of Confederates east of the Mississippi had deserted during the fall and early winter. On New Year's Eve, less than half the Confederacy's soldiers were present for duty with their units. Lee himself unsuccessfully requested that General E. Kirby Smith's Trans-Mississippi Army be transferred to Virginia.[30]

Grant's army and the threat it posed to Richmond seemed to be the sole concern of Lee and the paralyzed Confederate Government. They were slow to respond to the danger represented by Sherman and his resupplied 60,000-man army. Optimistically, Lee had sent one dispatch in which he spoke of achieving two incompatible goals: stopping Sherman and holding Charleston.[31] Doing both was unrealistic with the few Confederate troops available in the Carolinas. Besides Hardee's small force that had escaped Savannah, there were only local militia and the reassembled remnants of the Army of Tennessee, which had come northeast from Alabama to oppose Sherman.

Lee meanwhile was seeing his army melt away. On February 25 he wrote, "Hundreds of men are deserting nightly...."[32] Union Colonel Elisha Hunt Rhodes provided confirmation of that; he reported continuing Confederate desertions, including the arrival of ten deserters on February 21 and one hundred and sixty of them on February 25. Between

February 15 and March 18, there were 3,000 deserters from Lee's army, a loss of eight percent.[33] The situation became so bad that in March Lee reported 1,094 desertions in a ten-day period, and one entire brigade left en masse. That month a North Carolina captain wrote, "Most of the desertions, lately, have been caused by letters from home."[34] During March numerous regimental and brigade commanders requested the Confederate Adjutant's Office in Richmond to drop from the rolls captains and lieutenants who had deserted. William Marvel calculated that, between March 10 and April 9, between 14,400 and 20,400 of Lee's soldiers deserted.[35]

These desertions were not simply due to the strains of trench warfare and life. A major factor was the impact of Sherman's campaign: it caused a reduction of food and supplies coming to Lee's Army, and, as Bevin Alexander observed, it resulted in "letters from home, which reflected the despair and helplessness of families and friends who had watched Sherman's unchecked progress and witnessed the destruction of their property."[36] Lee's manpower situation became so desperate that in January he and Davis agreed to exchange their black prisoners and in March the Confederate Congress belatedly passed a pathetically ineffective bill to recruit black soldiers that required slave-owners' consent and did not even provide for emancipation.[37]

THE CAPTURE OF WILMINGTON

Because of the continued incompetence of Major General Benjamin Butler, Wilmington, North Carolina, remained open to blockade-runners as 1865 began. After Sherman had captured Atlanta and Mobile had been blocked, Grant approved use of troops in an amphibious assault to close Wilmington. Grant designated Brigadier General Godfrey Weitzel to command the army component of the assault, but Butler shocked him by exercising his seniority and assuming command. In response to the Union threat, Lee had sent a division of troops to defend the city; President Davis overruled Lee's choice of a commander and put his friend, Braxton Bragg, in command there instead of his enemy, P. G. T. Beauregard. When Davis designated Bragg to defend Wilmington, a Virginia newspaper opined, "Braxton Bragg has been ordered to Wilmington. Goodbye Wilmington."[38]

On Christmas Eve, Butler exploded a naval vessel near Fort Fisher, guarding the approach to Wilmington, in an effort to destroy that fort. As early as December 3 Grant had expressed his skepticism about the exploding-ship tactic: "Owing to some preparations Admiral Porter and Gen. Butler are making to blow up Fort Fisher, and which, whilst I hope for the best, do not believe a particle in...." The ship explosion was a fiasco—as was Butler's Christmas Day amphibious assault on Fort Fisher.[39]

On December 28 Lincoln inquired of Grant, "... please tell me what you now understand of the Wilmington expedition, present & prospective." An angry Grant responded, "The Wilmington expedition has proven a gross and culpable failure.... Delays and free talk of the object of the expedition enabled the enemy to move troops to Wilmington to defeat it. After the expedition sailed from Fort Monroe three days of fine weather was squandered, during which the enemy was without a force to protect himself. Who is to blame I hope will be known." Grant was priming the president to at long last fire Butler.[40]

Infuriated that Butler had ignored his orders to at least besiege the fort, Grant urged Lincoln to relieve Butler of his command. In early January 1865 Lincoln finally approved removal of that political general, who had, in the words of Chris Fonvielle, a "singular blend of arrogance and military ineptitude" and, in the words of Chester Hearn, "had given [Lincoln] nothing but trouble and military disasters." After his January 8 relief as department commander, Butler unsurprisingly jumped over Grant and Stanton to ask Lincoln's permission to publish his own report on "the Wilmington affair." Fully supporting Grant, the president responded that Butler's preliminary report had been returned to Grant at his request and "Of course, leave to publish, cannot be given, without inspection of the paper, and not then, if it should be deemed to be detrimental to the public service." After revising his endorsement on the report, Grant requested its publication.[41] Butler's next predictable move was to take his case to the Joint Committee on the Conduct of the War; on January 13 Lincoln approved his coming to Washington to testify.[42]

Having approved Sherman's plans for a march through the Carolinas, Grant was determined not only to close Wilmington to Confederate commerce but also to capture and open it as a means of resupplying Sherman via the Cape Fear River and Wilmington's three railroads. Grant designated Brigadier (Brevet Major) General Alfred H. Terry as Butler's replacement to cooperate with Admiral Porter in taking Fort Fisher and Wilmington.

On January 13, Terry landed his 9,000 troops four miles north of the fort. The next day Porter softened the Confederate land defenses by shelling the fort's guns protecting that side. On January 15, Terry and Porter continued their coordination and successfully stormed the weakened fort with a combined force of soldiers, sailors, and marines. Bragg, who had ignored numerous pleas from Fort Fisher for reinforcements, simply returned to Richmond.[43]

For the additional manpower needed to complete the capture of Wilmington, Grant assigned General Schofield and his 23rd Corps, which only recently had come east from Tennessee. Schofield, who superseded Terry as the Union commander by virtue of his seniority, arrived with one division on February 7 and began his advance on February 11. A combined naval and ground assault resulted in the February 19 capture of Fort Anderson, closer to the city. The Union forces continued their assaults and approached the city. Bragg returned from Richmond just in time to evacuate the Confederacy's last major port city on the night of February 21–22.[44]

The fall of Wilmington opened three rail routes for possible resupply of Sherman's ongoing advance into the Carolinas. Grant sent railroad rolling stock by water from Virginia to reinforce and supply Sherman. The city's fall also opened the Cape Fear River, which immediately was used to supply Sherman at Fayetteville. Conversely, no more foreign supplies would come to Lee or Johnston through the Union blockade.[45] Grant's investment of troops in the Wilmington campaign, therefore, paid real dividends. As Fonvielle concluded, "The fall of Wilmington did not end the Confederacy, but it hastened its downfall by guaranteeing the success of Sherman's Carolinas Campaign."[46]

The Wilmington campaign's success after Butler's departure demonstrated the correctness of his removal. His removal fulfilled Grant's long-standing desire to be rid of another incompetent political general. In February 1865 Grant blocked an attempt by Butler to become provost marshal of Charleston. With the presidential election behind him, Lincoln consented to Grant's continued downgrading and exclusion of the problematic political general.[47]

SHERMAN MARCHES THROUGH THE CAROLINAS

On February 1 Sherman left Savannah for the major offensive thrust of 1865. His men were eager to wreak havoc in South Carolina. One Union soldier exclaimed, "Here is where treason began, and by God, here is where it will end!"[48] Sherman wrote to Halleck that he almost trembled at the fate of South Carolina.[49] With that fervor, Sherman's soldiers advanced through the wintry swamps of southern South Carolina at a pace that amazed their opponents. They headed for the South Carolina capital of Columbia while cavalry bluffed movements toward Augusta, Georgia, on the left and Charleston, South Carolina, on the right.[50]

As he had in 1864, Sherman still had concerns about the possibility of Lee shifting troops to oppose his advance:

> ... the only serious question that occurred to me was, would General Lee sit down in Richmond (besieged by General Grant), and permit us, almost unopposed, to pass through the States of South and North Carolina, cutting off and consuming the very supplies on which he depended to feed his army in Virginia, or would he make an effort to escape from General Grant, and endeavor to catch us inland somewhere between Columbia and Raleigh?[51]

The answer was the same as in 1864: Lee would not move any troops from his beloved Virginia to oppose Sherman. He did allow the 14,000 troops who had been defending Fort Fisher, Wilmington, and its environs to remain in North Carolina.[52]

Virtually unopposed, therefore, Sherman raced over the rivers and through the swamps of South Carolina to the capital at Columbia. The only delays were to rebuild burned bridges, corduroy roads, and tend off cavalry skirmishers. About one third of Columbia burned on February 17; controversy still exists as to whether the wind-driven fire's primary cause was Confederates' torching of their cotton stockpiles or arson by drunken Union soldiers and other looters—both of which occurred. Sherman's juggernaut moved on.[53]

Sherman's march on Columbia cut many of the railroad connections to Charleston and compelled the military evacuation of that "Cradle of the Confederacy" on February 15. Beauregard positioned his forces forty-five miles north of Columbia to protect Charlotte, North Carolina. Sherman, however, moved northeast toward Goldsboro and unification with Schofield and at least 21,000 soldiers who previously had entered North Carolina to capture Wilmington and were now moving inland.[54]

As Sherman approached North Carolina and then moved from one Carolina to the other, Jefferson Davis reluctantly allowed Lee to reinstate Davis's old enemy, Joseph Johnston, as commander of the remnants of the Army of Tennessee, Hardee's Corps, Hampton's cavalry, and ultimately Bragg's Department of North Carolina. Thus, it was not until February 22 that Lee recalled Johnston to once again serve as commander of the Army of Tennessee. Lee optimistically ordered him to "Concentrate all available forces and drive back Sherman."[55]

On March 1, 1865, Johnston proposed that Lee bring a large number of his troops to North Carolina to join Johnston in defeating Sherman. Grant and Sherman had been concerned about such a merger even before they began their simultaneous campaigns in May 1864. Sherman said that, "if Lee is a soldier of genius, he will seek to transfer his army from Richmond to Raleigh or Columbia; if he is a man simply of detail, he will remain where he is, and his speedy defeat is sure." Lee declined to move against Sherman until the Federals had crossed the Roanoke River, a mere fifty-five miles south of Petersburg. At the time of his proposal, Johnston had about 21,000 troops to take on Sherman's forces: 60,000 soldiers of

Sherman's own and perhaps another 30,000 with Schofield coming inland from the North Carolina coast. Lee and Johnston's Confederate armies would lose separately.[56]

On March 8 to 10, Bragg's 8,500 troops halted Schofield's westward movement at Kinston, North Carolina. The delay was only temporary because Sherman's overwhelming force was moving farther northeast with little hindrance. He took Fayetteville on March 11, crossed the Cape Fear and Black rivers, and continued northeast toward a rendezvous with Schofield at Goldsboro. Grant earlier had selected Goldsboro as Sherman's goal because it was the junction of two railroads, the Wilmington & Weldon and the Atlantic and North Carolina, that would facilitate troop and supply movements from Wilmington, New Bern, and Morehead City on the coast.[57]

Slocum's left wing of Sherman's army was delayed by Hardee's troops at Averasboro between the Black and Cape Fear rivers on March 15 and 16.[58] Then on March 19 to 21, two isolated divisions of that wing were attacked by Johnston's combined forces at Bentonville. Sherman's forces incurred 1,500 casualties while inflicting 2,600 on the Confederates. Seeking to avoid a costly end-of-the-war frontal assault on Johnston's lines, Sherman passed up an opportunity to reinforce a breakthrough by one of his divisions.[59]

To avoid the merging Federal forces, Johnston retreated north to Smithfield. As a result, on March 23 Sherman and Schofield merged their forces at Goldsboro into a 90,000-man threat to Johnston's less than 20,000 troops. Sherman's army thus completed its 425-mile march, which Bevin Alexander described as "the greatest march in history through enemy territory."[60]

UNION PROGRESS IN VIRGINIA

Things were going no better for the Confederates in the Shenandoah. The forces of both Early and Sheridan had been reduced by winter transfers to the Richmond area. Sheridan decided to end Confederate occupation of any part of the Valley and promptly did so. He moved south on February 25 and pushed aside Early's cavalry at Mount Crawford on

March 2. The next day Sheridan decimated Early's infantry at Waynes-
boro. Early retreated through the Blue Ridge Mountains toward Charlottesville, thereby ending any Confederate army presence in the valley
that had once been its primary breadbasket in the East.

On the Petersburg front, meanwhile, Grant was making survival more
difficult for the Army of Northern Virginia. On February 5 to 7 Grant
pushed back the Confederates at Hatcher's Run on the far western end
of the line below and west of Petersburg and then extended both his line
and, consequently, the Confederate line an additional two miles. Grant's
army was closer than ever before to the Southside Railroad and the Boydton Plank Road, key supply routes for Lee's army.[61] Grant's continual
extension of his line was weakening Lee's defensive strength by stretching
out his defenders. In August 1864 Lee had about 65,000 soldiers defending a twenty-seven-mile front—2,500 men per mile. By March 1865,
however, Lee was defending a thirty-five-mile front with 53,000 troops—
a greatly reduced 1,500 men per mile.[62]

Not only was Grant lengthening and weakening Lee's line, he also
was fortifying his own so efficiently that he freed up men to launch the
final campaign of the war. David W. Lowe explained this development:

> In the war's last months, Federal engineers strengthened every
> fort on the Petersburg front into a self-sufficient fortress capa-
> ble of meeting an assault from any direction. Artillery fields
> of fire were carefully refined, using diverse facings and restrict-
> ing embrasures to generate the maximum degree of mutual
> support among the forts. The engineers proposed to denude
> the connecting parapets of troops and place the brunt of
> defense on the artillery and garrisons of 150–300 men—about
> 900 men per mile of front—certainly the most efficient use of
> entrenchments of the war.[63]

As the war moved toward its conclusion, Lincoln and Davis, realizing
that neither was going to yield on the issues of union and slavery, maneuvered to make each other appear blameworthy for the failure to negotiate
an end to the war. With political powerhouse Francis Preston Blair Sr. as

the go-between (with a through-the-lines pass issued by Lincoln) in January 1865, Davis agreed to a conference "to secure peace to the two countries" and Lincoln agreed to an informal conference to secure "peace to the people of our one common country." Davis overlooked their one/two-country difference, which Blair had pointed out to him, and appointed three peace commissioners, but Lincoln instructed his military commanders in Virginia to block any commissioners not willing to accept "one common country" as the basis for talks.[64]

When Major Thomas T. Eckert, sent by Lincoln (through Grant and Ord) to meet with the Confederate commissioners, did block them from proceeding farther through Union lines, Grant met with two of them and then indirectly advised Lincoln that his approach might be a mistake. Grant wrote Stanton, "I am convinced, upon conversation with Messrs [Alexander H.] Stevens [sic] and [Robert M.T.] Hunter [two of the Confederate commissioners] that their intentions are good and their desire sincere to restore peace and union.... I fear now their going back without any expression from anyone in authority will have a bad influence.... I am sorry however that Mr. Lincoln cannot have an interview with the two named in this despatch [sic] if not all three now within our lines." Here was Grant providing political advice to Lincoln—advice that Lincoln later told Congress changed his purpose. Lincoln told Grant to tell the commissioners he would meet them and advised Secretary Seward, that, "[i]nduced by a despatch [sic] from Genl Grant," he would meet Seward at Fortress Monroe. The president then journeyed to Hampton Roads and joined Seward for four hours of discussions with the three Confederate officials on February 3. The Hampton Roads Peace Conference terminated without any agreement because of the intractable position of the two sides on the dual issues of union and slavery. Lincoln, negotiating from a position of strength, refused to even consider any armistice short of an end to the war on Union terms.[65]

Thus, Grant had entered the political arena by undertaking discussions with the Confederate commissioners and then advising Lincoln to change his mind and meet with them because of the negative political impact of not doing so. When asked by the House of Representatives for a full report on the peace conference, Lincoln graciously asked Grant for permission to release a copy of his February 1 dispatch advising against a rejection of the commissioners. The president concluded, "I think the despatch [sic] does you credit while I do not see that it can embarrass you. May I use it?" Grant immediately gave his permission "if you desire to do so" and explained that the wire "was marked 'confidential' in contra distinction to official dispatches but not to prevent such use being made of it as you or the Secretary of War might think proper." The president included that wire in an extensive February 10 report to the House on the Hampton Roads Conference.[66]

Lincoln took the precaution of advising Grant, "Let nothing which is transpiring, change, hinder, or delay your Military movements, or plans." Just to be sure, Lincoln wrote and Stanton signed a telegram to Grant reiterating that concept: "The President desires me to repeat that nothing transpired, or transpiring with the three gentlemen from Richmond, is to cause any change[,] hindrance or delay, of your military plans or operations."[67]

Lincoln and Stanton took other steps to ensure that Grant was in control of matters of military consequence. On February 7, Grant wired Stanton that a trader named Laws was at City Point with a load of coffee and sugar plus a Treasury Department permit to trade it for ten thousand bales of cotton. Grant opined, "I have positively refused to adopt this mode of feeding the Southern army unless it is the direct order of the President." Stanton immediately replied,

> The President directs that you will regard all trade permits, licenses, or privileges of every kind, by whomsoever signed…as subject to your authority and approval as commander of the U.S. forces in the field, and such permits as you deem prejudicial to the military service by feeding or supporting the rebel armies…you may disregard and annul, and if necessary to the public safety seize the property of the traders. In short, the President orders that you "as being responsible for military results, must be allowed to be judge and master on the subject of trade with the enemy."

Sometime later the trader appealed to the president, who drafted a meeting summary to Grant: "To-night Mr. Laws calls on me, and I have told him, and now tell you that the matter, as to his passing the lines is under your control absolutely; and that he can have any relaxation you choose to give him & none other."[68] Lincoln similarly deferred to Grant on a whiskey-trading issue even when the Illinois governor supported the trading mission.[69] The next month Lincoln continued deferring to Grant on possible trading-with-the-enemy activities even when close associates of Lincoln were involved and appealed personally to the president. Grant exercised authority from the president to suspend much of the trading otherwise authorized under Treasury permits.[70]

At about the same time, the growing closeness of Lincoln and Grant was demonstrated by their sensitive handling of a personal matter dear to the president. On January 19, 1865, he wrote to Grant about his son Robert:

> Please read and answer this letter as though I was not President, but only a friend. My son, now in his twenty second year, having graduated at Harvard, wishes to see something of the war before it ends. I do not wish to put him in the ranks, nor yet to give him a commission, to which those who already have served long, are better entitled, and better qualified to hold. Could he, without embarrassment to you, or detriment to the service, go into your Military family with some nominal rank, I, and not the public, furnishing his necessary means? If no, say so without the least hesitation, because I am as anxious, and as deeply interested, that you shall not be encumbered as you can be yourself. Yours truly A. Lincoln

Two days later Grant responded, "... I will be most happy to have him in my Military family in the manner you propose...." Grant suggested that Robert be appointed a captain and explained why. As a result of Lincoln's diplomatic request and Grant's accommodating response,

Robert was appointed a captain and assistant adjutant general of volunteers on Grant's staff on February 11 and served in that capacity until his June 10 resignation.[71]

While Lincoln and Grant were exchanging wires about Robert Lincoln's February 22 arrival at Grant's headquarters, the president also asked for Grant's support ("Can not you help me out with it?") of a military prisoner exchange sought by powerhouse editor Horace Greeley. Greeley wanted the exchange to the Confederacy of Brigadier General Roger A. Pryor, whom Grant had wanted held. Lincoln asked for Grant's help and added, "I can conceive that there may be a difference to you in days; and I can keep him a few days to accommodate on that point." Lincoln's focus on the timing of the exchange apparently had been accurate because Grant responded, "Send Pryor on here and we will exchange him; He can do us no harm now."[72] This is yet another example of how the two leaders were working together hand in glove.

Although Lincoln trusted Grant's military judgment, he was not above questioning the general on military matters. Thus, on February 25, he wired Grant about a dispatch from Sheridan to Grant in which Sheridan had said, "will be off on Monday.... The cavalry officers say the cavalry never was in such good condition. I will leave behind about 2,000 men, which will increase to 3,000 in a short time." Lincoln focused on the words "will leave behind about 2,000 men" and expressed his and Stanton's "considerable anxiety." He continued, "Have you well considered whether you do not again leave open the Shenandoah-valley entrance to Maryland and Pennsylvania?—or, at least, to the B & O. Railroad?" Grant responded that the soon-to-be-3,000 cavalry were in addition to all of Sheridan's infantry and that Union movement toward the enemy would protect the railroad and the two named states. That same day Sheridan advised Stanton that he was leaving 12,000 to 14,000 men on the B&O in addition to troops in Harpers Ferry and the Shenandoah Valley. The next day a relieved Lincoln backed off and advised Grant: "Subsequent reflection, conference with Gen. Halleck, your despatch [sic], and one from Gen. Sheridan, have relieved my anxiety; and so I beg that you will dismiss any concern you may have on my account, in the matter of my last despatch [sic]."[73]

On military administrative matters, Lincoln was fully cooperative. For example, he delayed for three months submitting the annual report of the secretary of war to Congress so that Grant would have time to finish his own report for inclusion.[74]

Into the last full month of the war, Lincoln continued to rely upon Grant for news from the Richmond newspapers. In early March, when no reports were received for two straight days, Lincoln asked Grant about the omission: "Did you not receive [the papers]? If not, does it indicate anything?" Grant responded that the papers were being received daily but "[n]o bulletins were sent Tuesday or Wednesday because there was not an item of either good or bad news in them." To provide some substance, he added, "There is every indication that Genl Sherman is perfectly safe. I am looking every day for direct news from him." Grant was aware of Lincoln's concern about the out-of-contact Sherman, who was campaigning northward through the Carolinas. Only a day after Grant's wire, Lincoln gave the following remarks in response to an inauguration-eve serenade: "Sherman went in at Atlanta and came out right. He has gone in again at Savannah, and I propose three cheers for his coming out gloriously."[75]

On that same day before his second inauguration, Lincoln unsurprisingly demonstrated that he continued to be in full control of diplomacy involving the Confederacy. Grant had forwarded to Stanton a March 2 letter to Grant from Lee concerning the possibility of a military convention:

> Lieut Genl Longstreet has informed me that in a recent conversation between himself and Maj Genl Ord as to the possibility of arriving at a satisfactory adjustment of the present unhappy difficulties, by means of a military convention. Genl Ord stated that if I desired to have an interview with you on the subject you would not decline, provided I had authority to act. Sincerely desiring to leave nothing untried which may put an end to the calamities of war, I propose to meet you at such convenient time and place as you may designate with the hope that upon an interchange of views it may be found

practicable to submit the subjects of controversy between belligerents to a convention of the kind mentioned. In such event I am authorized to do whatever the result of the proposed interview may render necessary or advisable.[76]

Lincoln wasted no time in squelching Lee's proposal. He wrote the body of a telegram sent from Stanton to Grant:

The President directs me to say to you that he wishes you to have no conference with General Lee unless it be for the capitulation of Gen. Lee's army, or on some minor, and purely, military matter. He instructs me to say that you are not to decide, discuss, or confer upon any political question. Such questions the President holds in his own hands; and will submit them to no military conferences or conventions. Meantime you are to press to the utmost, your military advantages.[77]

In no uncertain terms, Lincoln, with some prodding from Stanton at a cabinet meeting, recognized a dichotomy between military and political matters, particularly in a diplomatic context, and asserted his control over the latter.[78] His actions also may have been a measure of how deep the wounds were in Lincoln's mind from his experiences with McClellan.

The next day Lincoln began his second term with a brief but eloquent inaugural address. He paid tribute to the military success the last year had brought: "The progress of our arms, upon which all else chiefly depends, is as well known to the public as myself; and it is, I trust, reasonably satisfactory and encouraging to all. With high hope for the future, no prediction in regard to it is ventured." After a short discourse on the intimate connection between slavery and the war, the president memorably concluded, "With malice toward none; with charity for all; with firmness in the right, as God gives us to see the right, let us strive on to finish the work we are in; to bind up the nation's wounds; to care for him who shall have borne the battle, and for his widow, and his orphan—to do all which may achieve and cherish a just, and a lasting peace, among ourselves, and with all nations."[79]

A few days later Lincoln bolstered their friendly relations by sending Grant the gold medal Congress had ordered struck and presented to him in gratitude for his services. The president's message to Grant concluded, "Please accept, for yourself and all under your command, the renewed expression of my gratitude for your and their arduous and well-performed public service."[80]

Lincoln's liberality in releasing Rebel soldiers who took a loyalty oath (similar to his sympathetic treatment of court-martialed soldiers sentenced to death)[81] caused anguish to Grant. On March 8 the general complained to Stanton about "rebel prisoners...allowed to take the oath of allegiance and go free." He said the practice was wrong and added, "No one should be liberated on taking the oath...who has been captured while bearing arms against us, except where persons of known loyalty vouch for them." Grant argued that those willing to take such an oath were the best candidates for prisoner exchanges, not simple release.

The next day Lincoln took the blame for such releases but said he only did it upon receiving assurances from primarily border state congressmen that it was safe to release the particular individuals. He admitted to Grant, "The number I have discharged has been rather larger than I liked"—perhaps fifty a day recently and perhaps a thousand Missourians and Kentuckians in 1864. Lincoln concluded, "...I believe what I have done in this way has done good rather than harm." Grant immediately replied that he was satisfied that oath-takers were not automatically being released but rather required special permission.[82] Grant had made his point but must have realized the president would continue his liberal releases in hopes of facilitating post-war reconstruction in the border states.

Perhaps to address Grant's manpower concerns and certainly to implement a new law, the president shortly thereafter issued a proclamation pardoning deserters who returned to service with their assigned units by May 10, 1865, and served their original enlistment periods and additional time equal to that lost by desertion.[83] Manpower issues dominated Lincoln's March 17 speech to an Indiana regiment. The president focused on a recent, desperate and unsuccessful Confederate attempt to arm some of their slaves. Lincoln mocked the effort and asserted that it showed the

Rebels were drawing "upon their last branch of resources." He concluded, "I am glad to see the end so near at hand."[84]

LINCOLN COMES TO GRANT'S HEADQUARTERS

As Grant sensed the war was reaching its climax, he invited the president to come to his front. On the morning of March 20, the general wired the president, "Can you not visit City Point for a day or two? I would like very much to see you and I think the rest would do you good." That same day, an eager Lincoln responded, "Your kind invitation received. Had already thought of going immediately after the next rain. Will go sooner if any reason for it. Mrs. L. and a few others will probably accompany me. Will notify you of exact time, once it shall be fixed upon." On March 21 Lincoln advised his son Robert that he expected to leave for City Point at 1 p.m. on March 23; two days later he sent similar notice to Grant as he was departing Washington. By the next day, March 24, Lincoln, his wife, son Tad, a bodyguard, and military escort had reached City Point.[85]

Lincoln wanted to be close to Grant as his army closed in on Lee. There, at the juncture of the Appomattox and James rivers, where Grant had established a virtual city to support his army, Lincoln huddled with Grant, Sherman, and Porter on March 27 or 28, or possibly both, to discuss how to end the war and how to reunite the country. An uninvited Sherman, unaware of Lincoln's visit, had decided on his own to come from North Carolina to visit Grant. The four men met on board the president's vessel, the *River Queen*, for significant discussions. Because of Lincoln's concerns about Sherman being absent from his command, Sherman left by 4 p.m. on March 28.[86]

Lincoln expressed his fears that both Lee and Johnston (now commanding the Rebels in North Carolina) would slip away to continue the war indefinitely—possibly using guerilla warfare. Grant and Sherman shared his concerns. Grant later described this time as "the most anxious of my experience." He wrote, "I was afraid, every morning, that I would awake from my sleep to hear that Lee had gone...and the war might be prolonged another year."[87] Lincoln inquired whether more bloodshed was going to be necessary; his generals responded that the ever-aggressive Lee was likely to bring on at least one more desperate and bloody battle. A worried Lincoln, desperate to end the fighting and begin reconciliation, provided them with guidance (sometimes called the *River Queen* Doctrine): "... get the deluded men of the rebel armies disarmed and back to their homes.... Let them once surrender and reach their homes, [and] they won't take up arms again.... Let them all go, officers and all; I want submission and no more bloodshed.... I want no one punished; treat them liberally all around. We want those people to return to their allegiance to the Union and submit to the laws."[88]

The Lincolns had arrived at City Point just in time to be near a Confederate attack. In a desperate attempt to force Grant to shorten his lines and perhaps aid an escape of Lee's army to North Carolina, Lee launched a March 25 pre-dawn assault from his Petersburg lines on Fort Stedman. Although initially successful in capturing that fort (perhaps because the Union defenders thought the attackers were the usual deserters coming over to their lines), the Confederate attackers were driven back or surrounded by an immediate counterattack and deadly crossfire from every direction—particularly from the well-positioned nearby forts. Some survivors retreated without 4,000 of their comrades who were killed, wounded, or captured. Grant's army had lost a few more than a thousand men. That was to be Lee's last offensive.[89]

An unexcited Lincoln offhandedly advised Stanton that morning, "Robert just now tells me there was a little rumpus up the line this morning, ending about where it began." Later the president told Stanton he was five miles from the action and had seen what appeared to be the reported 1,600 Rebel prisoners. In fact, the president had visited the battlefield, seen the bodies of slain men and horses, and commented that he "had seen of the horrors of war" and hoped this battle "was the beginning of the end."[90] The next day Lieutenant Colonel Elisha Hunt Rhodes wrote a fuller account:

> We had a very exciting day yesterday. At daylight the Rebels charged upon Fort Stedman on the 9th Corps front and got possession. Our division was ordered to march to the relief

of the 9th Corps. The distance was about five miles, and we
made it at a double quick most of the time and arrived in
season to see a Division commanded by [Brigadier] Gen. John
[F.] Hartranft of Penn. recapture the fort with many prisoners.
We got a good shelling as we passed the Rebel forts and lost
two horses from our division.[91]

The failure of Lee's desperate assault on Fort Stedman affected both Lee
and Grant. Lee finally argued to Davis that his army should attempt to
join with Johnston to defeat Sherman and then turn on Grant. On the
other side of the lines, Grant sensed an enhanced opportunity to end the
stalemate. On the 24th, he had issued orders to Meade for a movement
by Ord and Sheridan that was to begin on the 29th with Ord bringing
three divisions from the far right to the far left of Grant's lines. Grant said
that the movement was "for the double purpose of turning the enemy
out of his present position around Petersburg, and to insure the success
of the Cavalry under general Sheridan…in its efforts to reach and destroy
the South Side and Danville rail-road[s]." Lee's losses at Fort Stedman
improved the prospects for success on the Union far left.[92]

Using Ord's men to fill the lines vacated by the Second Corps, Grant
completed the shift of manpower to create a mobile force of Major General Andrew A. Humphreys' Second and Warren's Fifth infantry corps
plus Sheridan's 9,000-man cavalry corps. With that force, Grant intended
to finally get around the Confederate right flank and cut off the Southside
and Danville railroads, the last ones supplying, respectively, Petersburg
and Richmond. The Union troops started moving west on the 27th, and
Lee sent Major General Fitzhugh Lee's cavalry and Major General George
E. Pickett with five brigades of infantry to oppose them. By moving at
least 5,500 cavalry and 5,000 infantry southwest out of the Petersburg
fortifications, Lee was fulfilling one of Grant's goals: drawing the Confederates into a fight with few, if any, fortifications.[93]

On March 29 Elisha Hunt Rhodes expressed anticipation of a movement and confidence in his commanders: "Still on picket and very quiet,
although every man is on the alert. Something is about to happen. We
are all ready to move, and if I did not know our leaders I should feel that

we were in trouble and about to retreat. But I feel sure that the enemy are about to leave Petersburg, and we are held in readiness to pursue them."[94] That day Grant left Lincoln at City Point and proceeded west to be near the fighting he was initiating. The president's last words to Grant and his departing party were: "Good-bye, gentlemen. God bless you all! Remember, your success is my success."[95]

The president stayed behind at City Point to await the results of Grant's offensive. He was there with Tad—but not Mary. She had been sent back to Washington after throwing a fit and delivering an angry tirade when the young wife of one of Grant's generals accompanied the president on a review of troops. Unfortunately, the insecure and jealous Mary Todd Lincoln often was a burden to the president; in contrast, the secure and loving Julia Dent Grant was a comfort to the general, who seemed to need her presence in order to perform at his best. In any event, Lincoln kept his absent wife updated by telegraph on the exciting events as they unfolded.[96]

Also on March 29 two of Warren's Fifth Corps divisions moved into positions on the key Boydton Plank Road as a result of their success at the Battle of Lewis's Farm. Encouraged by this development, Grant told Sheridan to forget a railroad raid and instead work with the Fifth Corps to turn the Confederate flank. When Sheridan asked instead for the Sixth Corps, with which he had worked in the Shenandoah Valley, Grant pointed to the Fifth Corps' position closer to Sheridan and declined his request. Four times that day Grant wired Lincoln about his situation and military developments. The final one answered Lincoln's question about the location of the Rebel attack.[97]

The Fifth Corps stayed in place on March 30 because of heavy rain, the issuance of three days' rations, and confusion about orders. That evening Lincoln told Stanton, "I begin to feel that I ought to be at home, and yet I dislike to leave without seeing nearer to the end of General Grant's present movement. He has now been out since yesterday morning, and although he has not been diverted from his programme, no considerable effect has yet been produced, so far as we know here."[98] The president's impression was accurate, and the situation worsened at first the next day.

On March 31, at White Oak Road (Gravelly Run or Hatcher's Run), Warren allowed two of his four divisions to be separately attacked and routed before he finally drove back Confederate Major General Bushrod R. Johnson's infantry division across White Oak Road. The action, however, did prevent Johnson from reinforcing Pickett, who faced Sheridan farther west. Grant and Meade took critical note of Warren's performance and wondered why he had allowed the enemy troops to entrench after their retreat.[99]

That day Grant oversaw the combat and kept the nearby president advised of developments. First, at midday he wired him that the enemy had driven back Warren's left to Boydton Plank Road, a Union counter-attack was about to begin, he hoped to more than recover the lost ground, and "heavy Rain & horrid roads have prevented the Execution of my designs or attempting them up to this time...." Late that day Grant was able to raise the president's spirits by reporting, "Our troops...turned & drove the Enemy in turn & took the White Oak Road which we now have. This gives us the ground occupied by the Enemy this morning. I will send you a rebel flag captured by our troops in driving the Enemy back." Lincoln reiterated Grant's messages in a telegram he sent to Stanton that evening.[100]

DINWIDDIE COURT HOUSE AND FIVE FORKS

To the west of the Fifth Corps on that same day, Pickett and Fitzhugh Lee hit Sheridan's strung-out 9,500 troopers hard in the Battle of Dinwiddie Court House[101] and forced them back until Sheridan actively oversaw a last-ditch stand to avoid collapse. Although he had been stymied by Pickett from reaching Five Forks, Sheridan saw an opportunity and that evening told one of Grant's aides, "[Pickett's] force is in more danger than I am in—if I am cut off from the Army of the Potomac, it is cut off from Lee's army, and not a man in it should ever be allowed to get back to Lee."[102]

Nearby, Colonel Rhodes heard the fighting and wrote, "The fight has raged all day on the 2nd Corps front to our left, and we have been under arms waiting for something to turn up. It means fight within a few hours, and may God give us a victory. Grant knows what he is doing and I am willing to trust him to manage Army affairs."[103] Rhodes would not be disappointed.

On the evening of March 31 Grant agreed with Sheridan's assessment of Pickett's isolation and vulnerability. Therefore, Grant, through Meade, ordered Warren to withdraw a division and send it to reinforce Sheridan. Meade at first sent only a brigade, but within hours Grant accepted a Meade recommendation and ordered Warren to move his entire corps west to strike Pickett. Due to delayed and confused orders and the prior destruction of a key bridge, Warren's Corps arrived on the morning of April 1 well after Sheridan expected them. As soon as he was ordered to reinforce Sheridan, Warren had told Meade that he would have to build a replacement bridge over the swollen Gravelly Run; that forty-foot bridge was completed at 2 a.m. the next day. Sheridan, unaware of Warren's difficulties, wanted to attack immediately but had to delay until the arrival of all Warren's troops. Warren inexplicably and foolishly waited three hours before personally reporting to Sheridan at 11 a.m., and Sheridan's anger at Warren increased as the day progressed.[104]

During the night, Pickett had learned of the approach of Warren's infantry, which threatened to isolate him, and withdrew from Dinwiddie Court House back to a more secure line at Five Forks. During that movement, Pickett received a forceful and unfriendly message from Robert E. Lee: "Hold Five Forks at all hazards. Protect road to Ford's Depot and prevent Union forces from striking the Southside Railroad. Regret exceedingly your forced withdrawal, and your inability to hold the advantage you gained."[105] Lee correctly understood the value of Five Forks in protecting the Southside Railroad, but he probably failed to appreciate the difficult situation faced by Pickett with only about 10,000 soldiers defending a mile and three-quarter line and opposed by an increasingly superior adversary.[106]

At 4 p.m., the Battle of Five Forks finally got under way. Sheridan's 9,000 cavalry, generally dismounted, manned the bulk of the attacking Union line and took the brunt of the Rebel defenders' fire. To Sheridan's right, Warren's 12,000 troops were to come in on the left flank of Pickett's infantry. Because of an erroneous map and faulty reconnaissance,

Warren's troops were misaligned and got into the fight only after changing the direction of their march. Warren desperately directed his divisions
toward the fighting and even chased down one that had marched well
past the battle. Brigadier General Joshua Chamberlain worked with
Sheridan on the front lines to throw all available troops into the struggle
as Pickett's leaderless troops bravely held on but finally broke and ran.
One reason they broke is that the bulk of Warren's troops finally appeared
on their flank and rear. Occupied at a nearby shad bake, Pickett and
Fitzhugh Lee learned of the battle from couriers. Pickett got through to
Five Forks to participate in the rout while Lee was trapped behind Hatch-
er's Run with Rosser's cavalry.[107]

Throughout the day on April 1, Grant kept Lincoln posted on the
fast-moving developments. By 9:15 a.m. Lincoln was reading that Warren
had been sent to support Sheridan. Grant summarized the early morning
situation: "I had much hopes of destroying the force detached by the
Enemy so far to our rear I have not yet heard the result but I know that
Sheridan took the offensive this A.M." The latter was at best an overstate-
ment of Sheridan's morning situation because by late morning Grant had
"nothing special to report" and bemoaned the quicksand road conditions
that had required fifty-six hours to move six hundred teams of horses a
mere five miles with twelve hundred men assisting. In mid-afternoon
Grant passed to Lincoln a dispatch from Lieutenant Colonel Horace
Porter indicating that Sheridan had achieved some initial success at Five
Forks and that Warren's entire corps was about to enter the fray. Lincoln
thanked Grant for the updates and forwarded the information to Seward
and Stanton.[108]

After the prior night's delayed march by Warren's Fifth Corps,
although primarily the fault of Meade and a missing bridge, Grant had
authorized Sheridan to relieve Warren of command. After Warren's
"tardy" arrival, his misdirected attack, and his absence from the front
lines while he retrieved his errant divisions, Sheridan used that authority.
When Warren's chief of staff reported to Sheridan late in the battle,
Sheridan told him, "By God, sir, tell General Warren he wasn't in the
fight." When a subordinate suggested that he rethink his decision,

Sheridan roared, "Reconsider, hell! I don't reconsider my decisions. Obey the order!" At 7 p.m. a messenger brought Warren written orders replacing him as corps commander with Brigadier General Charles Griffin, who was promptly promoted to major general.[109]

With the sacking of Warren, Grant had completed a clean sweep of all his senior commanders except Meade as he entered the final phase of the war. A. A. Humphreys had succeeded the ailing Hancock as Second Corps commander; Wright had replaced the dead John Sedgwick (victim of a Rebel sharpshooter) at the Sixth Corps; John G. Parke had replaced Burnside, who had long commanded the Ninth Corps; John Gibbon had replaced Baldy Smith at the 24th Corps, and Ord had replaced the incompetent Butler as Commander of the Army of the James.[110] All involved were major generals. The new leadership guaranteed there would be no hesitation in the war's last days.

Sheridan's cavalry and Warren's infantry had achieved a great victory at Five Forks, devastated Pickett's command, killed or wounded more than five hundred, taken between 2,000 and 2,500 prisoners, turned Lee's right flank, and opened the way to the Southside Railroad. Remnants of Pickett's five brigades were in full retreat, and Grant ordered artillery fire all along the line in anticipation of a full-scale attack the next day. After receiving the news of the Sheridan/Warren victory from Porter, Grant quietly retired to his tent, drafted orders, and then announced to the celebrating officers, "I have ordered a general assault along the lines."[111]

From his position nearer the front, Grant ensured that Lincoln, back at City Point, was kept abreast of developments. At 9:30 p.m. on April 1 he wired Colonel Theodore S. Bowers at City Point that Sheridan had "carried everything before him" and that one of his officers "reports that he has captured three brigades of infantry and a train of wagons and is now pushing up his success." Grant concluded, "I have ordered everything else to advance and prevent a concentration of the enemy against Sheridan. Several batteries were captured. The prisoners captured will amount to several thousand."[112] Lincoln relayed all this information to his wife and Stanton in a telegram at 7:45 on the morning of April 2.[113]

BREAKTHROUGH AT PETERSBURG

April 2 was a critical day in the history and ultimate demise of the Army of Northern Virginia. Following up on the victory at Five Forks the preceding day, Union troops captured Sutherland Station on the Southside Railroad, four miles east of Five Forks, and thereby severed Lee's lifeline. More significantly, Union forces executed Grant's order for an all-out assault on the Confederate lines at Petersburg, which he assumed would be weakened by Lee's manpower shifts to the west. Grant also attacked to preclude any possible counterattack on Five Forks by the ever-aggressive Lee.[114]

Wright's Sixth Corps exploited a weakness where a creek breached the Confederate line, used a 14,000-man wedge to attack at first light (about 4:40 a.m.) along a one-mile front, and by 5:15 a.m. had achieved a complete breakthrough. Alongside Wright, Ord's and Humphreys's Corps were likewise successful in overrunning the Confederate lines in their fronts. At midday, Grant's forces assaulted two Confederate forts at Petersburg; they captured one, and the defenders of the other then fled. Lee sent President Davis a message, saying "I think it is absolutely necessary that we should abandon our position to-night...." It was delivered to Davis as he attended Sunday services in Richmond. Davis immediately began preparations for the Confederate Government and treasury to leave Richmond by rail.[115]

Grant's well-conceived assault broke Lee's line, killed Lieutenant General A. P. Hill, compelled the evacuation of Petersburg and Richmond, and sent Lee's army in a westward retreat. He accomplished these tasks with fewer casualties than he inflicted on the Rebels. While Grant may have suffered casualties of about 4,000, Lee's army lost between 5,000 and 5,500—about ten percent of Lee's remaining force. As A. Wilson Greene concluded, "The engagements of April 2 doomed the Confederate war effort in Virginia."[116]

Grant continued to keep the president apprised of the swiftly moving developments. At 8:25 a.m. he wired Assistant Adjutant General Theodore S. Bowers that Wright, Humphreys, and Ord had all broken through the Rebel lines, Ord's men were tearing up the Southside Railroad, and

Sheridan was closing in on Petersburg from the west. A little over two hours later, Grant reported advances and numerous gun, fort, and prisoner captures by the Sixth, Second, and Twenty-fourth corps. Again, Lincoln shortly thereafter reiterated all that information to Stanton in two separate telegrams.[117]

Late in the afternoon, Grant again reported to Bowers on his army's sweeping success. He stated that his men were in a continuous line that would soon have both ends anchored on the Appomattox River above and below Petersburg and estimated the capture of 12,000 men and fifty artillery pieces. He closed with an invitation to Lincoln: "I think the President might come out and pay us a visit to-morrow." Lincoln, who passed Grant's report on to Stanton, immediately accepted Grant's invitation in a telegram filled with praise: "Allow me to tender to you, and all with you, the nations [*sic*] grateful thanks for this additional, and magnificent success. At your kind suggestion, I think I will visit you to-morrow."[118]

That same evening Lincoln advised Mary of Grant's success, the visit invitation and acceptance, and the good health of Tad and himself.[119] The next morning (April 3) Grant sent a wire advising that Petersburg had been evacuated and another one stating, "Say to the President that an officer and escort will attend him, but as to myself I start toward the Danville road with the army. I want to cut off as much of Lee's army as possible."[120]

Early that morning Lincoln advised Stanton that Grant had reported Petersburg evacuated and Richmond likely so. He added that Grant was pushing forward to cut off Lee's retreat and that he (Lincoln) would "start to him in a few minutes." The last few words alarmed Stanton, who immediately responded, "I congratulate you and the nation on the glorious news in your telegram just recd. Allow me respectfully to ask you to consider whether you ought to expose the nation to the consequence of any disaster to yourself in the pursuit of a treacherous and dangerous enemy like the rebel army. If it was a question concerning yourself only I should not presume to say a word. Commanding Generals are in the line of their duty in running such risks. But is the political head of a nation in the same condition [?]"[121]

Lincoln responded in a manner that probably did not reassure Stanton: "Thanks for your caution; but I have already been to Petersburg, staid [sic] with Gen. Grant an hour & a half and returned here. It is certain now that Richmond is in our hands, and I think I will go there to-morrow. I will take care of myself."[122] At Petersburg, the president had met Grant in a deserted house, shook his hand, and said, "Do you, General, know that I have had a sort of sneaking idea for some days that you intended to do something like this?" When the president inquired about Sherman's possible role, his fellow Westerner Grant, perhaps surprisingly to Lincoln, explained that he wanted the Eastern army alone to "vanquish their old enemy" without handing the opportunity to politicians to take away any credit from them. In his memoirs, Grant said, "Mr. Lincoln said he saw that now, but had never thought of it before, because his anxiety was so great that he did not care where the aid came from so the work was done."[123]

Before departing for Richmond on April 4, Lincoln advised Stanton of good news he was receiving from Major General Godfrey Weitzel in Richmond and Grant at "Southerland Station," ten miles west of Petersburg. Lincoln quoted a wire from Grant indicating that Sheridan and others had picked up 1,500 to 1,800 prisoners and stating, "The majority of the arms that were left in the hands of the remnant of Lee's army are now scattered between Richmond and where his troops are. The country is also full of stragglers, the line of retreat marked with artillery, ammunition, burned or charred wagons, caissons, ambulances, &c."[124]

Lincoln then proceeded on his dangerous April 4 and 5 visits to the smoldering ruins of Richmond, where he was greeted as a savior by the black population. Most whites watched him from behind their curtains. While walking the streets, the president told the local Union commander, General Weitzel, "If I were in your place, I'd let 'em up easy, let 'em up easy."

Some whites, as represented by Judge John A. Campbell (purporting to speak for the state legislature), were anxious to bring the fighting to a close. The judge met with Lincoln, who then provided him with a written statement containing three conditions for peace: restoration of Union authority everywhere, the end of slavery, and "no cessation of hostilities short of an end of the war, and the disbanding of all force hostile to the government."[125] The president later sent a letter to General Weitzel directing him to allow and protect a meeting of the members of the Virginia legislature for the purpose of withdrawing Virginia troops from combat.[126] The legislators never met before Grant's capture of Virginia's troops, and thus Lincoln ultimately withdrew and countermanded his earlier directions to Weitzel.[127]

While delicately trying to encourage peace, Lincoln advised Grant of the ongoing discussions with Campbell to ensure the two of them were not working at cross-purposes. He told Grant that the Virginia legislature might convene to withdraw its troops and that he had authorized Weitzel to allow them to meet so long as they attempted nothing hostile to the U.S. To clarify the impact of these actions and keep their political and military functions separate, the president concluded:

> I do not think it very probable that anything will come of this; but I have thought best to notify you, so that if you should see signs, you may understand them. From your recent despatches [sic] it seems that you are pretty effectually withdrawing the Virginia troops from opposition to the government. Nothing I have done, or probably shall do, is to delay, hinder, or interfere with you in your work.[128]

GRANT PURSUES LEE TO APPOMATTOX

Before abandoning Richmond, Lee ordered the burning of large quantities of Confederate supplies in the city. The resulting fires burned much of Richmond. As Grant's troops occupied the city on April 3, Lee's army fled westward. The Appomattox Campaign had begun.[129]

The Rebel troops generally followed the Appomattox River on their ninety-mile retreat, which ended at Appomattox Court House. Although trying to hasten their retreat, the Rebels were slowed by having to cross and re-cross the river and its tributary creeks. Their flight was accompanied by Union cavalry and infantry moving on their left flank in order to keep them from moving toward North Carolina and Johnston—as well as by Union forces following directly behind them.

Lee's plan was to have his forces head for Amelia Court House on the Richmond and Danville (R&D) Railroad, where Lee later claimed rations and supplies were supposed to be waiting. None were there, however, when the Confederates arrived. Expecting boxcars of rations at Amelia Court House, Lee and his soldiers instead found boxcars filled with ammunition and artillery supplies. It is quite possible that Lee's staff, specifically Colonel Walter Taylor, had failed to issue an order for rations and needed supplies in the haste of evacuating Richmond (and Taylor's haste to get to his evening wedding on April 2). More significantly, Lee had to wait an extra day at Amelia Court House for Ewell's column, which was delayed by a missing pontoon bridge in crossing the Appomattox River.[130]

Having consumed most of the one-day rations with which they had departed Richmond, Lee and his weakening army moved farther west in search of food. Lee's predicament was worsened by the fact that some of Grant's cavalry had already gotten ahead of his troops and were eight miles southwest at Jetersville astride the R&D. Even farther southwest, by the morning of April 6, Ord's Army of the James was at Burke (Burkeville Junction), where the R&D joined the Southside Railroad.[131]

Meanwhile, Sheridan at Jetersville had wired Grant to join him there. With a few staff and a cavalry escort of only fourteen, Grant hastily rode sixteen miles on unsecured Virginia back-roads to get near the scene of the action. Arriving at Jetersville, he sensed victory as he learned that Sheridan was closing in on Lee with his cavalry and three corps of infantry. A still-concerned Grant expressed his worries about Lee's next course of action: "Lee's surely in a bad fix. But if I were in his place, I think I could get away with part of the army. I suppose Lee will." Early on April 6 Grant sent Sheridan on a northwest sweep to get in front of Lee and ordered another infantry corps to press the rear of Lee's army. The trap was being set.[132]

With the R&D forcefully blocked, Lee had no choice but to leave the southwesterly R&D and head due west. Hoping to find supplies from Lynchburg on the Southside Railroad northwest of Burke, Lee ordered a forced march westward toward Farmville. But disaster befell his army on April 6 when Anderson's and Early's divisions fell behind and were trapped at Sayler's (Sailor's) Creek by Sheridan's cavalry and the Second and Sixth Union corps. Five hours of fierce fighting ensued, and the Rebels were overwhelmed. Afterward, overlooking the battlefield, Lee exclaimed, "My God, has the army dissolved?" He did lose more than a quarter of it that day. The Confederates lost most of their wagon train, had about 2,000 killed or wounded, and had another 7,000 (including at least nine generals) taken prisoner—at a cost to Grant of only 1,200 casualties.[133]

That same day (April 6) Lee's survivors at last found rations in railcars on the Southside Railroad at Farmville. They had only partially removed the rations when the arrival of trailing Federal soldiers ended that operation. The railcars were moved west toward Appomattox Station, and Lee's remaining forces crossed the Appomattox River for the last time.[134]

Lee, however, now found his army trapped between the Appomattox and James rivers. His soldiers headed west once again—this time toward a place called Appomattox Court House. But Phil Sheridan's cavalry was well ahead of them. He had captured the trainloads of Rebel rations at Appomattox Station on the Southside Railroad and blocked any farther advance by Lee's army.

Sheridan wired news of his success to Grant. He claimed the capture of six Rebel generals and several thousand prisoners. He concluded, "If the thing is pressed I think Lee will surrender." From Burkeville Station, Grant at 11:45 p.m. forwarded Sheridan's telegram to Lincoln. The next morning Lincoln sent it to Stanton. A short while later Lincoln sent Stanton copies of positive battle reports from Generals Meade, Humphreys, and Wright.[135]

At 11 a.m. on April 7, the president, just before departing for Washington, sent Grant a succinct wire in which he repeated Sheridan's concluding remark and urged Grant to bring the fighting to a close: "Gen. Sheridan says 'If the thing is pressed I think that Lee will surrender.' Let the thing be pressed."[136] In two succinct sentences, Lincoln told Grant to end the war.

Grant recognized that the human chess-match was nearly over and on the afternoon of April 7 made his first overture to Lee:

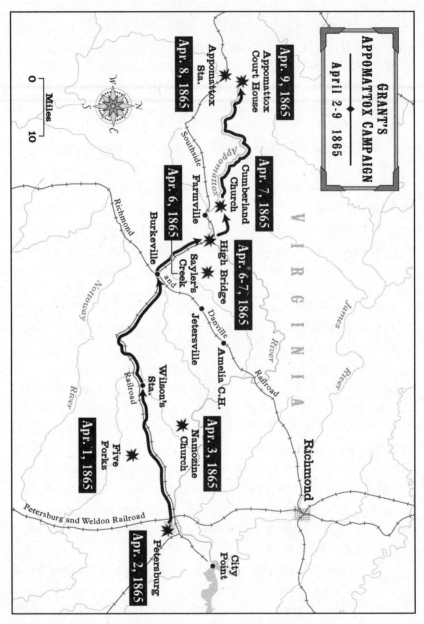

Map by David Deis, Dreamline Cartography, Northridge, California

General,

The result of the last week must convince you of the hopelessness of further resistance on the part of the Army of Northern Va. in this struggle. I feel that it is so and regard it as my duty to shift from myself, the responsibility of any further effusion of blood by asking of you the surrender of that portion of the C. S. Army known as the Army of Northern Va.[137]

That night, his Army's third consecutive night of marching, Lee responded with an inquiry about the terms Grant would allow:

General, I have recd your note of this date. Though not entertaining the opinion you express of the hopelessness of further resistance on the part of the Army of N. Va. I reciprocate your desire to avoid useless effusion of blood & therefore before Considering your proposition ask the terms you will offer on condition of its surrender.[138]

Lee's response was delayed by delivery difficulties and did not arrive until the morning of April 8. Grant promptly responded with a minimal requirement:

Your note of last evening, in reply to mine of same date, asking the conditions on which I will accept the surrender of the Army of N. Va. is just received. In reply I would say that peace being my great desire there is but one condition I insist upon, namely: that the men and officers surrendered shall be disqualified for taking up arms again, against the Government of the United States, until properly exchanged.

I will meet you or will designate Officers to meet any officers you may name for the same purpose, at any point agreeable to you, for the purpose of arranging definitely the terms upon which the surrender of the Army of N. Va. will be received.[139]

In a response to Grant that night, Lee expressed an unrealistic view that the end was not necessarily imminent but then reluctantly agreed to a meeting with Grant:

> General, I recd at a late hour your note of today—In mine of yesterday I did not intend to propose the Surrender of the Army of N. Va—but to ask the terms of your proposition. To be frank, I do not think the emergency has arisen to call for the Surrender of this Army; but as the restoration of peace should be the Sole object of all, I desired to know whether your proposals would lead to that end. I cannot therefore meet you with a view to Surrender the Army of N— Va— but as far as your proposal may affect the C. S. forces under my Command & tend to the restoration of peace, I should be pleased to meet you at 10 A m tomorrow on the old stage road to Richmond between the picket lines of the two armies—[140]

Although Lee may not yet have been willing to accept the inevitable, several of his officers were. They held an informal council, and one of them, Brigadier General William Nelson Pendleton, approached Longstreet about advising Lee to surrender. Refusing to do so, Longstreet responded, "If General Lee doesn't know when to surrender until I tell him, he will never know."[141]

In a nearby house, Grant, suffering from an anxiety-driven migraine headache, read Lee's response and concluded, "It looks as if Lee still means to fight."[142] The next morning, however, it became clear that the time for surrender had arrived. As Confederates attempted a massive breakout under orders from Lee and challenged Sheridan's cavalry, they clearly observed six infantry brigades of Ord's Army of the James behind the cavalry and poised to attack. The Second, Fifth, and Sixth corps all were circling Lee's beleaguered army. Escape was not possible. Grant had Lee's army bottled up.[143]

Earlier that same morning, before the final military confrontation, Grant had declined to meet Lee on Lee's terms. Instead, based on his instructions from Lincoln, Grant rejected Lee's peace discussion overture in a note he sent to Lee:

> Your note of yesterday is received. As I have no authority to treat on the subject of peace the meeting proposed for 10 a.m. to-day could lead to no good. I will state however General that I am equally anxious for peace with yourself and the whole North entertains the same feeling. The terms upon which peace can be had are well understood. By the South laying down their Arms they will hasten that most desirable event, save thousands of human lives and hundreds of Millions of property not yet destroyed.
>
> Sincerely hoping that all our difficulties may be settled without the loss of another live [*sic*] I subscribe myself...[144]

After receiving Grant's response and observing and receiving reports of his army's surrounded condition, Lee finally decided to surrender and went into the Union lines looking for Grant. As Lee went through the Union lines under a flag of truce, he belatedly remembered that the outgunned Confederates facing Ord and others ought to send out a flag of truce of their own. As Lee directed, Longstreet sent an officer with the white flag as a Federal offensive was about to start. That officer was accompanied back to the Rebel lines by a brash Union cavalry commander, Major General George A. Custer, who made a pompous demand for the Confederate army's unconditional surrender. When Custer repeated his demand to Longstreet, the First Corps commander dressed down Custer and told him he could either wait for Lee or attack. A humbled Custer returned to his lines, and all awaited developments at the highest level.[145]

When he was unable to find Grant, Lee wrote to him: "General: I received your note of this morning on the picket line, whither I had come to meet you and ascertain definitely what terms were embraced in your proposal of yesterday with reference to the surrender of this army. I now request an interview in accordance with the offer contained in your letter of yesterday, for that pu[r]pose."[146]

Their subordinate officers quickly arranged for the historic meeting of Grant and Lee in Appomattox Court House at the home of Wilmer McLean. The unfortunate McLean had moved to that hitherto peaceful town after his home had been hit by artillery during the First Battle of Bull Run (Manassas) in 1861. During the rather awkward meeting, Grant extended generous terms to Lee. He paroled Lee's 28,000 remaining men and allowed his officers to keep their horses. The only condition was that the Confederates not again take up arms against the United States. After confirming Lee's acceptance of his terms, Grant asked for writing materials and reduced the terms to writing on the spot. He verbally agreed to Lee's additional request that any artilleryman or cavalryman who had brought his own horse to war could take one horse back home; Grant said that would help in the planting of crops. At Lee's request, Grant ordered Sheridan to provide rations for Lee's men. They then signed the surrender agreement, and Lee departed.[147]

Grant had a good sense of Lincoln's desire to end the fighting and pave the way for peaceful reconciliation. Thus, when he negotiated surrender terms with Lee at Appomattox Court House, Grant moved beyond purely military stipulations and addressed civilian issues. Richard F. Selcer concluded that Grant exceeded his military authority by conceding that "each officer and man will be allowed to return to their homes not to be disturbed by U.S. authority so long as they observe their parole and the laws in force where they may reside." Selcer observed, "Here, Grant was on thin ice, but he had the confidence of knowing the president felt the same way. He also had the imposing authority of his own immense reputation to reinforce his language. In other words, he had little fear of being overruled by the politicians in Washington."[148] On the basis of their meeting on the *River Queen*, Grant was aware of the president's desire for reconciliation with the South. Furthermore, they both shared a fear of protracted guerilla warfare. Grant himself had concluded, "To overcome a truly popular, national resistance in a vast territory without the employment of truly overwhelming force is probably impossible."[149]

Although there were about a hundred other engagements elsewhere before all fighting ceased, Lee's surrender to Grant on April 9, 1865, effectively ended the Civil War. Once again Grant had achieved his goal with a reasonable loss of men. During the entire expanded Appomattox Campaign, about 9,000 of Grant's 113,000 soldiers (8 percent) were killed or wounded as they broke through the Petersburg lines and pursued Lee to Appomattox. They killed or wounded almost 7,000 of Lee's 50,000 troops (13.5 percent) and took thousands of prisoners along the way.[150]

In the chase from Petersburg to Appomattox Courthouse, Grant used about 80,000 troops to pursue more than 50,000 Confederates. William Marvel described how, on April 9, Confederate General Gordon claimed in an address to his troops that Lee surrendered only 8,000 troops to Grant's 60,000 and thus started the myth of Appomattox Campaign numbers relied upon by defenders of the "Lost Cause." Rejecting claims by Lee's adjutant, Colonel Walter Taylor, that Lee faced 6:1 odds and had only 25,000 troops as the Appomattox pursuit began, Marvel carefully reviewed the official records and other sources and concluded that Lee started the chase with between 51,000 and 57,000 men. Marvel pointed out that the numbers of Gordon and Taylor are difficult to reconcile with the published list of 28,231 Confederates who surrendered and were paroled at Appomattox. Similarly, Marvel demolished Taylor's claim that Grant had 162,000 troops and instead concluded that Grant started the chase with about 80,000 men—less than a two-to-one edge.[151] Thus, Lee still had a significant force at his disposal as he abandoned Petersburg and Richmond, but Grant's aggressive pursuit with a somewhat larger force quickly brought Lee's army to bay.

As Assistant Secretary of War Charles A. Dana concluded, "Grant in eleven months secured the prize with less loss than his predecessors suffered in failing to win it during a struggle of three years."[152] Grant was persistent, aggressive, dogged, and determined, but he rarely incurred unnecessary casualties. During the Appomattox Campaign, as was his usual practice, he maneuvered his army and avoided frontal assaults as best he could and attacked when he believed he had to. With Lee's surrender, Grant had demonstrated that he knew what had to be done to achieve victory, and he had done it.

Lincoln finally returned to Washington on April 8. On April 11 he gave his last public address to a crowd celebrating Lee's surrender. The president said a call for national thanksgiving was being drafted and would be promulgated. He did not live long enough to do so. He spoke of his recent trip to City Point and Richmond and then praised Grant: "I myself was near the front, and had the high pleasure of transmitting much of the good news to you; but no part of the honor, for plan or execution, is mine. To Gen. Grant, his skilful [sic] officers, and brave men, all belongs." In the balance of his speech, Lincoln said no purpose was served by speculating on whether the Southern states were or were not in the Union. He was more interested in quickly moving toward restoring them to "their proper practical relation with the Union" and urged acceptance of a new Louisiana constitution that abolished slavery, provided black and white public schools, and authorized legislative approval of voting rights for blacks. On a broader scale, he concluded, "In the present 'situation,' as the phrase goes, it may be my duty to make some new announcement to the people of the South. I am considering, and shall not fail to act, when satisfied that action will be proper."[153] An assassin's bullet would preclude such a presidential announcement.

Grant returned to Washington on April 13. A relieved Lincoln invited him, Stanton, and their wives to join Mary and Lincoln for an English comedy at Ford's Theatre the next evening. Grant, but not Stanton accepted. However, Julia Grant, not a fan of Mary's, and Stanton, who wisely counseled against Grant and Lincoln being together at a public event, convinced the general to also decline the invitation. A disappointed Lincoln eventually recruited Major Henry Rathbone and his fiancée, Clara Harris, to accompany the Lincolns to Ford's on Good Friday evening, April 14.

When newspapers erroneously reported that the Lincolns and Grants would attend the performance of *Our American Cousin* at Ford's, John Wilkes Booth thought he might be able to kill both the president and the general. However, the Grants took a train to New Jersey a few hours before the play started, and the two men never saw each other again.

CHAPTER 13

LINCOLN AND GRANT: THE WINNING TEAM

———•◆•———

The unheralded accomplishment of Lincoln and Grant was to balance the civilian-military relationship nearly as perfectly as it could be; that, along with winning the war, may be the greatest legacy these two handed down to us. To understand the reasons for their astounding mutual Civil War success, it is necessary to examine their similar personality traits, their interpersonal respect and loyalty, and major aspects of their working relationship.

PERSONAL TRAITS

Beyond their shared backgrounds as Westerners from the Ohio River Valley border state country, Lincoln and Grant shared many traits that resulted in Union victory. An overview of their common traits was provided by General Horace Porter in his *Campaigning with Grant*:

Although their appearance, their training, and their characteristics were in striking contrast, yet [Lincoln and Grant] had
many traits in common, and there were numerous points of
resemblance in their remarkable careers. Each was of humble
origin, and had been compelled to learn the first lessons of life
in the severe school of adversity. Each had risen from the people,
possessed an abiding confidence in them, and always retained a
deep hold upon their affections.... Both were conspicuous for
the possession of that most uncommon of all virtues, common
sense. Both despised the arts of the demagogue, and shrank from
posing for effect, or indulging in mock heroics.[1]

Their most significant common personal traits were humility, decisiveness, clarity of communication, moral courage, and perseverance.

HUMILITY

In an era when oversized personalities were the norm, Lincoln and
Grant's humble natures were disparaged by many of their contemporaries. However, Colonel Eaton, who knew them both, was intrigued by
the humility of each: "Grant and Lincoln were alike in the unassuming
qualities of their greatness—a trait which seems to be characteristic of
most really great men. In America it sometimes takes the guise of perhaps
too little respect for the formalities attaching to a high office, but on the
whole it springs from an unconscious recognition of essentials which we
shall do well to cherish."[2] Grant's casualness about his uniform and
Lincoln's openness to White House visitors from all walks of life showed
their disdain for formalities. But, more importantly, neither let his ego
get in the way of goal accomplishment.

Grant's modesty was a distinguishing trait. One of his acquaintances
described him as "a man who could remain silent in several languages."
Adam Badeau, his military secretary, discussed his mix of humility and
decisiveness:

Not a sign about him suggested rank or reputation or power.
He discussed the most ordinary themes with apparent interest,

and turned from them in the same quiet tones, and without a shade of difference in his manner, to decisions that involved the fate of armies, as if great things and small were to him of equal moment. In battle, the sphinx awoke. The outward calm was even then not entirely broken; but the utterance was prompt, the ideas were rapid, the judgment was decisive, the words were those of command. The whole man became intense, as it were, with a white heat.[3]

Grant's humility enabled him to appreciate the different perspective of enlisted volunteers. As Jean Edward Smith observed, "Having survived a number of years on the bottom rung in civil life, [Grant] had developed an instinctive feel for how civilians behaved," and adjusted his expectations of them accordingly.[4] Gary Gallagher noted a widespread wartime belief that Grant "personified the best of American virtues" and quoted an Iowa soldier who wrote in June 1863 of his unassuming character: "Gen Grant has passed around the lines several times, but in his old white hat and unpretending appearance we seem to forget such a man could be the very man we love to honor...."[5]

After his exposure to Grant, Charles Dana wrote to Washburne, "My impressions concerning Grant do not differ from yours. I tell everybody that he is the most modest, the most disinterested, and the most honest man I have ever known."[6] After Grant had been in Washington less than two months, John Hay wrote, "The stories of Grant's quarrelling with the Secretary of War are gratuitous lies. Grant quarrels with no one."[7] As Grant and his army continued south through Virginia during the Overland Campaign, Lincoln praised Grant's modesty in a public address: "There is enough yet before us requiring all loyal men and patriots to perform their share of the labor and follow the example of the modest General at the head of our armies, and sink all personal considerations for the sake of the country." At the same time a Philadelphia newspaper described Grant as "truly modest, as are all great men."[8]

Even more impressive was the humility of the sixteenth president of the United States. His attitude toward others contrasted sharply with that of his egotistic counterpart, Jefferson Davis, who managed to feud on a personal basis throughout the war with his cabinet, his generals, the Confederate congress, Southern governors, and newspaper editors.[9] Most remarkable was Lincoln's post-Vicksburg letter to Grant in which he stated, "... when you turned Northward East of the Big Black, I feared it was a mistake. I now wish to make the personal acknowledgment that you were right, and I was wrong."[10] Not many presidents would even have considered such an admission and apology. The letter is Exhibit A of Lincoln's humility.

The next year, at the August 31, 1864, nadir of his wartime political fortunes, Lincoln demonstrated his humility to a large audience, a 100-day Ohio regiment on its way home after serving in Virginia. While urging those soldiers to stand firm in defense of their country, the president said, "Nowhere in the world is presented a government of so much liberty and equality. To the humblest and poorest amongst us are held out the highest privileges and positions. The present moment finds me at the White House, yet there is as good a chance for your children as there was for my father's."[11] The great president portrayed himself as no better than the family members of these Midwestern soldiers.

Their Ohio River Valley origins may have been one reason for Lincoln's and Grant's humility. Exposure to, and experience with, the diverse political and social views among their families, friends and associates in the border states of their origins distinguished them from so many antebellum Americans who knew only the hardline positions of either the North or South on the slavery-related issues that divided the nation. This phenomenon was noted by Joe Fulton: "A man of the border state, Lincoln could see all sides, could feel the Civil War and all of its issues founded on race and place in his very bones."[12] The same thing could be said about Grant. Unlike so many of their countrymen at the time, both Lincoln and Grant were not certain of the absolute correctness of particular social and political views, and this open-mindedness made them stop, think, and be humble.

This trait was observed in both men by Colonel Eaton: "One of the most remarkable traits which they had in common was their open-mindedness. Grant occasionally manifested the stubbornness which was part of his equipment as a soldier in ways which were criticized at the

time, but my own personal experience with him and with Mr. Lincoln
led me to feel that they had unusually 'willing' minds—willing in the
sense of their readiness to revise their points of view, to accept new evidence, to turn back and undo, if necessary, so the truth should better be
served. This quality involved in both an almost absolute freedom from
personal pique."[13]

Whatever the causes, both Lincoln and Grant demonstrated a humility that reflected their skepticism, open-mindedness and ability to work
without the hindrance of egocentric behavior that characterized so many
other leading politicians (Seward, Chase, Jefferson Davis) and generals
(McClellan, McClernand, Frémont, Butler) of the Civil War era.

DECISIVENESS

Both Lincoln and Grant were decisive. Lincoln's decisiveness as
president was first demonstrated when he resisted the advice of his
general-in-chief and cabinet in ordering the resupplying of Fort Sumter
in April 1861. He understood the need to stand firm and to place the
onus of initiating war on the Confederates by announcing his intention
to resupply the fort in the heart of Charleston harbor.

In a similar manner, the president disregarded the nearly unanimous
views of his cabinet that he should sack McClellan after that general had
played a major role in causing the Union defeat at Second Manassas in
August 1862. He realized that, at a time of total chaos enveloping two
Union armies in the vicinity of the nation's capital, McClellan's ability
to reorganize the armies and the soldiers' admiration for him were
critical to regaining equilibrium in that time of crisis. He put McClellan
in command of the forces in the Washington area, a well-organized army
quickly emerged and those troops were soon on their way to a strategic
victory in the Antietam Campaign.[14]

Perhaps the best examples of Lincoln's decisiveness involve his handling of the emancipation issue. He understood the critical nature of the
issue and would not be pressured into precipitous steps nor precluded
from decisive, revolutionary action when he deemed it appropriate. Thus,
early in the war, he quickly and decisively overruled emancipation declarations by Generals Frémont and David Hunter and advised them that

he retained that important decision-making power for himself. On July 22, 1862, he told his cabinet he was going to issue an emancipation proclamation, and exactly two months later he did so five days after the Battle of Antietam—much to the consternation of a huge majority of Northern Democrats.

Lincoln appreciated decisiveness in others. During Grant's first interview with him, Lincoln said he was not a military man and would not interfere, but he was opposed to procrastination. That certainly would not be a problem with Grant, who firmly believed in the value of decisiveness.

Grant was as decisive as Lincoln could have desired. That trait was so obvious that early in the war Rebel General Richard Ewell was purported to have warned his colleagues, "I should fear [Grant] more than any of their officers I have heard of. He is not a man of genius, but he is clear-headed, quick and daring."[15] Whether Ewell uttered these words is uncertain, but they reflect a widespread contemporaneous view of Grant. For example, Lincoln's top two secretaries later opined, "[Grant] always had an opinion, and that opinion was positive, intelligible, practical."[16]

Early in the war, as soon as Rebel General Leonidas Polk violated Kentucky's neutrality and seized Columbus, Kentucky, Grant proceeded to seize the critical Ohio river junction towns of Paducah and Smithland, Kentucky, without waiting for approval from his theater commander. Very familiar with that geographic area, Lincoln appreciated the value of Grant's decisive actions.

Just a few months later, immediately after capturing Fort Donelson and a Rebel army, Grant took another decisive action. While General-in-Chief McClellan and theater commanders Halleck and Buell dithered and debated about whether there should be a movement and who should move against the vital city of Nashville, Grant simply issued an order to some of Buell's troops to do so. They did, Nashville fell, and Grant earned some enmity from his fellow generals.

Colonel James F. Rusling of the Quartermaster General's staff recalled an incident demonstrating Grant's deliberate decisiveness. In the winter of 1863–64, a quartermaster officer approached Grant for approval of millions of dollars of expenditures for the coming Atlanta campaign, and

Grant approved the expenditure after briefly examining the papers involved. Questioning Grant's swift decision, the officer asked him if he was sure he was right. Grant replied, "No, I am not, but in war anything is better than indecision. We must decide. If I am wrong we shall soon find it out and can do the other thing. But not to decide wastes both time and money and may ruin everything."[17]

In discussing Grant's positive effect on the mindset of the usually victorious Army of the Tennessee, Steven E. Woodworth pointed to his prompt and decisive counterattack at Shiloh: "Perhaps in part at least it was not so much that Grant infused confidence into his army as that he refrained from destroying—by timid campaigning—the confidence of men who knew they had survived the worst the enemy had to throw at them."[18]

Decisiveness can be a two-sided coin. As indicated, Grant believed it was better to make a wrong decision rather than no decision at all. On at least three occasions (Fort Donelson, Shiloh, and Jubal Early's 1864 Raid), his decisive focus on attacking the enemy caused him to overlook the enemy's own plans. As a result, the Confederates, respectively, almost escaped his trap at Donelson, almost destroyed his army at Shiloh, and succeeded in reaching the outskirts of Washington. In the first two instances, however, his mid-battle decisiveness prevented disaster and resulted in Union victories. In the third, he sent sufficient troops to repel, although not destroy, Early's force. Grant's decisiveness was not always correct; the second assault at Vicksburg and the attack at Cold Harbor are the best examples of incorrect decisions.

Lincoln recognized and valued Grant's decisiveness. After Grant had come east to command all the Union armies, the president told one of his secretaries, "[Grant's] the quietest little fellow you ever saw.... The only evidence you have he's in any place is that he makes things git! Wherever he is, things move!"[19]

Outstanding examples of Grant's decisiveness and Lincoln's recognition of it occurred during the Vicksburg Campaign. Against the advice of his subordinates and with no approval from his superiors, Grant decided to cross the Mississippi below Vicksburg and march to Jackson and then Vicksburg with an outnumbered army and with virtually no supply line in the midst of enemy territory. After these daring and decisive moves had succeeded, the president described them as part of "one of the most brilliant [campaigns] in the world." After the surrender of Vicksburg, Lincoln told Grant that he originally thought his unilateral moves within Mississippi were a mistake but he had been wrong.

Grant's decisiveness translated into the "matter-of-fact steadiness" and "hard-driving aggressiveness" noted by Woodworth. His aggressiveness is discussed below as part of his perseverance. In summary, Lincoln and Grant demonstrated their decisiveness throughout the Civil War.

CLARITY OF COMMUNICATION

Lincoln's and Grant's decisiveness was reflected in their lucid writings. Both Lincoln and Grant were effective communicators and produced documents that were paradigms of clarity and inspiration.

In that respect, they were sons of the West (now the Midwest), which is known for plain speaking. This talent served them both well. Grant could appreciate the depth of Lincoln's homey expressions while most Easterners saw them only as signs of a country bumpkin. As Lincoln historian Don Fehrenbacher observed, "Above all, Lincoln was a self-made man in his mastery of the English language, increasingly visible in a lean but moving eloquence that contrasted sharply with the florid oratory of the age."[20]

Lincoln "triumphed not on the battlefield...but with the most powerful weapon at his disposal: his pen."[21] His Gettysburg Address and Second Inaugural Address, both written by Lincoln himself, are two of the greatest literary and oratorical masterpieces in American history. The first encapsulated the meaning of the Civil War as it had evolved, and the second sent a message of reconciliation coupled with profound but judicious condemnation of slavery. Lincoln, the Great Communicator, is a keystone of U.S. presidential history, and his talents as a writer and speaker need not be expounded upon here.

The ability to clearly communicate in writing was a trait that distinguished Grant from most other Civil War generals. Unlike those of Lee[22] and many other generals on both sides, Grant's orders were lucid and unambiguous—even when issued in the heat of battle.[23] General Meade's chief of staff commented that "there is one striking feature of Grant's orders; no matter how hurriedly he may write them on the field, no one ever has the slightest doubt as to their meaning, or even has to read them over a second time to understand them."[24]

Nicolay and Hay observed, "[Grant's] usefulness and superiority were evinced by the clearness and brevity of his correspondence, the correctness of routine reports and promptness of their transmission, the pertinence and practical quality of his suggestions, the readiness and fertility of expedient with which he executed orders."[25] English military historian John Keegan noted that Grant had "the gift of dictating clear orders without hesitation in a steady stream," was a gifted writer, and had a gift of communication.[26]

Brevet Brigadier General Horace Porter, an aide to Grant, described Grant's drafting of a flurry of orders after his arrival at Chattanooga: "His work was performed swiftly and uninterruptedly, but without any marked display of nervous energy. His thoughts flowed as freely from his mind as the ink from his pen; he was never at a loss for an expression, and seldom interlined a word or made a material correction."[27] Porter similarly observed Grant, during the Union breakthrough at Petersburg, sitting on the ground at the foot of a tree "busy...writing orders to officers conducting the advance" while under enemy fire.[28] R. Steven Jones said, "Historians have always regarded Grant's orders as some of the clearest in the war, rarely leaving room for misunderstanding or misinterpretation."[29]

One reason that Grant's orders were lucid is that they were simple. His oral and written orders tended to be simple and goal-oriented with the means of execution left to the discretion of his subordinates. Jean Edward Smith concluded, "The genius of Grant's command style lay in its simplicity. Better than any Civil War general, Grant recognized the battlefield was in flux. By not specifying movements in detail, he left his subordinate commanders free to exploit whatever opportunities developed."[30]

Their individual writing abilities enabled Grant and Lincoln to communicate well with many—especially with each other. Brooks Simpson has described their mutual "matter-of-fact, common-sense communications...reflecting the mutual respect of the president and the general."[31]

MORAL COURAGE

Once they made decisions, neither Lincoln nor Grant had any reluctance to quickly implement them. They did so because both had moral courage. Colonel Eaton commented that both men had character:

> In my association with Lincoln and with Grant, I think what impressed me most was the fact that their greatness rested in both cases upon the simple and fundamental elements of character. Both were essentially [the same] in morals and in intellect. Both were normal men first and great men afterwards. They met as adequately the demands of their private, personal relationships as they did the exactions of the great National issues with which the genius of each contended. They were the same magnanimous, self-sacrificing, noble, and tender-hearted men wherever and by whomsoever they were met.[32]

A distinguishing feature of Grant was what he himself called "moral courage." His friend William T. Sherman observed this trait in Grant:

> But I tell you where he beats me, and where he beats the world. He don't care a damn for what the enemy does out of his sight.... He uses such information as he has, according to his best judgment. He issues his orders and does his level best to carry them out without much reference to what is going on about him.[33]

As James McPherson pointed out, moral courage went beyond the physical courage that Grant had demonstrated while carrying out Mexican War attacks under the command of others:

> This was a quality different from and rarer than physical courage.... Moral courage involved a willingness to make decisions

and give the orders. Some officers who were physically brave shrank from this responsibility because decision risked error and initiative risked failure. This was George B. McClellan's defect as a commander; he was afraid to risk his army in an offensive because he might be defeated. He lacked the moral courage to act, to confront that terrible moment of truth, to decide and to risk.[34]

General Fuller said, "In the Vicksburg campaign Grant's moral courage has seldom been equalled, certainly seldom surpassed."[35] A one-time subordinate, Major General Jacob D. Cox, said, "[Grant's] quality of greatness was that he handled great affairs as he would little ones, without betraying any consciousness that this was a great thing to do."[36] T. Harry Williams noted that Grant's approach was to "seek out the enemy and strike him until he is destroyed"—an approach that required "a tremendous will and a dominant personality."[37] Grant had both.

Joan Waugh focused on Grant's character:

> A much more persuasive analysis is that Grant's painful experience with financial and personal failure accounted for his unusually strong character displayed under the stresses of wartime. A man was judged by the quality of his character in the nineteenth century. Character was the culmination of estimable qualities possessed by an individual but also implied "the estimate attached to the individual by the community." Allan Nevins claimed Grant "gained his place in the American pantheon not by intellectual power.... He gained it by character." Much later, Brooks D. Simpson echoed Nevins, arguing, "Grant's generalship was shaped as much by character as it was by intellect."[38]

Grant's character probably was strengthened by his struggles with alcohol—struggles more present in the 1850s than during the Civil War, when they were more the figment of others' imaginations. Persistent rumors of his alleged drunkenness plagued Grant throughout the war.

Although he may have inherited alcoholic tendencies from his grandfather, been greatly affected by a little alcohol, and had a drinking problem when separated from his family, Grant is never known to have been drinking—let alone drunk—during battle or at other than quiescent times during the war.[39]

The stories about his drinking or being drunk during the war were "usually circulated by dishonest war contractors, corrupt subordinates, or jealous rivals whom Grant had reprimanded, dismissed, or supplanted."[40] Recollections about Grant's drinking during the war may have been exaggerated by reporter Sylvanus Cadwallader, who was noted for inaccuracies and self-promoting exaggerations, and by John Rawlins, who wanted credit for being the watchdog over Grant's drinking.[41] James McPherson concluded that

> [Grant's] predisposition to alcoholism may have made him a better general. His struggle for self-discipline enabled him to understand and discipline others; the humiliation of prewar failures gave him a quiet humility that was conspicuously absent from so many generals with a reputation to protect; because Grant had nowhere to go but up, he could act with more boldness and decision than commanders who dared not risk failure.[42]

Grant also paid a heavy price for his outward confidence and perseverance. As Winik commented, "It wasn't just the [alleged] episodic binge drinking, but the unbearable migraine headaches that necessitated chloroform treatments, the sleeplessness, the physical illnesses that manifested considerable emotional strain."[43] Again and again during the war, Grant suffered bouts of depression. Overcoming these seems to have further strengthened his character.

A critical part of Grant's character was what Bruce Catton described as Grant's military realism. He learned as early as Belmont and Fort Donelson that in every hotly-contested battle there is a critical time when both armies are exhausted and the battle is in the balance and that "the one which can nerve itself for one more attack at such a time is very likely to win." Grant applied that lesson again at Shiloh, Champion's Hill and Chattanooga.[44] It was his character and moral courage that enabled him to act so decisively under pressure.

Significantly, Grant met Lincoln's character test. Colonel Eaton described a July 1863 interview with Lincoln in which the president inquired deeply about Grant: "... the President...seemed to be doing all in his power to measure the personal character of prominent men. He gauged the strength of his armies by their leaders.... true to his habit he let slip no opportunity by which he might gain a clearer view of the character of the man [Grant] he was dealing with...."

Few would question the character and moral courage of Lincoln himself. Working his way up from abject poverty to the presidency required courage and diligence as he educated himself, worked a variety of commercial jobs, became a leading lawyer in his state, and jousted in the down-and-dirty Illinois and national political arenas. He escaped from his humble beginnings "by force of will."[45] His character and moral courage sustained the Union cause in the Civil War as he became the moral backbone of the North and saw the war through to victory when so many others were willing to quit. Lincoln also had the character to stand up and fight for blacks' equality and freedom at a time when such a position was less than popular.

Although Lincoln was tenacious in his determination to win the war, he knew that doing so would not be easy. The price he paid for putting his whole soul into the struggle was internal anxiety. Lincoln's physical ailments throughout the course of his presidency reflected that anxiety. At various times he suffered from depression, or melancholia, and severe, disabling headaches. Winik observed, "[H]e was a man so prone to depressions and a fathomless gloom that he once mourned, 'I laugh because I cannot weep,'" and "From Sandburg to Hofstadter and Oates and Donald, all wonderfully capture the depths of Lincoln's depressions and moroseness."[46] Friends or associates noticed Lincoln's depression or melancholy at various times in his life—such as after Anne Rutledge died, when he returned home from his congressional stint in Washington in 1849,[47] and many times during the Civil War.[48]

He suffered sleepless nights and experienced nightmarish dreams. In the week before his death, he revealed to his wife Mary a haunting dream in which he had discovered his own catafalque in the East Room with a crowd of mourners who told him the president had been assassinated.[49] Such a dream was not unexpected for a man whose life was in constant danger. His struggles against these demons appear to have made him an even stronger man.

Both Lincoln and Grant were iron-willed, and their characters, especially their moral courage, were a major factor in the North's winning the Civil War.

PERSEVERANCE

A dominant and significant trait shared by Lincoln and Grant was perseverance. Once either had decided to undertake a course of action, he persevered until that action had been accomplished. Despite the fact that both of them saw their popularity rise and fall with the ebb and flow of public opinion during the war, each one persevered in tenaciously striving to preserve the Union and win the war.

Winik described Lincoln's inner strength: "Reaching deep down into the wellspring of his soul, no man was more fervent in his belief in the Union; no man loved his country, North as well as South, as much as Lincoln. And no man was more concerned about not simply winning the war, but about keeping the country and the nation together." Winik then concluded Lincoln had survived the "brittle highs and soaring lows of the war" (including massive casualties, incompetent generals, draft riots, and brutal press and political attacks) by virtue of his tenacity: "Dogged tenacity. It is a simple explanation for greatness. But, in Lincoln's case, also probably quite true."[50]

Winik supported his "dogged tenacity" argument with 1860s quotations from Lincoln's dispatches. For instance, to Grant on the James River, he wrote: "Hold on with a bull-dog grip and chew & choke, as much as possible." To Washburne, urging no compromise on prohibiting extension of slavery into territories in December 1860: "Hold firm, as with a chain of steel." To Grant about the Shenandoah Valley in 1864:

"Watch it every day, and hour, and force it."[51] Perseverance was a trait Lincoln recognized and praised in Grant. After Chattanooga, for example, Lincoln praised Grant and his soldiers for their "skill, courage, and perseverance."

Dogged perseverance, including a disinclination to retrace his steps, also was an important aspect of Grant's character. Grant's determination was demonstrated on numerous occasions, including his counterattack on the second day of Shiloh, his numerous efforts to capture Vicksburg, his successful efforts to drive the Rebels out of Chattanooga and Tennessee, his continuing south against Lee and Richmond after the Battle of the Wilderness (to the joy of his soldiers), and his crossing of the James River shortly after the disaster at Cold Harbor. As McPherson said, "In crisis situations during combat, Grant remained calm. He did not panic. He persevered and never accepted defeat even when he appeared to be beaten."[52]

Again, in 1864–65, Grant demonstrated his perseverance (Gordon Rhea called it "persistence") as he carried out his campaign of adhesion against Lee's Army of Northern Virginia and achieved all his goals within a year.[53] As he explained in his official reports, "The battles of the Wilderness, Spotsylvania, North Anna, and Cold Harbor, bloody and terrible as they were on our side, were even more damaging to the enemy, and so crippled him as to make him wary ever after of taking the offensive."[54] That comment was typical of Grant's "refusal to treat reverses as defeats."[55]

Just after the Battle of the Wilderness, Lincoln commented on Grant's tenacity: "I believe if any other General had been at the head of that army it would now have been on this side of the Rapidan [after retreating]... The great thing about Grant... is his perfect coolness and persistency of purpose.... He has the grit of a bull dog! Once let him get his 'teeth' in, and nothing can shake him off.... It is the dogged pertinacity of Grant that wins." At that same time, the *Chicago Tribune*, comparing him to Lee, said, "He understands Northern character, and reposes entire confidence in the pluck and endurance of his soldiers," noted his "cold, imperturbable tenacity," and concluded Grant would "adhere to a grip with the vigor of a mastiff. It is Grant's lion heart that wins. Lee is a valiant man; but his courage is not perfectly awful like that of his opponent."[56]

Even a critic of Grant's tactics noted his perseverance on significant matters: "Tactically rigid, strategically flexible, grand-strategically unrelenting—such was the generalship of U. S. Grant."[57] James R. Arnold summed up Grant's determination and focus throughout the war: "Grant was a simple man who dealt with the facts as he found them. While his contemporaries saw war in all its complexities and too often took counsel of their fears, from Belmont to Appomattox Grant saw the main chance, stuck to it, and thus led his armies to victory."[58]

Steven Woodworth described Grant and his Army of the Tennessee as "steady, hard-driving, can-do, and aggressive,"—traits of the Midwest[59] that cumulatively constituted perseverance and tenacity. Winik cited some of Grant's well-known statements to demonstrate his tenacity. For instance, after Shiloh: "I gave up all hope of saving the Union except by complete conquest." At the Wilderness: "Whatever happens, there will be no turning back." Between the Wilderness and Spotsylvania: "I will fight Lee if it takes all summer." Winik concluded:

> Grant had a kind of built-in shock absorber that permitted him in life and in war to survive the setbacks, the defeats, the humiliations, and, of course, the heartbreaking number of deaths. One cannot help but be struck by his tenacious resolve, his detached but tightly focused energy, his unwavering determination and gritty pugnacity.... Peel back his shy, composed demeanor and you find a core of cold steel.... In the hundreds of war photographs of Grant, you can glimpse multiple expressions and many sentiments, but one: He never looks defeated.... Even after Cold Harbor,...there would be no turning back, no retreat, no sign of weakness.[60]

Toward the end of the Overland Campaign, Lincoln addressed the Great Central Sanitary Fair in Philadelphia and tied together the perseverance of Grant with his own tenacity: "General Grant is reported to have said, I am going through on this line if it takes all summer. This war has taken three years...I say we are going through on this line if it takes three years more." Only days later, when Lincoln visited Grant outside Richmond, Grant assured the president, "I am just as sure of going into Richmond as I am of any future event. It may take a long summer day, but I will go in." Lincoln was encouraged by Grant's "persistent confidence" and convinced he would press on till the job was finished. Clearly the perseverance of each of them reinforced that of the other and made them a relentless team to be reckoned with.

SUMMARY OF PERSONAL TRAITS

To sum it up, the president and his leading general shared a set of core qualities that were grounded in their common background. A hardscrabble life begun on the Western frontier produced in both of them the balance that comes from the humility engendered by an untamed wilderness and the open-mindedness needed to overcome those challenges. Thus balanced, they were able to recognize opportunities, consider multiple alternative courses of action and communicate their decisions in clear and simple language. Their decisiveness was strengthened by their moral courage; once they decided what should be done, they did it without fear of the consequences. Finally, they persevered in their courses of action and continued toward their goals even if that continuation required weeks, months or years of dogged determination.

INTERPERSONAL RELATIONS

Individually, Lincoln and Grant had the personal traits necessary to be successful. But it was the merging of their talents that produced phenomenal results. The basis for this merger was the increasing respect they had for each other as the war progressed and their loyalty to each other throughout those challenging years. Their mutual respect and loyalty deserve separate examination.

MUTUAL RESPECT

Perhaps their strongest reinforcing and shared trait was Lincoln and Grant's respect for each other. Their similar backgrounds were a real asset. As John Waugh has concluded, "McClellan never reciprocated Lincoln's personal regard for him. It was unlikely that they ever could have been fast friends, their backgrounds were so dissimilar—Lincoln the rough-hewn man of the frontier, McClellan the descendant of eastern gentility."[61] Grant and Lincoln did not have that problem.

Rather, they both came from humble backgrounds. After more than a year of working closely with the president, Grant's respect for Lincoln was unbounded. During the East Room funeral service for the martyred president, Grant sat alone at the head of the casket and openly wept. He later described that day as the saddest of his life.[62]

Lincoln watched his fellow Illinoisan with interest beginning in late 1861 and began developing increasing respect for him during 1862. Grant won so much respect for his victories at forts Henry and Donelson in February 1862 that Lincoln did not take any action against him after the bloodbath at Shiloh that partially resulted from Grant's negligence before the battle. As James M. McPherson concluded, "Perhaps the greatest contribution Lincoln made to the successful strategy of Union forces in the Western theater, and eventually in the war as a whole, was to stick with Grant through thick and thin when others wanted to get rid of him."[63]

As the aggressive, daring Grant produced critical victories at Vicksburg and Chattanooga, Lincoln recognized his value as a general and his potential as a presidential candidate. The latter respect and concern led Lincoln to consult mutual acquaintances about Grant's possible desire to be president—both before and after his ascent to general-in-chief.

One of those acquaintances was Colonel John Eaton, who assured Lincoln that Grant did not want to oppose Lincoln and was impressed with Lincoln's great confidence in his best general. Eaton quoted Lincoln as saying, "... since Grant has assumed command on the Potomac, I have made up my mind that whatever is possible to have done, Grant will do, and whatever he does n't [sic] do, I don't believe is to be done. And now we sleep at night." Eaton noted that Grant reciprocated Lincoln's respect by reacting violently to the suggestion that Grant might run for president and declaring that Lincoln's reelection was as important as military success.

Both were comfortable with each other's role and had the highest respect for the other.

Unlike McClellan, Beauregard, Joseph Johnston, and many other Civil War generals, Grant made it his business to get along with his president. In the words of Thomas Goss, "Unlike many of his fellow commanders, Grant was willing to support the political goals of the administration as they were presented to him."[64] That cooperation included tolerating political generals, such as McClernand, Sigel, Banks, and Butler, until Grant had given them enough rope to hang themselves and provide the president with political cover when they were sacked.

Michael C. C. Adams explained Grant's willingness to work with Lincoln: "Grant's freedom from acute awareness of class may also partially explain his excellent working relationship with Lincoln. Grant was one of the few top generals who managed to avoid looking down on the common-man President. He took his suggestions seriously and benefited accordingly."[65] Grant's loyalty was rewarded when Lincoln allowed him to designate colonels and generals for promotion and to remove the remaining unsuccessful political generals—especially after Lincoln's 1864 reelection.[66]

Lincoln and Grant were each other's most loyal supporters in the turbulent days leading up to the Union (Republican) Party convention in early June 1864. Although Lincoln's foes were pushing for Grant's nomination, the president said he would be content with Grant's nomination if he "could be more useful than I in putting down the rebellion" and often said that Grant could have the nomination if he took Richmond. An uninterested Grant responded, "Lincoln is just the man of all others whom the country needs, and his defeat would be a great national calamity."

LOYALTY

Lincoln and Grant's mutual loyalty, observed Eaton, was crucial to their relationship: "The loyalty which in both men was such a marked trait, was nowhere better exemplified than in their relationship toward one another. Their confidence in each other was, I think, unlimited. At a time when appalling ignorance and misapprehension prevailed in regard to the facts which underlay the great questions, these two men saw eye to eye, and recognized the essential elements in the issues that were presented."[67]

Lincoln's loyalty to Grant was affirmed by those who reported his remarks about not being able to spare Grant because he was a fighter and about providing whiskey to his other generals (in response to allegations about Grant's drinking). The significance of Lincoln's protection of Grant cannot be overemphasized. James M. McPherson said, "Had it not been for Lincoln's support [after Shiloh], the Grant of history would not have existed—and perhaps neither would the Lincoln of history."[68]

In December 1862, Lincoln demonstrated his loyalty to Grant even while countermanding Grant's notorious and foolish General Orders No. 11, in which he expelled all Jews from his department. Halleck passed to Grant the almost father-like concern of the president to soften the blow to Grant: "The president has no objection to your expelling traitors and Jew peddlers, which I suppose was the object of your order; but, as it in terms proscribed an entire religious class, some of whom are fighting in our ranks, the President deemed it necessary to revoke it."[69]

Grant's decisiveness, aggressiveness and mistakes made him vulnerable to attacks from jealous Union generals, aggrieved reporters, and an assortment of politicians and other civilians. Therefore, there were numerous occasions during the war when Lincoln displayed his loyalty to Grant by protecting him from such criticism. These times included the post-Donelson period when Halleck curiously detained Grant at Fort Henry, the aftermath of Bloody Shiloh, the long winter of failures between 1862 and 1863 in the Vicksburg area, and the casualty-filled Overland Campaign of mid-1864. Washburne confirmed that Lincoln stood "like a wall of fire" between Grant and his critics, and Lincoln reportedly said in 1865 that he had defended Grant after Shiloh from "Washington friends, who fight battles with their tongues instead of swords far from the enemy."[70]

Perhaps the best statement of Lincoln's loyalty to Grant came when Grant was under intense attack for the 1862–63 failures in moving on or vitiating Vicksburg. The president said, "I think Grant has hardly a friend left, except myself. What I want, and what the people want, is generals who will fight battles and win victories. Grant has done this and I propose to stand by him."[71] A little while later, after Grant had succeeded in reaching Vicksburg, the ecstatic president fulfilled that proposal and exclaimed, "Grant is my man and I am his the rest of the war!"[72]

The president's loyalty to Grant did have its limits. While still supporting Grant in the early days of 1863, Lincoln hedged his bet by sending Charles Dana to report back on Grant's personal and professional behavior. The general recognized what Dana's function was, treated him graciously and openly, and converted him to a friendly go-between with Lincoln. When Grant later was being touted for promotion to three stars and general-in-chief, Lincoln was concerned that Grant might have presidential ambitions. The astute general overcame those concerns by seeing that Lincoln received a copy of his letter stating, "Nobody could induce me to think of being a presidential candidate, particularly so long as there is a possibility of having Mr. Lincoln reelected."

Grant repaid Lincoln's loyalty by fully supporting all the president's major decisions and policies. As discussed below, their working relationship was greatly facilitated by Grant's adherence to and implementation of Lincoln's national policy, national strategy and military strategy initiatives. These initiatives included aggressive offensive warfare, war on Southern resources, pursuit and destruction of enemy armies, emancipation, use of black troops, and retention of political generals.

Because Grant's own success was based on a combination of common sense and intelligence, not on pre-war fame and scholarship, said Russell Weigley, he was unique in respecting and communicating with civilian superiors like Lincoln without pretension or condescension.[73] Gary Gallagher perceptively observed, "Unlike George B. McClellan,...Grant accepted that he must always defer to civilian superiors. He thus stood steadfastly in the tradition of George Washington, something his fellow citizens recognized and applauded."[74]

In summary, Lincoln and Grant came from a common background and derived from it common personality traits. These traits allowed them to recognize each other's inherent virtues, and this recognition provided the fertile ground for the solid trust that grew between them.

This trust—as evidenced by their mutual respect and loyalty—was the basis for a successful partnership in which they sometimes acted as co-equal partners and other times deferred to each other. The respect and loyalty Lincoln and Grant had for each other, in addition to their shared traits, provided a firm basis for a positive working relationship.

WORKING RELATIONSHIP

James McPherson provided a useful basic framework for analyzing Lincoln's and Grant's similar approaches to the major issues they faced. He argued that Lincoln's ideas and performance evolved during the war in areas of policy, national strategy, military strategy, operations and tactics.[75] The same can be said of Grant. Also critical to success in the field were military personnel decisions concerning manpower in the field and the management of Union general officers. To understand the basis and nature of Lincoln's and Grant's mutually supportive actions, therefore, it is critical to examine how they cooperated in the areas of national policy, military strategy, military operations and tactics, military personnel decisions concerning manpower in the field, and military personnel decisions concerning Union generals.

NATIONAL POLICIES

A primary reason for their successful partnership was that each knew his responsibilities. Lincoln controlled the policy and political arenas while Grant controlled many, but certainly not all, military matters. Lincoln himself spelled out this dichotomy when he told Grant, while precluding a substantive meeting between Grant and Lee in March 1865, that he was "not to decide, discuss, or confer upon any political question." It was clear that "Lincoln was principally responsible for shaping and defining policy."[76] On rare occasions, Grant provided Lincoln with political advice (such as encouraging the Hampton Roads Peace Conference in February 1865), but it was just that—advice.

Lincoln's performance as commander-in-chief was brilliant. As Harold Holzer concluded, "Though he could claim no real military leadership experience when the war began, most historians agree that by war's end,

Lincoln had become perhaps the nation's most skillful commander-in-chief ever. He triumphed not on the battlefield... but with the most powerful weapon at his disposal: his pen."[77] Triumphs on the battlefield came from his best general, Ulysses Grant.

Lincoln's overall policy, said McPherson, changed from preservation of the unified nation with slavery still permitted in fifteen states to preservation of a union in which slavery was abolished.[78] As the president changed his policies, such as those on emancipation and use of black soldiers, Grant adjusted to and accommodated them. Brooks Simpson observed that "Grant... believed that it was his duty to execute administration directives, not create new policies that challenged established ones."[79] In summary, Grant took his marching orders from the president and, unlike too many other generals, neither pushed the president to change his policies, criticized them, nor attempted to undermine them.

Independently, Grant's own political antennae also kept him from "retreating" back up the Mississippi River to begin a fresh campaign against Vicksburg or moving back toward Washington after Overland Campaign "setbacks" because of the negative public reaction and morale impact such a regressive movement would provoke among his soldiers and the public.[80]

Where Lincoln's political policies conflicted with Grant's military policies, Lincoln made the final decision. For example, the president followed a policy of liberally releasing Confederate prisoners who took loyalty oaths (particularly if they were from border states) despite the general's strong views on depriving the Confederacy of every possible soldier. Usually, as in that case, Grant willingly accommodated the president's major policy decisions and made them part of his military policies. An excellent example is their shared views on the recruitment and use of blacks as Union soldiers, which is discussed below under "Military Personnel Decisions: Manpower in the Field."

As in other areas, Lincoln and Grant concurred on a national strategy for winning the war. An enlightening example occurred in mid-1862, when Lincoln wrote to Secretary of State Seward about his views on what needed to be done by the Union: "What should be done is to hold what we have in the West, open the Mississippi, and take

Chatanooga [sic] & East Tennessee...."[81] Over the next year and a half, Grant did all those things. In the fall of 1862 he protected Union gains in northern Mississippi with victories at Iuka and Corinth, in the spring and summer of 1863 he opened the Mississippi by capturing Vicksburg, and in the fall of 1863 he drove the Confederates out of Chattanooga and East Tennessee.

McPherson accurately asserts that Lincoln's national strategy moved from attempted conciliation of the border states and Southern Unionists to "an all-out effort to destroy Confederate resources including slavery and to mobilize those resources for the Union." As the president's national strategy became more aggressive, Grant had no problem going along with it. After Shiloh, Grant had come to the realization that "complete conquest" of the Confederacy was going to be necessary. Grant was especially supportive in his active use of former slaves as Union laborers and then Union soldiers.

Once he understood that Lincoln wanted to reconcile with the South as quickly as possible after the war, Grant did what he could to carry out the president's policy. At Appomattox he extended generous terms to Lee, exceeded the terms of their formal agreement by allowing Lee's men (not just his officers) to retain their own horses and mules (so critical to returning home and farming), and even requested Lee to go to Washington to meet with Lincoln. Realizing that such a meeting would undermine his civilian superiors, Lee demurred but did promise to devote "his whole efforts to pacifying the country and bringing the people back to the Union." A satisfied Grant said he would carry that message to Lincoln.[82]

Earlier Grant had acquiesced to the president's disapproval of Grant's mid-1863 proposal to initiate a campaign against Mobile, the last open Confederate port on the eastern Gulf of Mexico. Lincoln had broader national policy concerns about the French installation of puppet dictator Maximilian in Mexico and wanted a movement that would protect Texas from French/Mexican aggression. After reiterating his reasons for a Mobile campaign, Grant conceded to Lincoln, "I see however the importance of a movement into Texas just at this time."

In both late 1863 and early 1864, Grant's recommendations for Mobile campaigns were trumped by Lincoln's policy to send diplomatic messages to Mexico and France—a policy that resulted in two miserably wasteful and unsuccessful campaigns by Banks in Texas and Louisiana. It seems as though, in those instances (involving both national policy and military strategy), Lincoln sent an army in the wrong direction under the wrong commander, delayed the conquest of Mobile, and possibly lengthened the war.

Right or wrong, however, on national policy matters, Lincoln made the decisions and Grant accommodated and implemented them. In doing so, "Grant displayed tact, political shrewdness, and an understanding of the nature of civil-military relations that did much to increase his influence with Lincoln."[83]

MILITARY STRATEGY

During the course of the war, Lincoln's military strategy fairly quickly moved from vague suppression of rebellion and capture of Confederate territory to an aggressive one of destroying enemy armies. Lincoln had unsuccessfully urged McClellan, Hooker, Buell, Rosecrans and Meade to pursue and destroy opposition armies,[84] but he had no need to do so with Grant. In 1863 Grant himself sought to learn why Meade had not effectively pursued Lee after Gettysburg. By 1864, Lincoln, Halleck and Grant all were focused on pursuing and destroying enemy armies. In fact, it was the similarity of Lincoln's and Grant's views on aggressive military strategy that played a major role in making Lincoln and Grant so successful as a team.

Their similar strategic approaches were demonstrated in early 1862. Brigadier General Grant took a professional risk when he went to St. Louis to unsuccessfully urge his theater commander, Major General Halleck, to authorize an expedition up the Tennessee and Cumberland Rivers against Confederate forts Henry and Donelson. Halleck cut him off and dismissed him. Within that same month, Lincoln issued his General Orders No. 1 directing forward movement by all Union forces, including specifically Grant's troops at Cairo. Halleck yielded and authorized Grant to proceed. The resulting forts Henry and Donelson victories thrust a sword into the Confederate left flank that significantly changed the war in the West. Grant and Lincoln both had recognized the opportunity for the North's first major victory and seized it.

Unlike most Union generals, who were reticent about taking advantage of the North's numerical superiority and unwilling to persistently invade the Confederacy that had to be conquered, Grant knew what had to be done and did it. Bruce Catton concluded, "Better than any other Northern soldier, better than any other man save Lincoln himself, [Grant] understood the necessity for bringing the infinite power of the growing nation to bear on the desperate weakness of the brave, romantic, and tragically archaic little nation that opposed it...."[85] General Cox observed, "[Grant] reminds one of Wellington in the combination of lucid and practical common-sense with aggressive bull-dog courage."[86]

Grant advanced aggressively and creatively, and he attacked with vigor while usually avoiding suicidal frontal attacks. In light of the large number of battles fought by his armies, the total of 94,000 killed and wounded suffered by his commands was surprisingly small—especially when compared with the 121,000 killed and wounded among the soldiers commanded by Robert E. Lee in a similar number of battles.[87]

In a recent study of Grant's use of military intelligence, William Feis disagreed with Sherman's conclusion that his friend Grant "don't care a damn for what the enemy does out of his sight." After analyzing Grant's increasing use of intelligence throughout the war, Feis concluded, "In reality, he cared a great deal about what the enemy did on the 'other side of the hill,' but, unlike Henry Halleck, George McClellan, or William Rosecrans, he refused to allow that concern to become an obsession in which the search for 'perfect' information became an end in itself, effectively stifling intuitive risk taking."[88]

Both Lincoln and Grant focused on pursuing, disrupting, capturing, and destroying enemy armies. As early as June 1863, Lincoln advised Hooker, "I think Lee's Army, and not Richmond, is your true objective point. Fight him when opportunity offers. If he stays where he is, fret him, and fret him."[89] As Grant's Fort Donelson victory showed and his Vicksburg Campaign was demonstrating, Grant by then already understood that enemy armies were his primary goal. By mid-war, Lincoln and Grant firmly agreed on this critical principle. Unlike McClellan, Hooker, Buell and Meade, who ignored Lincoln's admonitions to pursue and destroy enemy armies, and Halleck, who was satisfied with his hollow capture of Corinth, Grant believed in and practiced that approach, which was so critical to Union victory.[90] So long as the Confederacy had armies in the field, the war would continue.

Critical to Grant's success and Union victory in the war, therefore, was that Grant early in the war recognized the need to focus, and thereafter stayed focused, on defeating, capturing, or destroying opposing armies—not simply occupying geographic positions. He did not merely occupy Fort Donelson, Vicksburg, and Richmond. Instead he maneuvered his troops in such a way that he captured enemy armies in addition to occupying important locations.

From Fort Donelson to Vicksburg to Chattanooga to the Overland Campaign and Appomattox, Grant demonstrated time and again that disruption and elimination of enemy armies was his primary goal. From Sumter to Appomattox, Grant was the only Civil War general who captured an enemy army—and he did so three times (Fort Donelson, Vicksburg and Appomattox). Elimination of enemy armies was a critical shared goal of the president and his greatest general.

Having seen Lee's and other Rebel armies being allowed to escape so many times in the early years of the war, Lincoln was more cognizant than Grant of opportunities to destroy segments of Lee's army during the last year of the war. For example, the president saw Early's Raid on Washington as an opportunity to destroy his isolated Second Corps. Thus, he suggested (but declined to order) that Grant personally come from Richmond and bring all the troops he had to spare to Washington "and make a vigorous effort to destroy the enemie's [*sic*] force in this vicinity." Grant declined to come and expressed his belief that the Union troops being sent and others already there would be sufficient to prevent Early's return to Lee.

Lincoln graciously accepted Grant's decision but expressed his doubts about trapping Early with the leaders and force at hand. Lincoln proved correct, and Early escaped what could have been a deadly trap. Although Lincoln was deferential and patient during this episode, its outcome appears to have made him more forceful in future communications with Grant regarding Early and the threat his presence in the Shenandoah Valley posed to Washington.

They shared another common approach to military strategy. Early in the war, Lincoln unsuccessfully advised Halleck, Buell and other Union generals that the answer to Southern control of shorter, inside lines (enabling them to quickly transfer troops from one front to another) was to use superior Union resources to attack the Confederates in different places *simultaneously* so that they were not able to make inter-theater transfers.[91] In mid-1863, Lincoln provided that same advice to Rosecrans and was disappointed that "Old Rosey" somehow could not understand why it was better for him to attack when Rebel forces had been transferred out of his theater to oppose Grant's Vicksburg Campaign rather than waiting for them to return.

The one general who understood Lincoln was Grant. When he became general-in-chief, he devised a spring 1864 plan that called for five separate, simultaneous attacks by Grant and Meade in northeastern Virginia, Sherman in Georgia, Sigel in the Shenandoah Valley, Butler near Petersburg, and Banks in Louisiana and Alabama. Despite the incompetence and failures of the latter three generals, Grant and Sherman did manage to carry out their campaigns without Rebel reinforcements going from one theater to another (partly because of Lee's disinterest in any theaters but his own).[92] Hay noted that Lincoln had been "powerfully reminded, by General Grants [*sic*] present movements and plans, of his (Presidents [*sic*]) old suggestions so constantly made and as constantly neglected, to Buell & Halleck *et al* to move at once upon the enemy's old line so as to bring into action to our advantage our great superiority in numbers."[93]

Similarly, in late 1864 and 1865, when Grant's forces besieged Lee's troops in Richmond and Petersburg while Sheridan fought Rebels in the Shenandoah Valley, Grant would attack Lee's lines whenever he wanted to prevent reinforcements from being sent by Lee to the Shenandoah to fight Sheridan.

Beyond that, both men, as well as Sherman, came to realize that the Southern people and their resources, not just Southern armies, had to be defeated in order to win the war. Military historian Russell Weigley explained: "Grant almost by intuition, and Sherman by acute perception, recognized that the textbook precepts on the undoing of enemy armies, rooted to eighteenth-century warfare, did not fit their problem in the Civil War. They were fighting an angry people, not just armies. Therefore, they devised their own mode of war, carrying the fight to the enemy people as well as to his armies...."[94]

In his memoirs, Grant fully explained his change of attitude after the Battle of Shiloh:

> But when Confederate armies were collected which not only attempted to hold a line farther south, from Memphis to Chattanooga, Knoxville and on to the Atlantic, but assumed the offensive, and made such a gallant effort to regain what had been lost, then, indeed, I gave up all idea of saving the Union except by complete conquest. Up to that time it had been the policy of our army, certainly that part commanded by me, to protect the property of the citizens whose territory was invaded, without regard to their sentiments, whether Union or Secession. After this, however, I regarded it as humane to both sides to protect the persons of those found at their homes, but to consume everything that could be used to support or supply armies.[95]

Grant's conversion to warfare against the resources of the South was confirmed by his friend and former staff officer Adam Badeau, who published the first volume of a Grant biography in 1868. Badeau perceptively observed:

> A change thus came over the spirit of the North, and Grant embodied and represented this change. He saw that it was necessary to deprive the South of its resources as well as of its armies, for both were part of its military power. It was he who introduced and enforced the rule that all property useful to the enemy, adding to their strength, or assisting them to carry on the war, should be destroyed.... But, above all, he understood that he was engaged in a people's war, and that the people as well as the armies of the South must be conquered,

before the war could end. Slaves, supplies, crops, stock, as well as arms and ammunition—everything that was necessary in order to carry on the war, was a weapon in the hands of the enemy; and of every weapon the enemy must be deprived. This was a view of the situation which Grant's predecessors in the chief command had failed to grasp.... Grant's greatness consisted in his perception of this condition of affairs, and his adaptation of all his means to meeting it.[96]

The similar nature of Lincoln and Grant's approach to war was captured by Third Secretary William Stoddard on the day before Lincoln's renomination in early June 1864: "The war is pressed with terribly [sic] energy under the management of General Grant. He is an embodiment of the idea which President Lincoln grasped at the outset, and there can be no manner of doubt as to the result."[97]

Grant's armies incurred the bulk of their casualties in the Overland Campaign of 1864. In Gordon C. Rhea's words, "[t]he very nature of Grant's [offensive] assignment guaranteed severe casualties."[98] Although Meade's Army of the Potomac, under the personal direction of Grant, did suffer high casualties that year during its drive to Petersburg and Richmond, it inflicted an even higher percentage of casualties on Lee's army. In addition, that Federal army compelled Lee to retreat to a nearly besieged position at Richmond and Petersburg, which Lee had previously said would be the death-knell of his own army. Rhea concluded, "A review of Grant's Overland Campaign reveals not the butcher of lore, but a thoughtful warrior every bit as talented as his Confederate opponent."[99]

At the same time as he advanced on Lee's army and Richmond, Grant was overseeing and facilitating a coordinated attack against Confederate forces all over the nation, particularly Sherman's campaign from the Tennessee border to Atlanta. As he had hoped, Grant succeeded in keeping Lee from sending reinforcements to Georgia (although it is unlikely that doing so had ever crossed Lee's mind), Sherman's capture of Atlanta virtually ensured the crucial reelection of Lincoln, and Sherman ultimately broke loose on a barely contested sweep through Georgia and the Carolinas that doomed the Confederacy. Grant's 1864–65 nationwide coordinated offensive against the Rebel armies not only won the war but demonstrated that he was a national general with a broad vision.

As Rhea concluded, Grant provided the backbone and leadership that the Army of the Potomac had been lacking:

> ... it was a very good thing for the country that Grant came east. Had Meade exercised unfettered command over the Army of the Potomac, I doubt that he would have passed beyond the Wilderness. Lee would likely have stymied, or even defeated the Potomac army, and Lincoln would have faced a severe political crisis. It took someone like Grant to force the Army of the Potomac out of its defensive mode, and aggressively focus it on the task of destroying Lee's army.[100]

Grant, however, possibly erred in retaining Meade as commander of the Army of the Potomac instead of undertaking that responsibility himself. Having Grant and the less aggressive Meade both in the field with the same army sent mixed signals to the troops and probably contributed to the disasters at Cold Harbor and the Crater. An army in the field needs one commander, not two.

Jeffry Wert described how Grant's strategic vision and perseverance (described above) combined to reinforce each other: "On May 4, 1864, more than a quarter of a million Union troops marched forth on three fronts. There would be no turning back this time. This time, a strategic vision guided the movements, girded by an iron determination—the measure of Ulysses S. Grant's greatness as a general."[101] Williamson Murray saw the same traits: "Ulysses Simpson [sic] Grant was successful where other union generals failed because he took the greatest risks and followed his own vision of how the war needed to be won, despite numerous setbacks."[102]

On major military strategic matters, however, Grant did not hesitate to defer to Lincoln; this deference demonstrated that Lincoln was the senior partner in their successful partnership. In the period when Grant was being considered for promotion to general-in-chief, the commander-in-chief disapproved two of his military strategic proposals. He vetoed two separate movements from Chattanooga to both Atlanta and Mobile/ Montgomery because of the risk to eastern Tennessee, and he nixed a Norfolk-to-Raleigh advance because it would require taking troops from the area between Lee and Washington. These disapprovals reflected Lincoln's war-long concerns about securing and holding Unionist eastern Tennessee and protecting Washington. Thus, although Lincoln and Grant usually agreed on military strategy, Lincoln was in charge and Grant understood that fact and accepted it.

Fortunately for the Union, by 1863 at the latest, both Lincoln and Grant had a shared belief that an aggressive approach to utterly defeat the Confederacy was necessary to save the Union, and their common military strategy (combined with Lincoln's confidence in Grant) made Lincoln comfortable acting as commander-in-chief and allowing Grant to effectively perform his role as general-in-chief.[103] After March 1864 Lincoln was able to stop acting as his own general-in-chief because he finally had someone up to the task.

MILITARY OPERATIONS AND TACTICS

McPherson contended that Lincoln was significantly involved in strategic oversight but was not directly involved at the tactical level. That analysis is only partially correct. For example, in 1862 Lincoln was personally involved in the field in recapturing Norfolk and its shipyard, which McClellan had bypassed and ignored. There are other examples of Lincoln's involvement at the operational or tactical level.

One tactical area in which Lincoln frequently immersed himself was the testing and adoption of new weapons. He had a more open mind than the military bureaucracy and pushed for, and even participated in, such activities. He cleared the way for expedited construction of the USS *Monitor* just in time to halt the depredations of the CSS *Virginia*. On two evenings in August 1863, the president actually test-fired the new Spencer repeating, seven-shot rifle, a weapon that proved decisive in late-war Union victories.[104]

Also, in the gray area between broad military strategy and single-battle military tactics, the area of military operations (e.g., decisions on how many and which troops to use against a particular portion of the enemy army), Lincoln involved himself even after Grant came to the East. Because the president's involvement usually was appropriate, Grant generally deferred to his wishes or responded positively to his suggestions. At the same time, their close relationship allowed and encouraged Grant to explain why a suggestion might be inappropriate.

The classic example of Lincoln assuring Grant's control of military operations is his communication to Grant on the eve of the 1864 Overland Campaign. His key words were: "The particulars of your plans I neither know, or seek to know. You are vigilant and self-reliant; and pleased with this, I wish not to obtrude any constraints or restraints upon you.... If there is anything wanting which is within my power to give, do not fail to let me know it." While the first sentence conflicts with Lincoln's war-long practices (including his voraciously consuming virtually all message traffic at the War Department telegraph office), the assurances given were basically honored. Grant's friendly response to the president concluded, "Should my success be less than I desire, and expect, the least I can say is, the fault is not with you."

At that same crucial time, the president verbally expressed his joy at finally having a real general: "Grant is the first general I've had! He's a general!...[A]ll the rest...wanted me to be the general. Now it isn't so with Grant.... I'm glad to find a man who can go ahead without me.... He doesn't ask me to do impossibilities for him, and he's the first general I've had that didn't." To reinforce Grant's authority in the field, the president told Secretary Stanton to "leave him alone to do as he pleases." So, with Lincoln's blessing, Grant was in charge in the field for the rest of the war—except for some occasions when Lincoln provided persuasive advice of his own.

Beginning fairly early in the war, Lincoln consistently supported aggressive military operations and tactics. Generals who failed to demonstrate sufficient aggression, such as McClellan, Frémont, James Shields, Buell, Hunter, and Meade, were sacked or pushed aside for others.[105] In his numerous victories, Grant demonstrated the aggressiveness Lincoln desired. With whatever resources he had, Grant took the offensive from his first battle at Belmont, Missouri, in November 1861 until his last one at Appomattox, Virginia, in April 1865. In fact, his only large defensive battle, Shiloh, involved Grant's army being jeopardized because he had been so intent on planning an offensive that he carelessly ignored what the enemy might be planning against him.[106]

McClellan constantly frustrated Lincoln throughout 1861 and 1862 with his false assertions that his army was so outnumbered by Confederates (at least two-to-one) that he could not go on the offensive. On the contrary, Grant went on the offensive regardless of enemy strength and twice (Belmont and Vicksburg) used deceptive tactics to compensate for his numerical inferiority.

Similarly, the president often expressed his frustration about his many generals who kept calling for reinforcements. Grant was a refreshing change; he carried on with whatever forces he was assigned.[107] In fact, Lincoln said, "General Grant is a copious worker and fighter, but a very meager writer or telegrapher. [Grant] doesn't worry and bother me. He isn't shrieking for reinforcements all the time. He takes what troops we can safely give him... and does the best he can with what he has got."[108]

As related earlier, Lincoln raved about Grant to Stoddard because Grant, unlike his predecessors, did not demand "impossibilities" of his commander-in-chief. Grant, when later told of the president's remarks, reciprocated by explaining, "Well, it gives about my idea of the truth of what they call Lincoln's interference with military plans. He never interfered with me from the beginning to the end."[109] Their mutual respect and trust allowed each to perform his own role in the critical area of military operations and tactics.

Grant determined what the North needed to do to win the war and did it. Grant's record of unparalleled success—including Belmont, Forts Henry and Donelson, Shiloh, Iuka, Corinth, Raymond, Jackson, Champion's Hill, Vicksburg, Chattanooga, the Overland Campaign, Petersburg, and Appomattox—established him as the greatest general of the Civil War. In fact, in the middle of the war, Lincoln came to the same conclusion. Just after Grant started his siege of Vicksburg, the president told the press, "Where is anything in the old world that equals it [Grant's still incomplete campaign]? It stamps him as the greatest general of the age, if not of the world."[110]

As renowned Civil War scholar T. Harry Williams concluded, Grant was an enigma to many: "He hated war, and yet found his place there above all his fellows. No wonder he is difficult to understand, and no wonder he has not been more fully appreciated." While the strategy fascinated him, he loathed the actual slaughter.[111]

Grant won the war by excelling in three theaters. He fought six Confederate armies, defeated all of them, and captured three of them[112]— the only three captures of armies during the war until after Appomattox. He succeeded for two years in the Western and Middle theaters with amazingly minimal casualties—particularly when compared with those of his foes. He conquered the Mississippi Valley and chased the Confederates out of Chattanooga and Tennessee. His later casualties in the East were militarily acceptable considering that the presidential election demanded swift and aggressive action and that he defeated Lee, captured his army, and took Petersburg and Richmond—in less than one year after initiating the Overland Campaign.

Grant's aggressive Overland Campaign was just the type of operation Lincoln had been seeking and urging for the three prior years. He was impatient to finally finish the war and certainly to achieve as much success as possible prior to the November 1864 election. Of course, Grant has acquired the unfortunate and unfair label of "butcher" because of that 1864 campaign of adhesion he conducted against Robert E. Lee to secure final victory for the Union. Grant's dogged persistence as he moved beyond the Wilderness and Spotsylvania caused one Southerner to say, "We have met a man this time, who either does not know when he is whipped, or who cares not if he loses his whole army."[113] During that campaign, some described him as a "butcher" or "murderer."[114] However, as Russell F. Weigley concluded, "there is no good reason to believe that the Army of Northern Virginia could have been destroyed within an acceptable time by any other means than the hammer blows of Grant's army."[115]

That campaign represented a deliberate effort by Grant and Lincoln to take advantage of the fact that Lee had chewed up his Army of Northern Virginia during the prior two years and rendered it, and the Confederacy, vulnerable to a nationwide offensive campaign that would bring the hostilities to a final halt. Such an aggressive campaign inevitably would result in heavy Union losses, and, again in Weigley's words, "[i]t was the grim campaign to destroy the Confederacy by destroying Lee's army that was to give Grant his reputation as a butcher."[116] Despite that undeserved reputation, Grant was the most successful general of the Civil War and achieved his end-of-the-war success by partnering with America's greatest president.

Lincoln, however, did not stay entirely above the fray where military operations were concerned—especially those in the Shenandoah Valley, which continued to be a possible Rebel gateway to Washington. When Early came through that valley to threaten the capital in July 1864, Lincoln followed his progress, sought militia help, was not swayed by Grant's early assurances that all was under control, and advised Grant to come to the capital with reinforcements to destroy Early's force. Grant sent troops who arrived in time to save the capital but allowed Early to escape despite Grant's earlier statement that "I have great faith that the enemy will never be able to get back with much of his force." Lincoln had accurately predicted Early's escape.

After Early had returned to the Shenandoah, Hunter and Halleck had proven their inability to deal with the threat he posed to Washington, Lincoln had met with Grant about the Shenandoah problem, and Grant had convinced Lincoln to allow Sheridan to handle the problem, Lincoln was still not satisfied. Grant had advised Halleck that Sheridan was coming and added, "Unless Gen. Hunter is in the field in person I want Sheridan put in command of all the troops in the field with instructions to put himself south of the enemy and follow him to the death." Two days later a skeptical Lincoln wired Grant:

> This, I think, is exactly right, as to how our forces should move. But please look over the despatches [sic] you may have receved [sic] from here, even since you made that order, and

discover, if you can, that there is any idea in the head of any one here, of "putting our army South of the enemy" or of "[following] him to the death" in any direction. I repeat to you it will neither be done nor attempted unless you watch it every day, and hour, and force it.[117]

Lincoln had made his point. Two hours later Grant left for Washington. He met with and relieved Hunter. He placed Sheridan in charge of the Shenandoah, and Sheridan eventually cleaned out that valley for once and for all. This is a prime example of Lincoln actually intervening in Grant's military operations.

But the president was not through. After the fall of Atlanta, he again pressed Grant about the Shenandoah (which had become the focus of press attention after Atlanta's fall), where he saw Sheridan and Early deadlocked: "Could we not pick up a regiment here and there, to the number of say ten thousand men, and quietly, but suddenly concentrate them at Sheridan's camp and enable him to make a strike? This is but a suggestion."[118] A suggestion? Sure. Grant immediately went to visit Sheridan and pushed him into a decisive, aggressive Valley campaign.

Sheridan was so successful in pushing Early southward back up the valley that Lincoln thought Sheridan might be vulnerable. So he wrote Grant, "I hope it will lay no constraint upon you, nor do harm in any way, for me to say that I am a little afraid lest Lee sends re-enforcements to Early, and thus enables him to turn upon Sheridan." Grant assured him that he was attacking both ends of Lee's lines to prevent that from happening; he even caught a Rebel division in transition between Richmond and the Valley. It was not until Sheridan's decisive October 19, 1864, victory at Cedar Creek that Lincoln "gave it a rest."

More typical was Lincoln's letter to Sherman after he had reached Savannah in December 1864 at the end of his March to the Sea. The president inquired and deferred: "But what next? I suppose it would be safer if I leave Gen. Grant and yourself to decide." Lincoln stayed on top of Grant's operations to the end; his last written communication ever to Grant was sent on April 7, 1865: "Gen. Sheridan says 'If the thing is pressed I think Lee will surrender.' Let the *thing* be pressed."

It would be a mistake, therefore, to conclude that Lincoln was not involved in military operations. As a general rule, the president was content to make the major military strategic decisions after working with Grant on them and then to leave Grant free to conduct military operations with tactics of his own choosing. In the murkier area of military operations, particularly in the East, Lincoln did intervene on several occasions and Grant generally deferred to the president's suggestions and responded to his concerns. These arrangements proved to be quite successful.

MILITARY PERSONNEL DECISIONS: MANPOWER IN THE FIELD

Lincoln was impressed and pleased that throughout the war Grant, unlike many of Lincoln's other generals, was not whining about being outnumbered and forever requesting more troops. He noticed that Grant did what he could with what resources he had. Grant's ability to achieve success even when outnumbered in his theater was best demonstrated in the crucial opening weeks of his Vicksburg Campaign. He concentrated his forces brilliantly in each Vicksburg Campaign battle and thereby negated the Confederates' overall numerical superiority in that theater.

Especially after his promotion to general-in-chief, Grant's effective recognition and utilization of the North's superior resources distinguished him from most other Union generals. Gary Gallagher said, "The North always enjoyed a substantial edge in manpower and almost every manufacturing category, but none of Grant's predecessors proved equal to the task of harnessing and directing that latent strength. Grant's ability to do so stands as one of his greatest achievements."[119] James Arnold added, "When he massed for battle he brought every available soldier to the field, sublimating those secondary considerations that so often consumed the attention and resources of weaker generals."[120]

In fact, Grant was unique in fighting uncomplainingly with the soldiers he had on hand.[121] According to General Fuller, "[Grant] rarely complained, never asked for reinforcements, and went ahead and did the job with whatever resources were available."[122] Unlike McClellan and others, Grant did not grossly exaggerate the strength of his opponents in an effort to secure reinforcements, excuse inaction, or justify a potential defeat. Unlike Lee and McClellan, Grant rarely asked for reinforcements.[123] When Grant did ask for more troops, he did so in a subtle manner, such as, "The greater number of men we have, the shorter and less sanguinary will be the war. I give this entirely as my views and not in any spirit of dictation—always holding myself in readiness to use the material given me to the best advantage I know how."[124]

Both before and after becoming general-in-chief, Grant focused on efficient use of manpower. The more successful Grant was in advancing into Confederate territory, consistent with the Union's strategic goals, the more manpower he needed to establish garrisons and to provide logistical support for his front-line troops.[125] By late 1863 and in 1864, Grant decided to deal with this problem by conducting army-size raids with little or no logistical support, destroying the Confederate infrastructure, and reducing the need for garrisons and supply lines in his rear.[126] His efficiently moving on Vicksburg, sending Sherman on his Meridian Campaign, approving Sherman's March to the Sea, and reducing the Washington garrisons in 1864 all were consistent with this approach.

Lincoln supported Grant's focused and efficient use of troops. A good example occurred in early 1864 when Stanton objected to Grant's plan to move garrison troops out of Washington. The president sided with Grant and astutely said, "You and I, Mr. Stanton, have been trying to boss this job, and we have not succeeded very well with it. We have sent across the mountains for Mr. Grant, as Mrs. Grant calls him, to relieve us, and I think we had better leave him alone to do as he pleases."[127]

At about the same time, Grant was consulted about whether to accept 100-day troops that were being offered by Midwestern governors. He recommended accepting them if they did not count against states' draft quotas, and Lincoln approved. In August 1864 Halleck recommended that Grant move troops away from Richmond to Northern cities because of threatened anti-draft riots. Grant immediately objected that such transfers would hurt his and Sherman's efforts and should be avoided by using state militias. Fully concurring with Grant, Lincoln declined

Halleck's recommendation and sent Grant the famous "hold on with a bull-dog gripe [sic]" wire.

After Grant became general-in-chief, his and Lincoln's ideas about military manpower often coincided. When, in mid-July 1864, Grant recommended that the president issue a call for 300,000 more men for Union armies, Lincoln responded that he had issued a call for 500,000 the previous day, which, he added, presumably with a smile, "I suppose covers the case." Encouraging Grant's input, the president closed by writing, "Always glad to have your suggestions."

For the latter half of the war, Lincoln encouraged the recruitment and use of black soldiers and sailors to support the Union cause. Recruiting of blacks began in July 1862 under the authority of the confiscation acts and other laws. While McClellan, Sherman and others opposed the president on this issue, Grant immediately was fully supportive and worked with the president's appointees to maximize recruiting and utilization of black troops in his theater and later throughout the country. Grant's Western commands were noteworthy for their extensive use of black soldiers, and the general continued those policies on a national basis after becoming general-in-chief.

By November 1862 Grant had obtained approval from Stanton and Halleck (and presumably Lincoln) for use of refugee blacks as "teamsters, laborers, etc." in his army. The next month he expanded their use to serving as pioneers (field engineers) on railroads and steamboats and "in any way where their service can be made available." He designated Colonel Eaton general superintendent of contrabands with authority to organize their work and protect them and their families. By the spring of 1863, Grant was working with the adjutant general to expand blacks' services to performing military duties as soldiers.

On June 7, 1863, a thousand black soldiers under Grant's command repelled a vicious assault by 2,000 Confederates at Milliken's Bend near Vicksburg. The next month Grant assured Lincoln of his "hearty support" for arming blacks. In all, 70,000 Negroes served as Union soldiers in the Mississippi Valley. As more and more blacks joined the Union army, Lincoln pointed to their growing numbers (130,000 by April 1864, 130,000–150,000 by that August, and 140,000–150,000 by that

September) and continued to combat opposition to his black-soldier policies.[128] Grant's full support of Lincoln in this matter, which was dear to the president's heart, could not have failed to win the latter's lasting gratitude. In fact, in 1864 Lincoln pointed to Grant's commitment "to the policy of emancipation and employing Negro soldiers" as a reason why it would not make much difference which of them was president.

Use of black soldiers led to other manpower issues. Confederates killed numerous surrendering and surrendered black troops and their white officers at Fort Pillow, the Crater at Petersburg, Milliken's Bend and elsewhere. Official Confederate policy entailed a refusal to exchange those blacks who were "fortunate" enough to become prisoners of war. This refusal, insisted upon by Jefferson Davis and Robert E. Lee, caused both Lincoln and Grant to shut down prisoner-of-war exchanges. Undoubtedly, they had additional reasons for following this policy because one-on-one prisoner exchanges benefited the outmanned Rebels.[129]

On another prisoner-of-war issue, Lincoln acted alone and then apologized to Grant for having done so. Without consulting his general-in-chief, the president in September 1864 ordered Stanton to enlist in the Union army some Confederate prisoners who refused to be repatriated. When he learned that Grant opposed this action, Lincoln apologized for what he admitted was a "blunder," and presumably did not interfere when Grant recommended that the ex-prisoners be sent to faraway duty in New Mexico or Minnesota. Having erred once, Lincoln the next month deferred to Grant in advance on the issue of a small exchange of naval prisoners.

Before Grant was elevated to general-in-chief and while the mid-1863 siege of Vicksburg was ongoing, Grant and Lincoln did disagree on a significant military manpower issue. On July 2, 1863, Sherman asked Grant to use his influence with the president to have new recruits assigned to existing regiments instead of all-new units because doing so would minimize disease while increasing morale and military competence. In forwarding Sherman's letter to Lincoln with his positive endorsement, Grant added that Sherman's approach would save resources needed to equip new units and would quickly convert new recruits to old soldiers.

According to Charles B. Flood, "What he and Sherman got for their trouble was a letter to Grant from Halleck, saying that, as planned, two hundred thousand men would go into new regiments. Lincoln was still making military appointments [as new regimental commanders] as political favors." Halleck's response seemed more positive than Flood indicated. Although his response characteristically did chastise Grant for writing to the president outside proper military channels, Halleck did say that the course recommended by Grant would be carried out after the draft. Whatever Halleck was trying to tell Grant, the fact is that the Union continued to utilize new regiments instead of replenishing old ones—an approach that Lincoln favored for political purposes and Grant opposed for military reasons.[130]

Concerning military manpower in the field, despite these exceptions, Lincoln and Grant overall worked together amazingly smoothly. Until he was general-in-chief, Grant effectively used whatever manpower resources he had and did not bother anyone for more. After he was promoted to the top, Grant worked hand-in-hand with Lincoln to resolve manpower issues. As early and earnestly as anyone, Grant executed the president's policies on recruiting and using black soldiers—first in support roles and later in combat. With the help of the Confederacy's no-black-prisoner-exchange policy, Grant and Lincoln implemented a no-prisoner-swap policy that benefited the North militarily by depriving the undermanned Confederates of reinforcements but caused thousands of Union prisoners to die of disease and starvation in Rebel prison camps. All in all, military manpower was another area in which the two had no difficulty cooperating.

MILITARY PERSONNEL DECISIONS: THE GENERALS

Lincoln had—subject to Senate confirmation—the final say on who became Union generals. He used that authority to promote Grant on several occasions, including promotions rewarding his successes at Donelson, Vicksburg, and Chattanooga. Just as importantly, Lincoln increasingly deferred to Grant on military personnel matters (including the selection and relief of generals) as the war progressed—particularly after Grant's promotion to general-in-chief.

One instructive series of general officer–related developments involved the assignment of Grant to take command at Chattanooga in late 1863. As commander of the Army of the Cumberland, Rosecrans had lost the Battle of Chickamauga and retreated his army to Chattanooga, where it was trapped and virtually starving. Grant and two other armies were sent to the rescue. Three steps that followed shed light on the delicate and complicated nature of general officer assignments. First, Grant's orders were delayed until after a crucial Ohio election because of Rosecrans's popularity there. Second, Grant was authorized to relieve Rosecrans of command of his army. Third, Grant did so and replaced him with Thomas (who, in Grant's mind, probably unfairly was regarded as the lesser of two evils). By late 1863, Lincoln was increasing his trust in Grant on the handling of general officers, and Grant was using that discretion.

Their cooperation was a two-way street. In December 1863 Lincoln inquired whether Grant could find a position for Major General Robert Milroy, who had incurred two disastrous defeats the prior spring but was a favorite of the Indiana congressional delegation. A few months later Milroy was assigned to a minor position in Thomas's command. Likewise, in the spring of 1864, Lincoln requested a corps command in Sherman's army for the politically influential Major General Frank Blair. Grant and Sherman accommodated the request. Grant drew the line, however, when it came to his personal staff and rejected a Lincoln recommendation of an officer for such a position.

Prior to Grant's promotion to general-in-chief, many of Lincoln's selections of generals left much to be desired. Among the questionable ones were McClellan, Burnside, Hooker, Butler, Banks, Sigel, and arguably Halleck. From 1863 on, Grant successfully supported the promotions by Lincoln of Sherman and Sheridan to positions in which they played key roles in winning the war. Especially noteworthy was Lincoln's allowing Grant to bring the obscure Sheridan to the East as the Army of the Potomac's chief of cavalry. Both Lincoln and Grant failed in not earlier promoting George Thomas to major general in the regular army— due at least in part to Lincoln's reliance on Grant's recommendations and Grant's dislike for Thomas.

The major source of conflict in this vital area was the retention of political generals, such as the woefully incompetent Sigel, Banks, and Butler. It was not until their blatant failures in the Shenandoah, up the Red River, and near Wilmington, respectively, that Grant was able to relieve them from command. Even then, Grant tried to work with Lincoln to find less-than-embarrassing ways to move them out of active field commands. After Lincoln's reelection, the president understandably seemed less concerned about retaining political generals for their possible impact on the electorate.

Prior to their departures from their command positions, Banks and Butler posed serious problems for Grant. Realizing the president's political interest in retaining them at least until the 1864 elections, Grant handled them deftly. First, he arranged for Banks to be given a senior administrative position and to retain his theater command in Louisiana while he was stripped of his command of troops in the field. McPherson observed that the Banks "affair actually strengthened the bonds of understanding between Lincoln and Grant," who gained a greater appreciation of each other's concerns.

Later Grant tried the same gambit with Butler, who foiled the move by threatening to launch a political attack on Lincoln just before the Union Party convention in June 1864. After the November 1864 elections, Grant waited until Butler botched the first attack on Fort Fisher near Wilmington and then pounced; Lincoln then fully supported Grant's termination of Butler.

There was one major exception to the smooth-working Lincoln-Grant cooperation on the handling of generals. In late 1862 Lincoln's strong desire to utilize the recruiting skills of Illinois Democrat and Major General John McClernand and to retain him as a supporter of the war came close to jeopardizing Grant's command position and his Vicksburg Campaign. Lincoln overeagerly provided McClernand with substantial authority to launch his own Vicksburg Campaign. Only shrewd intervention by Stanton and Halleck, who both disliked McClernand, kept him from obtaining enough authority to derail Grant and his vital campaign. When McClernand realized he had been outmaneuvered, he complained to Lincoln, who threw his full support to Grant. After Grant's war-changing

Vicksburg victory, Lincoln never again did anything that would allow another officer to threaten Grant's position or authority.

In fact, McClernand himself became a prime example of that altered presidential position. After McClernand's first complaints to Lincoln, the president had given Grant authority to relieve McClernand. Despite several instances in which McClernand's behavior would have justified his relief, Grant patiently allowed him to remain in command of one of his corps. However, when McClernand publicly criticized the troops of his fellow corps commanders, Grant had had enough. He relieved him of command. Admitting that he should have done so earlier "for the good of the service," Grant contemporaneously explained that he had desired to "do the most I could with the means at my command, without interference with the assignments to command which the president alone was authorized to make" until the situation became intolerable.

Grant's deference to the president on this sensitive personnel matter was repaid by Lincoln, who denied McClernand's appeal and request for a court of inquiry. He explained to the relieved general, "I could do nothing without doing harm.... For me to force you back upon Gen. Grant, would be forcing him to resign." In the matter of generals, the president after Vicksburg fully supported Grant (except for retaining a handful of political generals as long as possible). Almost a year later Lincoln again denied a court-of-inquiry request from a general (Major General Stephen A. Hurlbut) who had been relieved of command by Grant and Sherman. Ironically, in July 1863, Lincoln had lent Grant a helping hand on a personnel matter involving that same general. Lincoln had urged Hurlbut to reconsider his request to resign. He said, "I also learn that an active command has been assigned to you by Gen. Grant." Hurlbut's resignation was not accepted at that time.[131]

When Grant, in mid-1864, pushed for the appointment of his protégé Phil Sheridan to command all Union troops in the Shenandoah Valley, Stanton and the president were unimpressed by the short, young and not-so-handsome Sheridan when he made courtesy calls on them. Nevertheless, the president overrode Stanton's and Halleck's objections and approved the appointment in deference to Grant, who insisted that Sheridan had "no superior as a general, either living or dead, and perhaps not an equal."[132] Not wholly convinced, Lincoln made the appointment temporary until Sheridan proved himself in battle against Early in the Valley.

Even when Lincoln personally liked a general, that general's career was not safe in the hands of Grant and Sherman as those two moved toward ultimate victory. Because the president personally liked Joe Hooker, Lincoln selected him to command the 11th and 12th corps when they moved from Virginia to reinforce Grant at Chattanooga. Lincoln explained to Meade, "I have not thrown Gen. Hooker away." But, under Grant, "Hooker found himself increasingly an outcast." Dana reported to Stanton that Grant believed Hooker's "presence here is replete with both trouble and danger." Grant and then Sherman tolerated Hooker because he was the president's choice and his troops liked him. Then, despite Hooker's record of success at Chattanooga and in the Atlanta Campaign, Sherman, in June 1864, selected the less successful, less troublesome and junior Major General Oliver O. Howard to succeed James B. McPherson (killed outside Atlanta on July 22, 1864) as an army commander. That insult caused Hooker to quickly resign. Lincoln did not second-guess this personnel decision with which he probably was not pleased.[133]

Perhaps even more significantly, Lincoln allowed Grant (and sometimes Halleck and Sherman) to harass and second-guess George Thomas as he dealt with Hood's invasion of Tennessee in late 1864 and to deprive Thomas of any meaningful role in bringing the war to a close in 1865. Lincoln had questioned and delayed Grant's attempt to unfairly relieve Thomas of command in mid-December 1864 (the delay actually preventing Thomas's relief), but otherwise he allowed Grant to avenge himself on Thomas for perceived slights dating at least from the Corinth Campaign of 1862.[134]

Before he earned his great flexibility on the use of generals, Grant had paid his dues while commanding in the Western and especially the Middle theaters. Although Grant became frustrated with incompetent political generals and those he perceived as lacking timely aggressiveness, he rehabilitated several Eastern generals who had been shipped elsewhere after less than glowing careers in the East. Among these generals who served at least somewhat successfully under Grant were Hooker, Howard, and Burnside.[135]

In summary, the delicate problem of handling political generals, which could have sharply divided Lincoln and Grant, was resolved by Grant's recognition and patient consideration of the president's political needs, as well as his creative use of face-saving organizational changes to accomplish his military goals while preserving the president's political prerogatives. At the same time, Lincoln recognized that his intervention in personnel assignments could negatively affect Grant's military efforts. Overall, their successful cooperation on issues relating to promotion, retention and assignment of generals was the result of mutual give-and-take by Lincoln and Grant.

· CONCLUSION

Lincoln and Grant's successful prosecution of the Civil War resulted from a combination of positive personality traits, extraordinary interpersonal respect and loyalty, and a cooperative working relationship.

Humility, decisiveness, clarity of communication, moral courage and perseverance were the critical traits these two men shared. Specifically, they were sufficiently humble that they were not hampered by swollen egos, made critical decisions in a timely manner, had the intestinal fortitude to implement those decisions, and finally had the dogged determination to accomplish the goals they had decided to achieve. They cemented their relationship by respecting and remaining loyal to each other.

In their working relationship, Lincoln directed national policy and even military strategy while Grant took charge of military operations and tactics—with significant input from Lincoln on military operations in 1864 and 1865. In handling military personnel decisions involving manpower in the field and general officers, the president and the general had an instinctive commonality of views and deferred to each other on a case-by-case basis that avoided ego- or policy-based disagreements.

In all these elements of their relationship, Lincoln and Grant demonstrated a unique ability to work together for the mutual goals they shared, especially the defeat of the confederate armies and the preservation of the Union. It is undeniable that, had the working relationship between these two influential men not taken root, the course of the Civil War—and indeed, American history—might have taken a drastically different route. These two amazing Westerners employed their personal strengths and developed a harmonious relationship that was directly responsible for winning the American Civil War.

ACKNOWLEDGMENTS

This book would not have been possible without the help and support of many people. As ever, the patience of my loving wife of fifty-plus years, Susan Weidemoyer Bonekemper, has been invaluable. We both remain inspired by the memory of, and encouragement from, her dad, Alfred W. Weidemoyer, who loved Civil War and World War II history.

Having learned from my prior four books that peer review is essential to a good book, I shared my draft manuscript with eleven outstanding historians, scholars, editors and writers. I have done my best to respond to or incorporate their ideas into this book.

The following reviewers of my manuscript prevented many blunders on my part and greatly enhanced the quality of this book. Allen Guelzo clarified my thinking on many issues, including civil-military relationships, Ulysses Grant's quartermaster experience, "total war," Henry Halleck's and Grant's strategic disagreements, the residual effects of George B. McClellan, the nature of Lincoln's and Grant's wives' personalities, Lincoln and Grant's constitutional legacy, and the significance of Grant's Florida, Missouri transformation. Steve Davis provided me with extensive comments on virtually every page of my manuscript; he provided a Southern perspective that hopefully tempered some of my conclusions, and he made so many valid inquiries that I could have written another book discussing all of them.

John Marszalek, John Foskett, and the late Carl Schenker all focused my attention on the complicated role played by Henry Halleck in the Lincoln-Grant relationship, the role of William T. Sherman, the possible benefits of Jubal Early's 1864 Raid, and numerous other personnel, military, and substantive issues. In partial response to John Marszalek's suggestion that I reformat the book, I have expanded the table of contents and the introduction to include and preview highlights of my last chapter, which explains the reasons for the success of the Lincoln-Grant team. Jonathan Noyalas compelled me to take a more thorough look at Phil Sheridan's Shenandoah Valley activities, especially the Battle of Cedar Creek.

Two of my former Department of Transportation colleagues, Elaine Economides Joost and Steve Farbman, provided invaluable editorial insights and clarifications. Elaine forced me to clarify my organization and presentation (especially concerning Lincoln's and Grant's communications skills) with extensive and creative comments on the entire text, and Steve again proved himself a master wordsmith with his incisive linguistic critique. Similarly helpful critical comments on the manuscript were provided by attorney and historian Mike Harrington (defending the interests of the Lone Star State), Ulysses S. Grant living historian Larry Clowers, and retired military intelligence officer Ed Powell.

David Deis of Dreamline Cartography, Northridge, California, deserves credit for all the lucid maps in this book.

Norm and Phyllis Sanford provided technical assistance on many occasions, and the Muhlenberg College library staff, especially Kelly Cannon, graciously and efficiently fulfilled all my research requests.

Critical to the quality of this manuscript has been the outstanding, professional, and detailed editing by Lauren Mann of Regnery Publishing.

While I am deeply indebted to all these people for their stellar contributions, I am solely responsible for any errors that remain in this volume.

NOTES

Introduction

1. Because this book focuses on the Civil War, it does not compare the Lincoln and Grant presidencies. On that topic, see Jean Edward Smith's "Abraham Lincoln and Ulysses S. Grant," in *Lincoln Revisited: New Insights from the Lincoln Forum* (New York: Fordham University Press, 2007), ed. John Y. Simon, Harold Holzer, and Dawn Vogel [hereafter *Lincoln Revisited*, Simon *et al.*], 80.

2. Americans were not the only ones facing these issues in the nineteenth century; Napoleon III helped cause his own downfall in Mexico by his determination to meddle at every level, while much of the success of the Prussians in 1864, 1866 and 1870–71 emerged out of the harmonious relationship established between Helmut von Moltke as the chief of the Prussian general staff, and Otto von Bismarck and King William I as the "political" leaders. The Moltke-Bismarck-William relationship is the great rival of the Lincoln-Grant relationship for smoothness of operation and success on the field.

3.   James M. McPherson, *This Mighty Scourge: Perspectives on the Civil War* (Oxford: Oxford University Press, 2007) [hereafter McPherson, *Mighty Scourge*], 110–11.

4.   See Doris Kearns Goodwin, *Team of Rivals: The Political Genius of Abraham Lincoln* (New York: Simon & Schuster, 2005) [hereafter Goodwin, *Team of Rivals*].

5.   See Edward H. Bonekemper III, *A Victor, Not a Butcher: Ulysses S. Grant's Overlooked Military Genius* (Washington: Regnery Publishing, 2004) [hereafter Bonekemper, *Victor*], republished as *Ulysses S. Grant: A Victor, Not a Butcher: The Military Genius of the Man Who Won the Civil War* (Washington: Regnery Publishing, 2010).

6.   As late as November 1864, Presidential Secretary John Hay referred to Michigan as part of "the West" while discussing presidential election returns. John Hay, *Inside Lincoln's White House: The Complete Civil War Diary of John Hay*, ed. Michael Burlingame and John R. Turner Ettlinger (Carbondale: Southern Illinois University Press, 1997) [hereafter Hay, *Diary*], Nov. 8, 1864, 246.

7.   Joe B. Fulton, *The Reconstruction of Mark Twain: How a Confederate Bushwhacker Became the Lincoln of Our Literature* (Baton Rouge: Louisiana State University Press, 2010) [hereafter Fulton, *Reconstruction of Twain*], 177.

8.   Lincoln's Annual Message to Congress, Dec. 1, 1862, *The Collected Works of Abraham Lincoln* (8 vols.), ed. Roy P. Basler (New Brunswick: Rutgers University Press, 1953) [hereafter *Works of Lincoln*], vol. 5, 518–37 at 528–29.

9.   Ibid.

10.   John Eaton, *Grant, Lincoln and the Freedmen: Reminiscences of the Civil War with Special Reference to the Work for the Contrabands and Freedmen of the Mississippi Valley* (New York: Negro Universities Press, 1969) (Reprint of New York: Longmans, Green, and Co., 1907) [hereafter Eaton, *Grant, Lincoln*], 88–89. Eaton was a Union chaplain who was ordered by Grant in November 1862 to take charge of fleeing blacks who entered Union lines in the Mississippi Valley Theater. He met with Lincoln and Grant separately on several occasions during the war.

11.   McPherson, *Mighty Scourge*, 138.

12.   James M. McPherson, *Tried by War: Abraham Lincoln as Commander in Chief* (New York: The Penguin Press, 2008) [hereafter McPherson, *Tried by War*], 5, 8.

13. Russell F. Weigley, "The Soldier, the Statesman, and the Military Historian," *Journal of Military History* 63, no. 4 (Oct. 1999): 807–22 [hereafter Weigley, "Soldier, Statesman"] at 812.

14. Russell F. Weigley, "The American Military and the Principle of Civilian Control from McClellan to Powell," *Journal of Military History* 57, no. 5 (Oct. 1993): 27–58 [hereafter Weigley, "American Military"] at 38–39.

15. Daniel E. Sutherland, "Abraham Lincoln, John Pope, and the Origins of Total War," *Journal of Military History* 56, no. 4 (Oct. 1992): 567–86 at 586. I disagree with the application of the term "total war" to the Civil War; that term more appropriately applies to the type of warfare used by the Germans, Japanese, and Russians in World War II when they collectively slaughtered millions of innocent civilians. There was no large- or even medium-scale systematic slaughter of civilians in the American Civil War.

16. William O. Stoddard, *Inside the White House in War Times: Memoirs and Reports of Lincoln's Secretary*, ed. Michael Burlingame (Lincoln: University of Nebraska Press, 2000) (reprint and expansion of New York: Charles L. Webster & Co., 1890) [hereafter Stoddard, *Inside the White House*], 125.

Chapter 1: Men of the West

1. Steven E. Woodworth, *Nothing But Victory: The Army of the Tennessee, 1861–1865* (New York: Alfred A. Knopf, 2005) [hereafter Woodworth, *Nothing But Victory*], ix–x.

2. William C., Harris, *Lincoln's Rise to the Presidency* (Lawrence: University Press of Kansas, 2007) [hereafter Harris, *Lincoln's Rise*], 7–8; Allen C. Guelzo, *Lincoln: A Very Short Introduction* (Oxford: Oxford University Press, 2009) [hereafter Guelzo, *Lincoln*], 12–13.

3. Milk sickness is poisoning caused by drinking milk from cows that have eaten white snakeroot.

4. Guelzo, *Lincoln*, 13; Harris, *Lincoln's Rise*, 8–9.

5. Michael Burlingame, *Abraham Lincoln: A Life*, vol. 1 (Baltimore: Johns Hopkins University Press, 2008) [hereafter Burlingame, *Lincoln*], 36–37.

6. Harris, *Lincoln's Rise*, 9–10 at 10; Guelzo, *Lincoln*, 18; Burlingame, *Lincoln*, vol. 1, 5.

7. Guelzo, *Lincoln*, 14; Burlingame, *Lincoln*, vol. 1, 11.

8. Harris, *Lincoln's Rise*, 10; Jay Winik, *April 1865: The Month That Saved America* (New York: Harper Collins, 2001) [hereafter Winik, *April 1865*], 232.

9. Burlingame, *Lincoln*, vol. 1, 31; Don E. Fehrenbacher, commentary in *Encyclopedia of American Biography*, ed. John A. Garraty (New York: Harper & Row, 1974) [hereafter Fehrenbacher commentary in Garraty, *Encyclopedia*], 666.

10. Guelzo, *Lincoln*, 19–21; Burlingame, *Lincoln*, vol. 1, 52–53, 56–57.

11. Winik, *April 1865*, 232–33.

12. Daniel Walker Howe, "Honest Abe: Abraham Lincoln and the Moral Character," *Foreign Policy Research Institute Newsletter* 13, no. 16 (June 2008), http://www.fpri.org/articles/2008/06/honest-abe-abraham-lincoln-and-moral-character [hereafter Howe, "Honest Abe"]; Donald, *Lincoln*, 64.

13. William C. Harris, *Lincoln and the Border States: Preserving the Union* (Lawrence: University Press of Kansas, 2011) [hereafter Harris, *Lincoln and the Border States*], 2.

14. Guelzo, *Lincoln*, 38–42.

15. Adam Badeau, *Military History of Ulysses S. Grant, from April, 1861, to April, 1865* (3 vols.) (New York: D. Appleton and Company, 1868) [hereafter Badeau, *Grant*], vol. 1, 7; Ulysses S. Grant, *Memoirs and Selected Letters: Personal Memoirs of U. S. Grant, Selected Letters 1839–1865* (New York: Literary Classics of the United States, Inc., 1990) (Reprint of 1885 edition) [hereafter Grant, *Memoirs*], 27.

16. Ibid., 28–29, 1122; Ezra J. Warner, *Generals in Blue: Lives of the Union Commanders* (Baton Rouge: Louisiana State University Press, 1964) [hereafter Warner, *Generals in Blue*], 183–84; John Y. Simon, ed., *The Papers of Ulysses Grant* (Carbondale: Southern Illinois University Press, 1967–2009) [hereafter *Papers of Grant*], vol. 1, 3–4; Jean Edward Smith, *Grant* (New York: Simon & Schuster, 2001) [hereafter Smith, *Grant*], 25; Bruce Catton, *U. S. Grant and the American Military Tradition* (Boston: Little, Brown and Company, 1954) [hereafter Catton, *Grant*], 15, 19.

17. Grant, *Memoirs*, 129.

18. Ibid., 31–35, 1122–23; Warner, *Generals in Blue*, 184.

19. Smith, *Grant*, 28.

20. Grant, *Memoirs*, 34–35. As a confidence-boosting tactic, he did wear a sword at the battles of Belmont, Fort Donelson, and Shiloh (where his scabbard deflected a projectile and may have saved his life), as well as at the beginning of the Overland Campaign.

21. Ibid., 36–39, 1123; Warner, *Generals in Blue*, 184; *Papers of Grant*, vol. 1, xxxvii.
22. Referred to hereafter by its popular name, the Mexican War.

Chapter 2: The Mexican War: A Military and Political Training Ground

1. Lincoln to W. Durley, Oct. 3, 1845, quoted and discussed in Richard Lawrence Miller, *Lincoln and His World: vol. 3: The Rise to National Prominence, 1843–1853* (Jefferson, NC: McFarland, 2011) [hereafter Lawrence, *Lincoln and World*, vol. 3], 51, 52.
2. Miller, *Lincoln and World*, vol. 3, 105.
3. Ibid., 115, 153–56.
4. Ibid., 116–17.
5. Ibid., 157–64.
6. Howe, "Honest Abe."
7. Miller, *Lincoln and World*, vol. 3, 165.
8. Ward Hill Lamon, *Recollections of Abraham Lincoln 1847–1865* (A.C. McClurg and Company, 1895) (2009 reprint by General Books) [hereafter Lamon, *Recollections*], 8–9.
9. Guelzo, *Lincoln*, 55; Miller, *Lincoln and World*, vol. 3, 206–12.
10. *Papers of Grant*, vol. 1, xxxvii.
11. Grant, *Memoirs*, 41–42.
12. Grant to Julia Dent, May 6, 1845, *Papers of Grant*, vol. 1, 43–45 at 43.
13. Richard Bruce Winders, *Polk's Army: The American Military Experience in the Mexican War* (College Station: Texas A&M University Press, 1997), 115.
14. Grady McWhiney and Perry D. Jamieson, *Attack and Die: Civil War Military Tactics and the Southern Heritage* (Tuscaloosa: The University of Alabama Press, 1982) [hereafter McWhiney and Jamieson, *Attack and Die*], 156.
15. Grant, *Memoirs*, 50.
16. Martin Dugard, *The Training Ground: Grant, Lee, Sherman, and Davis in the Mexican War (1846–1848)* (New York: Little, Brown and Co., 2008), 172–76; Smith, *Grant*, 42, 52.
17. Grant to Julia Dent, May 11, 1846, *Papers of Grant*, vol. 1, 84–87 at 86.
18. Grant, *Memoirs*, 65, 81, 1124; Smith, *Grant*, 56.
19. James M. McPherson, "The Unheroic Hero," *The New York Review of Books* LXVI, no. 2 (Feb. 4, 1999): 16–19 [hereafter McPherson, "Unheroic Hero"], 16–17.

20. Grant, *Memoirs*, 69–70. "Back of the famous soldier who was to go slouching off to the supreme moment of his career at Appomattox Court-house wearing a private's blouse, mud-stained pants and boots and no sword at all, stood somewhere the remembered example of Old Rough-and-Ready, who would have done it just the same way." Catton, *Grant*, 28.

21. Brian John Murphy, "Grant versus Lee," *Civil War Times* XLIII, no. 1 (April 2004): 42–49, 63–66 [hereafter Murphy, "Grant versus Lee"] at 45.

22. McPherson, "Unheroic Hero," 16; Grant, *Memoirs*, 83–85; Catton, *Grant*, 37. Polk's treatment of Taylor backfired: "General Taylor's victory at Buena Vista, February 22d, 23d, and 24th, 1847, with an army composed almost entirely of volunteers who had not been in battle before, and over a vastly superior force numerically, made his nomination for the Presidency by the Whigs a foregone conclusion." Grant, *Memoirs*, 85. Ironically, Polk, in May 1846, had initially replaced Scott with Taylor when Scott complained that Polk's interference placed him in "the most perilous of all positions, a fire upon my rear from Washington and the fire in front from the Mexicans." Joseph Wheelan, "Polk's Manifest Destiny," *The History Channel Magazine* 4, no. 1 (Jan./Feb. 2006): 41–45 at 43.

23. Smith, *Grant*, 67; James Marshall-Cornwall, *Grant as Military Commander* (New York: Barnes & Noble Books, 1995) (Reprint of 1970 edition) [hereafter Marshall-Cornwall, *Grant*], 31.

24. Grant, *Memoirs*, 85–128; McPherson, "Unheroic Hero," 16–17; Warner, *Generals in Blue*, 184. Among the Louisiana, Texas, and Mexico letters from Grant to Julia Dent in which he expressed his concern about her father's apparent disapproval of Grant's military career and failure to consent to their marriage were those of Jan. 12, 1845; July 6, 1845; Oct. 1845; Nov. 11, 1845; Nov.–Dec. 1845; Jan. 2, 1846; Feb. 5, 1846; Feb. 7, 1846; May 24, 1846; June 5, 1846; June 10, 1846; Dec. 27, 1846; Apr. 3, 1847; April 24, 1847; May 17, 1847; Grant, *Memoirs*, 40–42, 47–49, 58–60, 61–63, 64–66, 66–68, 69–70, 70–72, 72–74, 87–89, 90–91, 92–93, 118–20, 129–30, 131–33, 138–40. Among those letters to Julia reflecting efforts by Jesse Grant to persuade his son Ulysses to resign from the Army were those of Nov. 11, 1845; Jan. 12, 1846; June 5, 1846; May 17, 1847; Ibid., 64–66, 69–70, 90–91, 138–40. In another letter to her, Grant said, "Some time ago my Father had one of my letters published so hereafter I intend to be careful not to give them any news worth publishing." Nov. 7, 1846, Ibid., 116–18 at 117.

25. Kevin Anderson, "Grant's Lifelong Struggle with Alcohol: Examining the Controversy Surrounding Grant and Alcohol," *Columbiad: A Quarterly Review of the War Between the States* 2, no. 4 (Winter 1999): 16–26 at 18 [hereafter Anderson, "Grant's Struggle with Alcohol"]; Grant to Julia Dent, Feb. 7, 1846, *Papers of Grant*, vol. 1, 72–74 at 73.

26. *Papers of Grant*, vol. 1, 130–31; Grant, *Memoirs*, 1125–26.

27. Smith, *Grant*, 152.

28. Ibid., 64.

29. John Whiteclay Chambers II, ed., *The Oxford Companion to American Military History* (Oxford: Oxford University Press, 1999), 108; Smith, *Grant*, 631, fn 6 (citing Department of Defense figures). Another source states that 115,906 U.S. troops served in Mexico. Allan R. Millett and Peter Maslowski, *For the Common Defense: A Military History of the United States of America* (New York: Free Press, 1994), 653. That number seems unrealistically high.

30. Smith, *Grant*, 36, 64, 69.

Chapter 3: The Tumultuous 1850s: Approach of the Civil War

1. Miller, *Lincoln and World*, vol. 3, 220–23; John G. Nicolay and John Hay, *Abraham Lincoln: A History* (10 vols.) (New York: The Century Company, 1886, 1890, 1914) [hereafter Nicolay and Hay, *Lincoln*], vol. 5, 216.

2. Guelzo, *Lincoln*, 67–70.

3. Winik, *April 1865*, 237.

4. Guelzo, *Lincoln*, 81. Some of the votes were cast by holdover senators not up for reelection in 1858, and the districting did not reflect districts' 1858 populations.

5. William C. Harris, *Lincoln's Rise to the Presidency* (Lawrence: University Press of Kansas, 2007), 151–75.

6. Fehrenbacher commentary in Garraty, *Encyclopedia*, 666.

7. Harris, *Lincoln's Rise*, 184, quoting *Chicago Herald and Tribune*, Feb. 16, 1860.

8. William W. Freehling, *The Road to Disunion Volume II: Secessionists Triumphant* (Oxford: Oxford University Press, 2007), 329–30.

9. Harris, *Lincoln's Rise*, 213–14, 216.

10. Winik, *April 1865*, 240.

11. Anderson, "Grant's Struggle with Alcohol," 18–19; *Papers of Grant*, vol. 1, 195.

12. Grant to Julia Dent Grant, Aug. 9, 1852, *Papers of Grant*, vol. 1, 251–53.

13. Ibid., vol. 1, 311–15; Anderson, "Grant's Struggle with Alcohol," 19–20.

14. Charles Bracelen Flood, *Grant and Sherman: The Friendship That Won the Civil War* (New York: Farrar, Straus and Giroux, 2005) [hereafter Flood, *Grant and Sherman*], 7.

15. Grant to Julia Dent Grant, Feb. 2, 1854, *Papers of Grant*, vol. 1, 316–18.

16. Grant to Julia Dent Grant, Feb. 6, 1854, Ibid., 320–22.

17. Grant to Julia Dent Grant, Mar. 6 and 25, 1854, Ibid., 322–24, 326–28.

18. Ibid., 328–33. There is considerable dispute about whether Grant was drunk while serving as a paymaster at Humboldt, California. See James F. Epperson, Letter to Editor, *Columbiad* 3, no. 2 (Summer 1999): 8–9, citing the following from Charles Ellington's *The Trial of U. S. Grant*: "At this date, so far removed from the time in question, it is impossible to know whether the payroll episode did indeed take place." Jean Edward Smith concludes that circumstantial evidence indicates that the "story rings true." Smith, *Grant*, 87.

19. Anderson, "Grant's Struggle with Alcohol," 20–21. "Grant had served in the Army for fifteen years, performed well, and gained valuable experience. During those fifteen years, he had occasionally indulged in periods of drinking, but these generally had been confined to social occasions or when he had little to occupy his time and was separated from his family. There is no indication that prior to his resignation Grant drank more than was typical for a man of the time. Unfortunately, Grant incautiously allowed others to see him when inebriated, and he left the Army with a reputation as a heavy drinker." Ibid., 21.

20. Ibid., 1126–27; Warner, *Generals in Blue*, 184. Drinking problems may have been the immediate cause of Grant's resignation, and he may have had no more than a few off-duty drinking bouts during the Civil War. He had no drinking problem when he was with his wife, and when Grant was away from her his friend and chief-of-staff, John Rawlins, usually kept him from drinking. At least, that is Rawlins's claim. McPherson, "Unheroic Hero," 19.

21. Joan Waugh, *U. S. Grant: American Hero, American Myth* (Chapel Hill: University of North Carolina Press, 2009) [hereafter Waugh, *Grant*], 41.

22. Grant, *Memoirs*, 141–42, 1127–28; *Papers of Grant*, vol. 1, 336–55; Warner, *Generals in Blue*, 184.

23. Grant, *Memoirs*, 1128; Warner, *Generals in Blue*, 184; Anderson, "Grant's Struggle with Alcohol," 21.

24. Waugh, *Lincoln*, 46.

Chapter 4: Outbreak of the Civil War

1. Congressional Quarterly, *Presidential Elections, 1798–1996* (Washington: Congressional Quarterly, 1997) [hereafter CQ, *Elections*], 41, 93.

2. Ibid.

3. Grant, *Memoirs*, 143–52. Support for Grant's perception that slavery was the driving force behind secession is found in the secession ordinances of South Carolina, Mississippi, and Alabama, as well as the declarations of Georgia and Texas concerning the reasons for their secession. David S. Heidler and Jeanne T. Heidler, eds., *Encyclopedia of the American Civil War: A Political, Social, and Military History* (New York and London: W.W. Norton & Company, 2002) [hereafter Heidler and Heidler, *Encyclopedia*], 2240–52. Also, a pronounced emphasis on supporting slavery permeated the letters, speeches and writings of the commissioners sent by the early-seceding Confederate states to other states urging them to join the Confederacy. Charles B. Dew, "Apostles of Secession," *North & South* 4, no. 4 (Apr. 2001): 24–38; Charles B. Dew, *Apostles of Disunion* (Charlottesville: University Press of Virginia, 2001).

4. Lincoln to Lyman Trumbull, Dec. 10, 1860, *Works of Lincoln*, vol. 4, 149–50.

5. Grant, *Memoirs*, 152–55, 1128–29; Smith, *Grant*, 100–5.

6. Grant, *Memoirs*, 157–59; Anderson, "Grant's Struggle with Alcohol," 21; Smith, *Grant*, 105–7.

7. Grant, *Memoirs*, 160–62, 1129; Smith, *Grant*, 107–8.

8. Orders No. 7, June 18, 1861, *Papers of Grant*, vol. 2, 45–46.

9. Smith, *Grant*, 108–9.

10. Ibid., 111.

11. Grant, *Memoirs*, 163–65.

12. Ibid., 168–71, 1129. Grant's appointment as brigadier general was backdated to May 17, 1861, making him thirty-fifth in seniority in the U.S. Army (headed by Winfield Scott). Smith, *Grant*, 113.

13. Grant to Captain Speed Butler, August 23, 1861, *Papers of Grant*, vol. 2, 131. The "Pillow" reference is to Confederate Brigadier General Gideon J. Pillow, who gained notoriety in the Mexican War for having a ditch dug on the wrong side of his fortifications.

14. Smith, *Grant*, 116.

15. Grant, *Memoirs*, 171–73, 1129; Smith, *Grant*, 117–18.

16. Donald J. Roberts II, "Belmont: Grant's First Battle," *Military Heritage* 2, no. 6 (June 2001): 40–49 [hereafter Roberts, "Belmont"] at 43.

17. Grant, *Memoirs*, 172–75, 1129; Smith, *Grant*, 118–20. In addition to notifying Frémont of his intended move on Paducah, Grant also sent a telegram to the speaker of the Kentucky legislature advising him of the Confederate occupation of Columbus in violation of that Commonwealth's neutrality. Grant, *Memoirs*, 176; Smith, *Grant*, 119.

18. William Feis, *Grant's Secret Service: The Intelligence War from Belmont to Appomattox* (Lincoln, Nebraska: The University of Nebraska Press, 2002) [hereafter Feis, *Grant's Secret Service*], 21–25.

19. Nicolay and Hay, *Lincoln*, vol. 5, 48–49 at 49.

20. Harris, *Lincoln and the Border States*, 107.

21. William F. Fox, *Regimental Losses in the American Civil War, 1861–1865: A Treatise on the Extent and Nature of the Mortuary Losses in the Union regiments, with Full and Exhaustive Statistics Compiled from the Official Records on File in the State Military Bureaus and at Washington* (Dayton: Morningside House, Inc., 1985) (Reprint of Albany: Brandow Printing Company, 1898) [hereafter Fox, *Regimental Losses*], 543, 549.

22. Grant, *Memoirs*, 185–86; Roberts, "Belmont," 49; Smith, *Grant*, 130–32; Hattaway and Archer, *How the North Won*, 53.

23. Flood, *Grant and Sherman*, 74.

24. Lincoln to McClernand, November 10, 1861, and note, *Works of Lincoln* vol. 5, 20–21.

Chapter 5: Lincoln Protects Grant

1. Nicolay and Hay, *Lincoln*, vol. 5, 103–7; Halleck to Grant, Jan. 6, 1862, *The War of Rebellion: A Compilation of the Official Records of the Union and Confederate Armies* (128 vols.) (Washington: Government Printing Office, 1880–1901) [hereafter OR], Ser. I, VII, 533–34; Grant to Halleck, Jan. 8, 1862, Ibid., 537–38, *Papers of Grant*, vol. 4, 3–4 at 3.

2. Nicolay and Hay, *Lincoln*, vol. 5, 111–12.

3. Lincoln to Simon Cameron, Jan. 4, 1862, in *The Collected Works of Abraham Lincoln: Supplement 1832–1865*, ed. Roy P. Basler (Westport, CT: Greenwood Press, 1974), 118.

4. Nicolay and Hay, *Lincoln*, vol. 5, 107; Lincoln to Buell and Halleck, Jan. 13, 1862, OR, Ser. I, VII, 928–29.

5. John F. Marszalek, *Commander of All Lincoln's Armies: A Life of General Henry W. Halleck* (Cambridge, MA: Belknap Press of Harvard University Press, 2004) [hereafter Marszalek, *Halleck*], 116–17.

6.   Lincoln to Foote, January 23, 1862 and note, *Works of Lincoln*, V, 108; Lincoln to Stanton, January 24, 1862 and note, Ibid., vol. 5, 110; Grant to Halleck, Jan. 28 and 29, 1862, OR, Ser. I, VII, 121; Foote to Halleck, Jan. 28, 1862, Ibid., 120.

7.   President's General War Order No. 1, January 27, 1862, *Works of Lincoln*, vol. 5, 111–12. In December 1861 Lincoln had recommended that McClellan assault the Confederates in Northern Virginia; McClellan's failure to do so led to this order by Lincoln. Chester C. Hearn, *Lincoln, the Cabinet and the Generals* (Baton Rouge: Louisiana State University Press, 2010) [hereafter Hearn, *Lincoln, Cabinet, Generals*], 97.

8.   Nicolay and Hay, *Lincoln*, vol. 5, 108–10.

9.   Halleck to Grant, Jan. 30, 1862, OR, Ser. I, VII, 121; Grant to Halleck, Feb. 6, 1862, Ibid., 124. Halleck also may have been influenced by the Union victory at Mill Springs, Kentucky, in the theater of his Union rival Buell and by erroneous information from McClellan that Confederate General P. G. T. Beauregard was headed to Kentucky with fifteen regiments. Nicolay and Hay, *Lincoln*, vol. 5, 120.

10.   Lincoln to Halleck, Feb. 16, 1862, *Works of Lincoln*, vol. 5, 135; Nicolay and Hay, *Lincoln*, vol. 5, 189–91.

11.   Grant to Halleck, Feb. 16, 1862, OR, Ser. I, VII, 625. For more details on the Fort Donelson fighting and surrender, see Bonekemper, *Victor*, 27–34.

12.   Grant to Brig. Gen. George W. Cullum, Feb. 16, 1862, *Papers of Grant*, vol. 4, 223–25.

13.   Halleck to McClellan, Feb. 17, 1862, OR, Ser. I, VII, 628. Three days later Halleck followed up by wiring McClellan, "I must have command of the armies in the West.... Lay this before the President and Secretary of War. May I assume the command? Answer quickly." Halleck to McClellan, Feb. 20, 1862, Ibid., 641. John Marszalek noted, "Halleck was ready to accept congratulations for this string of victories, giving no public credit to the subordinates who had pushed him into action and actually carried out the assaults." Marszalek, *Halleck*, 118.

14.   Flood, *Grant and Sherman*, 89. The Senate confirmed Grant's nomination within two days. Carl R. Schenker Jr., "Grant's Rise from Obscurity," *North & South* 9, no. 3 (June 2006): 60–68 [hereafter Schenker, "Grant's Rise"] at 64.

15.   *Papers of Grant*, vol. 4, 272.

16.   Nicolay and Hay, *Lincoln*, vol. 5, 200.

17. Brooks D. Simpson, "Lincoln and Grant: A Reappraisal of a Relationship" in Frank J. Williams, William D. Pederson, and Vincent J. Marsala, *Abraham Lincoln: Sources and Style of Leadership* (Westport, CT: Greenwood Press, 1994), 109–23 [hereafter Simpson, "Lincoln and Grant"] at 111.

18. Nicolay and Hay, *Lincoln*, vol. 5, 305–11.

19. Halleck to Hunter, Feb. 19, 1862, OR, Ser. I, VII, 636.

20. McPherson, *Mighty Scourge*, 138; Carl R. Schenker Jr., "Ulysses in His Tent: Halleck, Grant, Sherman, and 'The Turning Point of the War'," *Civil War History* 56, no. 2 (June 2010): 175–221 [hereafter Schenker, "Ulysses in His Tent"] at 181. Inexplicably, Chester Hearn claimed that Halleck temporarily replaced Grant with Smith because he thought Grant had moved too slowly. Hearn, *Lincoln, Cabinet, Generals*, 104. Moving slowly was the last thing Grant was inclined to do. Halleck had reined him in before Henry/Donelson and claimed Grant thereafter had moved into Nashville without Halleck's permission.

21. Halleck to McClellan, March 3, 1862, OR, Ser. I, VII, 679–80; *Papers of Grant*, vol. 4, 320n.

22. Halleck to Grant, March 4, 1862, OR, Ser. I, X, Part II, 3; *Papers of Grant*, vol. 4, 319n.

23. McClellan to Halleck, OR, Ser. I, VII, 680; *Papers of Grant*, vol. 4, 320n (which also indicates that Stanton had approved McClellan's wire).

24. Halleck to McClellan, OR, Ser. I, VII, 682; *Papers of Grant*, vol. 4, 320n.

25. *Papers of Grant*, vol. 4, 320n.

26. Marszalek, *Halleck*, 118–19.

27. Grant to Halleck, March 7, 9 and 13, 1862, *Papers of Grant*, vol. 4, 331, 334, 353; Halleck to Grant, March 9, 10 and 13, 1862, OR, Ser. I, X, Part II, 22, 27, 32. See Schenker, "Ulysses in His Tent," 180–81.

28. Thomas to Halleck, March 10, 1862, OR, Ser. I, VII, 683.

29. Simpson, "Lincoln and Grant," 111.

30. Halleck to Grant, Match 13, 1862, OR, Ser. I, X, Part II, 32.

31. Halleck to Thomas, March 15, 1862, OR, Ser. I, VII, 683–84.

32. For a more sympathetic view of Halleck's role in this pre-Shiloh controversy, see Schenker, "Ulysses in His Tent," 180–81.

33. For details of the Battle of Shiloh, its casualties, and criticism of Grant in its aftermath, see Bonekemper, *Victor*, 37–57.

34. Nicolay and Hay, *Lincoln*, vol. 5, 331, quoting Whitlaw Reid, *Ohio in the Civil War*, vol. 1, 375. Famous reporter Reid wrote that this overheard conversation was, in his case, "the beginning of my belief in Grant's greatness."

35. Lincoln to Halleck, April 23, 1862, OR, Ser. I, XI, Part III, 10; Halleck to Lincoln, Ibid., Part I, 98–100.

36. Lincoln's Proclamation of Thanksgiving for Victories, April 10, 1862, *Works of Lincoln*, vol. 5, 185–86.

37. McPherson, *Tried by War*, 84–85.

38. McClure, *Lincoln*, 195–96.

39. Ward Hill Lamon, *Memorandum on Lincoln and Grant*, 6–7, cited in *Recollected Words of Abraham Lincoln*, ed. Don E. Fehrenbacher and Virginia Fehrenbacher (Stanford: Stanford University Press, 1996) [hereafter Fehrenbacher and Fehrenbacher, *Recollected Words*], 292; Lamon and Teillard, *Recollections of Lincoln*, 85. In their *Recollected Words* (xliii–liv), the Fehrenbachers devised a useful A-through-E system for classifying and evaluating the reliability of allegations that Lincoln had made certain statements.

40. Washburne to Grant, Jan. 24, 1864, *Papers of Grant*, vol. 9, 522–23n at 522n.

41. John Hay, *At Lincoln's Side: John Hay's Civil War Correspondence and Selected Writings*, ed. Michael Burlingame (Carbondale, IL: Southern Illinois University Press, 2000) [hereafter Hay, *At Lincoln's Side*], 20.

42. Simpson, "Lincoln and Grant," 111.

43. McPherson, *Mighty Scourge*, 138.

44. McPherson, *Tried by War*, 85.

45. Allen C. Guelzo, *Lincoln's Emancipation Proclamation: The End of Slavery in America* (New York: Simon & Schuster, 2004) [hereafter Guelzo, *Lincoln's Proclamation*], 113.

46. Halleck's Orders, April 28, 1862, OR, Ser. I, X, Part II, 138 and April 30, 1862, Ibid., 144; Nicolay and Hay, *Lincoln*, vol. 5, 337–38.

47. Marszalek, *Halleck*, 122–23.

48. Morton to Lincoln, May 23, 1862, *Works of Lincoln*, vol. 5, 231n; Lincoln to Halleck, May 24, 1862, Ibid., 231.

49. Nicolay and Hay, *Lincoln* vol. 5, 338–42 at 339.

50. Ibid., vol. 5, 234–38.

51. McClellan to Lincoln, June 5, 1862, *Works of Lincoln*, vol. 5, 261n; Lincoln to Halleck, June 5, 1862, Ibid., 260; Halleck to Lincoln, June 7, 1862, Ibid., 263n; Lincoln to McClellan, June 7, 1862, Ibid., 263.

52. Stanton to Halleck, OR, Ser. I, XVI, Part II, 69; Halleck to Stanton, June 30, 1862, OR, Ser. I, XIX, Part III, 279; Stanton to Halleck, June 30, 1962, Ibid., 280, Lincoln to Halleck, June 30, 1862, *Works of Lincoln*, vol. 5, 295; Halleck to Lincoln, June 30, 1862, Ibid., OR, Ser. I, XIX, Part

III, 285; Lincoln to Halleck, July 2, 1862, *Works of Lincoln,* vol 5., 300; Lincoln to Halleck, July 6, 1862, Ibid., 308.

53. Nicolay and Hay, *Lincoln,* vol. 5, 381, 420, 443.

54. McClellan to Stanton, June 28, 1862, OR, Ser. I, XI, Part I, 61.

55. Nicolay and Hay, *Lincoln,* vol. 5, 446–50.

56. Lincoln to Union Governors, July 3, 1862, *Works of Lincoln*, vol. 5, 304. Similarly, in his unissued June 30 draft call for troops, Lincoln had written, "the capture of New Orleans, Norfolk, and Corinth by the national forces has enabled the insurgents to concentrate a large force at and about Richmond...." Lincoln's unissued Call for Troops, June 30, 1862, Ibid., 293–94 at 293. On July 4, in another request to Halleck for troops for the East, the president stated, "Some part of the Corinth Army is certainly fighting McClellan in front of Richmond. Prisoners are in our hands from the late Corinth Army." Lincoln to Halleck, July 4, 1862, Ibid., 305.

57. Lincoln to Seward, June 28, 1862, Ibid., 291–92; Lincoln's Draft Call for Troops (not issued), June 30, 1862, Ibid., 293–94 and note; Lincoln's Call for 300,000 Volunteers, July 1, 1862, Ibid., 296–97 and note. During this same period, Lincoln called upon Congress to recognize Grant's ally, Captain Andrew H. Foote, for organizing the western flotilla and for his "gallantry at Fort Henry, Fort Donelson, Island Number Ten and at various other places." Lincoln to the Senate and House of Representatives, July 1, 1862, Ibid., 299. A month later he sent Foote a copy of a joint resolution doing that. Lincoln to Foote, August 1, 1862, Ibid., 352.

58. Lincoln to Stanton, Aug. 9, 1862, Ibid., 365; Lincoln to Andrew G. Curtin, Aug. 12, 1862, Ibid., 368.

59. Lincoln to Halleck, July 2, 1862, Ibid., 300; Halleck to Lincoln, July 2, 1862, Ibid., 301n.

60. Lincoln's Order Making Henry W. Halleck General-in-Chief, July 11, 1862, Ibid., 312–13.

61. Marszalek, *Halleck,* 129.

62. Lincoln's Order Making Henry W. Halleck General-in-Chief, July 11, 1862, Ibid., 312–13; Halleck to Lincoln, July 11, 1862, Ibid., 313n; Lincoln to Halleck, July 14, 1862, Ibid., 323; Lincoln to Halleck, July 15, 1862, Ibid., 323n.

63. Lance Janda, "Shutting the Gates of Mercy: The American Origins of Total War, 1860–1880," *Journal of Military History* 59, no. 1(Jan. 1995): 7–26 at 9, 13.

64. See full discussion in next chapter.

65. Lincoln's Proclamation Suspending the Writ of Habeas Corpus, September 24, 1862, *Works of Lincoln*, vol. 5, 436–37.
66. Record of Dismissal of John J. Key, September 26–27, 1862, Ibid., 442–43; Lincoln to John J. Key, Nov. 24, 1862, Ibid., 508.
67. Lincoln's Memorandum on Troops at Antietam, Oct. 1–3, 1862, Ibid., 448; Halleck to McClellan, Oct. 6, 1862, OR, Ser. I, XIX, Part I, 72; Lincoln to Halleck, Nov. 5, 1862, *Works of Lincoln*, vol. 5, 485. Lincoln's attempts to get McClellan moving included a long October 13 letter to McClellan about his "over-cautiousness" and the need to engage the enemy, as well as a famous message to McClellan that read, "I have just read your despatch about sore tongued and fatiegued [*sic*] horses. Will you pardon me for asking what the horses of your army have done since the battle of Antietam that fatigue anything?" Lincoln to McClellan, Oct. 13, 1862, Ibid., 460–61; Lincoln to McClellan, Oct. 25, 1862, Ibid., 474.
68. Lincoln's Memorandum on Furloughs, Nov. 1862, *Works of Lincoln*, vol. 5, 484.

Chapter 6: Emancipation and Military Use of Former Slaves

1. Nicolay and Hay, *Lincoln*, vol. 5, 216.
2. On March 6, 1862, for example, Lincoln had sent a message to Congress proposing that the United States provide financial aid to any state adopting gradual abolishment of slavery. Lincoln's Message to Congress, March 6, 1862, *Works of Lincoln*, vol. 5, 144–46. A week later he provided the Senate with calculations showing that the cost of compensated emancipation in the four border states and the District of Columbia (at $400 per slave) would be less than the cost of eighty-seven days of war. Lincoln to Senator James A. McDougal, March 14, 1862, Ibid., 160–61. But he voided an attempt by Major General David Hunter to free all slaves in Georgia, Florida, and South Carolina and specifically reserved such a decision to himself. Proclamation revoking General Hunter's Order of Military Emancipation of May 9, 1862, May 19, 1862, Ibid., 222–23. Lincoln's last major effort in this area was an oral and written appeal on July 12 to border state representatives; a majority of them rejected his plea. Lincoln's Appeal to Border State Representatives To Favor Compensated Emancipation, July 12, 1862, Ibid., 317–19 and note. Finally, he sent Congress a draft bill proposing to compensate states that abolished slavery. Lincoln to the Senate and House of Representatives, July 14, 1862, Ibid., 424. See also Nicolay and Hay, *Lincoln*, vol. 5, 201–17.

3.   Lincoln's First Draft of Emancipation Proclamation and notes, July 22, 1862, *Works of Lincoln*, vol. 5, 336–38.

4.   Lincoln to Greeley, August 22, 1862, Ibid., 388–89.

5.   Harold Holzer (ed.), *Lincoln on War: Our Greatest Commander-in-Chief Speaks to America* (Chapel Hill: Algonquin Books of Chapel Hill, 2011) [hereafter Holzer, *Lincoln on War*], 149–51.

6.   Lincoln's memorandum on recruiting Negroes, c. July 22, 1862, *Works of Lincoln*, vol. 5, 338 and note.

7.   Lincoln to Cuthbert Bullitt, July 28, 1862, Ibid., 344–46 at 345.

8.   Halleck to Grant, Aug. 2, 1862, OR, Ser. I, XVII, Part II, 150.

9.   Lincoln's Remarks to Deputation of Western Gentlemen, *New York Tribune*, August 5, 1862, reprinted in *Works of Lincoln*, vol. 5, 356–57.

10.   Lincoln's Meditation on the Divine Will, September 2, 1862, *Works of Lincoln*, vol. 5 , 403–4.

11.   McPherson, *Mighty Scourge*, 207.

12.   Lincoln's Preliminary Emancipation Proclamation, September 22, 1862, *Works of Lincoln*, vol. 5, 433–36 at 434.

13.   Ibid., 434–35.

14.   Lincoln to Grant and others concerning Louisiana, Oct. 14, 1862, Ibid., 462–63; Lincoln to Grant and others concerning Tennessee, Oct. 21, 1862, Ibid., 470–71.

15.   Lincoln to George Robertson, Nov. 20, 1862, Ibid., 502; Lincoln's Remarks to Union Kentuckians, Nov. 21, 1862, Ibid., 503–4 at 503.

16.   Lincoln's Annual Report to Congress, Dec. 1, 1862, Ibid., 518–37 at 520–21, 529–37.

17.   Eaton, *Grant, Lincoln*, 5, quoting Grant's Headquarters 13th Army Corps, Dept. of the Tennessee, Special Orders No. 15, Nov. 11, 1862.

18.   Ibid., 9–13.

19.   Ibid., 14–15.

20.   Grant to Halleck, Nov. 15, 1862, *Papers of Grant*, vol. 6, 315; Halleck to Grant, Nov. 16, 1862, Ibid., 315n.

21.   Grant's Headquarters 13th Army Corps Special Field Orders No. 4, Nov. 14, 1862 and Grant's Headquarters 13th Army Corps, Special Orders No. 21, Nov. 17, 1862 in Eaton, *Grant, Lincoln*, 20, 21.

22.   Eaton, *Grant, Lincoln*, 22–28, including Grant's Headquarters 13th Army Corps General Orders No. 13, Dec. 17, 1862, at 27–28.

23.   Lincoln's Emancipation Proclamation, January 1, 1863, *Works of Lincoln*, vol. 6, Jan. 1, 1863, 28–30 at 30.

24.   Eaton, *Grant, Lincoln*, 53–58.

25. Lincoln to Hunter, April 1, 1863, *Works of Lincoln*, vol. 6, 158.

26. Grant to Washburne, Aug. 31, 1863, *Papers of Grant*, vol. 9, 217–18 at 218.

Chapter 7: Grant Impresses Lincoln with Victory at Vicksburg

1. Lincoln to Halleck, July 13, 1862, *Works of Lincoln*, vol. 5, 322; Halleck to Buell, July 14, 1862, OR, Ser. I, XVI, Part II, 143.

2. Lincoln to Brigadier General Jeremiah T. Boyle, Sept. 7, 1862, *Works of Lincoln*, vol. 5, 408–9; Boyle to Lincoln, Sept. 7, 1862, Ibid., 409n, Boyle to Lincoln, Sept. 8, 1862, Ibid.; Lincoln to Buell, Sept. 7, 1862, Ibid., 409; Buell to Lincoln, Sept. 10, 1862, Ibid., 409n.

3. Lincoln to Grant, Oct. 8, 1862, Ibid., 453; Grant to Lincoln, October 10, 1862, Ibid.

4. See Bonekemper, *Grant and Lee: Victorious American and Vanquished Virginian* (Westport, CT: Praeger, 2008; republished, Washington, DC: Regnery History, 2012) [hereafter Bonekemper, *Grant and Lee*], 87–89; Peter Cozzens, *The Darkest Days of the War: The Battles of Iuka & Corinth* (Chapel Hill: University of North Carolina Press, 1997).

5. On July 10, 1862, Johnson had advised Lincoln, "… I am constrained to say one thing as I said to you repeatedly in the fall Genl Buell is not the man to redeem East Tennessee…." Johnson to Lincoln, July 10, 1862, *Works of Lincoln*, vol. 5, 303n.

6. Benson Bobrick, *Master of War: The Life of General George H. Thomas* (New York: Simon & Schuster, 2009) [hereafter Bobrick, *Master of War*], 125–26.

7. Woodworth, *Nothing But Victory*, ix–x.

8. Halleck protected Grant from what has been described as a "stunning lapse on the part of Abraham Lincoln," whose thinking was dominated on this occasion by political concerns. Flood, *Grant and Sherman*, 147–48 at 147. The late historian Carl Schenker commented to this author that Halleck's protection of Grant was an example of West Point solidarity.

9. Stanton Confidential Order re McClernand, Oct. 21, 1862, *Works of Lincoln*, vol. 5, 469; Lincoln's endorsement to McClelland on the order, Oct. 20, 1862, Ibid., 468.

10. Lincoln to Francis P. Blair, Jr., Nov. 17, 1862, Ibid., 498–99 (emphasis added); Stanton to McClernand, Nov. 15, 1862, OR, Ser. I, XVII, 348–49.

11. Lincoln to Samuel Treat, Nov. 19, 1962, *Works of Lincoln*, vol. 5, 501–2 at 501.

12.   Lincoln to Farragut, Nov. 11, 1862, Ibid., 495 and note.

13.   Lincoln to Halleck, Nov. 5, 1862, Ibid., 485; Lincoln to Halleck, Nov. 27, 1862, Ibid., 514–15. Lincoln's plan was rejected by Halleck and Burnside as too time-consuming. Ibid., 515.

14.   Lincoln's Congratulations to the Army of the Potomac, Dec. 22, 1862, Ibid., vol. 6, 13. The president's credibility among that army's troops may have been undercut by his erroneous statements that "… the attempt was not an error, nor the failure other than an accident.… I congratulate you that the number of [dead and wounded] is comparatively so small." Ibid. In fact, Burnside's foolish suicidal assaults at Marye's Heights were the primary cause of over 12,000 Union casualties compared to about 5,000 Rebel casualties. But the president felt compelled to congratulate an attacking Union army.

15.   Lincoln to Halleck, Jan. 1, 1863, Ibid., 31 and 32–33n.

16.   Burnside to Halleck, Jan. 5, 1863, OR, Ser. I, XXI, 944–45; Halleck to Burnside, Jan. 7, 1863, OR, Ser. I, XXI, 953–54; Lincoln to Burnside, Jan. 8, 1863, *Works of Lincoln*, vol. 6, 46.

17.   One temporary exception was Rosecrans's Middle Theater strategic success (and tactical draw) at Murfreesboro (Stone's River), Tennessee (Dec. 31, 1862–Jan. 2, 1863), for which Lincoln congratulated him. Lincoln to Rosecrans, Jan. 5, 1863, *Works of Lincoln*, vol. 6, 39. Lincoln later would be displeased with Rosecrans's slowness in pursuing Bragg's Confederates deeper into southeastern Tennessee.

18.   Lincoln to Banks, Nov. 22, 1862, Ibid., vol. 5, 505–6 at 505.

19.   Lincoln to Carl Schurz, Nov. 24, 1862, Ibid., 509–10.

20.   Grant to Halleck, Dec. 14, 1862, *Papers of Grant*, vol. 7, 29; McClernand to Lincoln and Stanton (two telegrams), Dec. 17, 1862, OR, Ser. I, XVII, Part II, 420; Stanton to McClernand, Dec. 17, 1862, Ibid.; General Orders No. 210, Dec. 18, 1862, Ibid., 432–33.

21.   Hearn, *Lincoln, Cabinet, Generals*, 169.

22.   Eaton, *Grant, Lincoln*, 25–26 at 26.

23.   Grant, *Memoirs*, 292–93; Meyers, "Two Generals," 36.

24.   McClernand to Lincoln, Jan. 7, 1863, *Works of Lincoln*, vol. 6, 71n.

25.   Lincoln to McClernand, Jan. 22, 1863, Ibid., 70. McClernand's case was not helped by the fact that only two weeks earlier Lincoln had rebuffed McClernand's implied criticism of the Emancipation Proclamation and his forwarding of dubious peace overtures from Confederate officers. Lincoln to McClernand, Jan. 8, 1863, Ibid., 48–49.

26.   Grant, *Memoirs*, 293–95.

27. Halleck to Grant, Jan. 21, 1863, OR, Ser. I, XXIV, Part I, 9.

28. Lincoln to Dix, Jan. 7, 1863, *Works of Lincoln*, vol. 6, 43, Jan. 29, 1863, Ibid., 83.

29. Symonds, Craig L., "Lincoln and His Admirals," in Simon *et al.*, *Lincoln Revisited*, 195–213 [hereafter Symonds, "Lincoln and Admirals"], at 211–12, citing Gideon Welles to David Porter, October 1, 1862, ONR, XXIII, 388; Beale, *Diary of Gideon Welles*, vol. 1, 157–58.

30. Porter had been involved in a Lincoln-Seward-Welles mix-up over whether to send a ship under Porter's command to Fort Pickens (at Pensacola) rather than Fort Sumter in April 1861. With an order from Lincoln in his pocket, Porter ignored a would-be countermanding order signed by Seward (which, unknown to Porter, Lincoln wanted Porter to obey). Symonds, "Lincoln and Admirals," 199–203.

31. Ibid., 212–13.

32. General Orders No. 11, Department of the Tennessee, Dec. 17, 1862, *Papers of Grant*, vol. 7, 50; Lutz, Stephen D., "General Orders, No. 11: Grant's Ignoble Act," *America's Civil War* XII, no. 7 (misprinted as 6) (March 2000): 50–56.

33. Halleck to Grant, Jan. 21, 1863, OR, Ser. I, XXIV, Part I, 9.

34. Rosecrans to Lincoln, March 16, 1863, OR, Ser. I, XXIII, part II, 146–47; Lincoln to Rosecrans, March 17, 1863, *Works of Lincoln*, vol. 6, 138–39 at 139.

35. Grant, *Memoirs*, 296.

36. Simpson, "Lincoln and Grant," 117.

37. Ibid., 296–97.

38. Edwin Cole Bearss, *Unvexed to the Sea: The Campaign for Vicksburg* (3 vols.) (Dayton: Morningside House, Inc., 1991) (Reprint of 1986 edition) [hereafter Bearss, *Vicksburg*], I, 431–50; Grant, *Memoirs*, 297–98; Winston Groom, *Shrouds of Glory. From Atlanta to Nashville: The Last Great Campaign of the Civil War* (New York: The Atlantic Monthly Press, 1995) [hereafter Groom, *Shrouds of Glory*], 89. During this undertaking, Grant asked Chaplain Eaton to check on the welfare of the black workers, whom Eaton found were "well supplied with food and blankets." Eaton, *Grant, Lincoln*, 44.

39. Bearss, *Vicksburg*, I, 467–78; Grant, *Memoirs*, 298–99.

40. Bearss, *Vicksburg*, I, 479–548; Grant, *Memoirs*, 299–301.

41. Bearss, *Vicksburg*, I, 549–95; Grant, *Memoirs*, 301–2; Groom, *Shrouds of Glory*, 89–90.

42. Grant, *Memoirs*, 303–305.

43.　Lincoln to Stanton, March 29, 1863, *Works of Lincoln*, VI, 155.

44.　James R. Arnold, *Grant Wins the War: Decision at Vicksburg* (New York: John Wiley & Sons, Inc., 1997) [hereafter Arnold, *Grant Wins*], 52.

45.　McClernand to Lincoln, March 15, 1863, Lincoln Papers, Library of Congress cited in McPherson, *Tried by War*, 167; Meyers, "Two Generals," 37.

46.　The general, unlike his brother, spelled his name without an "e" on the end.

47.　Joseph Medill to Washburne, Feb. 19, 1863, *Works of Lincoln*, vol. 7, 318–19n.

48.　Smith, *Grant*, 230–31.

49.　Alexander K. McClure, *Abraham Lincoln and Men of War-Times* (Philadelphia: Times Publishing Co., 1892), 196. McClure, however, is a questionable source for this and many other statements. Fehrenbacher and Fehrenbacher, *Recollected Words*, 314–15.

50.　Smith, *Grant*, 231; McPherson, *Tried by War*, 168.

51.　J. F. C. Fuller, *The Generalship of Ulysses S. Grant* (Bloomington: Indiana University Press, 1958) (Reprint of 1929 edition) [hereafter Fuller, *Generalship of Grant*], 134.

52.　Albert D. Richardson to Sydney Howard Gay, March 20, 1863, Fehrenbacher and Fehrenbacher, *Recollected Words*, 381; Halleck to Grant, April 2, 1863, OR, Ser. I, XXIV, Part I, 25.

53.　McPherson, *Mighty Scourge*, 139.

54.　Simpson, "Lincoln and Grant," 113.

55.　This was an attempt by Burnside to march the Army of the Potomac upriver along the Rappahannock River to cross it and move on Fredericksburg again. Horrible rainy weather turned the roads to impassable muck and forced cancellation of the movement.

56.　Burnside to Lincoln, Jan. 23, 1863, *Works of Lincoln*, vol. 6, 74–75n; Lincoln to Burnside, Jan. 23, 1863, Ibid., 74; Lincoln to Halleck, Jan. 25, 1863, Ibid., 77 and note; Halleck to Franklin, May 29, 1863, OR, Ser. I, XXI, 1008–9.

57.　Lincoln to Hooker, Jan. 26, 1863, *Works of Lincoln*, vol. 6, 78–79 at 79.

58.　Lincoln to Hooker, April 3, 1863, Ibid., 161 and note; Lincoln's Memorandum on Hooker's Plan of Campaign, c. April 6–10, 1863, Ibid., 164–65; Hooker to Lincoln, April 11, 1863, Ibid., 169n; Lincoln to Hooker, April 12, 1863, Ibid., 169; Lincoln to Hooker, April 14, 1863, Ibid., 173; Hooker to Lincoln, April 14, 1863, Ibid., 169n; Hooker to Lincoln, April 15, 1863, Ibid., 175–76n; Lincoln to Hooker, April 15, 1863, Ibid., 175;

Lincoln to Hooker, April 27, 1863, Ibid., 188; Hooker to Lincoln, April 27, 1863, Ibid., 188n, Hooker to Lincoln, Apr. 27, 1863, Ibid., 190n; Lincoln to Hooker, April 28, 1863, Ibid., 189–90.

59. Rosecrans to Lincoln, April 21, 1863, Ibid., 186n; Lincoln to Rosecrans, April 23, 1863, Ibid., 186.

60. Halleck to Grant, March 20, 1863, OR, Ser. I, XXIV, Part I, 22; March 24, 1863, Ibid.

61. Grant to Halleck, April 4, 1863, Ibid., 25–26.

62. Halleck to Grant, April 9, 1863, Ibid., 27–28 at 28.

63. Feis, *Grant's Secret Service*, 144–45.

64. Kenneth P. Williams, *Grant Rises in the West* (Lincoln: University of Nebraska Press, 1997) (2 vols.) (Originally vols. 3 and 4 of *Lincoln Finds a General: A Military Study of the Civil War* (New York: Macmillan, 1952) [hereafter Williams, *Grant Rises in the West*], vol. 2, 339; Dave Roth, "Grierson's Raid: A Cavalry Raid at Its Best, April 17–May 2, 1863," *Blue & Gray Magazine* X, Issue 5 (June 1993), 12–24, 48–65 [hereafter Roth, "Grierson's Raid"] at 13; Grant to Hurlbut, Feb. 13, 1863, *Papers of Grant*, Vol. 7, 316–17 at 317. For more details on Grierson's raid, see Bearss, *Vicksburg*, II, 187–236.

65. Arnold, *Grant Wins*, 87; Williams, *Grant Rises in the West*, vol. 2, 345.

66. Russell F. Weigley, *A Great Civil War: A Military and Political History, 1861–1865* (Bloomington and Indianapolis: Indiana University Press, 2000) [hereafter Weigley, *Great Civil War*], 265; Roth, "Grierson's Raid," 13, 64–65; Shelby Foote, *The Civil War: A Narrative* (3 vols.) (New York: Random House, 1958–1974) [hereafter Foote, *Civil War*], vol. 2, 334; Smith, *Grant*, 239; Arnold, *Grant Wins*, 87.

67. Feis, *Grant's Secret Service*, 146; Roth, "Grierson's Raid," 48–49.

68. Lincoln to Salmon P. Chase, May 13, 1863, *Works of Lincoln*, vol. 6, 213 and note.

69. Grant, *Memoirs*, 318; Weigley, *Great Civil War*, 265; Bruce Catton, *Grant Moves South* (Boston: Little, Brown and Company, 1960) [hereafter Catton, *Grant Moves South*], 422–24; Terrence Winschel, "Grant's March Through Louisiana: 'The Highest Examples of Military Energy and Perseverance'," *Blue & Gray Magazine*, XIII, Issue 5 (June 1996): 8–22 [hereafter Winschel, "Grant's March"] at 19; Woodworth, *Nothing But Victory*, 334.

70. Washburne to Lincoln, May 1, 1863, Lincoln Papers, cited in McPherson, *Tried by War*, 170.

71. For details and battle maps of the Battle of Port Gibson, see Terrence Winschel, "Grant's Beachhead for the Vicksburg Campaign: The Battle of Port Gibson, May 1, 1863," *Blue & Gray Magazine* XI, Issue 3 (Feb. 1994): 8–22, 48–56 [hereafter Winschel, "Grant's Beachhead"]; Arnold, *Grant Wins*, 101–18; and Bearss, *Vicksburg*, II, 353–407. For battle maps of the battles of Port Gibson, Raymond, and Jackson, see Keith Poulter, "Decision in the West: The Vicksburg Campaign, Part III," *North & South* 1, no. 4 (April 1998): 77–83 [hereafter Poulter, "Decision Part III"].

72. Grant, *Memoirs*, 321–24; Winschel, "Grant's Beachhead," 20–22, 48–55; Ed Bearss, "The Vicksburg Campaign: Grant Moves Inland," *Blue & Gray Magazine* XVIII, Issue 1 (October 2000): 6–22, 46–52, 65 [hereafter Bearss, "Grant Moves Inland"] at 6; Al W. Goodman Jr., "Grant's Mississippi Gamble," *America's Civil War* 7, no. 3 (July 1994): 50–56 [hereafter Goodman, "Grant's Gamble"] at 52–56; Woodworth, *Nothing But Victory*, 341–47. Even after the fall of Port Gibson, General Pemberton in Vicksburg had no idea what Grant was doing. He telegraphed his local commander, "Is it not probable that the enemy will himself retire tonight?" Goodman, "Grant's Gamble," 56.

73. Winschel, "Grant's Beachhead," 56.

74. Ibid.; Arnold, *Grant Wins*, 116–17; Michael B. Ballard, "Misused Merit: The Tragedy of John C. Pemberton," in Steven E. Woodworth, (ed.), *Civil War Generals in Defeat* (Lawrence: University of Kansas Press, 1999), 141–60 at 157; Woodworth, *Nothing But Victory*, 396.

75. Grant, *Memoirs*, 324–27; Bearss, "Grant Moves Inland," 6; Weigley, *Great Civil War*, 265.

76. Lincoln to Hooker, May 8, 1863, *Works of Lincoln*, vol. 6, 202–3.

77. Lincoln to Dix, May 11, 1863, *Works of Lincoln*, vol. 6, 210.

78. On May 3, Grant wrote to Halleck of Grierson's raid and concluded: "He has spread excitement throughout the State, destroyed railroads, trestle works, bridges, burning locomotives & rolling stock taking prisoners destroying stores of all kinds. To use the expression of my informant 'Grierson has knocked the heart out of the State.'" Grant to Halleck, May 3, 1863, *Papers of Grant*, vol. 8, 144.

79. Grant, *Memoirs*, 326–28; Bearss, "Grant Moves Inland," 6–7; Weigley, *Great Civil War*, 266.

80. Grant to Halleck, May 3, 1863, *Papers of Grant*, vol. 8, 145–48 at 147–48.

81. Poulter, "Decision III," 78.

82. Grant, *Memoirs*, 328–29; Bearss, "Grant Moves Inland," 7–8.

83. T. Harry Williams, *McClellan, Sherman and Grant* (New Brunswick: Rutgers University Press, 1962) [hereafter Williams, *McClellan, Sherman and Grant*], 95.

84. Buell, *Warrior Generals*, 247.

85. Grant to Sherman, May 9, 1863, *Papers of Grant*, vol. 8, 183–84.

86. Grant, *Memoirs*, 328, 330; Bearss, "Grant Moves Inland," 8, 11 (quote on 8). On May 10 Grant rejected a complaint from McClernand about "a very small number of teams" and pointed out that each corps had been provided with equal transportation. Grant to McClernand, May 10, 1863, *Papers of Grant*, vol. 8, 192–93 at 193.

87. Feis, *Grant's Secret Service*, 160.

88. Fuller, *Generalship of Grant*, 140–46.

89. Trudeau, Noah Andre, "Climax at Vicksburg," *North & South* 1, no. 5 (June 1998), 80–89 [hereafter Trudeau, "Climax at Vicksburg"] at 83.

90. For details on the Battle of Raymond, see Bearss, *Vicksburg*, II, 483–517.

91. Grant, *Memoirs*, 330–31; Bearss, "Grant Moves Inland," 8–21; Arnold, *Grant Wins*, 129–36; Fox, *Regimental Losses*, 544, 550.

92. Bearss, "Grant Moves Inland," 10; Smith, *Grant*, 245; William C. Davis, *Jefferson Davis: The Man and His Hour* (Baton Rouge: Louisiana State University Press, 1991), 501–4.

93. Grant, *Memoirs*, 332; Bearss, "Grant Moves Inland," 21–22; William B. Feis, "Charles S. Bell: Union Scout," *North & South* 4, no. 5 (June 2001): 26–37 [hereafter Feis, "Charles S. Bell"] at 28–29; Grant to McClernand, McPherson, and Sherman (three dispatches), May 12, 1863, *Papers of Grant*, vol. 8, 204–8; Grant to McClernand (two dispatches), May 13, 1863, Ibid., 208–9.

94. For a compelling argument that the loss of Vicksburg resulted from President Davis's ostrich-like behavior, Pemberton's incompetence, and Johnston's reluctance to fight, see Terrence J. Winschel, "A Tragedy of Errors: The Failure of the Confederate High Command in the Defense of Vicksburg," *North & South* 8, no. 7 (Jan. 2006): 40–49.

95. Grant, *Memoirs*, 333; Bearss, "Grant Moves Inland," 46–47.

96. Feis, *Grant's Secret Service*, 161.

97. For details on the Battle of Jackson, see Bearss, *Vicksburg*, II, 519–58.

98. Grant, *Memoirs*, 334–38; Bearss, "Grant Moves Inland," 47–51, 65; "The Opposing Forces in the Vicksburg Campaign," in Robert Underwood Johnson and Clarence Clough Buel, eds., *Battles and Leaders of the Civil War* (4 vols.) (New York: Thomas Yoseloff, Inc., 1956) (Reprint of Secaucus, New Jersey: Castle, 1887–8), vol. 3, 546–50 [hereafter "Opposing

Forces"] at 549; Weigley, *Great Civil War*, 267; Harold S. Wilson, *Confederate Industry: Manufacturers and Quartermasters in the Civil War* (Jackson: University of Mississippi Press, 2002), 192–93.

99. Feis, "Charles S. Bell," 29. Sherman's men tore up railroad ties and rails, set the ties on fire, heated the rails on those fires, and then bent the rails around trees and telegraph poles in what became known as "Sherman neckties." Bearss, "Grant Moves Inland," 52.

100. Grant, *Memoirs*, 340–41; Feis, *Grant's Secret Service*, 163; Ed Bearss, "The Vicksburg Campaign. Grant Marches West: The Battles of Champion Hill and Big Black Bridge," *Blue & Gray Magazine* XVIII, Issue 5 (June 2001), 6–24, 44–52 [hereafter Bearss, "Grant Marches West"] at 8–9. The Bearss article contains excellent maps of both those battles. For more details and battle maps on the Battle of Champion Hill, see Arnold, *Grant Wins*, 147–99 and Bearss, *Vicksburg*, II, 559–651.

101. Bearss, "Grant Marches West," 9–11.

102. Ibid., 16.

103. Ibid., 12, 16–19; Arnold, *Grant Wins*, 158–69.

104. Bearss, "Grant Marches West," 13, 20–21; Arnold, *Grant Wins*, 170–78.

105. Bearss, "Grant Marches West," 14, 21–24; Arnold, *Grant Wins*, 178–92; Foote, *Civil War*, vol. 2, 372–73.

106. Bearss, "Grant Marches West," 15, 44–45.

107. Grant, *Memoirs*, 342–48; Thomas L. Livermore, *Numbers & Losses in the Civil War in America:1861–65* (Millwood, New York: Kraus Reprint Co., 1977) (Reprint of Bloomington: Indiana University Press, 1957) [hereafter Livermore, *Numbers & Losses*], 99–100; Bearss, "Grant Marches West," 45.

108. Arnold, *Grant Wins*, 197–99; Foote, *Civil War*, II, 375; Grant, *Memoirs*, 349.

109. Grant, *Memoirs*, 349–50; Bearss, "Grant Marches West," 45; Freeman, Kirk, "Big Black River," *Military Heritage* 2, no. 3 (Dec. 2000): 76–85 [hereafter Freeman, "Big Black River,"] at 78–80; Al W. Goodman Jr., "Decision in the West (Part IV): Between Hell and the Deep Sea: Pemberton's Debacle at Big Black River Bridge," *North & South* 1, no. 5 (June 1998): 74–79 [hereafter Goodman, "Decision"] at 74–77.

110. For details and battle maps of the Battle of the Big Black River, see Freeman, "Big Black River"; Goodman, "Decision"; Arnold, *Grant Wins*, 225–32; and Bearss, *Vicksburg*, II, 653–89.

111. Grant, *Memoirs*, 350–53; Bearss, "Grant Marches West," 45–46; Freeman, "Big Black River," 81–85; Goodman, "Decision," 77–79; Dick

Barton, "Charge at Big Black River," *America's Civil War* 12, no. 4 (Sept. 1999): 54–61 [hereafter Barton, "Charge"].

112. Grant, *Memoirs*, 350–54; Bearss, "Grant Marches West," 49.

113. Grant, *Memoirs*, 354. In fact, Sherman had verbally and by letter urged Grant before the crossing of the Mississippi not to undertake the risky campaign with no base or line of supply. Grant was more concerned about the impact in the North if he appeared to be retreating by returning to Memphis to restart a presumably safer overland campaign against Vicksburg. As soon as Vicksburg was besieged, Sherman himself revealed his earlier opposition. But Grant was fully forgiving: "[Sherman's] untiring energy and great efficiency during the campaign entitle him to a full share of all the credit due for its success. He could not have done more if the plan had been his own." Grant, *Memoirs*, 364.

114. Russell F. Weigley, *The American Way of War: A History of United States Military Strategy and Policy* (New York: Macmillan Publishing Co., Inc., 1973) [hereafter Weigley, *American Way of War*], 139–40; Francis Vinton Greene, *This Mississippi* (New York: Charles Scribner's Sons, 1884), 170–71.

115. May 25, 1863 correspondence in the *Philadelphia Inquirer*, reprinted in the *Chicago Tribune*, May 29, 1863, and cited in Fehrenbacher and Fehrenbacher, *Recollected Words*, 11.

116. Among his many arguments to Davis, Lee contended that the oppressive Mississippi climate would cause Grant to withdraw from the Vicksburg area in June. Edward H. Bonekemper III, *How Robert E. Lee Lost the Civil War* (Fredericksburg, Virginia: Sergeant Kirkland's Press, 1998) [hereafter Bonekemper, *How Lee Lost*], 101.

117. Grant, *Memoirs*, 354–56; Bearss, *Vicksburg*, III, 753–873. The often unreliable *Chicago Times* reporter Sylvanus Cadwallader observed and said of McClernand's May 22 attack: "McClernand had commenced his attack. He expected to succeed. But that he ever carried any part of the fortifications on his front, as he signaled Grant he had already done, was absolutely false." Sylvanus Cadwallader, *Three Years with Grant* (New York: Alfred A. Knopf, 1956) [hereafter Cadwallader, *Three Years*], 92. Sherman agreed that McClernand had lied and thereby caused many additional casualties. William Tecumseh Sherman, *Memoirs of General William T. Sherman* (New York: D. Appleton and Co., 1889) (2 vols.) [hereafter Sherman, *Memoirs*], vol. 1, 355–56.

118. Grant, *Memoirs*, 588–89.

119. Fuller, *Generalship of Grant*, 154; Livermore, *Numbers & Losses*, 100; Grant, *Memoirs*, 358.

120. Woodworth, *Nothing But Victory*, 433–34.

121. Grant to Halleck, June 19, 1863, OR, Ser. I, XXIV, Part I, 43; Lincoln to Dix, June 24, 1863, *Works of Lincoln*, vol. 6, 293.

122. Grant to Lorenzo Thomas, June 26, 1863, OR, Ser. I, XXIV, Part I, 158–59. (emphasis added).

123. Lincoln to McClernand, Aug. 12, 1863, *Works of Lincoln*, vol. 6, 383; Ibid., 383–84; McClernand to Lincoln, Aug. 24, 1863, Ibid., 384n; Stanton to McClernand, Sept. 14, 1863, OR, Ser. I, XXIV, Part I, 169; McClernand to Lincoln, Jan. 14, 1864, *Works of Lincoln*, vol. 6, 384n.

124. Reports of this alleged event came from Chicago reporter Sylvanus Cadwallader, a very unreliable source, and Grant's Chief-of-Staff John Rawlins, who seemed to have positioned himself to take credit for stopping Grant's drinking.

125. B. A. Botkin, ed., *A Civil War Treasury of Tales, Legends and Folklore* (New York: Promontory Press, 1960) [hereafter Botkin, *Treasury*], 243–44. Lincoln's Third Secretary William O. Stoddard Jr. alleged that Lincoln said he would purchase a few barrels for some of the generals in the East. Stoddard to Charles G. Halpine, editor of the *New York Citizen*, Aug. 25, 1866, in Stoddard, *Inside the White House*, 149. Chaplain John Eaton said Lincoln told a similar story. He also described conversations with Grant in which the general described how a fellow officer and reporters with grievances against him spread false stories of his drinking while he commanded at Cairo. Eaton, *Grant, Lincoln*, 90, 101–2.

126. Grant, *Memoirs*, 359–60, 1134; James R. Arnold, *The Armies of U. S. Grant* (London: Arms and Armour Press, 1995) [hereafter, Arnold, *Armies of Grant*], 127; Chris E. Evans, "Return to Jackson: Finishing Stroke to the Vicksburg Campaign, July 5–25, 1863" *Blue & Gray Magazine* XII, Issue 6 (Aug. 1995): 8–22, 50–63 [hereafter Evans, "Return to Jackson"] at 12; Trudeau, "Climax at Vicksburg," 86.

127. McPherson, *Mighty Scourge*, 141, citing James F. Rusling, *Men and Things I Saw in Civil War Days* (New York, 1899), 16–17.

128. Grant, *Memoirs*, 368; Evans, "Return to Jackson," 12.

129. Grant, *Memoirs*, 369–70; Phillip A. B. Leonard, "Forty-seven Days. Constant bombardment, life in bomb shelters, scarce food and water, and rapidly accumulating filth were the price of resistance for the resolute Confederate citizens of besieged Vicksburg, Mississippi," *Civil War Times Illustrated* XXXIX, no. 4 (August 2000): 40–49, 68–69; Evans, "Return

to Jackson," 14; Smith, "Too Little," 44; Andrew Hickenlooper, "The Vicksburg Mine" in Johnson and Buel, *Battles and Leaders*, III, 539–42. Vicksburg residents' primary meats were mules and rats. Anonymous, "Daily Life during the Siege of Vicksburg," in William E. Gienapp, ed., *The Civil War and Reconstruction: A Documentary Collection* (New York: W.W. Norton and Company, 2001), 159–62.

130. Lincoln to Hurlbut, May 22, 1863, *Works of Lincoln*, VI, 226; Hurlbut to Lincoln, May 23, 1863, Ibid., 226n and OR, Ser. I, XXIV, Part III, 344.

131. Lincoln to Isaac N. Arnold, May 26, 1863, *Works of Lincoln*, vol. 6, 230–31 at 230.

132. Lincoln to Hooker, May 27, 1863, *Works of Lincoln*, vol. 6, 233; Lincoln to Rosecrans, May 27, 1863, Ibid.; Rosecrans to Lincoln, May 27, 1863, Ibid., 233n.

133. Lincoln to Rosecrans, May 28, 1863, Ibid., 236.

134. Halleck to Rosecrans, June 2, 1863, OR, Ser. I, XXIV, Part III, 376; Rosecrans to Halleck, June 2, 1863, Ibid., 376–77; Halleck to Rosecrans, June 11, 1863, Ibid., XXIII, Part I, 10; Rosecrans to Halleck, June 11, 1863, Ibid., 8; Halleck to Rosecrans, June 12, 1863, Ibid.

135. Lincoln to Grant, June 2, 1863, *Works of Lincoln*, vol. 6, 244; Grant to Lincoln, June 8, 1863, Ibid., 244n.

136. Lincoln to John A. Dix, June 6, 1863, Ibid., 252; June 8, 1863, Ibid., 254.

137. Eaton, *Grant, Lincoln*, 64.

138. Ibid., 64–71.

139. Lincoln to Hooker, June 5, 1863, *Works of Lincoln*, vol 6, 249; June 10, 1863, Ibid., 257.

140. Gideon Welles, *Diary of Gideon Welles* (3 vols.) (Boston and New York: Houghton Mifflin Company, 1911) [hereafter Welles, *Diary*], vol. 1, 364–65; Hearn, *Lincoln, Cabinet, Generals*, 168.

141. Hearn, *Lincoln, Cabinet, Generals*, 180.

142. Lincoln to Halleck, July 6, 1863, *Works of Lincoln*, vol. 7, 318.

143. Lincoln to Halleck, July 7, 1863, Ibid., 319; *Civil War Times* XLVI, no. 8 (Oct. 2007): 11. The original of this note, quoted verbatim in a contemporary wire from Halleck to Meade, was finally discovered in the National Archives in early 2007. Ibid.

144. Lincoln to Frederick F. Low, July 8, 1863, *Works of Lincoln*, vol. 6, 321; Lincoln to Lorenzo Thomas, July 8, 1863, Ibid., 321–22 at 322.

145. Eaton, *Grant, Lincoln*, 64–65, 88–93 at 88, 93.

146. Lincoln to Grant, July 13, 1863, *Works of Lincoln*, vol. 6, 326.

147. Lincoln did send a similar letter to Sherman after his capture of Savannah. In that letter, Lincoln also praised Thomas's defeat of Hood in Tennessee and ignored Sherman's allowing a Rebel force to escape from Savannah. Lincoln to Sherman, Dec. 26, 1864, Ibid., VIII, 181–82.

148. Lincoln to Grant, August 9, 1863, Ibid., vol. 6, 374; Grant to Lincoln, August 23, 1863, *Papers of Grant*, vol. 9, 195–97 at 195, 197.

149. Halleck to Meade, July 14, 1863, 1 p.m., OR, Ser. I, XXVII, Part I, 92; Meade to Halleck, July 14, 1863, 2:30 p.m., Ibid., 93; Halleck to Meade, July 14, 1863, 4:30 p.m., Ibid., 93–94.

150. Lincoln to Meade (not sent), July 14, 1863, *Works of Lincoln*, vol. 6, 327–28 at 328 (emphasis added).

151. Eaton, *Grant, Lincoln*, 94–95. Lincoln and Grant may have been too harsh on Meade, whose own army had been battered at Gettysburg and was not in the best condition to immediately pursue Lee's retreating army. In 1864 and 1865 they appear to have backed off and were content to allow Meade to continue to play a major role in the Eastern Theater.

152. For details on the Battle of Milliken's Bend, see Richard Lowe, "Battle on the Levee: The Fight at Milliken's Bend" in John David Smith, ed., *Black Soldiers in Blue: African American Troops in the Civil War Era* (Chapel Hill: University of North Carolina Press, 2003) [hereafter Smith, *Black Soldiers*], 107–35.

153. Ibid., 128; Guelzo, *Lincoln's Proclamation*, 248.

154. Charles A. Dana, *Recollections of the Civil War* (New York: Collier Books, 1898, 1963) [hereafter Dana, *Recollections*], 93–94.

155. For details, see Lawrence Lee Hewitt, "An Ironic Route to Glory: Louisiana's Native Guards at Port Hudson" in Smith, *Black Soldiers*, 78–106.

156. Lincoln to Stanton, July 21, 1863, *Works of Lincoln*, vol. 6, 342.

157. General Orders No. 252, July 30, 1863, Ibid., 357.

158. Lincoln to Grant, August 9, 1863, Ibid., 374; *Papers of Grant*, vol. 9, 197n; OR, Ser. I, XXIV, Part III, 584.

159. Grant's "heavyest blow" phrase caught Lincoln's attention, and he used it in an August 26 letter to James C. Conkling of Illinois. He wrote, "I know as fully as one can know the opinions of others, that some of the commanders of our armies in the field who have given us our most important successes, believe the emancipation policy, and the use of colored troops, constitute the heaviest blow yet dealt to the rebellion...." Lincoln to Conkling, Aug. 26, 1863, *Works of Lincoln*, vol. 6, 406–410 at 408–409.

160. Grant to Lincoln, August 23, 1863, *Papers of Grant*, vol. 9, 195–97 at 196–97; Henry Louis Gates Jr., *Lincoln on Race & Slavery* (Princeton: Princeton University Press, 2009), xli. Blacks had demonstrated their effectiveness and courage at Port Hudson on May 27, 1863, and at Milliken's Bend on June 7, 1863. Ibid.

161. Lincoln to Burnside, July 27, 1863, *Works of Lincoln*, vol. 6, 350. Grant returned the Ninth Corps to Burnside in a July 31 order. Ibid., note.

Chapter 8: Lincoln Calls on Grant to Save a Union Army

1. Grant to Halleck, July 24, 1863, OR, Ser. I, XXIV, III, 546–47.
2. Lincoln to Grant, Aug. 9, 1863, *Works of Lincoln*, vol. 6, 374.
3. Hay, *Diary*, August 9, 1863, 71.
4. Grant to Lincoln, Aug. 23, 1863, *Papers of Grant*, vol. 9, 195–97 at 195–96.
5. Hearn, *Lincoln, Cabinet, Generals*, 185.
6. Halleck to Grant, January 8, 1864, OR, Ser. I, XXXII, Part II, 40–43 at 41. Although the desperate Confederacy had recognized Maximilian as Mexico's emperor, the French ultimately abandoned him and he was captured and executed by Benito Juarez.
7. Halleck to Rosecrans, July 24, 1863 (two messages), OR, Ser. I, XXIII, Part II, 552; Rosecrans to Halleck, Aug. 1, 1863, Ibid., 585–86; Rosecrans to Lincoln, Aug. 1, 1863, *Works of Lincoln*, vol. 6, 378n.
8. Lincoln to Rosecrans, Aug. 10, 1863, Ibid., 377–78 at 377.
9. Rosecrans to Lincoln, Aug. 22, 1863, Ibid., 425n; Lincoln to Rosecrans, Aug. 31, 1863, Ibid., 424–25.
10. Lincoln to Halleck, Sept. 19, 1863, Ibid., 466–67 at 467. A month later Lincoln was still upset by Meade's failure to attack Lee; he said that this failure confirmed Lee in his belief that the Union had sent four, not just two, corps to Chattanooga. Lincoln to Halleck, Oct. 16, 1863, Ibid., 518.
11. The Confederate transfer of troops from Virginia to Georgia caught the Union hierarchy completely by surprise. On September 11, Halleck had advised Rosecrans, "It is reported here by deserters that a part of Bragg's army is re-enforcing Lee. It is important that the truth of this should be ascertained as early as possible." Halleck to Rosecrans, Sept. 11, 1863, OR, Ser. I, XXX, Part I, 148. The reinforcements, in fact, were moving the opposite way.
12. Lincoln to Halleck, Sept. 21, 1863, *Works of Lincoln*, vol. 6, 470–471.

13. Lincoln to Burnside, Sept. 21, 1863, 2 a.m., Ibid., 469; Sept. 21, 1863, 11 a.m., Ibid., 470; Sept. 25, 1863, Ibid., 480–81; Sept. 27, 1863, Ibid., 483; Sept. 27, 1863, Ibid., 484. Although Burnside had occupied Knoxville, a long-sought goal of Lincoln, that general had quickly lost the confidence of Lincoln, who wrote to him on September 25, "Yours of the 23rd. Is just received, and it makes me doubt whether I am awake or dreaming. I have been struggling for ten days...to get you to go to assist Gen. Rosecrans in an extremity, and you have repeatedly declared you would do it, and yet you steadily move the contrary way." Lincoln to Burnside, Sept. 25, 1863, Ibid., 480–81.

14. See, e.g., Lincoln to Grant, Oct. 8, 1862, Ibid., vol. 5, 453 and note.

15. Halleck to James H. Wilson, Oct. 3, 1863, *Papers of Grant*, vol. 9, 276–77n.

16. Lincoln to Rosecrans, Oct. 4, 1863, *Works of Lincoln*, vol. 6, 498.

17. Lincoln to Rosecrans, Oct. 12, 1863, Ibid., 510.

18. In a November 2, 1863 diary entry, Hay wrote that Lincoln told him Grant had relieved Rosecrans because he believed Rosecrans "never would obey orders"—a logical conclusion after their interplay at the last Battle of Corinth. Hay, *Diary*, 108.

19. McPherson, *Tried by War*, 196.

20. Dana to Stanton, Oct. 29, 1863, OR, Ser. I, XXXI, Part I, 72–73; Lincoln to Seward, Nov. 1, 1863, *Works of Lincoln*, vol. 6, 554.

21. Beauregard devised a plan for massive Confederate reinforcement of Chattanooga with 25,000 troops from Lee in Virginia and 10,000 from Joseph Johnston in Mississippi, but at an October 11 council of war Davis rejected the plan because Lee was not willing to provide more troops. Bonekemper, *How Lee Lost*, 142.

22. It appears that Longstreet and Lee wanted Longstreet to proceed from Knoxville back to Virginia but that Bragg and possibly Davis wanted Longstreet to return to Chattanooga after disposing of Burnside.

23. As of October 24, Lincoln was under the mis-impression that Lee had sent Ewell's corps to eastern Tennessee. Lincoln to Halleck, Oct. 24, 1863, *Works of Lincoln*, vol. 6, 534 and 534–35n.

24. Peter Cozzens, *The Shipwreck of Their Hopes: The Battles for Chattanooga* (Urbana: University of Illinois Press, 1994), 103–6, 390. See Jeffry D. Wert, *General James Longstreet: The Confederacy's Most Controversial Soldier: A Biography* (New York: Simon & Schuster, 1993), 338–39; Bonekemper, *How Lee Lost*, 142–44.

25. Lincoln's Proclamation Calling for 300,000 Volunteers, Oct. 17, 1863, Ibid., 523–24.

26. Lincoln's Order for Draft of 500,000 Men, Feb. 1, 1864, Ibid., vol. 7, 164; Lincoln's Order for Draft of 200,000 Men, March 14, 1864, Ibid., 245.

27. Lincoln to Burnside, Nov. 16, 1863, Ibid., 14; Burnside to Lincoln, Nov. 17, 1863, Ibid. note.

28. Lincoln's Gettysburg Address, Nov. 19, 1863, Ibid., 17–23 at 23.

29. Hay, *Diary*, 117.

30. Grant to Halleck, Nov. 23, 1863, OR, Ser. I, XXXI, Part II, 24, Nov. 24, 1863, Ibid.; Lincoln to Grant, Nov. 25, 1863, *Works of Lincoln*, vol. 7, 30.

31. Grant to Halleck, Dec. 6, 1863, OR, Ser. I, XXXI, Part III, 345.

32. Executive Mansion Announcement of Union Success in Tennessee (signed by Lincoln), Dec. 7, 1863, *Works of Lincoln*, vol. 7, 35.

33. Lincoln's Annual Address to Congress, Dec. 8, 1863, Ibid., 36–53 at 59.

34. Lincoln to Grant, Dec. 8, 1863, Ibid., 53.

35. Ibid., 53n, citing General Orders No. 7, Military Division of the Mississippi, Dec. 8, 1863.

36. Dennis W. Brandt, "A Question of Cowardice," *America's Civil War* 20, no. 2 (May 2007): 54–62 at 56.

37. Lincoln to Grant, Dec. 19, 1863, *Works of Lincoln*, vol. 7, 80 and note. For details on the life and career of Robert Milroy, see Jonathan A. Noyalas, *"My Will Is Absolute Law"): A Biography of General Robert H. Milroy* (Jefferson, North Carolina: McFarland, 2006).

38. Governor Thomas E. Bramlette to Lincoln, Jan. 5, 1864, *Works of Lincoln*, vol. 7, 109n; Lincoln to Bramlette, Jan. 6, 1864, Ibid., 109. Union General Foster had just received a complaint from General Longstreet about handbills distributed to Confederate soldiers inducing them to desert. Longstreet said, "I respectfully suggest, for your consideration, the propriety of communicating any views that your Government may have upon this subject through me." Longstreet to Foster, Jan. 3, 1864, OR, Ser. I, III, Part IV, 50–51. Foster responded, "I accept…your suggestion that it would have been more courteous to have sent these documents to you for circulation, and I embrace with pleasure the opportunity thus afforded to enclose to you twenty (20) copies of each of these documents and rely upon your generosity and desire for peace, to give publicity to the same among your officers and men." Foster to Longstreet, Jan. 7, 1864, Ibid. What a clever riposte! Even Longstreet must have smiled.

Chapter 9: Lincoln Elevates Grant to General-in-Chief

1.   Hearn, *Lincoln, Cabinet, Generals*, 209.
2.   Lincoln to the Senate, Dec. 8, 1863, *Works of Lincoln*, vol. 7, 56–57.
3.   Winfield Scott had been a brevet (honorary) lieutenant general.
4.   Halleck to Grant, January 8, 1864, OR, Ser. I, XXXII, Part II, 40–43 at 41.
5.   Lincoln to Elihu B. Washburne, Dec. 18, 1863, *Works of Lincoln*, 79 and note.
6.   Bruce Catton, *Grant Takes Command* (Boston: Little, Brown and Company, 1969) [hereafter Catton, *Grant Takes Command*], 93; Grant to Halleck, Dec. 7, 1863, *Papers of Grant*, vol. 9, 500–1.
7.   Grant to Halleck, OR, Ser. I, XXXII, Part II, 99–101; Halleck to Grant, Jan. 18, 1864, OR, Ser. I, XXXII, Part II, 126–27.
8.   Eaton, *Grant, Lincoln*, 116–21. A harbinger of Grant and Thomas's later falling-out can be found in Eaton's statement, "Of Thomas I remember [Grant] once said that one of the few qualities of a great general in which he was lacking was confidence in himself." Ibid., 118.
9.   Eaton, *Grant, Lincoln*, 119–21 at 121.
10.   Chase to Lincoln, Feb. 22, 1864, *Works of Lincoln*, vol. 7, 200–1n; Lincoln to Chase, Feb. 23, 1864, Ibid., 200; Feb. 29, 1864, Ibid., 212–13.
11.   Hay, *Diary*, 132–33 at 133.
12.   Grant to Washburne, Aug. 30, 1863, *Papers of Grant*, vol. 9, 217–18.
13.   Ibid., 543n; Simpson, *Grant*, 254–257; Ida M. Tarbell, *The Life of Abraham Lincoln*, 4 vols. (Springfield, Illinois: Lincoln History Society, 1903), vol. 3, 187–89; Halleck to Sherman, Feb. 16, 1864, OR, Ser. I, XXXII, Part II, 407–8 at 408.
14.   Halleck to Grant, Feb. 17 1864, OR, Ser. I, XXXII, Part II, 411–13 at 413.
15.   Ibid.
16.   R. Steven Jones, *The Right Hand of Command: Use & Disuse of Personal Staffs in the Civil War* (Mechanicsburg, PA: Stackpole Books, 2000) [hereafter Jones, *Right Hand*], 192.
17.   Simpson, "Lincoln and Grant," 114.
18.   *Works of Lincoln*, vol. 7, 234n; Nicolay and Hay, *Lincoln*, vol. 8, 340–41.
19.   Nicolay and Hay, *Lincoln*, vol. 8, 340–41.
20.   *Works of Lincoln*, vol. 7, 234.
21.   Ibid., 234–35n.
22.   Lincoln to Grant, March 10, 1864, Ibid., 235 and note; Smith, *Grant*, 294.
23.   Order Assigning Ulysses S. Grant to Command of the Armies of the United States, OR, Ser. I, XXXII, III, 83; *Works of Lincoln*, vol. 7, 236.

24. War Department General Orders No. 98, March 12, 1864, *Works of Lincoln*, vol. 7, 239–40.

25. Marszalek, *Halleck*, 197. "Halleck could now administer without commanding, which is essentially what he had been doing since his arrival in Washington in July 1862." Ibid.

26. McPherson, *Tried by War*, 8. See the last chapter of this book for a full discussion of their respective roles.

27. Lincoln's List of Candidates for West Point, c. March 10, 1864, *Works of Lincoln*, vol. 7, 235; Lincoln's Memorandum: Appointment of John D. C. Hoskins, Jan. 20, 1864, Ibid., 139 and note; Grant, *Memoirs*, vol. 1, 111–12.

28. Lincoln to Grant, March 15, 1864, *Works of Lincoln*, vol. 7, 248 and note. See also Lincoln to Stanton, April 21, 1864, Ibid., 307; Lincoln to the House of Representatives, April 28, 1864, Ibid., 319–20; and Lincoln to the House of Representatives, May 2, 1864, Ibid., 326–27.

29. Grant to Halleck, April —, 1864, Ibid., 300n; Lincoln to Halleck, April 16, 1864, Ibid., 300 and OR, Ser. I, XXXIV, Part III, 178.

30. Catton, *Grant Takes Command*, 139.

31. Lincoln to Grant, March 29, 1864, *Works of Lincoln*, vol. 7, 272; Grant to Lincoln, March 29, 1864, Ibid., 272n.

32. Lincoln to Stanton, April 5, 1864, Ibid., 287. Johnson had pleaded, "The papers state that Genl Buell is to be sent to Knoxville to take Command. I trust in god that Gen Buell will not be sent to Tennessee. We have been cursed with him here once and do not desire its repetition." Johnson to Lincoln, April 5, 1864, Ibid., 287–88n.

33. Sherman to Hurlbut, April 16, 1864, OR, Ser. I, XXXII, Part III, 381.

34. Ibid., 405–6.

35. Lincoln to Hurlbut, May 2, 1864, *Works of Lincoln*, vol. 7, 327.

36. Grant to Halleck, April 22, 25, 29, 30, 1864, Halleck to Grant, April 23, 26, 29 and May 3, 1864, OR, Ser. I, XXXIV, Part III, 252–53, 331, 357, 293, 331–32, 409–10; McPherson, *Tried by War*, 216–17.

37. McPherson, *Tried by War*, 217.

38. Lincoln to Albert G. Hodges, April 4, 1864, *Works of Lincoln*, vol. 7, 281–82.

39. Although the occurrence of a massacre was contested by Forrest, "Lost Cause" advocates, and others, the preponderance of the evidence indicates that Confederates did indeed massacre surrendering black troops at Fort Pillow. John Cimprich, "The Fort Pillow Massacre: Assessing the Evidence," in Smith, *Black Soldiers*, 150–68; Albert Castel, "The Fort Pillow

Massacre: A Fresh Examination of the Evidence," *Civil War History* 4 (March 1958): 37–50 at 45, 48–50.

40.   Lincoln to Cabinet members, May 3, 1864, *Works of Lincoln*, vol. 7, 328 and Ibid., 329n.

41.   Draft memorandum from Lincoln to Stanton, May 17, 1864, Ibid., 346–47 and note. See Nicolay and Hay, *Lincoln*, vol. 6, 478–84 for further discussion of the Fort Pillow massacre and White House reaction to it.

42.   Governors Brough, Morton, Yates, Stone and Lewis to Lincoln, April 21, 1864, *Works of Lincoln*, vol. 7, 312–13n. Four of the governors had met with Lincoln during the day on April 21 and were scheduled to meet with Lincoln, Stanton and Halleck that evening. Lincoln to Stanton, April 21, 1864, Ibid., 308.

43.   Grant to Stanton, April 21, 1864, *Papers of Grant*, vol. 10, 335. Grant was responding to Stanton's specific request whether the four governors' offer should be accepted or refused. Stanton to Grant, April 21, 1864, Ibid., 335n. Stanton's request, and thus Grant's answer, omitted Wisconsin.

44.   Stanton to Lincoln, April 22, 1864, Ibid., 312–13n; Lincoln to Stanton, April 23, 1864, Ibid., 312. On June 11, 1864, a 100-day unit, the 130th Ohio Regiment, came by the White House on the way to the front. *Works of Lincoln*, vol. 7, 388–89 and note, quoting the *New York Tribune*, June 13, 1864.

Chapter 10: Grant Goes on the Offensive with Lincoln's Full Support

1.   Rhea quoted in "Reconsidering Grant and Lee: Reputations of Civil War Generals Shifting," Associated Press, http://www.cnn.com/2003/SHOWBIZ/books/01/08/wkd.Grant.vs.Lee.ap/index.html [hereafter "Reconsidering Grant and Lee"].

2.   Rhea, "'Butcher' Grant," 46.

3.   Michael C. C. Adams, *Fighting for Defeat: Union Military Failure in the East, 1861–1865* (Lincoln: University of Nebraska, 1978, 1992) [hereafter Adams, *Fighting for Defeat*], 150.

4.   Bruce Catton, *This Hallowed Ground: The Story of the Union Side of the Civil War* (Garden City, New York: Doubleday & Company, Inc., 1956, 1962), 39–40.

5.   Eric A. Campbell, "'Slept in the mud, stood in the mud, kneeled in the mud," *America's Civil War* 15, no. 6 (January 2003): 50–55 at 54–55.

6. Brian Holden Reid, "Civil-Military Relations and the Legacy of the Civil War" in Susan-Mary Grant and Peter J. Parish, eds., *Legacy of Disunion: The Enduring Significance of the American Civil War* (Baton Rouge: Louisiana State University Press, 2003), 151–70 at 157.

7. Lincoln to Grant, April 30, 1864, *Works of Lincoln*, vol. 7, 324.

8. Grant to Lincoln, May 1, 1864, *Papers of Grant*, vol. 10, 380.

9. Stoddard, *Inside the White House*, 126.

10. Geoffrey Perret, *Ulysses S. Grant: Soldier & President* (New York: Random House, 1997) [hereafter Perret, *Grant*], 304.

11. Grant, *Memoirs*, 470–71.

12. Catton, "Generalship of Grant," 24. Richard J. Sommers said, "Prudent and competent, Meade would never have lost the war in Virginia, but, unaided, he would never have won it, either." Richard J. Sommers, *Richmond Redeemed: The Siege at Petersburg* (Garden City: Doubleday & Company, 1981) [hereafter Sommers, *Richmond Redeemed*], 437.

13. Robert N. Thompson, "The Folly and Horror of Cold Harbor," *Military History* 23, no. 8 (Nov. 2006): 38–45. Thompson demonstrates the problems caused by this bifurcated command structure—including, most notably, at Cold Harbor.

14. Smith, *Grant*, 292–94.

15. Grant, *Memoirs*, 480–81.

16. Jones, *Right Hand*, 59–60, 191–92, 219.

17. "Grant, Lincoln," 168–69.

18. Hay, *Diary*, 183.

19. Ibid., 191–92.

20. Marszalek, *Halleck*, 201–2.

21. Bruce Catton, *The Army of the Potomac: A Stillness at Appomattox* (Garden City, New York: Doubleday & Company, Inc., 1953), 37, 44–49.

22. See Bonekemper, *Victor*, 5, 258–59.

23. Grant, *Memoirs*, 478–79; Jeffry D. Wert, "All-out War," *Civil War Times* LXIII, no. 1 (April 2004), 34–40 [hereafter Wert, "All-out War"].

24. John Y. Simon, "Grant, Lincoln, and Unconditional Surrender," in Gabor S. Boritt, ed., *Lincoln's Generals* (New York and Oxford: Oxford University Press, 1994), 161–98 [hereafter Simon, "Grant, Lincoln"] at 168; Grant to Sherman, April 4, 1864, *Papers of Grant*, vol. 10, 251–53 at 253.

25. Herman Hattaway and Archer Jones, *How the North Won: A Military History of the Civil War* (Urbana and Chicago: University of Illinois Press, 1991) (Reprint of 1983 edition) [hereafter Hattaway and Jones, *How the*

North Won], 516–33; Grant to Meade, April 9, 1864, *Papers of Grant*, vol. 10, 273–75 at 274; Bonekemper, *How Lee Lost*, 145–46.

26. Thomas Lawrence Connelly and Archer Jones, *The Politics of Command: Factions and Ideas in Confederate Strategy* (Baton Rouge: Louisiana State University Press, 1973) [hereafter Connelly and Jones, *Politics of Command*], 179–81.

27. Grant, *Memoirs*, 471–73. Some historians plausibly contend that seizing Atlanta was a major or primary objective of Grant. Hattaway and Jones, *How the North Won*, 532.

28. Smith, *Grant*, 296.

29. Connelly and Jones, *Politics of Command*, 180–81.

30. John F. Marszalek, *Sherman: A Soldier's Passion for Order* (New York: Macmillan, Inc., 1993) [hereafter Marszalek, *Sherman*], 263.

31. Grant, *Memoirs*, 473.

32. Rhea, "'Butcher' Grant," 45.

33. Catton, "Generalship of Grant," 22–24.

34. Ibid., 201–3.

35. Thomas, *Lee*, 322; Lee to Davis, March 25, 1863; Robert E. Lee, *Lee's Dispatches: Unpublished Letters of General Robert E. Lee, C.S.A., to Jefferson Davis and the War Department of the Confederate States of America 1862–65*, ed. Douglas Southall Freeman (Baton Rouge: Louisiana State University Press, 1957) [hereafter *Lee's Dispatches*], 140–43.

36. Grant, *Memoirs*, 481–82; Feis, *Grant's Secret Service*, 203–5; Grant to Meade, April 9, 1864, *Papers of Grant*, vol. 10, 273–75 at 274.

37. Feis, *Grant's Secret Service*, 207.

38. Grant to Meade, April 9, 1864, *Papers of Grant*, vol. 10, 273–75 at 275.

39. Ibid., 538; Alfred C. Young, "Numbers and Losses in the Army of Northern Virginia," *North & South* 3, no. 3 (March 2000): 14–29 [hereafter Young, "Numbers and Losses"] at 19. During the course of the Overland Campaign, Lee received about 24,500 reinforcements from elsewhere. Ibid., 19.

40. Smith, *Grant*, 303–4.

41. Richard E. Beringer, Herman Hattaway, Archer Jones, and William N. Still Jr., *Why the South Lost the Civil War* (Athens: University of Georgia Press, 1986) [hereafter Beringer *et al.*, *Why the South Lost*], 316.

42. Rhea, "'Butcher' Grant," 47.

43. Even Confederate General Porter Alexander grudgingly conceded that Grant "was no intellectual genius, but he understood arithmetic." Edward Porter Alexander, *Fighting for the Confederacy: The Personal Recollections*

of General Edward Porter Alexander, ed. Gary W. Gallagher (Chapel Hill: University of North Carolina Press, 1989) [hereafter Alexander, *Fighting for the Confederacy*], 346.

44. The one glaring failure to tie down the Rebels was Jubal Early's breaking loose in July 1864; Lee, true to form, kept him in the Virginia Theater instead of using him to reinforce Atlanta.

45. Grant's 1864 Overland Campaign is described in detail in Noah Andre Trudeau, *Bloody Roads South: The Wilderness to Cold Harbor, May–June 1864* (Boston: Little, Brown and Co., 1989) [hereafter Trudeau, *Bloody Roads*]; Lowry, *No Turning Back*; Don Lowry, *Fate of the Country: The Civil War from June–September 1864* (New York: Hippocrene Books, 1992) [hereafter Lowry, *Fate of the Country*]; Gordon C. Rhea, *The Battle of the Wilderness, May 5–6, 1864* (Baton Rouge: Louisiana State University Press, 1994) [hereafter Rhea, *Wilderness*]; Gordon C. Rhea, *The Battles for Spotsylvania Court House and the Road to Yellow Tavern: May 7–12, 1864* (Baton Rouge: Louisiana State University, 1997) [hereafter Rhea, *Spotsylvania*]; Gordon C. Rhea, *To the North Anna River: Grant and Lee, May 13–25, 1864* (Baton Rouge: Louisiana State University Press, 2000) [hereafter Rhea, *North Anna River*]; Gordon C. Rhea, *Cold Harbor: Grant and Lee May 26–June 3, 1864* (Baton Rouge: Louisiana State University Press, 2002) [hereafter Rhea, *Cold Harbor*]; Richard Wheeler, *On Fields of Fury: From the Wilderness to the Crater: An Eyewitness History* (New York: HarperCollins Publishers, 1991) [hereafter Wheeler, *On Fields of Fury*]; Evander M. Law, "From the Wilderness to Cold Harbor" in *Battles and Leaders* IV, 118–44 [hereafter Law, "From the Wilderness to Cold Harbor"]; and Bonekemper, *Grant and Lee*, 177–98.

46. Lincoln's remarks at Marine Band concert, May 7, 1864, *Works of Lincoln*, vol. 7, 332, quoting *Washington Daily Times*, May 9, 1864.

47. Gideon Welles, May 7, 1864, *Diary*, II, 25; McPherson, *Tried by War*, 218, quoting Francis B. Carpenter, *Six Months at the White House with Abraham Lincoln* (New York: Hurd and Houton, 1866), 30.

48. Hearn, *Lincoln, Cabinet, Generals*, 218–19; Grant to Halleck, May 11, 1864, OR, Ser. I, XXXVI, Part II, 627.

49. Hay, *Diary*, May 9, 1864, 195.

50. The Wilderness was a tactical draw and arguably a strategic Union victory as Grant's army then moved closer to Richmond and forced Lee's to do the same.

51.   Lincoln's response to serenade, May 9, 1864, *Works of Lincoln*, vol. 7, 334 and note, quoting *Washington National Republican*, May 10, 1864.

52.   Lincoln to the Friends of Union and Liberty, May 9, 1864, *Works of Lincoln*, vol. 7, 333.

53.   Lincoln to Mrs. Sarah B. Meconkey, May 9, 1864, Ibid., 333 and note.

54.   Lincoln to Lewis Wallace, May 13, 1864, Ibid., 339–40 at 340 and note.

55.   McPherson, *Tried by War*, 221, quoting Noah Brooks, June 14, 1864 dispatch in July 9, 1864, *Sacramento Union;* Noah Brooks, *Lincoln Observed: Civil War Dispatches of Noah Brooks*, ed. Michael Burlingame (Baltimore: Johns Hopkins University Press, 1998), 113.

56.   Report of Lieutenant General Grant, Commanding Armies of the U.S., on Operations March 1864–May 1865, July 22, 1865, OR, Ser. I, XLVI, Part I, 11–60 at 19.

57.   Hay, *Diary*, May 22, 1864, 197–98.

58.   Simpson, "Lincoln and Grant," 115, 116.

59.   Grant to Halleck, July 7, 1864, OR, Ser. I, XL, Part III, 59; *Works of Lincoln*, 521n.

60.   Lincoln's Draft Order for Draft of 300,000 Men, May 17, 1864, *Works of Lincoln*, vol. 7, 344 and note. See also Lincoln to Chase, May 18, 1864, Ibid., 347, and Lincoln to John A. Dix, May 18, 1864, Ibid., 347–48 and note.

61.   Butler to Lincoln, May 16, 1864, Ibid., 347n; Lincoln to Butler, May 18, 1864, Ibid., 346.

62.   E. A. Paul to Lincoln, May 23, 1864, Ibid., 360n; Lincoln to Stanton, May 24, 1864, Ibid., 360; Stanton to Lincoln, Ibid.

63.   Grant to Halleck, May 23, 11 p.m., OR, Ser. I, XXXVI, Part III, 113–14; Lincoln to John Brough, May 24, 1864, *Works of Lincoln*, vol. 7, 359; Brough to Stanton, May 24, 1864, OR, Ser. III, IV, 405.

64.   Lincoln to Frederick A. Conkling *et al.*, June 3, 1864, *Works of Lincoln*, vol. 7, 374, responding to Conkling *et al.* to Lincoln, May 31, 1864, Ibid., 374n.

65.   Hearn, *Lincoln, Cabinet, Generals*, 223.

66.   Hearn, *Lincoln, Cabinet, Generals*, 223; Nicolay and Hay, *Lincoln*, vol. 9, 59.

67.   Hearn, *Lincoln, Cabinet, Generals*, 224.

68.   Nicolay to Hay, June 5, 1864, *Works of Lincoln*, vol. 7, 376–77n; Lincoln's endorsement on that letter, June 6, 1864, Ibid., 376; Hay to Nicolay, June 6, 1864, Ibid., 377–78n, citing Tyler Dennett, ed., *Lincoln and the Civil War in the Diaries and Letters of John Hay*, 186.

69. Hearn, *Lincoln, Cabinet, Generals*, 224–25.

70. William Dennison's remarks to Lincoln, June 9, 1864, reported in the *New York Tribune*, June 10, 1864, *Works of Lincoln*, vol. 7, 381n; Lincoln's reply to the notification committee, June 9, 1864, Ibid., 381. Lincoln formally accepted the nomination on June 27, 1864. Lincoln to William Dennison *et al.*, June 27, 1864, Ibid., 411.

71. Lincoln's reply to the National Union League delegation, June 9, 1864, as reported in the *New York Times, Herald,* and *Tribune,* June 10, 1864, Ibid., 384–85 at 385; Lincoln's response to Ohio delegation serenade, June 9, 1864, as reported in *New York Herald, Tribune,* and *New York Times,* June 10, 1864, Ibid., 384.

72. Lincoln's endorsement of June 6, 1864 on letter from Charles E. Sherman to Lincoln, June 6, 1864, Ibid., 376 and note.

73. Lincoln to the Senate and House of Representatives, June 8, 1864, Ibid., 380 and note.

74. Lincoln to Lorenzo Thomas, June 13, 1864, Ibid., 390; Thomas to Lincoln, June 13, 1864, Ibid., 390n.

75. For more information on the Battle of Cold Harbor, its casualties, the crossing of the James River and the initial Battle of Petersburg, see Bonekemper, *Grant and Lee*, 190–96, 310–11, 313.

76. Grant to Lincoln, June 14, 1864, OR, Ser. I, XL, Part II, 18–19, *Works of Lincoln*, vol. 7, 393n; Lincoln to Grant, June 15, 1864, Ibid., 393.

77. For details on Lee's delay in reinforcing P. G. T. Beauregard at Petersburg, see Bonekemper, *How Lee Lost*, 160–62.

78. Lincoln's speech at the Great Central Sanitary Fair, Philadelphia, June 16, 1864, Ibid., 394–96 at 395.

79. Ibid., 395–96.

80. Hay, *Diary*, June 21 and 23, 1864, 209, 210; Lincoln to Mary Todd Lincoln, June 24, 1864, *Works of Lincoln*, vol. 7, 406 and note quoting Orville H. Browning's *Diary*, June 26, 1864; Hearn, *Lincoln, Cabinet, Generals*, 220, citing Beale, *Diary of Edward Bates*, 378. In his letter to his wife, Lincoln left no doubt about whether Grant or Meade was in command of the Eastern Union troops: "Tad and I have been to Gen. Grant's army."

81. Lincoln to Edward Bates, June 24, 1864, *Works of Lincoln*, vol. 7, 404; Bates to Lincoln, July 14, 1864, Ibid., 405–6n; OR, Ser. III, IV, 490–93; Lincoln to Stanton, July 14, 1864, *Works of Lincoln*, vol. 7, 440.

82. J. Rutherford Worster to Lincoln, April 13, 1864, Ibid., 416n; Lincoln to Grant, June 29, 1864, Ibid., 416.

83. Lincoln to Grant, Aug. 29, 1864, Ibid., 523; Grant to Lincoln, Aug. 29, 1864, Ibid., 523–24n.

84. Pass from Lincoln to James R. Gilmore and James F. Jaquess, July 6, 1864, Ibid., 429; Lincoln to Grant, July 6, 1864, Ibid.

85. David Work, *Lincoln's Political Generals* (Urbana: University of Illinois Press, 2009) [hereafter, Work, *Lincoln's Political Generals*], 151–52.

86. Hearn, *Lincoln, Cabinet, Generals*, 220.

87. Work, *Lincoln's Political Generals*, 152–53. See later discussion of Lincoln's political problems in the summer of 1864.

88. McPherson, *Tried by War*, 223–24.

89. One of the first of these raids was a late June 1864 raid on the Richmond & Danville and Southside railroads by Brigadier General James H. Wilson with 5,500 cavalrymen. Although Wilson succeeded in destroying sixty miles of railroad track and disrupting Lee's supply flow for a month, he took considerable losses in getting back to Union lines. Philip L. Bolte, "An Earlier 'Bridge Too Far'," *North & South* 3, no. 6 (August 2000): 26–32.

90. Grant, *Memoirs*, 605; L. VanLoan Naisawald, "'Old Jubilee' Saves Lynchburg," *America's Civil War* 16, no. 2 (May 2003): 30–36, 72.

91. David Case, "The Battle That Saved Washington," *Civil War Times Illustrated* XXXVII, no. 7 (Feb. 1999): 46–56 [hereafter Case, "Battle,"] at 47. For details of Early's campaign, see Joseph Judge, *Season of Fire: The Confederate Strike on Washington* (Berryville, VA: Rockbridge Publishing Co., 1994) [hereafter Judge, *Season of Fire*];, Stephen E. Ambrose, *Halleck: Lincoln's Chief of Staff* (Baton Rouge: Louisiana State University Press, 1962, 1990), 179; Frank E. Vandiver, *Jubal's Raid: General Early's Famous Attack on Washington in 1864* (New York: McGraw-Hill Book Company, Inc., 1960).

92. Case, "Battle," 47–48; Benjamin Franklin Cooling, "Monocacy: The Battle That Saved Washington," *Blue & Gray Magazine* X, Issue 2 (Dec. 1992): 8–18, 48–60 [hereafter Cooling, "Monocacy"] at 13, 16.

93. Lincoln to John W. Garrett, July 5, 1864, *Works of Lincoln*, vol. 7, 424 and note; OR, Ser. I, XXXVII, Part II, 65–77.

94. For details on the Battle of Monocacy, see B. Franklin Cooling, *Monocacy: The Battle That Saved Washington* (Shippensburg, PA: White Maine Pub. Co., 2000); Judge, *Season of Fire*, 171–201; Eric J. Wittenberg, "Roadblock En Route to Washington," *America's Civil War* 6, no. 5 (Nov. 1993): 50–56, 80–82; Case, "Battle," 50–54; Cooling, "Monocacy," 48–55; Swift and Stephens, "Honor Redeemed," 42–44.

95. Lincoln to John W. Garrett, July 9, 1864, *Works of Lincoln*, vol. 7, 434; Garrett to Lincoln, July 9, 1864, 7:45 p.m., Ibid., 434n, OR, Ser. I, XXXVII, Part II, 138; Halleck to Wallace, July 9, 1864, 11:57 p.m., Ibid., 145.

96. Grant to Halleck, July 9, 6 p.m., Ibid., 437n.

97. Lincoln to Grant, July 10, 1864, 2 p.m., Ibid., 437.

98. Thomas Swann *et al.* to Lincoln, July 9, 1864, Ibid., 438n, OR, Ser. I, XXXVII, Part II, 140; Lincoln to Thomas Swann *et al.*, July 10, 9:20 a.m., Ibid., 437–38.

99. Grant to Lincoln, July 10, 1964, 10:30 p.m., Ibid., 438n.

100. Lincoln to Grant, July 11, 1864, 8 a.m., Ibid., 438.

101. Grant, *Memoirs*, 605–7, 614; Ted Alexander, "McCausland's Raid and the Burning of Chambersburg," *Blue & Gray Magazine* XI, Issue 6 (August 1994): 10–8, 46–61; Case, "Battle," 55–56.

102. Lincoln to Grant, July 12, 1864, 11:30 a.m., *Works of Lincoln*, vol. 7, 438; Grant to Lincoln, July 13, 1864, 12 M, Ibid., OR, Ser. I, XXXVII, Part II, 257.

103. Curtin to Lincoln, June 16, 1864, *Works of Lincoln*, vol. 7, 444n; Lincoln to Curtin, July 17, 1864, Ibid., 444.

104. Grant to Sherman, July 16, 1864, OR, Ser. I, XXXVIII, Part V, 149, *Works of Lincoln*, vol. 7, 444–45; Lincoln to Grant, July 17, 1864, Ibid., 444.

105. Hunter to Lincoln, July 17, 1864, Ibid., 445n; Lincoln to Hunter, July 17, 1864, Ibid., 445.

106. Lincoln to Hunter, July 23, 1864, Ibid., 456; Hunter to Lincoln, July 23, 1864, Ibid., 456n.

107. Marszalek, *Halleck*, 210–11; Hearn, *Lincoln, Cabinet, Generals*, 240–41.

108. Jonathan A. Noyalas, *The Battle of Cedar Creek: Victory from the Jaws of Defeat* (Charleston, SC: History Press, 2009, 2011) [hereafter Noyalas, *Cedar Creek*], 16.

109. Hattaway and Jones, *How the North Won*, 604.

110. Alexander, *Fighting for the Confederacy*, 440. Another Confederate leader saw those same possibilities: Brigadier General Josiah Gorgas, Chief of Confederate Ordnance, wrote: "I still think that my notions were correct at the outset of Sherman's movement when I advocated the detachment of 10,000 men to Georgia, even at the risk of losing Petersburgh [*sic*] & the Southern R.R. It would have ruined Sherman, & with his ruin, gone far to make the north tired of the war." Sarah Woolfolk Wiggins, ed., *The Journals of Josiah Gorgas 1857–1878* (Tuscaloosa: The University of Alabama Press, 1995) [hereafter, Wiggins, *Journals of Gorgas*], 143–44.

111. See Bonekemper, *Grant and Lee*, 203–4.

112. In his memoirs, Grant said of the change of command: "I know that both Sherman and I were rejoiced when we heard of the change." Grant, *Memoirs*, 632. In fact, Sherman had contemporaneously written to his wife, "I confess I was pleased at the change." Groom, *Shrouds of Glory*, 25.

113. Albert Castel, *Decision in the West: The Atlanta Campaign of 1864* (Lawrence: University Press of Kansas, 1992), 362; Stephen Davis, "Atlanta Campaign. Hood Fights Desperately. The Battles of Atlanta: Events from July 10 to September 2, 1864," *Blue & Gray Magazine* VI, Issue 6 (August 1989): 8, 11 [Davis believes Sherman's casualties were higher than cited here.]; Sam. R. Watkins, *"Co. Aytch," Maury Grays, First Tennessee Regiment; or, A Side Show of the Big Show* (Wilmington, NC: Broadfoot Publishing Company, 1987) (Reprint of 1952 edition and of Nashville: Cumberland Presbyterian Publishing House, 1882), 167–69, 174–75; Groom, *Shrouds of Glory*, 25; Marszalek, *Sherman*, 277; Thomas Lawrence Connelly, *Autumn of Glory: The Army of Tennessee, 1862–1865* (Baton Rouge: Louisiana State University Press, 1971, 1991) [hereafter Connelly, *Autumn of Glory*], 433; Hattaway and Jones, *How the North Won*, 609; McWhiney and Jamieson, *Attack and Die*, 21; Bonekemper, *How Lee Lost*, 166–70.

114. Bryce A. Suderow, "War Along the James," *North & South* 6, no. 3 (April 2003): 12–23.

115. Bryce A. Suderow, "Glory Denied: The First Battle of Deep Bottom, July 27th–29th, 1864," *North & South* 3, no. 7 (Sept. 2000): 17–32 [hereafter Suderow, "Glory Denied"].

116. Lincoln's Proclamation for 500,000 Volunteers and Backup Draft, July 18, 1864, *Works of Lincoln*, vol. 7, 448–49; Grant to Lincoln, July 19, 1864, OR, Ser. I, XXXVIII, Part II, 384, *Works of Lincoln*, vol. 7, 453n; Lincoln to Grant, July 20, 1864, Ibid., 452.

117. Sherman to Halleck, July 14, 1864 [two telegrams], OR, Ser. I, XXXVIII, Part V, 136–37; Lincoln to Sherman, July 18, 1864, *Works of Lincoln*, vol. 7, 449–50 at 450; Sherman to Lincoln, July 21, 1864, OR, Ser. I, XXXVIII, Part V, 210. In this same month, Sherman complained about two major general promotions; Lincoln sent him an explanation. Sherman to Inspector General James A. Hardie, July 25, 1864, OR, Ser. I, XXXVIII, Part V, 247, *Works of Lincoln*, vol. 7, 463–64n; Lincoln to Sherman, July 26, 1864, Ibid., 463. Lincoln had no similar second-guessing problems with Grant.

118. Grant to Lincoln, July 17, 1864, *Works of Lincoln*, vol. 7, 452n; Lincoln to Stanton, July 19, 1864, Ibid., 452.

119. Grant to Lincoln, July 25, 1864, *Papers of Grant*, vol. 11, 308–10; Stanton to Halleck, July 27, 1864, OR, Ser. I, XXXVII, Part II, 463.

120. Stanton to Grant, July 26, 1864, OR, Ser. I, XXVII, Part II, 444; Grant to Lincoln, c. July 27, 1864, *Works of Lincoln*, vol. 7, 470n; Lincoln to Grant, July 28, 1864, Ibid., 469; Lincoln to Grant, July 29, 1864, Ibid., 470; Grant to Lincoln, July 30, 1864, Ibid., 470n.

121. Grant, *Memoirs*, 607–12.

122. Grant to Meade, July 24, 1864, *Papers of Grant*, vol. 11, 305–307 at 306; Grant, *Memoirs*, 612–13; Hattaway and Jones, *How the North Won*, 614–15; Livermore, *Numbers & Losses*, 116; J. Michael Miller, "Strike Them a Blow: Lee and Grant at the North Anna River," *Blue & Gray* Magazine X, Issue 4 (April 1993): 12–22, 44–55 [hereafter Miller, "Strike Them"] at 53.

123. Lincoln to Hunter, July 30, 1864, *Works of Lincoln*, vol. 7, 472; Hunter to Halleck, July 30, 1862, OR, Ser. I, XXXVII, Part II, 511–12, *Works of Lincoln*, vol. 7, 472n.

124. Grant, *Memoirs*, 614–15; Grant to Halleck, August 1, 1864, *Papers of Grant*, vol. 11, 358–59 at 358; OR, Ser. I, XXXVII, Part II, 558; *Works of Lincoln*, vol. 7, 476n.

125. Lincoln to Grant, August 3, 1864, *Works of Lincoln*, vol. 7, 476; Grant, *Memoirs*, 615–16.

126. Grant to Lincoln, August 4, 1864, *Papers of Grant*, vol. 11, 360n; *Works of Lincoln*, vol. 7, 476n.

127. On August 5, Stanton sent a note to Lincoln saying "General Grant is at the Department. Shall he call to see you or will you see him here." Lincoln replied, "I will come over in a few minutes." Stanton to Lincoln, Aug. 5, 1864, *Works of Lincoln*, vol. 7, 482n; Lincoln to Stanton, Aug. 5, 1864, Ibid., 482.

128. Grant, *Memoirs*, 616–18; T. Harry Williams, *Lincoln and His Generals* (New York: Alfred A. Knopf, Inc., 1952) [hereafter Williams, *Lincoln and His Generals*], 331–33. Another occurrence undermined Hunter's authority. On August 1 Hunter ordered the arrest and shipment south of Confederate sympathizers in Frederick, Maryland. In response to immediate complaints, Lincoln suspended Hunter's order on August 3. On August 7 Hunter wired the president that he had merely been carrying out Grant's orders relayed to him by Halleck on July 17 and asked to be relieved of his command of the Department of West Virginia. Hunter's Special Order

No. 141, Aug. 1, 1864, *Works of Lincoln*, vol. 7, 477n; Lincoln to Stanton, Aug. 3, 1864, Ibid., 477; Hunter to Lincoln, Aug. 7, 1864, Ibid., 478n.

129. According to Sheridan, Lincoln and Stanton had doubts about Sheridan's youth and inexperience, but Lincoln accepted Grant's recommendation, "hoped for the best, and approved the temporary promotion of Sheridan." Hearn, *Lincoln, Cabinet, Generals*, 242–43.

130. Grant to Washburne, August 16, 1864, *Papers of Grant*, vol. 12, 16–17 at 16.

131. Ibid., 16–17.

132. 132

133. 133

134. Lincoln's interview with Alexander W. Randall and Joseph T. Mills, Aug. 19, 1864, *Works of Lincoln*, vol. 7, 506–8 at 506–7.

135. Lincoln's Reply to Loyal Colored People of Baltimore upon Presentation of a Bible, Sept. 7, 1864, *Works of Lincoln*, vol. 7, 542–43 at 542.

136. Lincoln's Order to Lieutenant Colonel Henry S. Huidekoper, 150th Pennsylvania Volunteers, Sept. 1, 1864, *Works of Lincoln*, vol. 7, 530 and note; Lincoln to Stanton, Sept. 20, 1864, Ibid., vol. 8, 14 and note; OR, Ser. III, IV, 680; Lincoln to Grant, Sept. 22, 1864, Ibid., 17 and note; Grant to Stanton, Sept. 25, 1864, Ibid., 17n and OR, Ser. III, IV, 744; Nicolay and Hay, *Lincoln*, vol. 5, 145–47.

137. Lincoln to Grant, Oct. 5, 1864, *Works of Lincoln*, vol. 8, 36 and note. See Welles, *Diary*, II, Oct. 4 and 5, 1864, 168–71.

138. Bryce A. Suderow, "'Nothing But a Miracle Could Save Us': Second Battle of Deep Bottom, Virginia, August 14–20, 1864," *North & South* 4, no. 2 (Jan. 2001): 12–32 [hereafter Suderow, "Nothing But Miracle"].

139. Halleck to Grant, Aug. 11, 1864, *Papers of Grant*, vol. 11, 424–25n; Grant to Halleck, August 15, 1864, Ibid., 424, *Works of Lincoln*, vol. 7, 499n; Lincoln to Grant, Aug. 17, 1864, *Papers of Grant*, vol. 11, 225n; *Works of Lincoln*, vol. 7, 499; Horace Porter, *Campaigning with Grant* (New York: The Century Company, 1897) (1981 Time-Life reprint) [hereafter Porter, *Campaigning with Grant*], 279.

140. Hearn, *Lincoln, Cabinet, Generals*, 230–33.

141. Ibid., 234–35.

142. Eaton, *Grant, Lincoln*, 185–86 at 186.

143. Ibid., 186–87; Lincoln's pass to Eaton to visit Grant, Aug. 12, 1864, *Works of Lincoln*, vol. 7, 492. At the same time, Lincoln signed a note asking Stanton to see Eaton, "whom Gen. Grant thinks is one of the best

contraband agents." Ibid. Eaton met with Stanton to discuss freedmen's issues in the Mississippi Valley. Eaton, *Grant, Lincoln*, 178–79.

144. Eaton, *Grant, Lincoln*, 190–91. In January 1865 Lincoln once again authorized Eaton to visit Grant at City Point. Lincoln's pass for John Eaton, Jan. 16, 1865, Ibid., 230; *Works of Lincoln*, vol. 8, 218.

145. Groom, *Shrouds of Glory*, 53.

146. *Works of Lincoln*, vol. 7, 532–34.

147. Groom, *Shrouds of Glory*, 54.

148. Grant to Sherman, Sept. 12, 1864, *Papers of Grant*, vol. 12, 154–55.

149. Grant, *Memoirs*, 602, 619; Margaret E. Wagner, Gary W. Gallagher, and Paul Finkelman, eds., *The Library of Congress Civil War Desk Reference* (New York: Simon & Schuster, 2002), 311.

150. Arthur W. Bergeron Jr., "The Battle of Mobile Bay and the Campaign for Mobile, Alabama," *Blue & Gray Magazine* XIX, Issue 4 (April 2002): 6–21, 46–54.

151. James M. McPherson, *Battle Cry of Freedom: The Civil War Era* (New York: Ballantine Books, 1988) [hereafter McPherson, *Battle Cry of Freedom*], 775.

152. Lincoln to Grant, Aug. 28, 1864, *Works of Lincoln*, vol. 7, 521; Grant to Lincoln, Aug. 29, 1864 (two telegrams), Ibid., 522n.

153. McPherson, *Tried by War*, 244; Lincoln to Grant, Sept. 12, 1864, *Works of Lincoln*, vol. 7, 548; Grant to Lincoln, Sept. 13, 1864, Ibid., 548n.

154. Grant, *Memoirs*, 620–21. For details of the 1864 Shenandoah Valley Campaign, see Jeffry D. Wert, *From Winchester to Cedar Creek: The Shenandoah Campaign of 1864* (Carlisle, PA: South Mountain Press, Inc., 1987).

155. Grant, *Memoirs*, 622; Lincoln to Sheridan, September 20, 1864, *Works of Lincoln*, vol. 8, 13; Hearn, *Grant, Cabinet, Generals*, 247.

156. Grant, *Memoirs*, 625.

157. Lincoln to Grant, Sept. 29, 1864, *Works of Lincoln*, vol. 8, 29; Grant to Lincoln, Ibid., 29n.

158. Feis, *Grant's Secret Service*, 246–49; Noah Andre Trudeau, "That 'Unerring Volcanic Firearm'," *Military History Quarterly* 7, no. 4 (Summer 1995): 78–87.

159. For details, see Noyalas, *Cedar Creek*.

160. Hearn, *Lincoln, Cabinet, Generals*, 248.

161. Curtin to Lincoln, October 17, 1864, *Works of Lincoln*, vol. 8, 50n; Lincoln to Curtin, Ibid., 50.

162. Lincoln's response to a serenade, Oct. 21, 1864, Ibid., 57–58 and note.

163. Grant, *Memoirs*, 628–30; Lincoln to Sheridan, October 22, 1864, *Works of Lincoln*, vol. 8, 73–74.

164. McPherson, *Battle Cry of Freedom*, 800. To accusations that Grant's no-exchange policy was the cause of many prison-camp deaths, Professor James Gillispie retorted that retaining Southern prisoners was the only security against a widespread Confederate policy of executing black prisoners and their white officers and that it also was intended to shorten the war by reducing the number of combatants—especially on the Rebel side. James Gillispie, Letter to Editor, *North & South 5*, no. 7 (Oct. 2002): 5–6. Gillespie greatly expanded on these points in James M. Gillispie, *Andersonvilles of the North: The Myths and Realities of Northern Treatment of Civil War Confederate Prisoners* (Denton: University of North Texas Press, 2008), 71–108.

Chapter 11: Lincoln Wins Reelection with Grant's Full Support

1. McPherson, *Mighty Scourge*, 207; John C. Waugh, *Reelecting Lincoln: The Battle for the 1864 Presidency* (New York: Crown Publishers, Inc., 1997), 339–42.

2. Welles, *Diary*, vol. 2, 130, 132.

3. Archer Jones, "Military Means, Political Ends," [hereafter Jones, "Military Means"] in Gabor S. Boritt, ed., *Why the Confederacy Lost* (New York: Oxford University Press, 1992) [hereafter Boritt, *Why the Confederacy Lost*], 43–77 at 48.

4. Wiggins, *Journals of Gorgas*, 66.

5. Longstreet to Brigadier General Thomas Jordan, March 27, 1864, quoted in McPherson, *Battle Cry*, 721.

6. McPherson, *Battle Cry*, 721.

7. David Herbert Donald, Jean Harvey Baker, and Michael F. Holt, *The Civil War and Reconstruction* (New York London: W.W. Norton & Company, 2001), 423, quoting *New York Sun*, June 30, 1889 (publishing historical documents on anti-Lincoln cabal of 1864).

8. James M. McPherson, "American Victory, American Defeat," in Boritt, *Why the Confederacy Lost*, 15–42 [hereafter McPherson, "American Victory"] at 40.

9. Donald, *Lincoln*, 529.

10. *Works of Lincoln*, vol. 7, 514; Nevins, Alan, *Ordeal of the Union* (8 vols.) (New York: Charles Scribner's Sons, 1947–50) [hereafter Nevins, *Ordeal of the Union*], vol. 8, 92–93.

11. Hay, *Diary*, Nov. 11, 1864, 247–48.

12. *Works of Lincoln*, vol. 7, 514n.

13. Ibid., 517–18n. Raymond went on to propose that peace proposals be made to Jefferson Davis on the basis of restoration of the Union and continuation of slavery. Lincoln disabused him of that notion at a September 25 meeting that included Seward, Stanton and new Treasury Secretary William P. Fessenden. Nicolay and Hay, *Lincoln*, vol. 9, 221.

14. Donald *et al.*, *Civil War*, 425.

15. John C. Waugh, *Lincoln and McClellan: The Troubled Partnership Between a President and His General* (New York: Palgrave Macmillan, 2010) [hereafter Waugh, *Lincoln and McClellan*], 198.

16. Holzer, *Lincoln on War*, 255.

17. William J. Miller, *Mapping for Stonewall: The Civil War Service of Jed Hotchkiss* (Washington: Elliott & Clark Publishing, 1993), 143.

18. McPherson, "American Victory," 39.

19. Nevins, *Ordeal of the Union*, vol. 8, 99–102.

20. Beringer *et al.*, *Why the South Lost*, photo between 274–75; Donald *et al.*, *Civil War*, 425.

21. Fuller, *Generalship of Grant*, 330.

22. Nevins, *Ordeal of the Union*, vol. 8, 103.

23. Fuller, *Generalship of Grant*, 330–1.

24. Blaine to Lincoln, Sept. 13, 1864, *Works of Lincoln*, vol. 8, 3n.

25. Lincoln's Memorandum of Pre-election Poll, c. Sept. 13, 1864, Ibid., 3.

26. Beringer *et al.*, *Why the South Lost*, 349.

27. Donald *et al.*, *Civil War*, 426.

28. Lincoln to Sherman, Sept. 19, 1864, *Works of Lincoln*, vol. 8, 11 and note.

29. Lincoln to Rosecrans, Sept. 26, 1864, Ibid., 24. Rosecrans assured him he was doing so and would continue to do so. Rosecrans to Lincoln, Oct. 3, 1864, Ibid., 24n.

30. Hearn, *Lincoln, Cabinet, Generals*, 257.

31. Lincoln to Gideon Welles (introduction of Charles Jones), Oct. 10, 1864, *Works of Lincoln*, vol. 8, 43 and note; Welles, *Diary*, II, Oct. 11, 1864, 175; Lincoln to Simon Cameron, Oct. 11, 1864, *Works of Lincoln*, vol. 8, 43; Cameron to Lincoln, Oct. 12, 1864, Ibid., 43–44n.

32. Lincoln to Grant, Oct. 12, 1864, Ibid., 45.

33. Morton to Lincoln and Stanton, Oct. 12, 1864, Ibid., 46–47n; Lincoln to Morton, Oct. 13, 1864, Ibid., 46; Morton to Lincoln and Stanton, Oct. 13, 1864, Ibid., 47n.

34. Estimated Electoral Vote in hand of President Lincoln, Oct. 13, 1864, Ibid., vol. 8, 46. On October 31, Lincoln issued a proclamation admitting Nevada (and its three electoral votes) to the Union. Proclamation Admitting Nevada into the Union, Oct. 31, 1864, Ibid., 83–84.

35. Lincoln's Sept. 27, 1864 and Grant's October 10, 1864 endorsement on September 27, 1864 letter from William H. Kent to Lincoln, Ibid., 26 and note.

36. Sherman to Lincoln, Sept. 26, 1864, Ibid., 27n; Lincoln to Sherman, Sept. 27, 1864, Ibid., 27; Sherman to Lincoln, Sept. 28, 1864, Ibid., 27n.

37. Lincoln's October 16, 1864 endorsement of P. J. J. October 15, 1854 letter to Seward, Ibid., 49 and note.

38. Lincoln's response to a serenade, Oct. 19, 1864, Ibid., 52–53.

39. Lincoln's Proclamation of Thanksgiving, Oct. 20, 1864, Ibid., 55–56 at 55.

40. Lincoln to McClure, Oct. 30, 1864, Ibid., 81; McClure to Lincoln, Nov. 5, 1864, Ibid., 81n.

41. Lincoln's Proclamation Admitting Nevada into the Union, Oct. 31, 1864, Ibid., 83–84.

42. Lincoln to Stanton, Nov. 3, 1864, Ibid., 89.

43. Lincoln's Order concerning LT A. W. White, Nov. 7, 1864, Ibid., 95.

44. Lincoln to Stanton, Nov. 5, 1864, Ibid., 91–92 and note at 91.

45. See telegrams from Lincoln to Seward in New York, Nov. 5, 6, and 8, 1862, Ibid., 91, 94, 97.

46. CQ, *Elections*, 94; Edward H. Bonekemper III, "Lincoln's 1864 Victory Was Closer Than It Looked," *Washington Times*, July 15, 2000. See more detailed analysis in "How Close Was the Election of 1864?" in Bonekemper, *Victor*, 325–32.

47. McPherson, *Battle Cry*, 804.

48. Hearn, *Lincoln, Cabinet, Generals*, 260.

49. Grant to Stanton, Nov. 9, 1864, *Works of Lincoln*, vol. 8, 100n; OR, Ser. I, XLII, Part 3, 570. Grant's wire included the first two columns of numbers. The last column was calculated from them by this author. "Lincoln's majority" was ascertained by Grant from subordinate commanders' reports to Meade. Or: Ibid., 560, 561, 564, 565, 567, 568, 569, 574, 576–77, 578.

50. Grant to Stanton, Nov. 10, 1864, *Papers of Grant*, vol. 12, 398.

51. Hay, *Diary*, Nov. 16, 1864, 251.

52. Donald *et al.*, *Civil War*, 427.

53. Lincoln's Responses to Serenades, Nov. 8 and 10, 1864, *Works of Lincoln*, vol. 8, 96, 100–1 at 101.

Chapter 12: Lincoln and Grant Win the War

1. Grant, *Memoirs*, 632–36; Grant to Sherman, Sept. 10, 1864, *Papers of Grant*, vol. 12, 144; Sherman to Grant, Sept. 10, 1864, Ibid., 144 note; Grant to Sherman, Sept. 12, 1864, Ibid., 154–55. Porter described the visit in Porter, *Campaigning with Grant*, 287–96.

2. Sherman to Grant, 11 a.m., October 11, 1864, *Papers of Grant*, vol. 12, 290n; Grant, *Memoirs*, 816. John Marszalek contends that Sherman had to convince Grant to allow him to undertake the unusual march. Marszalek, *Sherman*, 293–97.

3. Grant to Sherman, 11:30 p.m., October 11, 1864, *Papers of Grant*, vol. 12, 290n.

4. Grant, *Memoirs*, 652–53.

5. Ibid., 636–40.

6. Bobrick, *Master of War*, 266–67, 273, 280, 300, 305.

7. Grant, *Memoirs*, 631–38; Louis A. Garavaglia, "Sherman's March and the Georgia Arsenals," *North & South* 6, no. 1 (Dec. 2002): 12–22. For details of Sherman's March to the Sea, see Noah Andre Trudeau, *Southern Storm: Sherman's March to the Sea* (New York: Harper Collins, 2008); William R. Scaife, "Sherman's March to the Sea: Events from September 3 to December, 1864, Including the Occupation of Atlanta, More Battles with the Unpredictable John Bell Hood, the Burning of Atlanta, 'Marching Through Georgia,' and the Fall of Savannah," *Blue & Gray Magazine* VII, Issue 2 (Dec. 1989): 10–32, 38–42.

8. Grant, *Memoirs*, 648–50; Grant to Sherman, Dec. 3, 1864, *Papers of Grant*, vol. 13, 56–57 at 56.

9. When judged in light of Lincoln's and Grant's criticisms of McClellan after Antietam, Meade after Gettysburg, and Thomas after Nashville, Sherman's almost deliberately allowing Hardee to escape and fight again in the Carolinas was inexcusable, inconsistent with Union policy and, in the words of John Marszalek, "the only flaw in an otherwise excellent campaign." That error compounded his allowing Hood to escape after the capture of Atlanta. Marszalek continued, "Sherman never thought these escapes mattered. He had captured Atlanta, and he had taken Savannah, so Hood's and Hardee's escapes made no real difference. Sherman's priorities allowed the opposing army to withdraw in the face of superior force and did not require the victorious commander to destroy his opponent to be successful. In reality, he followed his own emotions. He hated the idea of killing Southern friends, yet he needed military successes to ensure the order necessary for his own personal success." Marszalek, *Sherman*, 308–9.

10. Grant, *Memoirs*, 651–52; Roger S. Durham, "Savannah: Mr. Lincoln's Christmas Present," *Blue & Gray Magazine* VIII, Issue 3 (Feb. 1991): 8–18, 42–53.

11. Grant, *Memoirs*, 652.

12. Lincoln to Sherman, Dec. 26, 1864, *Works of Lincoln*, vol. 8, 181–82 at 181.

13. Grant, *Memoirs*, 654–55; McWhiney and Jamieson, *Attack and Die*, 21; Groom, *Shrouds of Glory*, 156–224; Heidler and Heidler, *Encyclopedia*, 771–72.

14. See Bobrick, *Master of War*, 278–289.

15. Williams, *Lincoln and His Generals*, 342–44.

16. Grant, *Memoirs*, 655–61; McWhiney and Jamieson, *Attack and Die*, 21; Groom, *Shrouds of Glory*, 224–75; Gary W. Dolzall, "Enemies Front and Rear," *America's Civil War* 16, no. 2 (May 2003): 38–45; Jacob Dolson Cox, *Military Reminiscences of the Civil War* (2 vols.) (New York: Charles Scribner's Sons, 1900) [hereafter Cox, *Reminiscences*], vol. 2, 358–74; Lincoln to Thomas, Dec. 16, 1864, *Works of Lincoln*, vol. 8, 169.

17. Bobrick, *Master of War*, 295–307.

18. Williams, *Lincoln and His Generals*, 344–45.

19. Bobrick, *Master of War*, 302.

20. Lincoln to Seward, Nov. 17, 1864, *Works of Lincoln*, vol. 8, 114 and note.

21. Lincoln's Proclamation concerning the Blockade, Nov. 19, 1864, Ibid., 115.

22. Lincoln's Annual Message to Congress, Dec. 6, 1864, Ibid., 136–53 at 149.

23. Lincoln's Approval of Resolution Submitting Thirteenth Amendment to the States, Feb. 1, 1865, Ibid., 253 and note.

24. Lincoln's Proclamation Calling for 300,000 Volunteers, Dec. 19, 1864, Ibid., 171–72.

25. Lincoln to Sherman, Dec. 26, 1864, Ibid., 181–82 at 182.

26. Grant, *Memoirs*, 671–74. For example, the 10,000-man 23rd Corps was moved by river, rail, and sea from Clifton, Tennessee, to Wilmington in a rapid movement reminiscent of the late 1863 movement of the 11th and 12th corps from Virginia to Chattanooga. Report of Colonel Lewis B. Parsons, *Official Records*, XLVII, part 2 [S#99]; Longstreet, James, *From Manassas to Appomattox: Memoirs of the Civil War in America* (New York: Smithmark Publishers, Inc., 1994), 386–87.

27. Mark L. Bradley, "Last Stand in the Carolinas: The Battle of Bentonville, March 19–21, 1865," *Blue & Gray Magazine* XIII, Issue 2 (Dec. 1995): 8–22, 56–69 [hereafter Bradley, "Last Stand"] at 9.

28. Williams, *Lincoln and His Generals*, 347.

29. Grant to Sherman, December 18, 1864, *Papers of Grant*, vol. 13, 129–30 at 130; Mark Coburn, *Terrible Innocence: General Sherman at War* (New York: Hippocrene Books, 1993), 191–92.

30. Bell Irvin Wiley, *The Road to Appomattox* (Baton Rouge and London: Louisiana State University Press, 1994) (Reprint of Memphis: Memphis State College Press, 1956) [hereafter Wiley, *Road to Appomattox*], 85; Jones, "Military Means" in Boritt, *Why the Confederacy Lost*, 74; Beringer *et al.*, *Why the South Lost*, 333; Connelly, "Lee and the Western Confederacy," 123.

31. Connelly, *Autumn of Glory*, 529.

32. Emory M. Thomas, *Robert E. Lee: A Biography* (New York: W. W. Norton and Co., 1995), 348.

33. 33 Robert Hunt Rhodes, ed., *All for the Union: The Civil War Diary and Letters of Elisha Hunt Rhodes* (New York: Orion Books, 1991) (Originally published by Andrew Mowbray Incorporated in 1985) [hereafter Rhodes, *All for the Union*], 214–16, 349.

34. Wiley, *Road to Appomattox*, 72.

35. William Marvel, *Lee's Last Retreat: The Flight to Appomattox* (Chapel Hill and London: University of North Carolina Press, 2002) [hereafter Marvel, *Lee's Last Retreat*], 5–6, 205.

36. Bevin Alexander, *How Great Generals Win* (New York and London: W. W. Norton and Company, 1993) [hereafter Alexander, *How Great Generals Win*], 167.

37. Joseph T. Glatthaar, "Black Glory" in Boritt, *Why the Confederacy Lost*, 160; Thomas, *Lee*, 347; Beringer *et al.*, *Why the South Lost*, 373; Hattaway and Jones, *How the North Won*, 272; Bruce Levine, *Confederate Emancipation: Southern Plans To Free and Arm Slaves During the Civil War* (Oxford: Oxford University Press, 2006), 117–18.

38. Chris Fonvielle, "The Last Rays of Departing Hope: The Fall of Wilmington Including the Campaigns Against Fort Fisher," *Blue & Gray Magazine* XII, Issue 2 (Dec. 1994): 10–21, 48–62 [hereafter Fonvielle, "Last Rays"] at 16–19; Joe Zentner and Mary Syrett, "Confederate Gibraltar," *Military History* 19, no. 6 (Feb. 2003), 26–32, 73 [hereafter Zentner and Syrett, "Confederate Gibraltar"].

39. Ibid.; Grant to Sherman, Dec. 3, 1964, P*apers of Grant*, vol. 13, 56–57 at 56.

40. Lincoln to Grant, Dec. 28, 1864, *Works of Lincoln*, vol. 8, 187; Grant to Lincoln, Dec. 28, 1864, Ibid., 187n; OR, Ser. I, XLII, Part III, 1087; *Papers of Grant*, vol. 13, 177–78 at 177.

41. Fonvielle, "Last Rays," 20–21, 48–52; Hearn, *Lincoln, Cabinet, Generals*, 275; Butler to Lincoln, Jan. 19, 1865, *Works of Lincoln*, vol. 8, 207n; Lincoln to Butler, Jan. 10, 1865, Ibid., 207 and note; OR, Ser. I, XLVI, Part II, 97–98.

42. Lincoln to Butler, Jan. 13, 1865, *Works of Lincoln*, vol. 8, 214 and note.

43. Fonvielle, "Last Rays," 52–7.

44. Galveston, Texas, remained open but was a long distance from, and lacked rail connections to, the primary fighting.

45. Grant, *Memoirs*, 662–70, 680; Fonvielle, "Last Rays," 57–62; Zentner and Syrett, "Confederate Gibraltar," 26–32, 73.

46. Fonvielle, "Last Rays," 62.

47. Work, *Lincoln's Political Generals*, 156.

48. McPherson, *Battle Cry of Freedom*, 826.

49. Marszalek, *Sherman*, 320–21.

50. Grant, *Memoirs*, 675.

51. Sherman, *Memoirs*, 752.

52. Grant, *Memoirs*, 679–80.

53. Grant, *Memoirs*, 681–82. On the burning of Columbia, see E. Chris Evans, "'I Almost Tremble at Her Fate': When Sherman came to Columbia, South Carolina, secession's hotbed became a bed of coals," *Civil War Times Illustrated* XXXVII, no. 5 (Oct. 1998): 46–51, 60–67. Sherman's comment on the burning of Columbia was, "Though I never ordered it and never wished it, I have never shed many tears over the event, because I believe it hastened what we all fought for, the end of the war." Ibid. at 67.

54. Alexander, *How Great Generals Win*, 164.

55. Hattaway and Jones, *How the North Won*, 667.

56. Alexander, *How Great Generals Win*, 164–65, quoting Liddell Hart, *Sherman: Soldier, Realist, American*, 356 and Sherman, *Memoirs*, 271.

57. Cox, *Reminiscences*, vol. 2, 431–44; Bradley, "Last Stand," 10–12.

58. For details on the Battle of Averasboro, see Mark L. Bradley, "Old Reliable's Finest Hour: The Battle of Averasboro, North Carolina, March 15–16, 1865" *Blue & Gray Magazine* XVI, Issue 1 (Oct. 1998): 6–20, 52–57.

59. For full details and battle maps of the Battle of Bentonville, see Bradley, "Last Stand."

60. Alexander, *How Great Generals Win*, 166–67.

61. Arthur W. Bergeron Jr., "Three-day Tussle at Hatcher's Run," *America's Civil War* 16, no. 1 (March 2003): 30–37.

62. David W. Lowe, "Field Fortifications in the Civil War," *North & South* 4, no. 6 (Aug. 2001): 58–73 [hereafter Lowe, "Field Fortifications"] at 72.

63. Ibid.

64. Lincoln's pass for Francis P. Blair Sr., Dec. 28, 1864, *Works of Lincoln*, vol. 8, 188 and note; Lincoln to Blair, Jan. 18, 1865, Ibid., 220–21 at 221; Lincoln's endorsement on copy of that letter, Jan. 28, 1865, Ibid., 243.

65. Lincoln to Eckert, Jan. 30, 1865, Ibid., 246; Lincoln to Edward O.C. Ord (addressee changed to Grant by Stanton), Jan. 30, 1865, Ibid., 247; Eckert to Stephens, Campbell and Hunter, Jan. 30, 1865, Ibid., 248; Grant to Stanton, Feb. 2, 1865, Ibid., 282; Lincoln to Grant, Feb. 2, 1865, Ibid., 256; Lincoln to Seward, Feb. 2, 1865, Ibid.; Seward to Charles Francis Adams, Feb. 7, 1865, Ibid., 286–7n; McPherson, *Mighty Scourge*, 179–82; McPherson, *Tried by War*, 257–59.

66. Lincoln to Grant, Feb. 8, 1865, *Works of Lincoln*, vol. 8, 269; Grant to Lincoln, Ibid., 269–70n; Lincoln to the House of Representatives, Feb. 10, 1865, Ibid., 274–85.

67. Lincoln to Grant, Feb. 1, 1865, Ibid., 252; Stanton to Grant, Feb. 4, 1865, Ibid., 258.

68. Grant to Stanton, Feb. 7, 1865, Ibid., 267n; Stanton to Grant, Feb. 7, 1865, Ibid., 267–68n; Grant to Lincoln, Feb. [no day] 1865, Ibid., 267. It is unknown if the latter document was sent.

69. Lincoln to Grant, Feb. [c.11], 1865, Ibid., 288 and note.

70. Lincoln to Grant, March 8, 1865, Ibid., 343–44; Grant to Stanton, March 8, 1865, Ibid., 344n; Grant's Special Orders No. 48, March 10, 1865, Ibid., 344–45n; Lincoln to Grant, March 13, 1865, Ibid., 353 and note.

71. Lincoln to Grant, Jan. 19, 1865, Ibid., 223; Grant to Lincoln, Ibid., 223–24n. Grant explained that four experienced officers already on his staff were only captains or lieutenants and should not be outranked by Robert Lincoln.

72. Lincoln to Grant, Feb. 24, 1865, Ibid., 314 and note; Grant to Lincoln, Feb. 25, 1865, Ibid., 314n; Lincoln's Pass for Roger A. Pryor, Feb. 25, 1865, Ibid., 317.

73. Sheridan to Grant, Feb. 25, 1865, OR, Ser. I, XLVI, Part II, 701; Lincoln to Grant, Feb. 25, 1865, *Works of Lincoln*, 316; Grant to Lincoln, Feb. 26, 1865, *Papers of Grant*, vol. 14, 54; Sheridan to Stanton, Feb. 26, 1865, OR, Ser. I, XLVI, Part II, 711–12; Lincoln to Grant, Feb. 27, 1865, *Works of Lincoln*, vol. 8, 320–21.

74. Lincoln to Schuyler Colfax, March 2, 1865, Ibid., 328 and note; Lincoln to Hannibal Hamlin, March 2, 1865, Ibid., 329.

75. Lincoln to Grant, March 2, 1865, Ibid., 329; Grant to Lincoln, March 2, 1865, Ibid., 329n; Lincoln's response to a serenade, March 3, 1865, Ibid., 331, quoting *New York Tribune*, March 4, 1865.

76. Lee to Grant, March 2, 1865, Ibid., 331n.

77. Stanton to Grant, March 3, 1865, Ibid., 330–31.

78. Hearn, *Lincoln, Cabinet, Generals*, 287.

79. Lincoln's Second Inaugural Address, *Works of Lincoln*, vol. 8, 332–33.

80. Lincoln to Grant, March 7, 1865, Ibid., 339.

81. Thomas P. Lowry, *Merciful Lincoln: The President and Military Justice* (Thomas P. Lowry, 2009).

82. Grant to Lincoln, March 8, 1865, OR, Ser. I, XLVI, Part II, 887; Lincoln to Grant, March 9, 1865, *Works of Lincoln*, vol. 8, 347–48; Grant to Lincoln, Mar. 9, 1865, Ibid., 348n.

83. Lincoln's proclamation offering pardons to deserters, March 11, 1865, Ibid., 349–50.

84. Lincoln's speech to 140th Indiana Regiment, March 17, 1865, Ibid., 360–62 at 362, quoting *New York Herald*, March 18, 1865.

85. Grant to Lincoln, March 20, 1865, Ibid., 367n; Lincoln to Grant, Ibid., 367; Lincoln to Robert T. Lincoln, March 21, 1865, Ibid., 369; Charles B. Penrose to Stanton, March 24, 1865, Ibid., 373n; Lincoln to Stanton, March 25, 1865, Ibid., 373.

86. Carl R. Schenker Jr., "What Happened at City Point?" *North & South* 12, no. 5 (Jan. 2011): 11–13; Schenker, "Grant's Rise," 65.

87. Grant, *Memoirs*, 687–88.

88. Donald, *Lincoln*, 571–74.

89. Grant, *Memoirs*, 691–93; McWhiney and Jamieson, *Attack and Die*, 165; Marvel, *Lee's Last Retreat*, 9–11; Lowe, "Field Fortifications," 72; Fox, *Regimental Losses*, 548.

90. Winik, *April 1865*, 66.

91. Lincoln to Stanton, March 25, 1865, 8:30 a.m., *Works of Lincoln*, vol. 8, 373; Lincoln to Stanton, March 25, 1865, Ibid., 374; Rhodes, *All for the Union*, 221–22.

92. Grant, *Memoirs*, 693; Grant to Meade, March 24, 1865, *Papers of Grant*, vol. 14, 211–14 at 211.

93. Stephen W. Sears, *Controversies & Commanders: Dispatches from the Army of the Potomac* (Boston and New York: Houghton Mifflin Company, 1999) [hereafter Sears, *Controversies*], 263–64; Chris Calkins, "The Battle of Five Forks: Final Push for the South Side," *Blue & Gray Magazine* IX, no. 4 (April 1992): 8–22, 41–52 [hereafter Calkins, "Five Forks"] at 8–9.

94. Rhodes, *All for the Union*, 223.

95. Porter, *Campaigning with Grant*, 426.

96. Holzer, *Lincoln on War*, 284.

97. Calkins, "Five Forks," 10–11; Grant to Lincoln, March 29, 1865 (four telegrams), *Works of Lincoln*, vol. 8, 376–77n; Lincoln to Grant, March 29, 1865, Ibid., 376. Lincoln probably was following the action on maps at City Point—as he usually did at the War Department.

98. Lincoln to Stanton, March 30, 1865, *Works of Lincoln*, vol. 8, 377.

99. Curtis S. King, "Reconsider, Hell!," *MHQ: The Quarterly Journal of Military History* 13, no. 4 (Summer 2001): 88–95 [hereafter King, "Reconsider, Hell!"] at 88–92; Sears, *Controversies*, 269–71; Calkins, "Five Forks," 11–13.

100. Grant to Lincoln, March 31, 1865 (two telegrams), *Works of Lincoln*, vol. 8, 378–79n; Lincoln to Stanton, March 31, 1865 8:30 p.m., Ibid., 378.

101. For details of the Battle of Dinwiddie Court House, see Mark J. Crawford, "Dinwiddie Court House: Beginning of the End," *America's Civil War* 12, no. 1 (March 1999): 50–56 [hereafter Crawford, "Dinwiddie Court House"].

102. Crawford, "Dinwiddie Court House," 53–55; Calkins, "Five Forks," 16–17.

103. Rhodes, *All for the Union*, 224.

104. King, "Reconsider, Hell!," 92: Sears, *Controversies*, 272–74; Calkins, "Five Forks," 17–18.

105. Calkins, "Five Forks," 18.

106. Ibid., 18–22.

107. King, "Reconsider, Hell!," 92–93; Sears, *Controversies*, 279–81; Crawford, "Dinwiddie Court House," 56; Calkins, "Five Forks," 41–50; Sears, "Warren and Little Phil," 66–69.

108. Grant to Lincoln, April 1, 1865 (three telegrams), *Works of Lincoln*, vol. 8, 379–80n; Lincoln to Grant, April 1, 1865, 5:45 p.m., Ibid., 379; Lincoln to Seward and Stanton, April 1, 1865, Ibid., 380–81 and notes.

109. King, "Reconsider, Hell," 88, 94–95; Sears, *Controversies*, 281; William Marvel, "Retreat to Appomattox," *Blue & Gray Magazine* XXXVIII, Issue 4 (Spring 2001): 6–24, 46–54 [hereafter Marvel, "Retreat"] at 6; William Marvel, "Thorn in the Flesh," *Civil War Times Illustrated* XLI, no. 3 (June 2002): 42–49, 60–62; A. Wilson Greene, "April 2, 1865: Day of Decision at Petersburg," *Blue & Gray Magazine* XVIII, Issue 3 (Feb. 2001): 6–24, 42–53 [hereafter Greene, "April 2, 1865"] at 6; Sears, "Warren and Little Phil," 69–70.

110. Smith, *Grant*, 399n.

111. Calkins, "Five Forks," 50–51; Marvel, "Retreat," 6.

112. Grant to Colonel Theodore S. Bowers, April 1, 1865, OR, Ser. I, XLVI, Part III, 394; *Works of Lincoln*, vol. 8, 382n.

113. Lincoln to Mary Todd Lincoln (copy to Stanton), April 2, 1865, 7:45 a.m., *Works of Lincoln*, vol. 8, 381.

114. Grant, *Memoirs*, 702–3; Greene, "April 2, 1864," 12; Calkins, "Five Forks," 50–51.

115. Grant, *Memoirs*, 703–705; Greene, "April 2, 1864," 12–24, 42–50; Burke Davis, *The Long Surrender* (New York: Vintage Books, 1989), 21–32.

116. Greene, "April 2, 1865," 53.

117. Grant to Theodore S. Bowers, April 2, 1865, 8:25 a.m. and 10:45 a.m., *Works of Lincoln*, vol. 8, 382n and 383n; Lincoln to Stanton, April 2, 1865, 11 a.m. and 2 p.m., *Works of Lincoln*, 382–83, OR, Ser. I, XLVI, Part III, 446; Ibid., 447.

118. Grant to Bowers, April 2, 1865, 4:30 p.m., OR, Ser. I, XLVI, Part III, 449; Lincoln to Stanton, April 2, 1865, 8:30 p.m., *Works of Lincoln*, vol. 8, 383–84, OR, Ser. I, XLVI, Part III, 447; Lincoln to Grant, April 2, 1865, 8:15 p.m., *Works of Lincoln*, vol. 8, 383.

119. Lincoln to Mary Todd Lincoln, April 2, 1865, *Works of Lincoln*, vol. 8, 384, OR, Ser. I, XLVI, Part III, 447–48.

120. Grant to Bowers (two telegrams), April 3, 1865, a.m., OR, Ser. I, XLVI, Part III, 509.

121. Lincoln to Stanton, April 3, 1865, 8 a.m., *Works of Lincoln*, vol. 8, 384; Stanton to Lincoln, April 3, 1865, Ibid., 384–85n.

122. Lincoln to Stanton, April 3, 1865, 5 p.m., Ibid., 385.

123. Grant, *Memoirs*, vol. 2, 459–61.

124. Lincoln to Stanton, April 4, 1865, 7:30 a.m., *Works of Lincoln*, vol. 8, 385, quoting Grant to Lincoln, April 4, 1865, 3:20 a.m., Ibid.

125. Lincoln to Campbell, April 5, 1865, Ibid., 386.

126. Lincoln at City Point to Grant in the field, April 6, 1865, 12 M., Ibid., 388.

127. Lincoln to Weitzel, April 12, 1865, Ibid., 406–7.

128. Lincoln to Grant, April 6, 1865, 12 M, Ibid., 388.

129. For details on the Appomattox Campaign, see Marvel, *Lee's Last Retreat*; Marvel, "Retreat" [includes battle maps].

130. William Marvel contended that the missing pontoon bridge delayed Lee more than any missing rations. He blamed both on poor headquarters communication. Marvel, *Lee's Last Retreat*, 44–51, 207–208; William Marvel, "Many have offered excuses for the Confederate retreat to Appomattox, perhaps beginning with Robert E. Lee," *America's Civil War* 14, no. 3 (July 2001): 62–70 [hereafter Marvel, "Many Have Offered"] at 66–70. He also attacked the "myth" of the missing rations' significance and laid the probable blame for their absence at the doorstep of Lee's aide Walter Taylor. Marvel, *Lee's Last Retreat*, 207–213; Marvel, "Many Have Offered," 70.

131. Marvel, "Retreat," 8–11.

132. Winik, *April 1865*, 133–34.

133. Marvel, *Lee's Last Retreat*, 67–94; Gary Glynn, "Black Thursday for Rebels," *America's Civil War* 4, no. 5 (Jan. 1992), 22–29 [hereafter Glynn, "Black Thursday"]; Marvel, "Retreat," 13–20; Calkins, "Final Bloodshed at Appomattox," *America's Civil War* 14, no. 2 (May 2001): 34–40 [hereafter Calkins, "Final Bloodshed"] at 36; Fox, *Regimental Losses*, 549; Heidler and Heidler, *Encyclopedia*, 1710.

134. Marvel, "Retreat," 21–22.

135. Lincoln to Stanton, April 7, 1865, 8:35 a.m., *Works of Lincoln*, vol. 8, 389, containing or referencing copy of Sheridan to Grant, April 6, 1865; OR, Ser. I, XLVI, Part III, 640 and 610; Lincoln to Stanton, April 7, 1865, 9 a.m., *Works of Lincoln*, vol. 8, 390 91; OR, Ser. I, XLVI, Part III, 640.

136. Lincoln to Grant, April 7, 1865, 11 a.m., *Works of Lincoln*, vol. 8, 392.

137. Grant to Lee, April 7, 1865, *Papers of Grant*, vol. 14, 361.

138. Lee to Grant, April 7, 1865, Clifford Dowdey and Louis H. Manarin, *The Wartime Papers of R. E. Lee* (New York: Barnhall House, 1961) [hereafter *Papers of Lee*], 931–32 and *Papers of Grant*, vol. 14, 361 note. In the spirit of continued deification of Lee, editors Clifford Dowdey and Louis H. Manarin made editorial corrections to Lee's papers to make them

as perfect as possible. They failed to indicate they had done so. On the other hand, John Y. Simon republished Grant's correspondence as it was written (including all the errors). Simon similarly maintained the original accuracy of Lee's correspondence that he quoted in notes to Grant's correspondence. The Lee texts quoted here and below are the unedited Simon versions.

139. Grant to Lee, April 8, 1865, *Papers of Grant*, vol. 14, 367.

140. Lee to Grant, April 8, 1865, *Papers of Lee*, 932 and *Papers of Grant*, vol. 14, 367 note.

141. Douglas Southall Freeman, *Lee's Lieutenants: A Study in Command* (3 vols.) (New York: Charles Scribner's Sons, 1942–4) (1972 reprint), vol. 3, 721; Longstreet, *Memoirs*, 620.

142. Winik, *April 1865*, 143–44.

143. Marvel, "Retreat," 52–54; Calkins, "Final Bloodshed," 40.

144. Grant to Lee, April 9, 1865, *Papers of Grant*, vol. 14, 371.

145. Marvel, "Retreat," 54.

146. Lee to Grant, April 9, 1865, *Papers of Lee*, 932; *Papers of Grant*, vol. 14, 371n.

147. Marvel, *Lee's Last Retreat*, 180. Several of Grant's officers immediately bought the McLean parlor furniture as souvenirs. Ibid., 181.

148. Richard F. Selcer, "Battlefield Bulldog, Compassionate Conqueror," *Civil War Times* XLVI, no. 1 (Feb. 2007): 46–53 at 53.

149. Winik, *April 1865*, 153–54.

150. McWhiney and Jamieson, *Attack and Die*, 19, 158.

151. Marvel, *Lee's Last Retreat*, 184, 201–6; Marvel, "Many Have Offered," 62–66.

152. Dana, *Recollections*, 210–11.

153. Lincoln's Last Public Address, April 11, 1865, *Works of Lincoln*, vol. 8, 399–405.

Chapter 13: Lincoln and Grant: The Winning Team

1. Porter, *Campaigning for Grant*, 19–20.

2. Eaton, *Grant, Lincoln*, 310.

3. Badeau, *Grant*, vol. 2, 21.

4. Smith, *Grant*, 108–9.

5. Gary W. Gallagher, *The Union War* (Cambridge: Harvard University Press, 2011) [hereafter Gallagher, *Union War*], 133–34.

6. Dana to Washburne, Aug. 29, 1863, *Papers of Grant*, vol. 9, 218–19n.

7. Hay, *Diary*, April 28, 1864, 191.

8. *Philadelphia Daily Evening Bulletin*, June 7, 1864, 4, quoted in Gallagher, *Union War*, 134.

9. Wiley, *Road to Appomattox*, 78–96.

10. Lincoln to Grant, July 13, 1863, *Works of Lincoln*, vol. 6, 326.

11. Lincoln's Speech to 148th Ohio Regiment, Aug. 31, 1864, Ibid., 528–29 at 528.

12. Fulton, *Reconstruction of Twain*, 177.

13. Eaton, *Grant, Lincoln*, 312. His relationship with George Thomas seems to be an exception.

14. For details, see Edward H. Bonekemper III, *McClellan and Failure: A Study of Civil War Fear, Incompetence and Worse* (Jefferson, North Carolina: McFarland & Company, 2007), 95–122.

15. J. F. C. Fuller, *Grant and Lee: A Study in Personality and Generalship* (Bloomington: University of Indiana Press, 1957) (reprint of 1932 edition) [hereafter Fuller, *Grant and Lee*], 59. Although this purported and oft-repeated statement is intriguing, its utterance is doubtful. Donald C. Pfanz, Ewell's authoritative biographer, observed, "Ewell and Grant crossed paths on one or two occasions, but there is no evidence to suggest that they knew each other well. Barring prophetic inspiration, this statement must be dismissed as apocryphal." Donald C. Pfanz, *Richard F. Ewell: A Soldier's Life* (Chapel Hill: University of North Carolina Press, 1998), 589 fn 40.

16. Nicolay and Hay, *Lincoln*, vol. 5, 112.

17. Catton, *Grant Takes Command*, 105.

18. Steven E. Woodworth, "The Army of Tennessee and the Element of Military Success," *North & South* 6, no. 4 (May 2003), 44–55 at 52.

19. Stoddard, *Inside the White House*, 125.

20. Fehrenbacher, Don E. commentary in Garraty, *Encyclopedia*, 666.

21. Holzer, *Lincoln on War*, 178.

22. Bonekemper, *How Lee Lost*, 203.

23. McPherson, "Unheroic Hero," 17.

24. John Keegan, *The Mask of Command* (New York: Viking, 1987), 200. Grant probably modeled his orders on those of Zachary Taylor, of whom Grant wrote, "Taylor was not a conversationalist, but on paper he could put his meaning so plainly that there could be no mistaking it. He knew how to express what he wanted to say in the fewest well-chosen words." Grant, *Memoirs*, 95.

25. Nicolay and Hay, *Lincoln*, vol. 5, 111–12.

26. John Keegan, *The American Civil War: A Military History* (New York: Knopf, 2009), 329–30.

27. Porter, *Campaigning with Grant*, 7

28. Ibid., 447.

29. Jones, *Right Hand*, 111. Jones cited evidence that Grant wrote his own orders because he could write them more quickly than explain to a clerk or aide what he wanted written. Ibid., 111–12.

30. Smith, *Grant*, 202.

31. Simpson, "Lincoln and Grant," 119.

32. Eaton, *Grant, Lincoln*, 312.

33. Williams, *McClellan, Sherman and Grant*, 59.

34. McPherson, "Unheroic Hero," 18.

35. Fuller, *Generalship of Grant*, 190.

36. Cox, *Reminiscences*, vol. 2, 41.

37. Williams, *McClellan, Sherman and Grant*, 105–6.

38. Waugh, *Grant*, 47.

39. Anderson, "Grant's Struggle with Alcohol," 24; Perret, *Grant*, 262. "There is no evidence that he was under the influence at any moment of decision or that the habit interfered with his generalship. But the suspicion was always there, and it cropped up at regular intervals." Williams, *McClellan, Sherman and Grant*, 89. Those suspicions could have cost Grant promotions because "Lincoln was shy of alcoholics." Guelzo, *Lincoln*, 115.

40. McPherson, *Mighty Scourge*, 114.

41. Jones, *Right Hand*, 113–16.

42. McPherson, *Battle Cry of Freedom*, 588.

43. Winik, *April 1865*, 180 [Bracketed word added].

44. Catton, *Grant Moves South*, 217; Arnold, *Armies of Grant*, 108.

45. Fehrenbacher commentary in Garraty, *Encyclopedia*, 666.

46. Winik, *April 1865*, 241, 425.

47. Miller, *Lincoln and World*, vol. 3, 226.

48. Lamon, *Recollections*, 39, 54–56.

49. Winik, *April 1865*, 204–5.

50. Ibid., 242, 245.

51. Ibid., 247.

52. McPherson, *Mighty Scourge*, 110–11.

53. McPherson, "Unheroic Hero," 18–19; Rhea, *Cold Harbor*, 388.

54. OR, Ser. I, XLVI , Part I, 22.

55. Rhea, *Cold Harbor*, 388.

56. *Chicago Tribune*, May 14, 1864, 2, quoted in Gallagher, *Union War*, 134.

57. Sommers, *Richmond Redeemed*, 443.
58. Arnold, *Armies of Grant*, 275.
59. Woodworth, *Nothing But Victory*, ix–x.
60. Winik, *April 1865*, 179–80.
61. Waugh, *Lincoln and McClellan*, 218.
62. Winik, *April 1865*, 356–57.
63. McPherson, *Mighty Scourge*, 138.
64. Thomas J. Goss, *The War Within the Union High Command: Politics and Generalship During the Civil War* (Lawrence: University Press of Kansas, 2003) [hereafter Goss, *War*], 170.
65. Adams, *Fighting for Defeat*, 158.
66. Goss, *War*, 174–91.
67. Eaton, *Grant, Lincoln*, 313–14.
68. McPherson, *Tried by War*, 85.
69. Halleck to Grant, Jan. 21, 1863, OR, Ser. I, XXIV, Part I, 9.
70. Papers of Ward Hill Lamon, Memorandum on Lincoln and Grant, 6–7, as quoted in Fehrenbacher and Fehrenbacher, *Recollected Words*, 292.
71. Smith, *Grant*, 231.
72. McPherson, *Mighty Scourge*, 141, citing James F. Rusling, *Men and Things I Saw in Civil War Days* (New York, 1899), 16–17.
73. Weigley, "Soldier, Statesman," 812.
74. Gallagher, *Union War*, 135–36.
75. McPherson, *Tried by War*, 267.
76. Ibid., 5.
77. Holzer, *Lincoln on War*, 178.
78. Ibid.
79. Simpson, "Lincoln and Grant," 117.
80. T. Harry Williams, "The Military Leadership of North and South" in David Herbert Donald, ed., *Why the North Won the Civil War* (New York: Collier Books, 1960), 33–54 at 50–52.
81. Lincoln to Seward, June 28, 1862, *Works of Lincoln*, vol. 5, 291–92.
82. Winik, *April 1865*, 195.
83. Simpson, "Lincoln and Grant," 116.
84. McPherson, *Tried by War*, 267–68. Quite early in the war, before the Seven Days' Battle outside Richmond, however, Lincoln had told Stanton, "Richmond is the principal point for active operations." Lincoln to Stanton, June 8, 1862 in Holzer, *Lincoln on War*, 135–36 at 135. Within a few months, Lincoln refocused on the need to destroy Rebel armies.
85. Catton, *Grant Moves South*, 489.

86. Cox, *Reminiscences*, vol. 2, 41.

87. McWhiney and Jamieson, *Attack and Die*, 19, 22, 23, 158.

88. Feis, *Grant's Secret Service*, 267. Feis' conclusions appeared earlier in William B. Feis, "'He Don't Care a Damn for What the Enemy Does out of His Sight,'" *North & South* 1, no. 2 (Jan. 1998): 68–81.

89. Lincoln to Hooker, June 5, 1863, *Works of Lincoln*, vol. 6, 249; June 10, 1863, Ibid., 257.

90. James M. McPherson, "Lincoln and the Strategy of Unconditional Surrender," in Gabor S. Boritt, ed., *Lincoln, the War President: The Gettysburg Lectures* (New York: Oxford University Press, 1992), 29–62 at 45.

91. McPherson. *Tried by War*, 70–71, 268–69.

92. See Bonekemper, *Grant and Lee*, 261–63.

93. Hay, *Diary*, April 30, 1864, 193.

94. Russell F. Weigley, *Towards an American Army: Military Thought from Washington to Marshall* (New York: Columbia University Press, 1962), 80.

95. Grant, *Memoirs*, I, 368–69.

96. Badeau, *Grant*, vol. 3, 109, 642–44.

97. Stoddard, *Inside the White House*, 138.

98. Rhea, *Cold Harbor*, xii.

99. Gordon C. Rhea, "'Butcher' Grant and the Overland Campaign," *North & South* 4, no. 1 (Nov. 2000): 44–55 [hereafter Rhea, "'Butcher' Grant"] at 47.

100. Rhea *et al.*, "What Was Wrong?," 15.

101. Wert, "All-out War," 40.

102. Murray, Williamson, "In Praise of Sam Grant," *Military History Quarterly: The Quarterly Journal of Military History* 18, no. 4 (Summer 2006): 6–15 [hereafter Williamson, "Praise"] at 6.

103. Weigley, "American Military," 38–39.

104. Hay, *Diary*, 25.

105. McPherson, *Tried by War*, 268–69.

106. See Bonekemper, *A Victor, Not a Butcher*, xi–xviii.

107. See Bonekemper, *Grant and Lee*, 252–53.

108. Williams, *McClellan, Sherman and Grant*, 97–98.

109. Stoddard, *Inside the White House*, 126.

110. May 25, 1863 correspondence in the *Philadelphia Inquirer*, reprinted in the *Chicago Tribune*, May 29, 1863, and cited in Fehrenbacher and Fehrenbacher, *Recollected Words*, 11.

111. Williams, *McClellan, Sherman and Grant*, 105; Fuller, *Grant and Lee*, 63, 68.

112. Murphy, "Grant versus Lee," 49.

113. Hattaway, "Changing Face," 42.

114. Welles, *Diary*, vol. 2, 44–45; Jones, *Right Hand*, 200; Groom, *Shrouds of Glory*, 9. A 1993 article in *Blue & Gray Magazine* refers to the "butcher's bill" of the first two weeks of the Overland Campaign. Miller, "Strike Them," 13. On June 4, 1864, Navy Secretary Gideon Welles also wrote in his diary, "Still there is heavy loss, but we are becoming accustomed to the sacrifice. Grant has not great regard for human life." Welles, *Diary*, vol. 2, 45.

115. Weigley, *American Way of War*, 152.

116. Ibid., 142.

117. Lincoln to Grant, August 3, 1864, *Works of Lincoln*, vol. 7, 476; Grant, *Memoirs*, 615–16.

118. Lincoln to Grant, Sept. 12, 1864, *Works of Lincoln*, vol. 7, 548.

119. Gallagher, "'Upon Their Success'," 91.

120. Arnold, *Grant Wins*, 4.

121. Smith, *Grant*, 138.

122. Fuller, *Grant and Lee*, 81.

123. Williams, *Lincoln and His Generals*, 271.

124. Williams, *McClellan, Sherman and Grant*, 97.

125. Weigley, *American Way of War*, 130.

126. Hattaway and Jones, *How the North Won*, xvi.

127. Catton, *Grant Takes Command*, 139.

128. Lincoln to Albert G. Hodges, April 4, 1864, *Works of Lincoln*, vol. 7, 281–82 at 282; Lincoln to Charles D. Robinson, Aug. 17, 1864, Ibid., 499–501 at 500; Lincoln to Isaac M. Schermerhorn, Sept. 12, 1864, Ibid., vol. 8, 1–2 at 2.

129. See John David Smith, ed., *Black Soldiers in Blue: African American Troops in the Civil War Era* (Chapel Hill: University of North Carolina Press, 2003).

130. Sherman to Grant, June 2, 1863, OR, Ser. I, XXIV, Part III, 372–73; duplicate in OR, Ser. III, III, Part III, 386–88; Brooks D. Simpson and Jean V. Berlin, eds., *Sherman's Civil War: Selected Correspondence of William T. Sherman, 1860–1865* (Chapel Hill: University of North Carolina Press, 1999), 474–76; Grant to Lincoln, June 19, 1863, OR, Ser. III, III, 386; *Papers of Grant*, vol. 8, 395 (Grant's letter included this statement: "Taken in an economic point of view, one drafted man in an old regiment

is worth three in a new one."); Halleck to Grant, July 14, 1863, OR, Ser. III, III, 487; *Papers of Grant*, vol. 8, 397n; Flood, *Grant and Sherman*, 172–73.

131. Lincoln to Hurlbut, July 31, 1863, *Works of Lincoln*, vol. 6, 358 and 359n.
132. Noyalas, *Cedar Creek*, 16.
133. Sears, *Controversies*, 189–92; Lincoln to Meade, July 27, 1863, *Works of Lincoln*, vol. 6, 350; Dana to Stanton, Oct. 29, 1863, OR, Ser. I, XXXI, Part I, 73.
134. See Bobrick, *Master of War, passim.*
135. This practice contrasted with that of Lee, who "dumped" his less successful generals on other theaters.

BIBLIOGRAPHY

MEMOIRS, LETTERS, PAPERS, AND OTHER PRIMARY DOCUMENTS

Alexander, Edward Porter. *Fighting for the Confederacy: The Personal Recollections of General Edward Porter Alexander*. Edited by Gary W. Gallagher. Chapel Hill: University of North Carolina Press, 1989.

———. *The Military Memoirs of a Confederate*. New York: Charles Scribner's Sons, 1907.

Basler, Roy P., ed. *The Collected Works of Abraham Lincoln*. 8 vols. New Brunswick: Rutgers University Press, 1953.

———. *The Collected Works of Abraham Lincoln: Supplement 1832–1865*. Westport, CT: Greenwood Press, 1974.

Brooks, Noah. *Lincoln Observed: Civil War Dispatches of Noah Brooks*. Baltimore: Johns Hopkins University Press, 1998. Edited by Michael Burlingame.

Cadwallader, Sylvanus. *Three Years with Grant*. New York: Alfred A. Knopf, 1956. Published version of 1896 manuscript inaccurately titled *Four Years with Grant*.

Carpenter, Francis B. *Six Months at the White House with Abraham Lincoln*. New York: Hurd and Houton, 1866.

Cox, Jacob Dolson. *Military Reminiscences of the Civil War*. 2 vols. New York: Charles Scribner's Sons, 1900.

Dana, Charles A. *Recollections of the Civil War*. New York: Collier Books, 1898, 1963.

Davis, Jefferson. *The Rise and Fall of the Confederate Government*. 2 vols. New York: Da Capo Press, 1990. Reprint of 1881 edition.

Dowdey, Clifford and Manarin, Louis H. *The Wartime Papers of R. E. Lee*. New York: Barmhall House, 1961. Includes undisclosed editorial changes.

Eaton, John. *Grant, Lincoln and the Freedmen: Reminiscences of the Civil War with Special Reference to the Work for the Contrabands and Freedmen of the Mississippi Valley*. New York: Negro Universities Press, 1969. Reprint of New York: Longmans, Green, and Co., 1907.

Grant, Ulysses S. *Personal Memoirs of U. S. Grant*. 2 vols. New York: Charles L. Webster & Company, 1892 [copyrighted by Grant in 1885].

Hay, John. *At Lincoln's Side: John Hay's Civil War Correspondence and Selected Writings*. Edited by Michael Burlingame. Carbondale: Southern Illinois University Press, 2000.

———. *Inside Lincoln's White House: The Complete Civil War Diary of John Hay*. Edited by Michael Burlingame and John R. Turner Ettlinger. Carbondale: Southern Illinois University Press, 1997.

Johnson, Robert Underwood and, Clarence Clough Buel, eds. *Battles and Leaders of the Civil War*. 4 vols. New York: Thomas Yoseloff, Inc., 1956. Reprint of Secaucus, New Jersey: Castle, 1887–88.

Jones, J. B. *A Rebel War Clerk's Diary at the Confederate States Capital*. 2 vols. Philadelphia: J. B. Lippincott & Co., 1866. 1982 reprint.

Jones, J. William. *Personal Reminiscences of General Robert E. Lee*. Richmond: United States Historical Society Press, 1989. Reprint.

Lamon, Ward Hill and Dorothy Lamon Teillard. *Recollections of Abraham Lincoln 1847–1865*. A. C. McClurg and Company, 1895. 2009 reprint by General Books.

Lee, Robert E. *Lee's Dispatches: Unpublished Letters of General Robert E. Lee, C.S.A., to Jefferson Davis and the War Department of the Confederate States of America 1862–65*. Edited by Douglas Southall Freeman. Baton Rouge: Louisiana State University Press, 1957.

Longstreet, James. *From Manassas to Appomattox: Memoirs of the Civil War in America*. New York: Smithmark Publishers, Inc., 1994.

McClure, Alexander K. *Abraham Lincoln and Men of War-Times*.
Philadelphia: Times Publishing Co., 1892.

Nicolay, John G. *The Outbreak of Rebellion*. New York: Charles
Scribner's Sons, 1881. Reprint of Harrisburg: The Archive Society,
1992.

———, and John Hay. *Abraham Lincoln: A History*. 10 vols. New York:
The Century Company, 1886, 1890, 1914.

Porter, Horace. *Campaigning with Grant*. New York: The Century
Company, 1897. 1981 Time-Life reprint.

Rhodes, Robert Hunt, ed. *All for the Union: The Civil War Diary and
Letters of Elisha Hunt Rhodes*. New York: Orion Books, 1991.
Originally published by Andrew Mowbray Incorporated in 1985.

Sears, Stephen W., ed. *The Civil War Papers of George B. McClellan:
Selected Correspondence 1860–1865*. New York: Ticknor & Fields,
1989.

Sherman, William Tecumseh. *Memoirs of General W. T. Sherman*. New
York: Literary Classics of the United States, Inc., 1990. Reprint of
1885 second edition.

Simon, John Y., ed. *The Papers of Ulysses Grant*. 30 vols. Carbondale:
Southern Illinois University Press, 1967–2009.

Simpson, Brooks D. and Jean V. Berlin, eds. *Sherman's Civil War: Selected
Correspondence of William T. Sherman, 1860–1865*. Chapel Hill:
University of North Carolina Press, 1999.

Stoddard, William O. *Inside the White House in War Times: Memoirs
and Reports of Lincoln's Secretary*. Edited by Michael Burlingame.
Lincoln: University of Nebraska Press, 2000. Reprint and expansion
of New York: Charles L. Webster & Co., 1890.

Stoddard, William O., Jr. *William O. Stoddard: Lincoln's Third Secretary*.
New York: Exposition Press, 1955.

*The War of Rebellion: A Compilation of the Official Records of the Union
and Confederate Armies*. 128 vols. Washington, D.C.: Government
Printing Office, 1880–1901.

Watkins, Sam R. *"Co. Aytch," Maury Grays, First Tennessee Regiment;
or, A Side Show of the Big Show*. Wilmington, N.C.: Broadfoot
Publishing Company, 1987. Reprint of 1952 edition and of Nashville:
Cumberland Presbyterian Publishing House, 1882.

Welles, Gideon. *Diary of Gideon Welles*. 3 vols. Boston: Houghton Mifflin
Company, 1911.

Wiggins, Sarah Woolfolk (ed.). *The Journals of Josiah Gorgas 1857–1878*.
Tuscaloosa: The University of Alabama Press, 1995.

Woodward, C. Vann (ed.). *Mary Chesnut's Civil War*. New Haven: Yale University Press, 1981.

OTHER BOOKS AND PUBLICATIONS

Abbazia, Patrick. *The Chickamauga Campaign, December 1862–November 1863*. New York: Wieser & Wieser, Inc., 1988.

Adams, Michael C. C. *Fighting for Defeat: Union Military Failure in the East, 1861–1865*. Lincoln: University of Nebraska, 1978, 1992.

Alexander, Bevin. *How Great Generals Win*. New York: W. W. Norton & Co., 1993.

Ambrose, Stephen E. *Halleck: Lincoln's Chief of Staff*. Baton Rouge: Louisiana State University Press, 1962, 1990.

Arnold, James R. *The Armies of U. S. Grant*. London: Arms and Armour Press, 1995.

———. *Grant Wins the War: Decision at Vicksburg*. New York: John Wiley & Sons, Inc., 1997.

Badeau, Adam. *Military History of Ulysses S. Grant, from April, 1861, to April, 1865*. Vol. 1 of 3 vols. New York: D. Appleton and Company, 1868.

Bearss, Edwin Cole. *Unvexed to the Sea: The Campaign for Vicksburg*. 3 vols. Dayton: Morningside House, Inc., 1991. Reprint of 1986 edition.

Beringer, Richard E., Herman Hattaway, Archer Jones, and William N. Still Jr. *Why the South Lost the Civil War*. Athens, GA: University of Georgia Press, 1986.

Bobrick, Benson. *Master of War: The Life of General George H. Thomas*. New York: Simon & Schuster, 2009.

Bonekemper, Edward H., III. *Grant and Lee: Victorious American and Vanquished Virginian*. Westport, Connecticut: Praeger, 2008. Republished, Washington, DC: Regnery History, 2012.

———. *How Robert E. Lee Lost the Civil War*. Fredericksburg, VA: Sergeant Kirkland's Press, 1998

———. *McClellan and Failure: A Study of Civil War Fear, Incompetence and Worse*. Jefferson, NC: McFarland & Company, 2007.

———. *A Victor, Not a Butcher: Ulysses S. Grant's Overlooked Military Genius*. Washington: Regnery Press, 2004. [Republished as *Ulysses S. Grant: A Victor, Not a Butcher: The Military Genius of the Man Who Won the Civil War* (Washington: Regnery Publishing, 2010)].

Boritt, Gabor S., ed.. *Lincoln's Generals*. New York: Oxford University Press, 1994.

———. *Lincoln, the War President.* New York: Oxford University Press, 1992.

———, ed. *Why the Confederacy Lost.* New York: Oxford University Press, 1992.

Botkin, B. A., ed. *A Civil War Treasury of Tales, Legends and Folklore.* New York: Promontory Press, 1960.

Buell, Thomas B. *The Warrior Generals: Combat Leadership in the Civil War.* New York: Crown Publishers, Inc., 1997.

Burlingame, Michael. *Abraham Lincoln: A Life.* 2 vols. Baltimore: Johns Hopkins University Press, 2008.

Carnahan, Burrus. *Act of Justice: Lincoln's Emancipation Proclamation and the Law of War.* Lexington: University Press of Kentucky, 2007.

Castel, Albert. *Decision in the West: The Atlanta Campaign of 1864.* Lawrence: University Press of Kansas, 1992.

Catton, Bruce. *The American Heritage New History of the Civil War.* New York: Penguin Books USA, 1996.

———. *The Army of the Potomac: Glory Road.* Garden City, New York: Doubleday & Company, 1952.

———. *The Army of the Potomac: Mr. Lincoln's Army.* Garden City, NY: Doubleday & Company, 1951, 1962.

———. *The Army of the Potomac: A Stillness at Appomattox.* Garden City, NY: Doubleday & Company, 1953.

———. *Grant Moves South.* Boston: Little, Brown and Company, 1960.

———. *Grant Takes Command.* Boston: Little, Brown and Company, 1969.

———. *Terrible Swift Sword.* Garden City, NY: Doubleday & Company, 1963.

———. *This Hallowed Ground: The Story of the Union Side of the Civil War.* Garden City, NY: Doubleday & Company, 1956, 1962.

———. *U. S. Grant and the American Military Tradition.* Boston: Little, Brown and Company, 1954.

Chambers, John Whiteclay, II, ed. *The Oxford Companion to American Military History.* Oxford: Oxford University Press, 1999.

Coburn, Mark. *Terrible Innocence: General Sherman at War.* New York: Hippocrene Books, 1993.

Congressional Quarterly, Inc. *Presidential Elections, 1789–1996.* Washington, DC: Congressional Quarterly, Inc., 1997.

Connelly, Thomas Lawrence. *Army of the Heartland: The Army of Tennessee, 1861–1862.* Baton Rouge: Louisiana State University Press, 1967.

————. *Autumn of Glory: The Army of Tennessee, 1862-1865*. Baton Rouge: Louisiana State University Press, 1971, 1991.

————, and Archer Jones. *The Politics of Command: Factions and Ideas in Confederate Strategy*. Baton Rouge: Louisiana State University Press, 1973.

Cooling, Benjamin Franklin. *Forts Henry and Donelson: The Key to the Confederate Heartland*. Knoxville: The University of Tennessee Press, 1987.

————. *Jubal Early's Raid on Washington*. Fire Ant Books, 2008.

————. *Monocacy: The Battle That Saved Washington*. Shippensburg, PA: White Maine Publishing Co., 2000.

Cozzens, Peter. *The Darkest Days of the War: The Battles of Iuka and Corinth*. Chapel Hill: University of North Carolina Press, 1997.

————. *The Shipwreck of Their Hopes: The Battles for Chattanooga*. Urbana: University of Illinois Press, 1994.

Davis, Burke. *The Long Surrender*. New York: Vintage Books, 1989.

Davis, William C. *The Cause Lost: Myths and Realities of the Confederacy*. Lawrence: University Press of Kansas, 1996.

————. *Jefferson Davis: The Man and His Hour*. Baton Rouge: Louisiana State University Press, 1991.

Dew, Charles B. *Apostles of Disunion*. Charlottesville: University Press of Virginia, 2001.

Donald, David Herbert. *Lincoln*. New York: Simon & Schuster, 1995.

————, ed. *Why the North Won the Civil War*. New York: Macmillan Publishing Co., 1962.

————, Jean Harvey Baker, and Michael F. Holt, *The Civil War and Reconstruction*. New York: W. W. Norton & Company, 2001.

Dugard, Martin. *The Training Ground: Grant, Lee, Sherman, and Davis in the Mexican War (1846–1848)*. New York: Little, Brown and Co., 2008.

Eicher, David J. *The Civil War in Books: An Analytical Bibliography*. Urbana: University of Illinois Press, 1997.

————. *The Longest Night: A Military History of the Civil War*. New York: Simon & Schuster, 2002.

Engle, Stephen D. *The American Civil War: The War in the West 1861–July 1863*. Oxford: Osprey Publishing, 2001.

Fehrenbacher, Don E. and Virginia Fehrenbacher, eds. *Recollected Words of Abraham Lincoln*. Stanford: Stanford University Press, 1996.

Feis, William B. *Grant's Secret Service: The Intelligence War from Belmont to Appomattox*. Lincoln: University of Nebraska Press, 2002.

Fellman, Michael. *Citizen Sherman: A Life of William Tecumseh Sherman.* New York: Random House, 1995.

Fishel, Edwin C. *The Secret War for the Union: The Untold Story of Military Intelligence in the Civil War.* Boston: Houghton Mifflin, 1996.

Flood, Charles Bracelen. *Grant and Sherman: The Friendship That Won the Civil War.* New York: Farrar, Straus and Giroux, 2005.

Foote, Shelby. *The Civil War: A Narrative.* 3 vols. New York: Random House, 1958–1974.

Fox, William F. *Regimental Losses in the American Civil War, 1861–1865: A Treatise on the Extent and Nature of the Mortuary Losses in the Union regiments, with Full and Exhaustive Statistics Compiled from the Official Records on File in the State Military Bureaus and at Washington.* Dayton: Morningside House, Inc., 1985 (Reprint of Albany: Brandow Printing Company, 1898).

Freehling, William W. *The Road to Disunion, Volume II: Secessionists Triumphant.* Oxford: Oxford University Press, 2007.

Freeman, Douglas Southall. *Lee's Lieutenants: A Study in Command.* 3 vols. New York: Charles Scribner's Sons, 1942–44 (1972 reprint).

———. *R. E. Lee.* 4 vols. New York: Charles Scribner's Sons, 1934–45.

Fuller, J. F. C. *The Generalship of Ulysses S. Grant.* Bloomington: Indiana University Press, 1958. Reprint of 1929 edition.

———. *Grant and Lee: A Study in Personality and Generalship.* Bloomington: Indiana University Press, 1957. Reprint of 1933 edition.

Fulton, Joe B. *The Reconstruction of Mark Twain: How a Confederate Bushwhacker Became the Lincoln of Our Literature.* Baton Rouge: Louisiana State University Press, 2010.

Furgurson, Ernest B. *Not War But Murder: Cold Harbor 1864.* New York: Alfred A. Knopf, 2000.

Gallagher, Gary W. *The American Civil War: The War in the East 1861–May 1863.* Oxford: Osprey Publishing, 2001.

———, ed. *The Spotsylvania Campaign.* Chapel Hill: University of North Carolina Press, 1998.

———. *The Union War.* Cambridge: Harvard University Press, 2011.

———, ed. *The Wilderness Campaign.* Chapel Hill: University of North Carolina Press, 1997.

Garraty, John A., ed. *Encyclopedia of American Biography.* New York: Harper & Row, 1974.

Gates, Henry Louis, Jr. *Lincoln on Race & Slavery.* Princeton: Princeton University Press, 2009.

Gienapp, William E., ed. *The Civil War and Reconstruction: A Documentary Collection*. New York: W. W. Norton and Company, 2001.

Glatthaar, Joseph T. *The American Civil War: The War in the West 1863–1865*. Oxford: Osprey Publishing, 2001.

———. *Partners in Command: The Relationships Between Leaders in the Civil War*. New York: Macmillan, 1994.

Goodwin, Doris Kearns. *Team of Rivals: The Political Genius of Abraham Lincoln*. New York: Simon & Schuster, 2005.

Goss, Thomas J. *The War Within the Union High Command: Politics and Generalship During the Civil War*. Lawrence: University Press of Kansas, 2003.

Gott, Kendall D. *Where the South Lost the War: An Analysis of the Fort Henry–Fort Donelson Campaign, February 1862*. Mechanicsburg, PA: Stackpole Books, 2003.

Grant, Susan-Mary, and Peter J. Parish, eds. *Legacy of Disunion: The Enduring Significance of the American Civil War*. Baton Rouge: Louisiana State University Press, 2003.

Greene, Francis Vinton. *This Mississippi*. New York: Charles Scribner's Sons, 1884.

Groom, Winston. *Shrouds of Glory: From Atlanta to Nashville: The Last Great Campaign of the Civil War*. New York: The Atlantic Monthly Press, 1995.

Guelzo, Allen C. *Abraham Lincoln: Redeemer President*. Grand Rapids: Eerdsman Publishing, 2003.

———. *The Crisis of the American Republic: A History of the Civil War and Reconstruction Era*. New York: St. Martin's Press, 1995.

———. *Lincoln and Douglas: The Debates That Defined America*. New York: Simon & Schuster, 2009.

———. *Lincoln's Emancipation Proclamation: The End of Slavery in America*. New York: Simon & Schuster, 2004.

———. *Lincoln: A Very Short Introduction*. Oxford, Oxford University Press, 2009.

———, and Michael Lind. *Abraham Lincoln as a Man of Ideas*. Carbondale: Southern Illinois University Press, 2009.

Guernsey, Alfred H., and Henry M. Alden, eds. *Harpers Pictorial History of the Civil War*. New York: The Fairfax Press, 1977. Reprint of *Harpers Pictorial History of the Great Rebellion in the United States*. New York: Harper & Brothers, 1866.

Hagerman, Edward. *The American Civil War and the Origins of Modern Warfare: Ideas, Organization, and Field Command*. Bloomington: Indiana University Press, 1992.

Harris, William C. *Lincoln and the Border States: Preserving the Union*. Lawrence: University Press of Kansas, 2011.

———. *Lincoln's Rise to the Presidency*. Lawrence: University Press of Kansas, 2007.

Hassler, Warren W., Jr. *Commanders of the Army of the Potomac*. Baton Rouge: Louisiana State University Press, 1962.

Hattaway, Herman, and Archer Jones. *How the North Won: A Military History of the Civil War*. Urbana: University of Illinois Press, 1991. Reprint of 1983 edition.

Hearn, Chester C. *Lincoln, the Cabinet and the Generals*. Baton Rouge: Louisiana State University Press, 2010.

Heidler, David S., and Jeanne T. Heidler, eds. *Encyclopedia of the American Civil War: A Political, Social, and Military History*. New York: W. W. Norton & Company, 2002.

Heleniak, Roman J., and Lawrence L. Hewitt, eds. *The Confederate High Command & Related Topics: The 1988 Deep Delta Civil War Symposium*. Shippensburg, PA: White Mane Publishing Co., 1990.

Holzer, Harold, ed. *Lincoln on War: Our Greatest Commander-in-Chief Speaks to America*. Chapel Hill: Algonquin Books of Chapel Hill, 2011.

Johnson, Clint. *Civil War Blunders*. Winston-Salem: John F. Blair, 1997.

Jones, Archer. *Civil War Command & Strategy: The Process of Victory and Defeat*. New York: The Free Press, 1992.

———. *Confederate Strategy from Shiloh to Vicksburg*. Baton Rouge: Louisiana State University Press, 1991.

Jones, R. Steven. *The Right Hand of Command: Use & Disuse of Personal Staffs in the Civil War*. Mechanicsburg, PA: Stackpole Books, 2000.

Jordan, David M. *"Happiness Is Not My Companion": The Life of General G. K. Warren*. Bloomington: Indiana University Press, 2001.

———. *Winfield Scott Hancock: A Soldier's Life*. Bloomington: Indiana University Press, 1996.

Judge, Joseph. *Season of Fire: The Confederate Strike on Washington*. Berryville, VA: Rockbridge Publishing Co., 1994.

Keegan, John. *The American Civil War: A Military History*. New York: Knopf, 2009. Marred by numerous errors.

———. *The Face of Battle*. New York: Dorset Press, 1986. Reprint of New York: The Viking Press, 1976.

_____. *Fields of Battle: The Wars for North America*. New York: Alfred A. Knopf, 1996.

_____. *The Mask of Command*. New York: Viking, 1987.

Kiper, Richard L. *Major General John Alexander McClernand: Politician in Uniform*. Kent, Ohio: Kent State University Press, 1999.

Lamers, William M. *The Edge of Glory: A Biography of General William S. Rosecrans, U.S.A.* Baton Rouge: Louisiana State University Press, 1999. Reprint and expansion of New York: Harcourt, Brace & World, 1961.

Lawson, Melinda. *Patriot Fires: Forging a New American Nationalism in the Civil War North*. Lawrence: University Press of Kansas, 2002.

Levine, Bruce. *Confederate Emancipation: Southern Plans To Free and Arm Slaves During the Civil War*. Oxford: Oxford University Press, 2006.

Lewis, Lloyd. *Captain Sam Grant*. Boston: Little, Brown and Company, 1950.

Livermore, Thomas L. *Numbers & Losses in the Civil War in America: 1861–65*. Millwood, New York: Kraus Reprint Co., 1977. Reprint of Bloomington: Indiana University Press, 1957.

Longacre, Edward G. *General Ulysses S. Grant: The Soldier and the Man*. New York: Da Capo Press, 2006.

Long, David E. *The Jewel of Liberty: Abraham Lincoln's Re-election and the End of Slavery*. New York: Da Capo Press, 1997. Reprint of Mechanicsburg, PA: Stackpole Books, 1994.

————. *Grant's Cavalryman: The Life and Wars of General James H. Wilson*. Mechanicsburg, PA: Stackpole Press, 1996. Originally *From Union Stars to Top Hat*, 1972.

Lossing, Benson. *A History of the Civil War, 1861–65, and the Causes That Led up to the Great Conflict*. New York: The War Memorial Association, 1912.

Lowry, Don. *Fate of the Country: The Civil War from June–September 1864*. New York: Hippocrene Books, 1992.

————. *No Turning Back: The Beginning of the End of the Civil War: March-June, 1864*. New York: Hippocrene Books, 1992.

Lowry, Thomas P. *Merciful Lincoln: The President and Military Justice*. Thomas P. Lowry, 2009.

Marshall-Cornwall, James. *Grant as Military Commander*. New York: Barnes & Noble Books, 1995. Reprint of 1970 edition.

Marszalek, John F. *Commander of All Lincoln's Armies: A Life of General Henry W. Halleck*. Cambridge: Belknap Press of Harvard University Press, 2004.

————. *Sherman: A Soldier's Passion for Order*. New York: Macmillan, Inc., 1993.

Marvel, William. *Lee's Last Retreat: The Flight to Appomattox*. Chapel Hill: University of North Carolina Press, 2002.

Matloff, Maurice, ed. *American Military History*. Washington, DC: U.S. Army Center of Military History, 1985.

McDonough, James Lee. *Chattanooga: A Death Grip on the Confederacy*. Knoxville: University of Tennessee Press, 1984.

McFeely, William. *Grant: A Biography*. New York: W. W. Norton & Company, 1981.

McKenzie, John D. *Uncertain Glory: Lee's Generalship Re-Examined*. New York: Hippocrene Books, 1997.

McMurry, Richard M. *Two Great Rebel Armies: An Essay in Confederate Military History*. Chapel Hill: University of North Carolina Press, 1989.

McPherson, James M. *Battle Cry of Freedom: The Civil War Era*. New York: Ballantine Books, 1988.

————. *This Mighty Scourge: Perspectives on the Civil War*. Oxford: Oxford University Press, 2007.

————. *Tried by War: Abraham Lincoln as Commander in Chief*. New York: Penguin Press, 2008.

McWhiney, Grady, and Perry D. Jamieson. *Attack and Die: Civil War Military Tactics and the Southern Heritage*. Tuscaloosa: University of Alabama Press, 1982.

McWhiney, Grady, ed. *Grant, Lee, Lincoln and the Radicals: Essays on Civil War Leadership*. New York: Harper & Row, 1966. Reprint of Chicago: Northwestern University Press, 1964.

Miers, Earl Schenck. *The Last Campaign: Grant Saves the Union*. Philadelphia: J. B. Lippincott Company, 1972.

————. *The Web of Victory: Grant at Vicksburg*. Baton Rouge: Louisiana State University Press, 1984. Reprint of New York: Alfred Knopf, 1955.

Miller, Richard Lawrence. *Lincoln and His World: Vol. 3: The Rise to National Prominence, 1843–1853* Jefferson, NC: McFarland, 2011.

Miller, William J. *Mapping for Stonewall: The Civil War Service of Jed Hotchkiss*. Washington: Elliott & Clark Publishing, 1993.

Millett, Allan R., and Peter Maslowski. *For the Common Defense: A Military History of the United States of America*. New York: Free Press, 1994.

Mitchell, Joseph B. *Decisive Battles of the Civil War*. New York: Ballantine Books, 1955.

Morris, Roy, Jr. *Sheridan: The Life and Wars of General Phil Sheridan.*
    New York: Crown Publishers, Inc., 1992.

Nevins, Alan. *Ordeal of the Union.* 8 vols. New York: Charles Scribner's
    Sons, 1947–50.

Nolan, Alan T. *Lee Considered: General Robert E. Lee and Civil War
    History.* Chapel Hill: University of North Carolina Press, 1991.

Noyalas, Jonathan A. *The Battle of Cedar Creek: Victory from the Jaws of
    Defeat.* Charleston, SC: History Press, 2009, 2011.

———. *"My Will Is Absolute Law": A Biography of General Robert H.
    Milroy.* Jefferson, North Carolina: McFarland, 2006.

———. *Plagued by War: Winchester, Virginia During the Civil War.*
    Leesburg, VA: Gauley Mount Press, 2003.

———. *Stonewall Jackson's 1862 Valley Campaign: War Comes to the
    Homefront.* Charleston, South Carolina: History Press, 2010.

Perret, Geoffrey. *A Country Made by War: From the Revolution to
    Vietnam—the Story of America's Rise to Power.* New York: Random
    House, 1989.

———. *Ulysses S. Grant: Soldier & President.* New York: Random House,
    1997.

Pfanz, Donald C. *Richard F. Ewell: A Soldier's Life.* Chapel Hill: University
    of North Carolina Press, 1998).

Phisterer, Frederick. *Statistical Record of the Armies of the United States.*
    Edison, New Jersey: Castle Books, 2002. Reprint of 1883 book.

Pollard, Edward A. *The Lost Cause. A New Southern History of the War of
    the Confederates.* New York: Gramercy Books, 1994. Reprint of New
    York: E. B. Treat & Company, 1866.

Rhea, Gordon C. *The Battle of the Wilderness May 5–6, 1864.* Baton
    Rouge: Louisiana State University Press, 1994.

———. *The Battles for Spotsylvania Court House and the Road to Yellow
    Tavern, May 7–12, 1864.* Baton Rouge: Louisiana State University
    Press, 1997.

———. *Cold Harbor: Grant and Lee May 26–June 3, 1864.* Baton Rouge:
    Louisiana State University Press, 2002.

———. *To the North Anna River: Lee and Grant May 13–25, 1864.* Baton
    Rouge: Louisiana State University Press, 2000.

Roland, Charles P. *An American Iliad: The Story of the Civil War.*
    Lexington: University Press of Kentucky, 1991.

Ross, Ishbel. *The General's Wife: The Life of Mrs. Ulysses S. Grant.* New
    York: Dodd, Mead and Company, 1959.

Rowland, Thomas J. *George B. McClellan and Civil War History in the*

Shadow of Grant and Sherman. Kent, OH: Kent State University Press, 1998.

Royster, Charles. *The Destructive War: William Tecumseh Sherman, Stonewall Jackson, and the Americans*. New York: Vintage Books, 1993.

Scott, Robert Garth. *Into the Wilderness with the Army of the Potomac*. Bloomington: Indiana University Press. 1985.

Sears, Stephen W. *Controversies & Commanders: Dispatches from the Army of the Potomac*. Boston: Houghton Mifflin Company, 1999.

———, ed. *The Civil War: The Best of American Heritage*. New York: American Heritage Press, 1991.

Simon, John Y., Harold Holzer, and Dawn Vogel, eds. *Lincoln Revisited: New Insights from the Lincoln Forum*. New York: Fordham University Press, 2007.

Simpson, Brooks D. *Ulysses S. Grant: Triumph Over Adversity, 1822–1865*. Boston: Houghton Mifflin Company, 2000.

Simpson, Harold B. *Hood's Texas Brigade: Lee's Grenadier Guard*. Fort Worth: Landmark Publishing, Inc., 1970. Vol. 2 of four-volume set on Hood's Texas Brigade.

Smith, Gene. *Lee and Grant: A Dual Biography*. New York: Promontory Press, 1984.

Smith, Jean Edward. *Grant*. New York: Simon & Schuster, 2001.

Smith, John David, ed. *Black Soldiers in Blue: African American Troops in the Civil War Era*. Chapel Hill: University of North Carolina Press, 2003.

Sommers, Richard J. *Richmond Redeemed: The Siege at Petersburg*. Garden City: Doubleday & Company, 1981.

Steere, Edward. *The Wilderness Campaign*. New York: Bonanza Books, 1960.

Stern, Philip Van Doren. *Robert E. Lee: The Man and the Soldier*. New York: Bonanza Books, 1963.

Stewart, George R. *Pickett's Charge: A Microhistory of the Final Attack at Gettysburg, July 3, 1863*. Boston: Houghton Mifflin Co., 1959.

Swinton, William. *Campaigns of the Army of the Potomac*. New York: Richardson, 1866.

Tarbell, Ida M. *The Life of Abraham Lincoln*. 4 vols. Springfield, Illinois: Lincoln History Society, 1903.

Thomas, Emory M. *Robert E. Lee: A Biography*. New York: W. W. Norton and Co., 1995.

Tidwell, William A., James O.Hall, and David Winfred Gaddy. *Come

Retribution: The Confederate Secret Service and the Assassination of Lincoln. Jackson: University Press of Mississippi, 1988.

Time-Life Books Editors. *Voices of the Civil War: Second Manassas*. Alexandria, VA: Time-Life Books, 1995.

Trudeau, Noah Andre. *Bloody Roads South: The Wilderness to Cold Harbor, May-June 1864*. Boston: Little, Brown and Co., 1989.

———. *Gettysburg: A Testing of Courage*. New York: HarperCollins, 2002.

———. *The Last Citadel: Petersburg, Virginia June 1864–April 1865*. Baton Rouge: Louisiana State University Press, 1991.

———. *Out of the Storm: The End of the Civil War, April–June 1865*. Boston: Little, Brown and Company, 1994.

———. *Southern Storm: Sherman's March to the Sea*. New York: Harper Collins, 2008.

Vandiver, Frank E. *Jubal's Raid: General Early's Famous Attack on Washington in 1864*. New York: McGraw-Hill Book Company, Inc., 1960.

Virginia Civil War Trails. *Lee vs. Grant: The 1864 Campaign*. Richmond, undated.

Wagner, Margaret E., Gary W. Gallagher, and Paul Finkelman, eds. *The Library of Congress Civil War Desk Reference*. New York: Simon & Schuster, 2002.

Wallace, Willard M. *Soul of the Lion: A Biography of General Joshua L. Chamberlain*. Gettysburg: Stan Clark Military Books, 1991. Reprint of Edinburgh, New York: Thomas Nelson & Sons, 1960.

Walsh, George. *"Whip the Rebellion": Ulysses S. Grant's Rise to Command*. New York: Tom Doherty Associates, 2005.

Ward, Geoffrey C., Ric Burns, and Ken Burns. *The Civil War: An Illustrated History*. New York: Alfred A. Knopf, 1990.

Warner, Ezra J. *Generals in Blue: Lives of the Union Commanders*. Baton Rouge: Louisiana State University Press, 1964.

———. *Generals in Gray: Lives of the Confederate Commanders*. Baton Rouge: Louisiana State University Press, 1959.

Waugh, Joan. *U. S. Grant: American Hero, American Myth*. Chapel Hill: University of North Carolina Press, 2009.

Waugh, John C. *The Class of 1846: From West Point to Appomattox: Stonewall Jackson, George McClellan and Their Brothers*. New York: Warner Books, Inc., 1994.

———. *Lincoln and McClellan: The Troubled Partnership Between a President and His General*. New York: Palgrave Macmillan, 2010.

———. *Reelecting Lincoln: The Battle for the 1864 Presidency*. New York: Crown Publishers, 1997.

Weber, Thomas. *The Northern Railroads in the Civil War, 1861–1865*. Bloomington: Indiana University Press, 1999. Reprint of 1952 edition.

Weigley, Russell F. *The American Way of War: A History of United States Military Strategy and Policy*. New York: Macmillan, 1973.

———. *A Great Civil War: A Military and Political History, 1861–1865*. Bloomington: Indiana University Press, 2000.

———. *Towards an American Army: Military Thought from Washington to Marshall*. New York: Columbia University Press, 1962.

Weir, William. *Fatal Victories*. Hamden, Connecticut: Archon Books, 1993.

Welles, Gideon. *Diary of Gideon Welles*. 3 vols. Boston: Houghton Mifflin Company, 1911.

Werstein, Irving. *Abraham Lincoln Versus Jefferson Davis*. New York: Thomas Y. Crowell Company, 1959.

Wert, Jeffry D. *A Brotherhood of Valor: The Common Soldiers of the Stonewall Brigade*. New York: Simon & Schuster, 1999.

———. *From Winchester to Cedar Creek: The Shenandoah Campaign of 1864*. Carlisle, Pennsylvania: South Mountain Press, 1987.

———. *General James Longstreet: The Confederacy's Most Controversial Soldier: A Biography*. New York: Simon & Schuster, 1993.

———. *The Sword of Lincoln: The Army of the Potomac*. New York: Simon & Schuster, 2005.

Wheeler, Richard. *On Fields of Fury: From the Wilderness to the Crater: An Eyewitness History*. New York: HarperCollins, 1991.

Wiley, Bell Irvin. *The Road to Appomattox*. Baton Rouge: Louisiana State University Press, 1994. Reprint of Memphis: Memphis State College Press, 1956.

Williams, Frank J., William D. Pederson, and Vincent J. Marsala. *Abraham Lincoln: Sources and Style of Leadership*. Westport, CT: Greenwood Press, 1994.

Williams, Kenneth P. *Grant Rises in the West*. 2 vols. Lincoln: University of Nebraska Press, 1997. Originally vols. 3 and 4 of *Lincoln Finds a General: A Military Study of the Civil War*, New York: Macmillan, 1952.

———. *Lincoln Finds a General: A Military Study of the Civil War*. Vol. 1. Bloomington: Indiana University Press, 1985. Reprint of 1949 edition.

———. *Lincoln Finds a General: A Military Study of the Civil War*. Vols. 2 and 5. New York: Macmillan, 1959. Reprint of 1949 edition.

Williams, T. Harry. *Lincoln and His Generals*. New York: Alfred A. Knopf, Inc., 1952.

———. *McClellan, Sherman and Grant*. New Brunswick: Rutgers University Press, 1962.

Wills, Brian Steel. *A Battle from the Start: The Life of Nathan Bedford Forrest*. New York: HarperPerennial, 1992.

Wilson, Harold S. *Confederate Industry: Manufacturers and Quartermasters in the Civil War*. Jackson: University of Mississippi Press, 2002.

Winders, Richard Bruce. *Polk's Army: The American Military Experience in the Mexican War*. College Station: Texas A&M University Press, 1997.

Winik, Jay. *April 1865: The Month That Saved America*. New York: HarperCollins, 2001.

Woodworth, Steven E., ed. *Civil War Generals in Defeat*. Lawrence: University of Kansas Press, 1999.

———, ed. *Davis and Lee at War*. Lawrence: University Press of Kansas, 1995.

———, ed. *Grant's Lieutenants from Cairo to Vicksburg*. Lawrence: University Press of Kansas, 2001.

———. *Jefferson Davis and His Generals: The Failure of Confederate Command in the West*. Lawrence: University Press of Kansas, 1990.

———. *Nothing But Victory: The Army of the Tennessee, 1861–1865*. New York: Alfred A. Knopf, 2005.

Work, David. *Lincoln's Political Generals*. Urbana: University of Illinois Press, 2009.

PERIODICAL ARTICLES

Anderson, Kevin. "Grant's Lifelong Struggle with Alcohol: Examining the Controversy Surrounding Grant and Alcohol," *Columbiad: A Quarterly Review of the War Between the States* 2, no. 4 (Winter 1999): 16–26.

Barton, Dick, "Charge at Big Black River," *America's Civil War* 12, no. 4 (Sept. 1999): 54–61.

Bearss, Ed. "The Vicksburg Campaign. Grant Marches West: The Battles of Champion Hill and Big Black Bridge," *Blue & Gray Magazine* XVIII, issue 5 (June 2001): 6–24, 44–52.

———. "The Vicksburg Campaign: Grant Moves Inland," *Blue & Gray Magazine* XVIII, issue 1 (October 2000): 6–22, 46–52, 65.

Bergeron, Arthur W., Jr. "The Battle of Mobile Bay and the Campaign for Mobile, Alabama," *Blue & Gray Magazine* XIX, issue 4 (April 2002): 6–21, 46–54.

———. "Three-day Tussle at Hatcher's Run," *America's Civil War* 16, no. 1 (March 2003): 30–37.

Bolte, Philip L. "An Earlier 'Bridge Too Far'," *North & South* 3, no. 6 (August 2000): 26–32.

Bonekemper, Edward H., III. "Lincoln's 1864 Victory Was Closer Than It Looked," *Washington Times*, July 15, 2000.

Bradley, Mark L. "Last Stand in the Carolinas: The Battle of Bentonville, March 19–21, 1865," *Blue & Gray Magazine* XIII, issue 2 (Dec. 1995): 8–22.

———. "Old Reliable's Finest Hour: The Battle of Averasboro, North Carolina, March 15–16, 1865" *Blue & Gray Magazine* XVI, issue 1 (Oct. 1998): 6–20, 52–57.

Brandt, Dennis W. "A Question of Cowardice," *America's Civil War* 20, no. 2 (May 2007): 54–62.

Calkins, Chris. "The Battle of Five Forks: Final Push for the South Side," *Blue & Gray Magazine* IX, no. 4 (April 1992): 8–22, 41–52.

———. "Final Bloodshed at Appomattox," *America's Civil War* 14, no. 2 (May 2001), 34–40.

Campbell, Eric A. "'Slept in the mud, stood in the mud, kneeled in the mud,'" *America's Civil War* 15, no. 6 (January 2003): 50–55 at 54–55.

Case, David. "The Battle That Saved Washington," *Civil War Times Illustrated* XXXVII, no. 7 (Feb. 1999): 46–56.

Castel, Albert. "The Fort Pillow Massacre: A Fresh Examination of the Evidence," *Civil War History* 4 (March 1958): 37–50.

Cooling, Benjamin Franklin. "Monocacy: The Battle That Saved Washington," *Blue & Gray Magazine* X, issue 2 (Dec. 1992): 8–18, 48–60.

Crawford, Mark J. "Dinwiddie Court House: Beginning of the End," *America's Civil War* 12, no. 1 (March 1999): 50–56.

Davis, Stephen. "Atlanta Campaign. Hood Fights Desperately. The Battles of Atlanta: Events from July 10 to September 2, 1864," *Blue & Gray Magazine* VI, issue 6 (August 1989), 8, 11.

Dew, Charles B. "Apostles of Secession," *North & South* 4, no. 4, (Apr. 2001), 24–38.

Dolzall, Gary W. "Enemies Front and Rear," *America's Civil War* 16, no. 2 (May 2003): 38–45.

Durham, Roger S. "Savannah: Mr. Lincoln's Christmas Present," *Blue & Gray Magazine* VIII, issue 3 (Feb. 1991): 8–18, 42–53.

Epstein, Robert M. "The Creation and Evolution of the Army Corps in the American Civil War," *Journal of Military History* 55, no. 1 (Jan. 1991), 21–46.

Evans, E. Chris. "'I Almost Tremble at Her Fate': When Sherman came to Columbia, South Carolina, secession's hotbed became a bed of coals," *Civil War Times Illustrated* XXXVII, no. 5 (Oct. 1998): 46–51, 60–67.

———. "Return to Jackson: Finishing Stroke to the Vicksburg Campaign, July 5–25, 1863," *Blue & Gray Magazine* XII, issue 6 (Aug. 1995): 8–22, 50–63.

Feis, William B. "Charles S. Bell: Union Scout," *North & South* 4, no. 5 (June 2001): 26–37.

———. "'He Don't Care a Damn for What the Enemy Does out of His Sight,'" *North & South* 1, no. 2 (Jan. 1998): 68–81.

Fonvielle, Chris, "The Last Rays of Departing Hope: The Fall of Wilmington Including the Campaigns Against Fort Fisher," *Blue & Gray Magazine* XII, issue 2 (Dec. 1994): 10–21, 48–62.

Freeman, Kirk. "Big Black River," *Military Heritage* 2, no. 3 (Dec. 2000): 76–85.

Garavaglia, Louis A. "Sherman's March and the Georgia Arsenals," *North & South* 6, no. 1 (Dec. 2002): 12–22.

Glynn, Gary. "Black Thursday for Rebels," *America's Civil War* 4, no. 5 (Jan. 1992): 22–29.

Goodman, Al W., Jr. "Decision in the West (Part IV): Between Hell and the Deep Sea: Pemberton's Debacle at Big Black River Bridge," *North & South* 1, no. 5 (June 1998): 74–79.

———. "Grant's Mississippi Gamble," *America's Civil War* 7, no. 3 (July 1994): 50–56.

Greene, A. Wilson. "April 2, 1865: Day of Decision at Petersburg," *Blue & Gray Magazine* XVIII, issue 3 (Feb. 2001): 6–24, 42–53.

Howe, Daniel Walker. "Honest Abe: Abraham Lincoln and the Moral Character," *Foreign Policy Research Institute Newsletter* 13, no. 16 (June 2008) at www.fpri.org

Janda, Lance. "Shutting the Gates of Mercy: The American Origins of Total War, 1860–1880," *Journal of Military History* 59, no. 1 (Jan. 1995), 7–26.

King, Curtis S. "Reconsider, Hell!" *MHQ: The Quarterly Journal of Military History* 13, no. 4 (Summer 2001): 88–95.

Leonard, Phillip A. B. "Forty-seven Days.Constant bombardment, life in bomb shelters, scarce food and water, and rapidly accumulating filth were the price of resistance for the resolute Confederate citizens of besieged Vicksburg, Mississippi," *Civil War Times Illustrated* XXXIX, no. 4 (August 2000): 40–49, 68–69.

Lowe, David W. "Field Fortifications in the Civil War," *North & South* 4, no. 6 (Aug. 2001): 58–73.

Lutz, Stephen D. "General Orders, No. 11: Grant's Ignoble Act," *America's Civil War* XII, no. 7 (misprinted as 6) (March 2000): 50–56.

Marvel, William. "Retreat to Appomattox," *Blue & Gray Magazine* XXXVIII, issue 4 (Spring 2001): 6–24, 46–54.

———. "Thorn in the Flesh," *Civil War Times Illustrated* XLI, no. 3 (June 2002): 42–49, 60–62.

McPherson, James M. "The Unheroic Hero," *The New York Review of Books* LXVI, no. 2 (Feb. 4, 1999): 16–19.

Miller, J. Michael. "Strike Them a Blow: Lee and Grant at the North Anna River," *Blue & Gray Magazine* X, issue 4 (April 1993): 12–22, 44–55.

Murray, Williamson. "In Praise of Sam Grant," *Military History Quarterly: The Quarterly Journal of Military History* 18, no. 4 (Summer 2006), 6–15.

Naisawald, L. VanLoan. "'Old Jubilee' Saves Lynchburg," *America's Civil War* 16, no. 2 (May 2003): 30–36, 72.

Poulter, Keith. "Decision in the West: The Vicksburg Campaign, Part III," *North & South* 1, no. 4 (April 1998): 77–83.

Powles, James M. " New Jersey's Western Warriors," *America's Civil War* 14, no. 4 (Sept. 2001): 46–52.

"Reconsidering Grant and Lee: Reputations of Civil War Generals Shifting," Associated Press, http://www.cnn.com/2003/SHOWBIZ/books/01/08/wkd.Grant.vs.Lee.ap/index.html.

Rhea, Gordon C. "'Butcher' Grant and the Overland Campaign," *North & South* 4, no. 1 (Nov. 2000): 44–55.

Roberts, Donald J., II. "Belmont: Grant's First Battle," *Military Heritage* 2, no. 6 (June 2001): 40–49.

Roth, Dave. "Grierson's Raid: A Cavalry Raid at Its Best, April 17–May 2, 1863," *Blue & Gray Magazine* X, issue 5 (June 1993): 12–24, 48–65.

Scaife, William R., "Sherman's March to the Sea: Events from September 3 to December, 1864, Including the Occupation of Atlanta, More Battles with the Unpredictable John Bell Hood, the Burning of Atlanta, 'Marching Through Georgia,' and the Fall of Savannah," *Blue & Gray Magazine* VII, issue 2 (Dec. 1989): 10–32, 38–42.

Schenker, Carl R., Jr. "The Grant-Halleck-Smith Affair," *North & South* 12, no. 1 (Feb. 2010): 11–12.

———. "Grant's Rise from Obscurity," *North & South* 9, no. 3 (June 2006): 60-68.

———. "Ulysses in His Tent: Halleck, Grant, Sherman, and 'The Turning Point of the War," *Civil War History* 56, no. 2 (June 2010): 175–221.

———. "What Happened at City Point?," *North & South* 12, no. 5 (Jan. 2011): 11–13.

Selcer, Richard F. "Battlefield Bulldog, Compassionate Conqueror," *Civil War Times* XLVI, no. 1 (Feb. 2007): 46–53.

Suderow, Bryce A. "Glory Denied: The First Battle of Deep Bottom, July 27th–29th, 1864," *North & South* 3, no. 7 (Sept. 2000): 17–32.

———. "'Nothing But a Miracle Could Save Us': Second Battle of Deep Bottom, Virginia, August 14–20, 1864," *North & South* 4, no. 2 (Jan. 2001): 12–32.

———. "War Along the James," *North & South* 6, no. 3 (April 2003): 12–23.

Sutherland, Daniel E. "Abraham Lincoln, John Pope, and the Origins of Total War," *Journal of Military History* 56, no. 4 (Oct. 1992): 567–86.

Thompson, Robert N. "The Folly and Horror of Cold Harbor," *Military History* 23, no. 8 (Nov. 2006): 38–45.

Trudeau, Noah Andre. "Climax at Vicksburg," *North & South* 1, no. 5 (June 1998): 80–89.

———. "That 'Unerring Volcanic Firearm'," *Military History Quarterly* 7, no. 4 (Summer 1995): 78–87.

Weigley, Russell F. "The American Military and the Principle of Civilian Control from McClellan to Powell," *Journal of Military History* 57, no. 5 (Oct. 1993): 27–58.

———. "The Soldier, the Statesman, and the Military Historian," *Journal of Military History* 63, no. 4 (Oct. 1999): 807–22.

Wert, Jeffry D. "All-out War," *Civil War Times* LXIII, no. 1 (April 2004): 34–40.

Wheelan, Joseph. "Polk's Manifest Destiny," *The History Channel Magazine* 4, no. 1 (Jan./Feb. 2006): 41–45.

Winschel, Terrence. Energy and Perseverance'," *Blue & Gray Magazine* XIII, issue 5 (June 1996): 8–22.

———. "Grant's Beachhead for the Vicksburg Campaign: The Battle of Port Gibson, May 1, 1863," *Blue & Gray Magazine* XI, issue 3 (Feb. 1994): 8–22, 48–56.

————. "A Tragedy of Errors: The Failure of the Confederate High Command in the Defense of Vicksburg," *North & South* 8, no. 7 (Jan. 2006): 40–49.

Wittenberg, Eric J. "Roadblock En Route to Washington," *America's Civil War* 6, no. 5 (Nov. 1993): 50–56, 80–82.

Woodworth, Steven E. "The Army of Tennessee and the Element of Military Success," *North & South* 6, no. 4 (May 2003): 44–55.

Young, Alfred C. "Numbers and Losses in the Army of Northern Virginia," *North & South* 3, no. 3 (March 2000): 14–29.

Zentner, Joe and Mary Syrett, "Confederate Gibraltar," *Military History* 19, no. 6 (Feb. 2003): 26–32, 73.

INDEX